Foundations of Computer Security

David Salomon

Foundations of Computer Security

With 45 Figures

 Springer

Professor David Salomon (emeritus)
Computer Science Department
California State University
Northridge, CA 91330-8281
USA
email: david.salomon@csun.edu

British Library Cataloguing in Publication Data
A catalogue record for this book is available from the British Library

Library of Congress Control Number: 2005932091

ISBN-10: 1-84628-193-8   e-ISBN 1-84628-193-8
ISBN-13: 978-1-84628-193-8

Printed on acid-free paper

Printed in the United States of America   (HAM)

9 8 7 6 5 4 3 2 1

Springer Science+Business Media
springeronline.com

Dedicated to the many anonymous users and experts who serve with zeal and dedication in the unending war of computer security.

There isn't an author who doesn't take their [sic] books personally.

—Muriel Spark, *A Far Cry From Kensington* (1988).

Preface

GENTLE READER. Your interest in this book is understandable. Computer security has become one of the most important areas in the entire discipline of computing. Computers today are used not only in the home and office, but in a multitude of crucial and sensitive applications. Computers control long distance telephone conversations, the flow of information on the Internet, the distribution of electrical power to cities, and they monitor the operations of nuclear power plants and the performance of space satellites, to name just a few important applications.

We have become used to these small, quiet machines that permeate our lives and we take them for granted, but from time to time, when they don't perform their tasks, we immediately become aware that something has gone terribly wrong. Considering the complexity of today's computers and their functions, and considering especially the physical hazards that abound in the world, it is a wonder that our computers function at all, yet we expect them to be reliable and we entrust them with more and more delicate, sensitive, and complex assignments.

It is easy to disrupt a computer. Just brush your elbow accidentally against your desk and you may spill your cup of coffee on your computer. A power loss lasting a fraction of a second may lead to a head crash of the hard disk, resulting in a complete loss of the disk and all its data. Carelessness on the part of operators or administrators in a large computations center can cause a costly loss of data or even physical damage to expensive equipment. Yet all these dangers (and there are many more like them) pale in comparison with the many types of intentional criminal damage that we have come to expect and that we collectively associate with the field of computer security.

A term closely related to computer security is computer crime. A computer crime is an incident of computer security in which a law is broken. Traditionally, computer crime has had a low profile. After all, in a computer crime there are no smoking guns, no blood-stained victims, and no getaway cars. Often, such a crime is solved just by sheer accident. In contrast, computer security is a high-visibility discipline because it involves most of us.

Experience has shown that the more sophisticated a civilization is, the more vulnerable it is to natural or man-made disruptions. A tree that fell on power lines in

Ohio in August 2004 plunged 50 million people from Detroit to New York into darkness. A computer glitch at an airport on 26 December 2004 (the day this paragraph was written) caused the cancellation of 1100 flights of Comair, a subsidiary of Delta Air Lines, and similar examples abound. Our civilization depends more and more on computers, which is why any disruption of our computers is at least inconvenient and at worst catastrophic.

In the past, computer security violations, such as viruses and DoS (denial of service, Section 7.5) attacks were caused by hackers, most of whom were believed to be young adults who did this for fun or enjoyed the feeling of power and notoriety. However, it seems that this situation is rapidly changing. Security experts are warning that future attacks on computers may be planned and funded by terrorists (better called cyberterrorists) and may be devastating. A powerful hurricane, a huge earthquake, or a tsunami may kill many and wreak untold havoc, but a large-scale, concerted attack on key computers may bring the economy of an entire country to its knees, even though no one may actually get killed.

The reason for such dire predictions is our experience with computer security in the last two decades. We know that a single computer virus, perhaps written and released by a teenager living in a remote town in a distant country, can propagate quickly, infect a vast number of computers within hours, and cause economic damage in the billions (of Dollars, Euros, or whatever currency is affected).

Today, computers are responsible for the distribution of electrical power and for routing telephone conversations. They store information on passenger and cargo flights, on large cash transfers between banks, and on military plans, to name just a few crucial applications. It is generally agreed that a well-organized attack that takes over several important, sensitive computers may cause at least a temporary collapse of an entire country.

What makes this kind of attack attractive to organized terrorists is that it can be carried out from the comfort of their homes. There is no need to actually go anywhere, to obtain and use dangerous nuclear or chemical materials, or to smuggle anything across international borders. The fact that we depend so much on computers may be crucial to our future survival, and the least that we can do now is to learn as much as possible about potential threats to computers and how to defend against them.

> Virus writing is a crazy activity. People who write viruses just don't consider the consequences of their actions. At the same time, I believe in the American constitution, and the first amendment, which gives people freedom to write and to talk, so I don't have a problem in the larger sense of people discussing or studying viruses.
>
> —Peter Tippett (Symantec) in [Virus bulletin 05] May 1994 issue.

There is an ongoing debate about whether newly-discovered security holes and vulnerabilities in operating systems and communications software should be made public. Publicizing a security weakness allows users to avoid it until a patch is issued or a solution is found. On the other hand, it gives the bad guys ideas. So far, advocates of public exposure have had the upper hand, with the result that any item of news about a new computer security problem ignites a race between attackers and defenders. The following is a list of some of those races:

■   SNMP flaw. A flaw in the Simple Network Management Protocol (SNMP) leaves open many network devices to attack. The flaw has not been widely exploited.

■   Microsoft SQL vulnerability. A hole in a common component of Microsoft's SQL database software leaves PCs open to remote attack. Six months after it was found, the vulnerability was exploited by the slammer worm (see year 2003 in Appendix B).

■   Microsoft RPC flaw. In July 2003, Microsoft published details of a flaw in the remote procedure call (RPC) functions of Windows. About three weeks later, the MSBlast worm arrived and exploited this flaw to infect as many as 10 million computers.

■   Microsoft LSASS flaw. A hole in Local Security Authority Subsystem Service (LSASS) exposed personal computers running the Windows operating system. A month after it was revealed, the sasser worm hit the Internet and spread among computers that still had this hole (see year 2004 in Appendix B).

■   iFrame flaw. In late October 2004, a security researcher discovered the existence of a flaw in Internet Explorer, a popular Web browser (page 61). Hackers with nothing better to do immediately exploited the vulnerability to compromise personal computers running this software.

Three types of persons are involved in computer security: experts who study this field and recommend preventive measures and solutions, the general public, which suffers from the breakdown of computer security, and the (mostly anonymous) perpetrators of the various misdeeds and attacks. Most of these perpetrators are known as *hackers*, which is why this important, popular term is discussed here.

From the dictionary

Expert: someone widely recognized as a reliable source of knowledge or skill whose judgement is accorded authority and status by the public or their peers.

===================== **The Hacker** =====================

Madame Curie once said "En science, nous devons nous intéresser aux choses, non aux personnes [In science, we should be interested in things, not in people]." Things, however, have since changed, and today we have to be interested not just in the facts of computer security and crime, but in the people who perpetrate these acts. Hence this discussion of hackers.

Over the centuries, the term "hacker" has referred to various activities. We are familiar with usages such as "a carpenter hacking wood with an ax" and "a butcher hacking meat with a cleaver," but it seems that the modern, computer-related form of this term originated in the many pranks and practical jokes perpetrated by students at MIT in the 1960s. As an example of the many meanings assigned to this term, see [Schneier 04] which, among much other information, explains why Galileo was a hacker but Aristotle wasn't.

A hack is a person lacking talent or ability, as in a "hack writer." Hack as a verb is used in contexts such as "hack the media," "hack your brain," and "hack your reputation." Recently, it has also come to mean either a kludge, or the opposite of a kludge, as in a clever or elegant solution to a difficult problem. A hack also means a simple but often inelegant solution or technique. The following tentative definitions are quoted from the jargon file ([jargon 04], edited by Eric S. Raymond):

1. A person who enjoys exploring the details of programmable systems and how to stretch their capabilities, as opposed to most users, who prefer to learn only the minimum necessary.

2. One who programs enthusiastically (even obsessively) or who enjoys programming rather than just theorizing about programming.

3. A person capable of appreciating hack value.

4. A person who is good at programming quickly.

5. An expert at a particular program, or one who frequently does work using it or on it; as in "a Unix hacker." (Definitions 1 through 5 are correlated, and people who fit them congregate.)

6. An expert or enthusiast of any kind. One might be an astronomy hacker, for example.

7. One who enjoys the intellectual challenge of creatively overcoming or circumventing limitations.

8. [deprecated] A malicious meddler who tries to discover sensitive information by poking around. Hence "password hacker" and "network hacker." The correct term for this sense is cracker (which stands for criminal hacker).

Today's computer hacker is often an expert in a computer-related field who finds a way to exploit a weakness or a vulnerability in a certain component of that field. This component may be a piece of hardware, part of the operating system, or a software application. Not all hackers are experts and not all are malicious. A notable example is Linus Torvalds, the creator of the well-known, free Linux operating system. Many Linux users will agree that this activity of Torvalds is a hack, but everyone (except commercial competitors) agrees that it is useful.

> I think any time you expose vulnerabilities it's a good thing.
> —Janet Reno

Some security experts claim that today's computer hackers should be termed crackers or intruders, but the general public and the media seem to love the term hacker. The word "cracker" is used to designate someone who breaks the security code of software, so that it can be used without pay. The term "intruder" is commonly used to indicate a person who breaks into a remote computer.

The following classification of the various hacker categories is informal and is by no means universally accepted.

■   The highest category of hacker may be a brilliant programmer (although such a hacker may prefer the title of guru, cracksman, or wizard). Someone who is intimately familiar with a certain communications program, protocol, operating system, or encryption algorithm. Such a person can identify weaknesses or vulnerabilities and then come up with a clever, original way of penetrating a computer and inflicting damage. Alternatively, such an expert may develop ways and means to plug up security holes in software, or even completely rewrite a weak routine or procedure to make it invulnerable.

■ The next category is that of the good programmer. Such a person hears of a new security threat, for example, a new type of virus, and may decide to "improve" it. A good programmer can disassemble the code of a virus, read and understand it, and come up with more "efficient" ways of employing the basic principle of the virus. Such a person may also be a good guy (a white-hat hacker) and work as a security expert. Disassembling and reading the code of a virus uncovers the vulnerabilities the virus exploits and leads directly to eliminating them.

■ A script kid is a hacker with little or no programming skills who simply follows directions created by a higher-rank hacker or who uses a cookbook approach without fully understanding the principles and details of what he is constructing.

■ A hacktivist is an activist who employs hacking to promote a cause. In 1995, a virus attached a political message "Stop all French nuclear testing in the Pacific" to the footer of letters printed from Microsoft Word, so users who trusted the computer and didn't check their printouts became unwilling supporters of a cause.

■ A sneaker or a gray-hat is a hacker who breaks security for altruistic motives or other non-malicious reasons. The darker the hat, the more the ethics of the activity should be considered dubious.

■ The least harmful hacker is the white-hat type. This term is often used to describe self-appointed security gurus who attempt to break into computers or networks in order to find security flaws and inform the owners/administrators of the problem.

The following is a list of "tools of the trade," methods, approaches, and special software used by hackers to gain unauthorized access to data, to computers, and to entire computer installations:

■ Rogue software. These are computer programs especially designed to propagate among computers and either inflict damage or collect data and send it back to the hacker. They are also known as malware. The chief types of rogue software are viruses, worms, Trojan horses, and the various kinds of spyware. Each is described in one paragraph below.

Virus (Chapter 2, a term borrowed from biology). A program that invades a computer and embeds itself inside a host program, where it replicates and propagates from computer to computer, infecting each in turn. A virus spreads by infected removable disks, or over a network.

Worm. A program that exploits weaknesses in an operating system or in communications software in order to replicate itself on other computers on a network. A worm does not reside in a host program. Worms are discussed in Chapter 3.

Trojan horse. A program that seems useful, but has a backdoor, installed by its creator and employed later to gather information or to damage software. Examples are programs that mimic login sequences or that fool a user into downloading and executing them by claiming to be useful applications. This type of rogue software is described in Chapter 4.

Spyware is the general name assigned to a whole range of nasty software that runs on a computer, monitors its users' activities, collects information such as keystrokes, screen dumps, and file directories, and either saves this information or sends it to a remote location without the knowledge or consent of the computer owner. Spyware is described in Chapter 9.

■   Scanning. This term refers to software and equipment that methodically probes computers on the Internet for vulnerabilities. Two of the main tools used for this purpose are a vulnerability scanner and a sniffer. They are described here.

Vulnerability scanner. A program designed to quickly check computers on a network for known weaknesses. A port scanner (Section 7.2) is a special case. It is a program that attempts to find open ports on a target computer or ports that are available to access the computer. A firewall is a piece of hardware or software that defends computers from intruders by closing off all unused ports.

Sniffer. A program that captures passwords and other data while the data is in transit either within the computer or between computers or routers on a network.

■   Exploit. A ready-to-run program that takes advantage of a known weakness. These can often be found in hackers' newsgroups.

■   Social engineering. A general term for methods that exploit human weaknesses. A hacker may discover someone's password by calling and pretending to be an official, by looking over someone's shoulder while a password is being typed, or by sending email that pauses as an official notice asking for sensitive information. Bribing and blackmailing are also included in this class. Even though no special software may be needed and no software weakness is exploited, this is still a powerful tool used by many miscreants. Social engineering (page 204) is a wide class that includes, among others, the following methods:

Shoulder spying (or shoulder watching or surfing). A hacker enters a secure computer installation or a restricted computer lab (often disguised as a pizza delivery man) and looks behind users' shoulders for passwords typed by them or being taped to the sides of computer monitors.

Optical spying. The hacker watches from a nearby room or building, perhaps with a binocular, and tries to read keystrokes typed by legitimate users.

Scavenging (or dumpster diving). Hackers have been known to collect trash and examine it for passwords and credit card numbers (see also page 205).

■   Side-channel attacks. A hacker can spy on a secure installation "from the side" by capturing and listening to information that is continuously and unintentionally leaked by electronic devices inside. The basis of this approach is the well-known fact that people are nosy and machines are noisy. Side-channel methods are discussed in Section 1.1, but the following are typical examples.

Eavesdropping. A hacker, often disguised as a telephone company repair man, enters a computer room and plants devices that later transmit to him useful data on the activities of users. Such devices may include radio transmitters, acoustic microphones (Section 1.1.1), and cameras.

Acoustic keyboard eavesdropping. This recent, sophisticated approach to spying employs the little-known fact that each key in a keyboard emits a slightly different sound when pressed. Recording the sounds of keys with a sensitive microphone may enable a hacker to analyze them by computer and discover the actual keys pressed by a user. A similar approach is to use a high-gain antenna outside a building to receive the electromagnetic waves emitted by CRT monitors inside and analyze them to recreate the displays. These methods are discussed in Section 1.1.1.

Root kit. A program especially designed to hide the fact that a computer's security has been compromised. A root kit may replace an operating system program, thereby making it impossible for the user/owner to detect the presence of the intruder by looking at activity inside the computer.

Leet (l33t speak). Slang used by hackers to obfuscate discussions in newsgroups and other "gathering places" on the Internet. Examples of leet are "warez" (for pirated software), "pr0n" for pornography, and "sploitz" for exploits. See Appendix A.

A honeypot is the name of the opposite tool. A honeypot is a server that acts as a decoy, attracting hackers in order to study their methods and monitor their activities. Security workers use honeypots to collect valuable information about new methods and tricks employed by hackers to break into computers.

Hacker motivation and psychology. Why does someone become a hacker? In most cases, hacking involves much study (of programming, communications protocols, and the internal workings of operating systems), expense (the hacker must have a computer and normally also Internet connection), time, and effort.

We all hear about teenagers, high-school kids who spend days in front of a computer, trying to hack into another computer for the satisfying feeling of achievement, of (false) success. This type of hacker, who "works" for the challenge of penetrating a secure computer or a secret computer installation, for the sheer pleasure and the rush of adrenalin, may also be an adult. There are many known cases of disgruntled employees who plant a time bomb in sensitive software and schedule it to go off when they are terminated. Another category is a computer-savvy person who hears about successful hacking episodes and decides to try and make money this way. Spies are also potential hackers. A spy may acquire a great deal of useful information by hacking into a military computer and can do it "from the comfort of his home." A case in point is discussed by [Stoll 88, 90, 04]. Various kinds of terrorists, both home grown and foreigners, are also believed to be active in hacking, because this is one activity that causes much harm with relatively small risk for the hacker. Finally, there is organized crime, as the following quote (from [Brenner 02]) makes clear:

"The Internet is still in its infancy, but we have already seen large segments of human activity migrate wholly or partially into cyberspace, a trend that will only accelerate. Criminal activity has also moved into cyberspace, and this, too, is a trend that will only accelerate; lawbreakers will shift much of their activity into cyberspace because it will increasingly be the venue where illicit profits are to be made and because it offers operational advantages."

Computer crime is perpetrated not just by hackers. Many honest people who have access to computers with important data are tempted to commit a crime in order to enrich themselves. Inevitably, some yield to the temptation. The following story from the 1960s (which may even be true) is just one of many examples. A low-level programmer in a bank had noticed that the quarterly interest payments on the many savings accounts held by the bank (there were tens of thousands of such accounts) were computed to four decimal places, then rounded off. Thus, anything above $0.0075 was rounded up to the next cent and any amount below that was truncated to the nearest cent. In other words, anything below three quarters of a cent earned in interest was going back to the bank. The programmer simply modified the source code of the program that did these computations, directing it to send all this extra money to his account. The story (there are many versions of it) goes on to say that the programmer was unmasked only because he bought an expensive car, too expensive for his salary, and parked it prominently in the bank's parking lot. This story may or may not be true, but in response to it many banks have instituted a policy that requires each programmer to take his annual vacation every year, at which time any software the programmer worked on is scrutinized by special auditors.

⋄ **Exercise Pre.1:** Who audits the auditors?

(A joke. Today, after decades of inflation, it is even possible for a bank programmer to simply take a penny or two from each bank account without the account's owner noticing or caring about the loss, and channel this money to his private account. Before going on vacation, the programmer can clean his program for the benefit of the auditors. While on vacation, the programmer enjoys the extra money. Upon returning, the program can be doctored again. Naturally, this author does not condone such behavior, but it helps to improve the vacation patterns of low-paid bank programmers. On second thought, is this just a joke?)

Another, even more bizarre story is about a pair of programmers who started appearing to work in a matching pair of Rolls-Royces. The company's executives immediately became suspicious and started an investigation. When the pair heard of it, they promptly bolted. However, in spite of a long and careful investigation, nothing untoward was ever discovered. If the two programmers were guilty, they managed to completely cover their tracks, and got scared needlessly.

In the early days of hacking and breaking into computers, some security experts maintained that "hackers have done less damage to corporate computer systems than overflowing lavatories." Today, such a claim seems ludicrous. The damage done to computers, to networks, to individuals, and to the economy is getting worse and has become a global concern. Fighting it involves governments, law enforcement agencies, and security experts all over the world.

For more information, see *How to Become a Hacker* and *Brief History of Hackerdom* by Eric Raymond [Raymond 04].

Not all computer crime and attacks are perpetrated by hackers. Much harm is done by insiders, trusted employees who do it for a variety of reasons. This is the human side of computer security. The history of computer crime is riddled with stories about users who take their frustration out on the computer. They drop it on the floor, shoot it, pound it with a hammer, and even urinate on it, just to vent their feelings and frustration. Some employees strike at their machines as a way to get back at the boss, while others act out of political convictions and allow their fellow party members to sabotage equipment. However, the main reason for insider computer crime is money. An employee or a trusted consultant suddenly realize they have enough knowledge to induce a computer into printing a check, transferring money to their account, or releasing information that can later be sold (such as a mailing list or credit card numbers) and this temptation may prove too much. Such a treacherous insider suddenly turns into a living Trojan horse, as dangerous as those discussed in Chapter 4. The best an employer can do to defend against such employees is to compartmentalize information, to make sure an employee knows only as much as he or she needs to know for their jobs. This policy is difficult to implement in practice, it adversely affects employees' morale and productivity, and it is not full proof.

We have all heard of bank robbers, but one of the most notorious bank robbers, one who kept the title "biggest computer fraud" in the Guinness Book of World Records [Guinness 04] from 1978 to 1999, was someone called Stanley Rifkin, a name most of us would have trouble recognizing. He is virtually forgotten today, perhaps because he didn't use a gun in his exploit and didn't even hack the bank's computer. He was a consultant to the now defunct Security Pacific National Bank in Los Angeles and in this capacity he learned some of the codes used by bank personnel to make large money transfers. He used this knowledge to call the employees in the wire transfer room, pretending to be Mike Hansen, a member of the bank's international department, and con them into transferring ten million dollars to a temporary account that he had previously opened. He later transferred the money to Switzerland and used it to buy diamonds that he then smuggled back to the United States. He was caught by the FBI very quickly, but only because he had bragged about his exploit to his lawyer, trusting the confidentiality of attorney-client relations. The lawyer notified the FBI and Rifkin was arrested. The final twist of this story is that the bank didn't even miss the money when notified by the FBI of the successful solution of this crime.

⋄ **Exercise Pre.2:** Imagine that you are an operator of a large computer. You've been with the company for years, and you have suddenly been switched to the night shift, forcing you to sleep during the day so you rarely get to see your family. You don't want to quit, because in just a few years you'd be eligible for retirement. What can you do to improve your lot?

FBI: Why do you rob banks?
Willie Sutton: Because that's where the money is.
   http://www.fbi.gov/libref/historic/famcases/sutton/sutton.htm.

Computer security: an example

The following incident illustrates the serious nature of Internet security, hacking, and cyber vandalism. On 1 April 2001, a Chinese military jet collided with an American spy plane. The Chinese pilot was killed and the American plane was crippled and had to land in Chinese territory. The crew of 24 was held by China and released 11 days later.

The diplomatic row between the two countries was well publicized, short lived, and did not lead to any long-term animosity. In contrast, the cyber war between Chinese and American hackers was less known, was very intense, and has inflicted much damage to Web sites on both sides. American hackers started scanning Chinese Web sites, looking for vulnerabilities that make it possible to deface or hijack a site. A typical attack ended up leaving offending messages on the target site.

In response, a Chinese hacking group calling itself the Honker (Chinese for "red user") Union of China decided to retaliate. The Honker Web site [honker 04] prompted its members for action with the message "We are obligated to strike back with utmost force after such provocation by American hackers." The group managed to disable many American Web sites and left pro-China messages in others. Among the victims were the Department of Labor, Department of Health and Human Services, and the Web site of the United States Surgeon General. The White House Historical Association Web site (`http://www.whitehousehistory.org/`) was also defaced, presumably because the Chinese assumed it to be a government site (it is a charitable nonprofit institution dedicated to the understanding, appreciation, and enjoyment of the White House).

To an outside observer, this and similar incidents serve as a useful lesson. They do not involve any physical casualties, while keeping Web site owners and administrators on their toes. To the victims, however, this affair seemed at best an annoyance.

About this book

This book is intended as a starting point for those familiar with basic concepts of computers and computations who would like to extend their knowledge into the realm of computer and network security. The book is primarily a textbook for undergraduate classes on computer security. It is mostly nonmathematical and makes no attempt to be complete. The only prerequisite for understanding the material presented here is familiarity with the basic concepts of computers and computations such as (1) the organization of data in bits and bytes, (2) data structures (arrays, trees, and graphs), and (3) network concepts such as IP numbers, input/output ports, and communications protocols.

Timing. The many phrases "at the time of this writing" found in the book refer to the period from October 2004 to mid 2005 during which this book was written.

Special features that enhance the textbook aspect of the book are the many exercises sprinkled throughout the text, the virus timeline (Appendix B), and the Glossary. Another attractive feature is the jokes (check the index). There are no riddles.

A note on references. The text refers to many resources using notation of the form [Thompson 84] where the 2-digit number is a year. All the references are listed in the Bibliography and many are Web sites. As we all know, Web sites tend to have a relatively short life, so by the time this book is in your hands, many of the references may be broken links. However, given the context of a reference, an Internet search engine may locate a cached copy of the original page or a similar page. Don't give up easily.

An interesting (and, I believe, also original) feature of this book is its minimal use of the vague term "system." This word is used only (1) in connection with well-defined or commonly-used terms such as "operating system," "file system," and "notational system," (2) when it is part of names of organizations, or (3) when it is included in a quotation. Many texts use this vague term liberally, thereby confusing the reader. Sentences such as "In addition, the blah flood may exhaust system memory, resulting in a system crash. The net result is that the system is unavailable or nonfunctional," are confusing. Instead of "system" the author should specify what is being discussed, whether it is a computer, a piece of software, a router, or something else. Here is what William Strunk [Strunk 18] has to say about this term.

System. Frequently used without need.	
Dayton has adopted the commission system of government	Dayton has adopted government by commission
The dormitory system	Dormitories
	—William Strunk Jr., *The Elements of Style.*

While I was at it, I also avoided the use of the cliché "basically," employing "essentially" or "fundamentally" instead.

On the other hand, the term "user" is a favorite in this book.

> Why is it drug addicts and computer aficionados are both called users?
> —Clifford Stoll.

Following is a short description of the chapters and appendixes of the book.

- Chapter 1 is a collection of topics that have to do with the physical security of computer hardware, computer networks, and digital data. The topics discussed cover a variety of issues ranging from computer theft and static electricity on carpets to laptop security.

- Chapter 2 is the first of the chapters on rogue software (the term *malware* is often also used). The chapter is devoted to computer viruses, and it covers all the important aspects of this unusual type of software. The various types of viruses, the way viruses propagate, the damage they may inflict (their payload), and the people who write them, are among the topics covered in this chapter.

- Another type of rogue software, namely worms, is the topic of Chapter 3. Techniques for worm propagation are discussed and the historically important Internet worm is described.

- Trojan horses are the topic of Chapter 4. The discussion concentrates on the types of damage done by this type of malware and on how Trojan horses are installed on a computer. Of special interest is Section 4.3 that describes an interesting technique for bugging or rigging a compiler. A Trojan horse can be embedded inside a compiler in such a way that certain programs compiled by it will be infected with the horse, yet nothing suspicious remains in the source code of the compiler itself and even a recompilation of the compiler does not get rid of the malicious software secretly embedded in it.

- Chapter 5 is full of examples of malware. About a dozen examples of viruses, worms, and Trojans are discussed and described in detail. Many (shorter) descriptions can be found in Appendix B.

- The important topics of preventing malware and defending against it make up Chapter 6. Among the methods discussed in this chapter are backing up files, antivirus software and its applications, activity monitors, vaccines, and file permissions. The interesting topic of hoaxes is also included in this chapter.

■   Network security is the topic of Chapters 7 through 10. Chapter 7 starts this important subject with a detailed discussion of important threats that relate to networks. Topics such as port scanning, spoofing, password cracking, firewalls, and denial of service (DoS) are described and analyzed.

■   Chapter 8 concentrates on authentication. Both local and remote methods for authentication are included. Of special interest are the biometric authentication techniques of Section 8.2.

■   Spyware, the topic of Chapter 9, is a relatively new threat and is already serious enough to merit its own discussion and methods of defense. Material on spyware and terrorism and on remote reporting is also included, as are several varieties of spyware such as adware and researchware.

■   Chapter 10 tries to familiarize the reader with the growing crime of identity theft. The topic of phishing is also covered in detail, including examples.

■   Privacy and trust in the online world are the topics of Chapter 11. General privacy concerns as well as children's privacy and safety are discussed, together with how to generate trust in visitors to Web sites (and how to keep it). Notice that privacy issues are also discussed in Section 1.5.

■   Chapter 12 is an introduction to cryptography and how it works. The chapter starts with the concepts of cipher and code and follows this by examples of old monoalphabetic and polyalphabetic ciphers. The important method of the one-time pad and the problem of key distribution are discussed next. The chapter continues with the principles of public-key cryptography, RSA encryption, and the all-important secure socket layer (SSL) protocol.

■   Appendix A introduces "l33t Speak" (pronounced "leet"), a language or a notational system widely used by hackers.

■   Appendix B is a detailed virus timeline. The history of viruses and other types of rogue software is traced from its infancy in the late 1940s to the present day (early 2005), stressing "firsts" such as the first stealth virus and the first boot sector infector.

The book's Web site, with an errata list and BibTEX information, is part of the author's Web site, located at `http://www.ecs.csun.edu/~dsalomon/`. Domain name `www.DavidSalomon.name` has been registered and is used as a mirror. The author's email address is `dsalomon@csun.edu`, but ⟨*anyname*⟩`@DavidSalomon.name` is an alternative address.

Disclaimer. This is not a fact-free book. A book like this could not have been written without the help of many people, but this book was! As a result, the author is the only one responsible for both the correct and useful material in the book and for the many errors that may or may not be discovered in the future.

Lakeside, California   David Salomon

I offer this advice without fee; it is included in the price of this book.
—Muriel Spark, *A Far Cry From Kensington* (1988).

Contents

Preface —————————————————————————— vii

Introduction ————————————————————— 1

1   **Physical Security** ———————————————— 15

    1.1   Side-Channel Attacks   15
    1.2   Physical Threats   20
    1.3   Laptop Security   26
    1.4   Disaster Recovery Planning   28
    1.5   Privacy Protection   29

2   **Viruses** ————————————————————— 33

    2.1   Operating Systems   34
    2.2   Computer Viruses   36
    2.3   Virus Writers   40
    2.4   Virus Propagation   43
    2.5   Virus Classification   46
    2.6   Boot Sector Viruses   48
    2.7   File Infector Viruses   51
    2.8   Companion Viruses   55
    2.9   Multipartite Viruses   56
    2.10   Macro and Script Viruses   57
    2.11   Infected Images   59
    2.12   Virus Life Cycle   62
    2.13   Viruses and UNIX   65
    2.14   Viruses and the Macintosh   65
    2.15   Viruses and the Amiga   66
    2.16   Virus Replication   66
    2.17   Virus Payload   66
    2.18   Virus Organization   74
    2.19   Virus Naming   75

2.20	Virus Hiding Methods	76
2.21	Polymorphism	80
2.22	Virus Stealth Techniques	83
2.23	Interrupts and Viruses	84
2.24	Trapdoors	88

3   Worms _____ **91**

3.1	Code Red I	93
3.2	Worming Techniques	95
3.3	Proposing a CCDC	105
3.4	The Internet Worm	108

4   Trojan Horses _____ **113**

4.1	Applications of Trojans	114
4.2	Installing a Trojan	116
4.3	Rigging a Compiler	118

5   Examples of Malware _____ **125**

5.1	The Lehigh Virus	125
5.2	The Brain Virus	126
5.3	The Michaelangelo Virus	127
5.4	The SirCAM Virus	128
5.5	The Melissa Virus	129
5.6	Scores Virus	130
5.7	Swiss Amiga Virus	131
5.8	Christmas Card Virus	131
5.9	VBS.KAK Worm	132
5.10	The Cruncher Virus	133
5.11	Opener Virus	134
5.12	MTX Worm/Virus	135

6   Prevention and Defenses _____ **139**

6.1	Understanding Vulnerabilities	139
6.2	Defenses Against Malware	144
6.3	Anti-Virus Software	145
6.4	Backups and Such	155
6.5	Hoaxes	160

7   Network Security _____ **163**

7.1	Internet Vulnerabilities	163
7.2	Port Scanning	164
7.3	Spoofs	165
7.4	Spam	169
7.5	Denial of Service	181
7.6	Firewall Basics	184

8   Authentication _____ **189**

8.1	Local Authentication	190
8.2	Biometric Techniques	190
8.3	Passwords	196

9   Spyware _____ **211**

9.1	Introduction and Definition	212
9.2	RIAA and Spyware	215
9.3	Terrorism and Spyware	217
9.4	Political Contributions	218
9.5	Distribution of Spyware	219
9.6	Remote Reporting	222
9.7	Adware	225
9.8	Spyware?	226

10   Identity Theft _____ **231**

10.1	Introduction	232
10.2	Shredding	236
10.3	Internet Cookies	238
10.4	Phishing	239
10.5	The Homograph Threat	245

11   Privacy and Trust _____ **247**

11.1	Privacy Issues	248
11.2	Online Privacy	251
11.3	Children's Privacy	253
11.4	Trust	258

12   Elements Of Cryptography _____ **263**

12.1	Principles of Cryptography	264
12.2	Kerckhoffs's Principle	265
12.3	Polybius's Monoalphabetic Cipher	266
12.4	Polybius's Polyalphabetic Cipher	268
12.5	The One-Time Pad	269
12.6	The Key Distribution Problem	271
12.7	Diffie–Hellman–Merkle Keys	272
12.8	Public-Key Cryptography	273
12.9	RSA Cryptography	274
12.10	SSL: Secure Socket Layer	278

A   l33t Speak _____ **285**

B   Virus Timeline _____ **289**

Concluding Remarks _____ **305**

Answers to Exercises _____ **311**

Glossary _____ **327**

Bibliography _____ **343**

Index _____ **357**

LIFF (n.). A book, the contents of which are totally
belied by its cover. For instance, any book the dust jacket
of which bears the words. "This book will change your life."

—Douglas Adams, *The Meaning of Liff* (1984)

Introduction

The first microprocessors appeared in the early 1970s and were immediately employed in personal computers. A popular question in those early years was: Why would anyone want a computer at home? Typical answers were: To balance your checking account, to store your recipes, and to help you compute your taxes. It was only a few years later, when many already owned personal computers, that computer owners discovered the real reasons for the usefulness of their machines. We buy and use personal computers mainly because they provide us with communications and entertainment.

Games, initially primitive, were written for the early personal computers and became a powerful selling tool in the hands of computer salespersons because of the entertainment they provided. The development of email in the 1970s and of the World Wide Web in the 1980s have turned computers into tools for communications, which is why they became the common household appliances they are today. Most owners of home computers use their computers to play games and to communicate, to send and receive email, and to browse the Internet. Relatively few users perform computations, benefit from a personal data base, or know how to use a spreadsheet.

Once personal computers became a part of our lives, it had quickly been realized that like many other technological advances, computers and data networks have their dark side. Security problems in the form of malicious programs, loss of privacy, and floods of unwanted advertisement and spam, have popped up immediately and have become a way of life for virtually every computer user.

⋄ **Exercise Intro.1:** What industry is the biggest user of computers?

Definitions. The dictionary defines security as "the quality or state of being free from danger" or "measures taken to guard against espionage or sabotage, crime, attack, or escape." This book explores some of the ways computers and computer networks are put at risk by perpetrators, hackers, and other wrongdoers. The terms "attack" and "threat" are used here to identify any activity that aims to gain access to computers for malicious purposes. The terms "security hole," "weakness," and "vulnerability" refer to a state that can be exploited for such an attack (some would even say that a security hole *invites* an attack).

For the purposes of computer security, there are two types of people, insiders (employees) and outsiders (nonemployees). Figure Intro.1 shows the three classes of computer security and crime caused by each of the two types plus the special class of threats that are not directly caused by humans, namely accidents.

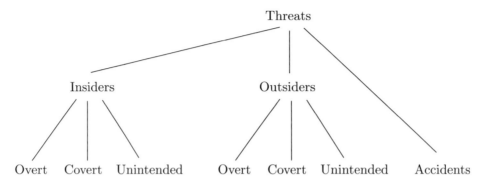

Figure Intro.1: Seven Classes of Computer Security and Crime.

The seven classes are as follows:

■   Insiders overt. Overt actions by insiders are often performed by disgruntled employees and result in destruction of data and equipment. However, this class is small compared to the other six.

■   Insiders covert. Generally, insiders have more information about a place of work than outsiders, which is why they can wreak more havoc. Thus, this class corresponds to serious threats and criminal actions.

■   Insiders unintended. Employees make errors and can also neglect their duties. Consequently, this class encompasses actions such as wrong inputs, wrong data, damage as a result of extreme temperatures or other harsh conditions, and interruption of vital services.

■   Outsiders overt. Physical attacks on computer and network facilities belong in this class as are also DoS attacks (page 181).

■   Outsiders covert. This wide class consists of the various types of rogue software sent from the outside to a personal computer or to a large computer facility.

■   Outsiders unintended. It is fairly rare that an outsider will harm a computer or data unintentionally.

■   Finally, there are accidents. They always happen, not just in the computing field. Accidents are caused either by nature, such as earthquake or flood, or indirectly by humans (see the "insiders unintended" class).

> History is a jangle of accidents, blunders, surprises and absurdities, and so is our knowledge of it, but if we are to report it at all we must impose some order upon it.
> —Henry Steele Commanger, *The Nature and the Study of History*, 1966.

There are many different types of computer security threats and problems, but they can be classified into three large classes as follows:

- Physical security. A personal computer can be stolen. A large computer center can be broken into and equipment taken. Fire, electrical surges, and floods can damage computer hardware and network connections and cause loss of data. These and other physical threats are discussed in Chapter 1.

- Rogue software. We have all heard of computer viruses. Small, sneaky programs that invade our computers and spread quickly and silently. Viruses are just one aspect of the general threat posed by rogue software. This topic, which also includes worms and Trojan horses, is discussed in Chapters 2 through 6.

- Most computers are connected to networks, and most local networks are connected to the Internet. Thus, there is a large class of computer security threats that are related to networks and fall under the category of network security. This wide area of security includes threats such as port scanning, spoofing, password cracking, spyware, and identity theft and is the topic of Chapters 7 through 9.

Almost nonexistent two decades ago, computer security is now a vast, complex, and important field. This book is just one of many books, articles, reports, and other publications that discuss, explain, and analyze the various aspects of and approaches to computer security. The feature that makes this book special is its reliance on the keyword "compromise." This word is employed here in two meanings as follows:

1. Computer security is a compromise. The more security is needed, the less convenient it is for users to use their computers.

2. An attacker has to find only one security weakness to compromise an entire computer installation or many computers worldwide and cause extensive psychological and financial damage to users, their identities, software, and personal and commercial data.

Any security threat or vulnerability described in this book can be reduced, managed, solved, or overcome in some way, but the solution makes it more difficult or less convenient to use the computer, the network, or a particular operating system or program. This view of security as a compromise or a tradeoff is the key to understanding computer and network security.

Anyone who has ever tried to manage accounts on mainframes or local area networks (LANs) will recognize that there is a constant battle between the aspects of security and user friendliness in computer use. This tension arises from the definition of the two functions. If a computer is easy to use, it is easy to misuse. If a password is hard to guess, it is hard to remember. If access to information is simple for the owner, it is simple for the cracker.

—David Harley et al., *Viruses Revealed*, 2001.

Why does the problem of computer security exist? Why are computers so vulnerable to attacks and so easy to damage? This book offers four reasons, but the reader may come up with more.

Reason 1. Computers are fast, accurate, and powerful in certain tasks such as computing, searching, and manipulating data, while being inadequate and inefficient in other tasks, most notably in anything requiring intelligence.

The field of artificial intelligence is almost as old as the modern electronic computer. Researchers have been trying since the 1950s to teach computers how to solve real-world problems such as recognizing patterns, playing games against a human opponent, and translating natural languages, all without success. Today, after half a century of effort, computers can recognize handwriting, can identify speech commands, and can prove certain types of mathematical theorems, but are not good at any of these tasks. Computers have recently become good at beating chess masters at their own game, but only because they (the computers) are fast enough to analyze every possible move in a reasonable time, not because they understand chess.

Thus, computers are fast, reliable, and very useful, but are not very intelligent, which makes them victims of (computer) crime. Even humans, who are much more intelligent, (too?) often fall prey to clever schemes designed to take their money, so it is no wonder that the problem of computer security is serious and is getting worse.

◇ **Exercise Intro.2:** Computers are fast, reliable, and very useful, but are not very intelligent. With this in mind, can they be trusted?

Reason 2. It is easier to break computer security than to build fully secure computers. A modern computer has many security weaknesses and a hacker has to find only one in order to do harm. A security worker, on the other hand, has to find and correct *all* the security holes, a virtually impossible task. This situation is a special case of the general rule discussed in the answer to exercise 2.15.

Reason 3. A computer is controlled by its operating system and modern operating systems are extremely complex. A systems programmer designs an operating system with a view towards making it easy to use, but as we already know, the easier it is to use a computer, the less secure it is. Today's modern graphical user interface (GUI) operating systems are designed around several layers where the user interacts with the top level and the hardware is controlled by the bottom level. Each level controls the one below it and it is this organization in levels that allows malware to hide from the user and perform its operations in relative obscurity and safety.

At the time of this writing (late 2004 and early 2005), operating systems have become so complex that hackers constantly find ways to exploit vulnerabilities and security holes in them. Quite often, such holes are discovered by honest users who then notify the maker of the operating system, resulting in a patch or an update being promptly issued to solve that problem, only for a new hole to be quickly discovered. The following warning, found on the Internet in late October 2004, is typical. It shows how difficult it is to identify a security vulnerability, because it may occur in rare circumstances. Don't worry about the details, just keep in mind that this announcement is typical.

Security Update 2004-10-27 addresses a security hole in Apple Remote Desktop:
Available for: Apple Remote Desktop Client 1.2.4 with Mac OS X 10.3.x
CVE-ID: CAN-2004-0962

Impact: An application can be started behind the loginwindow and it will run as root. Description: For a system with these following conditions

Apple Remote Desktop client installed
A user on the client system has been enabled with the Open and quit applications privilege
The username and password of the ARD user is known
Fast user switching has been enabled
A user is logged in, and loginwindow is active via Fast User Switching
If the Apple Remote Desktop Administrator application on another system is used to start a GUI application on the client, then the GUI application would run as root behind the loginwindow. This update prevents Apple Remote Desktop from launching applications when the loginwindow is active. This security enhancement is also present in Apple Remote Desktop v2.1. This issue does not affect systems prior to Mac OS X 10.3.

Reason 4. In addition to the complexity and vulnerability of operating systems, there is another factor that affects the behavior of a computer, namely the Internet and its protocols. Most personal computers and mainframes are connected to the Internet and enjoy the benefits of communications that it confers. In order for many computers to communicate, there is a need for communications standards, which is why various communications protocols had to be developed. Such a protocol is a set of rules that specify the individual steps of a complete Internet session. Thus, all the computers that send, forward, and receive email have to execute the same protocol. Similarly, transferring files between computers requires a protocol. The point is that the important Internet protocols were developed in the 1970s and 1980s, before Internet security became a global concern. This is why the security features included in the protocols are often weak. These protocols were examined by many experts and users who made contributions and proposed changes, but once such a protocol is approved and many programs are written to implement it, there is no way to go back and modify it. When a security hole is discovered, warnings are issued and programs are patched, but the underlying protocol is known to be weak.

The Ten Immutable Laws of Security (From [technet 04]).

Microsoft security workers investigate countless security reports every year and the 10 immutable laws of security [technet 04] listed here are based on their experience. The security issues discussed here are general and stem from the main weakness of computers, namely the lack of intelligence. They show that the best way to minimize security risks is to use common sense. Here is a summary of the 10 laws:

1: If someone can persuade you to run his program on your computer, it's not your computer anymore.

2: If someone can alter the operating system on your computer, it's not your computer anymore.

3: If someone has unrestricted physical access to your computer, it's not your computer anymore.

4: If you allow someone to upload programs to your website, it's not your website anymore.

5: Weak passwords defeat strong security.

6: A computer is only as secure as its owner/user is trustworthy.

7: Encrypted data is only as secure as the decryption key.

8: An out-of-date virus scanner is only marginally better than none at all.

9: Absolute anonymity isn't practical, in real life or on the Web.

10: Technology is not a panacea.

And here are the same laws in more detail:

Law 1: If someone can persuade you to run his program on your computer, it's not your computer anymore.

It doesn't take much knowledge to understand that when a computer program runs, it will do exactly what it is programmed to do, even if it is programmed to be harmful. When you elect to run a program, you let it control your computer. Once a program is running, it can do anything that a user program can do on the computer. It could collect your keystrokes and save them or send them outside. It could open your text files and change all the occurrences of "will" to "won't" in some of them. It could send rude emails to all your addressees. It could install a virus or other rogue software. It could create a backdoor that lets a fraudster control your computer remotely. It could dial up a long-distance number and leave you stuck with the bill. It could even erase your hard disk.

Which is why it is important to never run, or even download, a program from an untrusted source, where "source," means the person who wrote it, not the person who gave it to you. There's a nice analogy between running a program and eating a sandwich. If a stranger walked up to you and offered you a sandwich, would you eat it? Probably not. How about if your best friend gave you a sandwich? Maybe you would, maybe you wouldn't, it depends on whether she made it or found it lying in the street. Using common sense in the security of your computer means to apply the same critical thought to a program that you would to a sandwich.

Law 2: If someone can alter the operating system on your computer, it's not your computer anymore.

An operating system is a program (rather, a set of programs) that provide important services and also supervise users. As such, the operating system must be more powerful than users' programs. Thus, letting someone modify your operating system is like letting them have more power in your computer than you do. Operating system routines must be powerful, which implicitly makes them trusted. The owner and users of the computer must trust those routines, which is why anyone who manages to corrupt them can gain complete control.

A perpetrator gaining operating system privileges can log into the computer locally or remotely, obtain users' passwords, change users' privileges, and in general do anything in the computer. The conclusion is again to use sound judgement before you let anyone mess up with your operating system.

Law 3: If someone has unrestricted physical access to your computer, it's not your computer anymore.

Someone who has access to your computer can deny you your computer's services simply by smashing it (this is an example of stone-age denial of service). More likely, the computer would be stolen, or even held for ransom. Having physical access makes it easy to install spyware, change the administrator's password, copy data off the hard disk, or do any other type of damage that's difficult or impossible to do from a distance. Any protection provided by the operating system is moot when a stranger has physical access to the computer.

◇ **Exercise Intro.3:** Think of an example of such damage.

Thus, a computer, personal or multiuser, should be physically protected in a way compatible with its value, but it's important to consider the value of the data in the computer, not just the market value of the hardware. Computers used in business and sensitive computers such as servers should be kept in a locked room and be physically protected. The list on Page 20 has more information on this topic.

Laptop computers are popular nowadays, and not only with their owners. Thieves target those machines because of their high price and availability. A laptop is normally taken out by its owner while traveling and is used in public places, thereby making it a potentially easy item to steal. Section 1.3 has more on laptop security.

Law 4: If you allow someone to upload programs to your Web site, it's not your Web site any more.

We already know that it is dangerous to let someone upload a program to your computer, but in most of these cases, the program is uploaded to a Web site and the uploader is permitted by the site's owner to run it. Long experience shows that Web site owners often allow visitors, out of the goodness of their heart or our of carelessness, to upload software and run it; a risky habit.

Security dictates that the owner of a Web site should limit the freedom of visitors. This is especially true in cases where the Web site is hosted by a large server that also hosts other sites. In such a case, a hacker who takes control of one site can extend his control to all the Web sites on the server. The owner of a large, shared server who wants to avoid trouble should therefore be security conscious.

Law 5: Weak passwords defeat strong security.

Section 8.3 discusses passwords, how they provide remote identification and authentication, and how important it is to select strong passwords. If you have an account on a remote computer and you select a weak password, chances are that someone will manage to crack or guess it. The strong security on the computer wouldn't protect you in such a case. If someone logs in as you, then the operating system treats him as you.

Security experts keep stating the surprising fact that many computer accounts have extremely weak passwords, such as the null password or one of the words "guest," "password," "admin," and "test."

The conclusion is obvious and unavoidable (but still ignored by many users). Select a strong password! It should include letters (both lowercase and uppercase), digits, and some punctuation marks. It should be long, and should be replaced often. Try not to write your password anywhere and don't tell it to anyone.

> Two people can keep a secret, but only if one of them is dead.
> —Benjamin Franklin.

Smartcards have been introduced a few years ago and can be used for authentication. Biometric products, such as fingerprint and retina scanners (Section 8.2), are also becoming more popular, but are still too expensive for common use.

Law 6: A computer is only as secure as its administrator is trustworthy.

The owner of a home personal computer is normally its administrator and sole user as well. A large, multiuser computer has many users and may be owned by a commercial entity, but it must have an administrator. The administrator is responsible for managing user accounts, installing software, searching for viruses, establishing security and usage policies, and perform any other tasks needed for a smooth run of the facility. It is obvious that the administrator is all powerful in the computer and that an untrustworthy administrator can create havoc in the computer installation.

Such an administrator can negate any security measures taken by the users, can install rogue software, can spy on the users, change their privileges and permissions, and turn off any security and protection features the operating system supports. In short, an untrustworthy administrator is the worst thing that can happen to computer security. An organization planning to acquire a large, multiuser computer should therefore start by hiring a trustworthy administrator. This person should have some experience working with large, multiuser computers and with computer security, but should most of all prove trustworthy. The references of each candidate for this position should be carefully checked and a complete background check should also be considered. In short, each candidate should be fully vetted. In addition, periodic checks of the administrator are also recommended.

There are methods to keep administrators countable. Often it is possible to have two, or even several administrators. Each should be assigned a user account, but with full privileges, instead of an administrator account. This way, the owner or an auditor can tell who did what on the computer. It also helps if the operating system allows to write a copy of all log files and audit information on a different computer. Each time software is installed or updated, one administrator should do the job, and another should later act as an auditor, checking the results.

Law 7: Encrypted data is only as secure as the decryption key.

Section 12.2 shows that an encryption algorithm can be made public (in fact, often has to be public if it is to be widely used) and the security of encryption depends on the encryption key. Thus, encryption keys have to be selected carefully and should be kept secret. Such a key should not be kept in the computer unless it is encrypted and protected by another key. When public-key cryptography (Section 12.8) is used, the private key should be protected in the same way.

Law 8: An out-of-date virus scanner is only marginally better than no virus scanner at all.

Anti-virus software is discussed on page 145, where it is stressed that this type of software has to be updated regularly, as new viruses are discovered and analyzed. Thus, anti-virus software is not for the lazy. A computer owner should check every day for new updates of this software, download and install them, and run the programs. A delay in installing a new update may mean an infection by a new virus, so a computer owner/user should start each day (as this author does) by looking up new virus information on the Internet. On a day a new virus is discovered, the user should be especially careful. No software should be downloaded and no email attachment opened until a new anti-virus update is issued and run.

Current anti-virus software normally checks for new updates automatically every time it is run. This is an important feature of the software and it shouldn't be disabled by users just to speed up the process of virus checking.

Law 9: Absolute anonymity isn't practical, in real life or on the Web.

Absolute anonymity in real life is impossible. From time to time we hear about people who cherish their privacy and try to avoid contact with others, especially the media. Howard Hughes is a classic example of such a recluse. There are those who try to stay completely anonymous, but even they have to interact with people, with the result that certain facts are eventually found out about them. Perhaps the best known example of an unknown person is the writer B. Traven, also known as Ret Marut, Hal Croves, and Traven Torsvan. He is the author of *The Treasure of the Sierra Madre* and many other novels. He lived in Mexico from about 1925 until his death in 1969, but despite many efforts to unravel his identity, we still don't know his real name and where and when he was born. Yet even this elusive character had to communicate with his publishers and movie directors, which is why today much is known about his life (see, for example, [Guthke 91]).

> I am freer than anybody else. I am free to choose the parents I want, the country I want, the age I want.
> —Rosa Elena Luján (Traven's widow) in the *New York Times*, 25 June 1990.

Merely appearing in public reveals your eye color and approximate height, weight, and age. Similarly, a chat with a stranger can reveal facts about yourself, your family, your profession, place of living, and your interests.

⋄ **Exercise Intro.4:** What other important fact can such a conversation yield to a stranger?

Identity theft is discussed in Chapter 10, where it is shown that maintaining anonymity and privacy is becoming more difficult and may already be impossible. Here are a few disguising techniques employed by those who are serious about maintaining their anonymity on the Internet. (1) Use network address translation to mask your real IP address. (2) Subscribe to an anonymizing email service (Section 11.2) that forwards your email with a different sender's address. (3) Use different ISPs for different purposes. (4) Visit certain Web sites only from public Internet cafes.

Such techniques and habits make it harder, but not impossible, for identity thieves to locate your personal information. The best way to protect your identity in this age of the Internet is to use common sense and to be careful.

Law 10: Technology is not a panacea.

Technology has been advancing rapidly in the last few decades. Many still remember the days without answering machines, cell telephones, or CDs. Yet technology has its downside too. We depend so much on computers that when something around us goes wrong, it is normally because of a computer glitch. We see our privacy slipping from under out feet. Many, especially the elderly, find it harder to learn how to use new gadgets. People are baffled by the rising threat of computer security. The phrase "the butler did it," much favored by mystery writers in the past, has been replaced with "it was a computer glitch/bug."

We simply have to live with the fact that technology is not the answer to all our problems, and that computers, wizards that they are, are not intelligent enough to defend themselves against wrongdoers. Security, especially computer security, must use policy in addition to technology. Security is a combination of technology and how it is used. Pest control professionals always disclaim "we do not exterminate pests, we just control them." Similarly, technology cannot solve the security problem, it can only keep it under control. We should look at security as a journey, not a destination.

⋄ **Exercise Intro.5:** There is nothing magical about 10, so try to come up with another law in the spirit of the above 10. (See also exercise 11.4.)

The discussion here shows that the task of achieving computer security involves common sense, encryption, legal means, various technical means such as passwords, parity bits, CRCs, and checksums, and lastly, keeping secrets. The book discusses the various types of threats to computers and networks and many of the technical means used as defenses. This is followed by a discussion of the principles of cryptography and current encryption methods and protocols. Common sense is also mentioned several times but this author isn't going to try to discuss it in any detail or to teach it. Finally, the next paragraph discusses secrets.

Some security problems can be solved or avoided by keeping certain things secret, but experience teaches us that keeping secrets is only a temporary solution, because we can tell people all kinds of secrets, but we cannot make them forget the secrets when they move, quit, are laid off, or get promoted. The physical analog is different. When we secure something with a lock and key, we can remove or replace the lock as needed. With human beings, though, secrets are not safe. A secret may be divulged accidentally or intentionally, and on the other hand it cannot be expunged from someone's memory even by the strictest order issued by a supreme authority. If at all possible, it is preferable to maintain security by technical means rather than by keeping secrets.

> The secret of teaching is to appear to have known all your life what you just learned this morning.
>
> —Anonymous

Resources for Computer Security

The best place to turn to, for resources and help in computer security, is the Internet, specifically, the Web. There are Web sites that provide historical information, discuss recent developments and threats, educate computer users, and offer tools and techniques for protection. It is very common to find in many Web sites security news and warnings such as the one quoted here (from 1 October 2004):

---

eEye has uncovered new security holes affecting a wide range of RealNetworks' media players, including the Mac version, according to Techworld. "The flaws could be exploited via a malicious Web page or a RealMedia file run from a local drive to take over a user's system or delete files, according to RealNetworks. The most serious of the three new bugs involves malformed calls, and could be exploited via a player embedded in a malicious site to execute arbitrary code. This bug affects RealPlayer 10, 10.5.... A second bug could also allow malicious code execution, but only via a local RM file, RealNetworks said. The bug affects several versions of RealPlayer and RealOne Player on Windows, Mac OS X and Linux."

However, the Word Wide Web also offers resources for hackers. Source code for various types of malicious programs, "success" stories of hackers, and information on weaknesses discovered in various operating systems, servers, and network software are available for the taking. Following is a short list of some "good" sites that offer reliable information and user education. In particular, any software downloaded from these resources stands a good chance of being uncontaminated.

- Perhaps the best overall site is the computer emergency response team, located at `www.cert.org`. This active organization, founded in 1988, is part of the software engineering institute of Carnegie-Mellon University, that receives reports from affected users and network administrators, and is often the first to distribute information on new threats.

- The national infrastructure protection center is a joint FBI and private sector body charged with protecting United States network and computer infrastructures. It is located at `www.nipc.gov`.

- The computer incident advisory capability (CIAC) is part of the United States department of energy. It is located at `www.ciac.org` and has uptodate information on attacks (real and hoaxes), as well as software tools.

- The system administration, networking, and security (SANS), at `www.sans.org`, whose mission is to help network administrators with certification, recent news, and training. The conferences on network security it organizes are highly respected.

- COAST—computer operations, audit, and security technology—is a multi-project, multiple investigator laboratory in computer security research in the Computer Sciences Department at Purdue University. It functions with close ties to researchers and engineers in major companies and government agencies. This organization is located at `www.cerias.purdue.edu/coast`.

- Counterpane Internet Security, located at `www.counterpane.com`, is a company that specializes in all aspects of Internet security. It was founded by the well-known security expert Bruce Schneier. The company provides sophisticated surveillance technology and the services of highly trained experts to help network users stay ahead of today's software vulnerabilities, malicious insiders, and attackers from the outside.

■   RSA Security, at `http://www.rsasecurity.com/` specializes in cryptography. The company develops new encryption methods and helps organizations protect private information and manage the identities of the people and applications accessing and exchanging that information.

■   Some hacker sites (those tend to be either useless or short lived) are the hacker quarterly (`http://www.2600.com/`), the chaos computer club (`http://www.ccc.de/`), and the hacker network (`http://www.hackernetwork.com/`).

■   A useful site with many virus descriptions, statistics, and a virus glossary is [f-secure 05].

■   [Webopedia 04] is a useful Web site that describes many Internet security issues.

■   [attrition 04] is a Web site maintained by volunteers and dedicated to Internet security. It collects information on many types of attacks, weaknesses, and errors in books on computer security. (This author hopes not to see this book listed in the attrition site.)

■   The various Internet search engines can always find useful sites. Search under "computer security," "network security," "internet security," or "hacker." For specific threats or to learn more about specific topics, try "Windows security," "virus," "unix security," or other key phrases. Much information (in fact, too much) can be had by subscribing to various mailing lists. Search under "security mailing list."

■   Needless to say, because of the importance of this topic, there is a huge number of books, in all areas of security, and at all levels. A quick search at `amazon.com` returns more than 78,000 titles for computer security and more than 81,000 for network security. The following is a list of a few popular books:

Security in Computing, Third Edition, Charles P. Pfleeger and Shari L. Pfleeger.
Exploiting Software: How to Break Code, Greg Hoglund and Gary McGraw.
Beyond Fear, Bruce Schneier.
Cryptography and Network Security: Principles and Practice (3rd Ed.), W. Stallings.
Network Security Essentials (Second Edition), William Stallings.
Computer Security: Art and Science, Matt Bishop.
Network Security: Private Communication in a Public World, Second Edition, Charlie Kaufman, et al.
Network Security: A Beginner's Guide, Second Edition, Eric Maiwald.
Computers Under Attack: Intruders, Worms, and Viruses, Peter J. Denning, ACM Press, New York, N.Y., 1990.
An Introduction to Computer Security: The NIST Handbook, Special Publication 800-12. A 290-page book in PDF format, available online at [NIST Handbook 04].
The following books concentrate on computer viruses.
Viruses Revealed, David Harley et al., Osborne/McGraw-Hill, 2001.

Robert Slade's Guide to Computer Viruses, 2nd edition, Robert M. Slade, Springer-Verlag 1996.

Dr. Solomon's Virus Encyclopedia, Alan Solomon S&S International, 1995.

A Short Course on Computer Viruses, 2nd edition, Frederick B. Cohen, New York, NY, John Wiley, 1994.

PC Security and Virus Protection Handbook, Pamela Kane, M&T Books, 1994.

A Pathology of Computer Viruses, David Ferbrache, Springer-Verlag, 1992.

Computer Virus Handbook, Harold J. Highland, Elsevier, 1990 (a little outdated).

Rogue Programs: Viruses, Worms, and Trojans, Lance Hoffman (ed.) Van Nostrand Reinhold (1990).

In addition to books, extensive literature on computer security is available online. As an example, the NSA has a number of documents on computer security at [NSA-SEC 05].

Last word: The best line of defense against all types of computer security is education and the use of technology, combined with good old common sense.

> Computer security is not a joke.
> —Ian Witten

1
Physical Security

What normally comes to mind, when hearing about or discussing computer security, is either viruses or some of the many security issues that have to do with networks, such as loss of privacy, identity theft, or how to secure sensitive data sent on a network. Computer security, however, is a vast discipline that also includes mundane topics such as how to physically protect computer equipment and secure it against fire, theft, or flood. This chapter is a short discussion of various topics that have to do with physical security.

1.1 Side-Channel Attacks

In order to whet the reader's appetite we start with a new, exotic area of physical threats termed *side-channel attacks*. At the time of this writing there aren't many references for this area, but [Shamir and Tromer 04] discuss several aspects of this topic.

A sensitive, secret computer installation may be made very secure. It may be surrounded by high electrified fences, employ a small army of guards, be protected by powerful firewalls complemented by watchful system programmers working three shifts, and run virus detection software continuously. Yet, it is possible to spy on such an installation "from the side" by capturing and listening to information that is continuously and unintentionally leaked by electronic devices inside. The basis of this approach is the well-known fact that people are nosy and machines are noisy.

First, a bit of history. One of the earliest side-channel attacks took place in 1956 when Britain's military intelligence (MI5) executed operation ENGULF that tapped (perhaps among others) the telephone of the Egyptian embassy in London to record the sound from its Hagelin cipher machines. The sound was used to determine the settings on the Hagelin machines [Wright 89]. A better-known side-channel attack was published by Wim Van Eck [van Eck 85] in 1985, that showed how to eavesdrop on a CRT by detecting its electromagnetic emission.

The following story (heard by this author back in the 1970s) illustrates the power of a side-channel attack.

In the early days of computing, punched cards were the main way to input data into a computer, and printers were the main output. Then came terminals with keyboards and printers, followed by terminals with keyboards and monitor screens. A CRT monitor works like a television tube. An electron beam is directed to a glass plate (the screen) that's coated with a phosphor compound. When the electrons hit the screen, their kinetic energy is converted to light, and a small dot flashes momentarily on the glass. The beam is then moved to another point on the screen, and the process continues until all the required information is displayed on the screen. The process is then repeated in order to refresh the glow on the screen.

An anonymous electronics engineer had an idea. He knew that an accelerated (and also decelerated) electric charge radiates, so he decided to try to detect and receive the radiation from a monitor screen with a small antenna and use it to reconstruct the information displayed on the screen. He drove
a van full of his equipment next to an office building where
workers were hunched at their computers and many monitors glowed, and within half an hour, a monitor screen in
the van showed the data displayed on one of the screens
in the building. This was a classic example of advanced
electronic eavesdropping applied in industrial spying. For
further discussion of this threat, see [Zalewski 05].

Modern monitors use LCDs or plasma screens that presumably don't radiate, but in the past, the only countermeasures to side-channel attacks were to either surround a computer room with a conductive material, to block any electromagnetic radiation from escaping, or to have a guarded, empty area around the entire building and move the parking lots away from the building.

The information that emanates naturally from a computer consists of electromagnetic radiation, sound, light from displays, and variations in power consumption.

It is intuitively clear that an idle CPU (i.e., a CPU that has executed a HLT instruction) requires less power than a busy CPU. Thus, measuring the power consumption of a CPU can tell a spy whether the CPU is busy or idle. Even more, power consumption depends on the instruction being executed, so while the CPU executes a loop it consumes a certain amount of power, and when it comes out of the loop its power consumption may change.

Our computers are electronic. They work by moving electrons between the various parts of the computer. A working CPU therefore emits electromagnetic radiation that can be detected outside the computer, outside the computer room, and even outside the computer building. A spy who knows the type of CPU being spied on can execute many programs on the same type of CPU, measure the radiation emitted, and thus associate certain patterns of radiation with certain types of computer operations, such as loops, idle, or input/output. Once such an association has been established, the spy can train a computer program to analyze radiation emitted by a spied computer and draw conclusions about the activity of the spied CPU at various times.

A CPU is an integrated circuit (IC, or a chip) enclosed in a ceramic or plastic container and has no moving parts. Yet, inside the container there are several parts (a cavity for the CPU chip, the chip itself, wires, and printed connections) and they vibrate, thereby generating sound. This type of acoustic emanation can be detected by a sensitive microphone and analyzed, similar to electromagnetic radiation, to provide clues on the state of the CPU. Experiments suggest that each type of CPU operation produces a characteristic sound—a typical acoustic signature. Thus, listening to the sound produced by a CPU that's busy all day encrypting secret messages may yield the encryption key (or keys) used by the operator; a significant achievement.

A CPU is normally part of a larger enclosure that has many other electronic parts and fans. These also emit sound waves and the computer room may also be noisy. This background noise complicates the analysis of sound waves emitted by the CPU, but it has been discovered that the latter sound is mostly above 10 kHz, whereas other sounds generated in and out of a computer are of much lower frequencies.

The sound created by a CPU depends on the CPU type, on the temperature inside the computer box, and on other environmental factors such as humidity. This fact complicates the analysis of sound waves from the CPU, but experiments conducted in various environments indicate that it is still possible to obtain useful information about the status of a CPU by analyzing what can be termed its *audio output*.

It is possible to absorb the sound emanated by a CPU by enclosing the computer box with a sound dampening material. An alternative is to generate artificial high-frequency sound outside the computer, to mask the sound that the spy is trying to capture and record. A more sophisticated technique is to absorb the sound emanated by the CPU and have another CPU running a different program to generate sound to foil any spy who may be listening outside. These considerations apply also to electromagnetic radiation emitted by the CPU.

A hard disk also generates sound because its head assembly moves in a radial direction to seek various cylinders. However, there is only a loose association between CPU input/output operations and the movements of the head, because of the use of cache memories and the fact that many CPUs work on several programs simultaneously (multitasking).

Researchers in this field feel that acoustic emanations are important and should be studied and fully understood, because it is harder to stop sound than to absorb electromagnetic waves. A common cold-war spying technique was to listen to a conversation in a closed room by directing a laser beam at a window and measuring its reflection from the glass pane that vibrates because of the sound waves inside.

An important class of side-channel attacks is the so-called *timing attacks*. A timing attack uses the fact that many important computational procedures take time that depends on the input. Thus, by measuring the time it takes to complete a procedure, a spy can learn something about the input to the procedure. An important example is the RSA encryption algorithm (Section 12.9). Part of this algorithm computes an expression of the form a^b where b is the encryption key. A simple method to compute an exponentiation is to multiply a by itself $b - 1$ times, so measuring the time it takes to compute a^b may give a spy an idea of the size of b and thus help in breaking a code. For a reference on timing attacks, see [Boneh and Brumley 04].

The idea of a side-channel attack is not limited to emanations from the CPU. The next section discusses an application to keystrokes, and there have also been attempts to exploit the sounds made by certain types of printers to reconstruct the information being printed. For a reference, see [Kuhn 04].

> It has long been a dream of cryptographers to construct a "perfect" machine.... The development in the last twenty years of electronic machines that accumulate data, or "remember" sequences of numbers or letters, may mean that this dream has already been fulfilled. If so, it will be the nightmare to end all nightmares for the world's cryptanalysts. In fact, the people who live in the vicinity of the National Security Agency think that there already are too many cipher and decoding machines in existence. The electronic equipment plays havoc with their television reception.
>
> —From [Moore and Waller 65].

1.1.1 Acoustic Keyboard Eavesdropping

Chapter 9 mentions keystroke loggers (or keystroke recorders) among other examples of spyware. A keystroke logger is a program that records every keystroke the user makes, and stores this data or transmits it to its owner (the spy). A similar concept is a screen capture, a program that periodically takes a snapshot of the monitor screen and saves it or transmits it outside. There are programs that identify and delete spyware, but spying on a computer can also be done physically. A crude idea is to try to spy on a computer user by looking behind their shoulder, but a more practical, more sophisticated technique is to install a miniature radio transmitter inside a keyboard, to transmit keystrokes to a nearby spy (See exercise Intro.3). Such a transmitter is a physical threat and cannot be detected by Spyware-removal software.

An even more sophisticated spying technique records keystrokes by listening to the sounds that individual keys make when pressed. Old timers in the computing field may remember that pressing a key on an old keyboard often resulted in two or more copies of the key read from the keyboard due to bouncing of the keys. In a modern keyboard, the keys are placed on top of a plastic sheet and different areas of this sheet vibrate differently (and therefore create different air vibrations, sounds) when a key is pressed. Thus, striking different keys generates different sounds (also the timing of keys varies, an A may take the keyboard slightly longer to produce than a B). The ear is not sensitive enough to hear the differences between sounds generated by different keys, but a good quality microphone is.

The idea of acoustic keyboard eavesdropping is for a spy to hide a microphone as close as possible to a keyboard, to record the sound made by the keys when pressed, to digitize the sound, and to send the audio samples to a computer program controlled by the spy. Experiments have demonstrated that a sensitive parabolic microphone can record keyboard sounds reliably from distances of up to 50 feet (about 17 meters) from the keyboard even in the presence of background noise.

Once the program learns to distinguish the individual sounds, it has to be trained so it can tell which key produces a given sound. In principle, the spy has to use another method, such as a keystroke logger, to capture many keystrokes, then feed the (ASCII codes of the) keys and the corresponding sounds to the program. In practice, however, it has been discovered that keyboards of the same make and model produce very similar sounds. Once the spy knows the kind of keyboard used by the victim, he may train his program on a keyboard of the same type, then feed it the sounds created by the poor victim's keyboard. If the program can recognize, say, 80% of the keystrokes of that keyboard, the spy can use his intelligence to guess the remaining keystrokes and employ this information to train the program further.

⋄ **Exercise 1.1:** Is it enough for a spy to detect 80% of a password?

Currently, such spying is exotic and (we hope) rare, but it is a dangerous development in the field of computer security because it is a physical threat and it cannot be recognized and blocked by software. Future developments may bring this type of spying to the attention (and the price range) of many would-be eavesdroppers, with unforeseen (and perhaps disastrous) consequences. A spy can often get to within 50 feet of his target's house by parking a car in the street, renting a room in a nearby house or adjacent apartment, or planting the microphone in a plant in the backyard. (Many front- and backyards have low-voltage lines to light the perimeter of the house at night, and this electricity may be tapped into to power the microphone.) In a place of work it may be easy to install a microphone in a desk next to the victim's desk or in an office adjacent to the victim's office, and such spying may be extremely difficult to detect.

At present it seems that computer hackers and criminals are not aware of this threat and continue to break into computers by means of viruses and by breaking firewalls. Admittedly, someone who wants to control a vast number of computers cannot use this method, but it may prove attractive to certain spies, especially those who currently install and use spyware. A list of potential spyware users can be found at the beginning of Chapter 9.

This vulnerability of keyboards can be eliminated by redesigning keyboards such that all keys would generate the same sound or very similar sounds. The technique of acoustic eavesdropping, however, is not limited to keyboards.

For a recent reference on this approach, see [Asonov and Agrawal 04].

The idea of eavesdropping on a typewriter keyboard, mentioned as coming from Dmitri Asonov ("Acoustic Keyboard Eavesdropping"), was anticipated decades ago by the National Security Agency. The radio waves created each time a key is struck on the keyboard of a teletypewriter or an electrical cipher machine differ from letter to letter. These can be detected and discriminated, thereby enabling the eavesdropper to understand the message before it is encrypted for transmission. The technique is code-named Tempest.

—David Kahn, *The New York Times*, 23 January 2005.

1.2 Physical Threats

▪   Surges in electrical power, often caused by lightning, may burn out electronic components in the computer. Solution: Use an uninterruptible power supply (UPS). Such a device regulates the incoming voltage and produces a clean output signal. If the voltage gets high, the UPS trims it. If the voltage drops, the UPS uses its internal battery to supply the computer with power for a few minutes, enough to either turn off the computer (typical for a home computer) or to start a generator (typical in a large installation, especially an installation that has to operate continuously, such as a hospital or a telephone exchange).

◇ **Exercise 1.2:** What can go wrong if power to the computer is suddenly turned off?

▪   Physical security of computer facilities. We constantly hear of damage done by computer viruses and other malicious programs, but the best virus protection software cannot prevent a home personal computer from being stolen (although it can help in its recovery, see Section 1.3). Thus, computer security starts by protecting the facilities that house computers and computer data. This problem is especially acute in industry. Many a company can be wiped out if its computers or especially if its sensitive data are stolen or damaged. Damage can be intentional, inflicted by a criminal or a disgruntled employee, or accidental, caused by fire, power failure, or broken air conditioning.

The solution is to physically protect this sensitive asset. A home should have an alarm system and power to the computer should go through an uninterrupted power supply (UPS). A commercial entity should have a secure computer facility, with controlled access, heavy doors, card-operated locks, security cameras, and an automatic fire system (using gas instead of water if possible). In addition, special care should be given to unconventional entry points, such as attics and air conditioning ducts. A modern office building often has a large attic above the ceiling of each floor. This space is handy for stringing wires inside the building, but can be used by a person to crawl into an otherwise secure room. A wide air-conditioning duct can be used for the same purpose and should therefore be secured by a heavy screen.

Other items, such as emergency lights, fireproof containers (for storing disks and papers), and proper training of personnel, are also important.

▪   Traditionally, fire is suppressed by water, but this causes damage to structures and equipment that may exceed the damage caused by the fire. For a while, a gas known as halon was used to extinguish fires in sensitive environments, but this was later found to deplete the ozone layer in the atmosphere. Modern replacements for water and halon are certain fluids that look like water but evaporate quickly. An example is the chemical NOVEC 1230 made by 3M [3M 04]. It can be used to protect delicate objects and electronic equipment from fire without damaging the items themselves.

Heat is only one type of damage caused by a fire. Smoke and soot particles resulting from a fire can compound the damage by contaminating removable disks, ruining the delicate mechanisms of magnetic disk and optical drives, and dirtying the electrical connections in keyboards. A case in point is the explosive eruption of Mount St. Helens in 1980, whose volcanic ash damaged computer equipment at large distances from the mountain.

Case study. The Pentagon is the United States' military headquarters. Located near Washington, D.C., the Pentagon has many computers and extensive networking equipment. Back in the 1970s, someone forgot to turn off a 300-watt light bulb in a vault where computer tapes were stored. The small bulb generated heat that had nowhere to go and started heating up the room and smoldering the ceiling. When the door was finally opened, the fresh air rushing into the room turned the high temperature to fire. The fire spread to several adjoining rooms and caused damage in the millions of dollars.

■   Theft should especially be mentioned, because personal computers are getting smaller and lightweight all the time and are therefore easy to steal. There is a school of thought in law enforcement that says that if you want to catch a thief, you should think like one. We hear about sophisticated hackers who write viruses and spyware, but an unsophisticated thief can cause much harm by stealing computers, because all the data in the computer disappears with the computer. Such data may be slow and expensive to replace and may also be private and sensitive. We should always keep in mind the simple, straightforward brute-force approach that computer thieves often adopt. Simply sneak in, take what you find, and get away quickly.

■   A facility that uses electronic locks and keys or other physical-identification devices to restrict access to certain areas should consider the following problem, known as piggybacking or tailgating. An intruder may wait at a locked door, perhaps holding disks, paper or other innocuous-looking stuff with both hands, trying to look legitimate and waiting for the door to open. When someone comes out of the restricted room, the intruder slips in while the door is still open. A guard can prevent such a problem, but this is an expensive solution. An alternative is to install a turnstile, or even a mantrap. The latter device is a two-door entrance where a person has to pass through two doors in order to enter or exit a restricted room. To enter, a person must pass through door A to a small space, the mantrap, and then open door B to the restricted room. The point is that door B will not open until door A is fully closed.

Figure 1.1 shows a possible design for a secure and safe computer installation. The operators' room (area 2) has a mantrap-controlled access to the outside and to the other rooms. The processor room (area 4) is easy to keep clean because access to it is through the network router room. Area 5, the disk and tape drives room, is kept even cleaner because access to it is through area 4. This is important because those drives have many moving parts. A lazy Susan (the circle) provides access to tapes and disks from their storage (area 6). Area 7 is a storage room for papers, forms, and spare parts. It also serves as temporary trash storage and houses the all-important shredders. The printers (and perhaps also binders, copiers, and collators), with their noise and paper particles, are insulated in area 8. The only area that contributes to weak security is the loading dock (area 9), because it has another outside access. However, access to the outside is important in cases of emergency, so this outside door is another example of the tradeoff between security and convenience.

◇ **Exercise 1.3:** Basements are easier to protect against unwanted entry. With this in mind, why is a basement a bad choice for a computer facility?

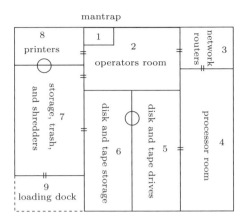

Figure 1.1: A Design For a Computer Installation.

■   Magnetic fields. Hard disks are magnetic storage. Data is recorded in small magnetic dots on the disk and is therefore sensitive to magnetic fields. (In contrast, CDs and DVDs are optical storage and are not sensitive to magnetism.) Experience shows that it is not enough to place a small magnet in your pocket and walk in a computer room, hoping to harm computers and data. Stronger fields are needed in order to adversely affect magnetic storage, but such fields exist. An old story, from the 1960s, tells of a computer tape storage room where tapes were always going bad. It took months until someone observed that the trouble affected only the tapes stored on the lower shelves. It turned out that the floor was cleaned periodically with a powerful vacuum cleaner that affected only those tapes.

■   A related concern is static electricity. Walking on a carpet often results in static electricity collected on shoes and clothing. This electricity is discharged when touching a conductor and may damage delicate electrical equipment. A computer room should have a tiled floor or at least anti-static carpeting.

■   User tracking. Imagine a facility with many computers and many workers, where a user may perform a task on a computer, move away to do something else, then step to the nearest computer to perform another task. A good example is a hospital with doctors and nurses treating patients and updating patient records all the time. Another example is a lab where tests (perhaps blood tests or forensic tests) are performed by workers, and a worker has to enter the results of a test into a computer. In such a situation, it is important to keep track of which employee used what computer, when and for what purpose. The simplest solution is to assign each user a password. The user has to log into the computer, perform a task, then log off. In the hospital example, where emergencies may and do occur often, such a procedure is too time consuming and unrealistic.

    A more sophisticated solution is to provide each user with a special, unique identification card (a key) and install in each computer special hardware (a lock) that can recognize such cards. The lock and key communicate by means of low-power radio transmissions, and each key contains a large (typically 32 bits) identification code. When a user arrives at a computer and starts using it, the lock recognizes the code on the key and immediately logs the user on. When the user walks away, the lock senses the loss of contact and immediately logs the user off. When no user is logged on, the computer cannot be used. In a sensitive environment, such as a military installation, this type of lock can be made even more secure by asking the user to provide a password in addition to carrying the key card. A commercial implementation of this technique, called XyLoc, is described in [ensuretech 04].

■ Physical protection of data. Data is normally stored on devices that are easily damaged or destroyed. Paper, magnetic disks, CDs and DVDs are sensitive to fire, magnetic fields, or scratches. Data stored on such devices deteriorates even under ideal storage conditions. Thus, data has to be physically protected, and this can be achieved by backing up sensitive data periodically, so a fresh backup is always at hand. A home computer should have two external disks (or rewritable CDs or DVDs), one kept at home and the other kept in a different location, such as a friend's home. Periodically, perhaps once a week, the computer owner should backup the data into the external disk located at home, and swap the two backup disks. This way, there is always a fresh (i.e., at most one week old) copy of the data kept at a remote location.

An even better strategy is to backup data every time a file is modified. Imagine a computer user, at home or in an office, working on a document that consists of text, numerical data, and illustrations. A word processor is used to create and edit the text, a spreadsheet may be used to construct and edit tables of data, and an illustration or painting program is the natural choice for creating digital images. Several of these files are modified by the user each day, and the safest way to work is to stop from time to time and back these files up on a small, temporary storage device, such as a zip disk or a flash memory. Once the weekly backup is done, the files on the temporary storage can be deleted. Backups are discussed in Section 6.4.

A company that depends on its digital data should also back it up on a regular basis, but may often use its local area network for this task. Data from an office or location A may be sent through the local network to another office B where it is stored as a backup, while at the same time data from B may be backed up in A.

In general, a computer user, whether an individual or an organization, should have a disaster-recovery plan based on regular and complete data backups. The plan (Section 1.4) should specify what to do if all the physical facilities are destroyed. New facilities may have to be rented in a hurry, new computers may have to be purchased or rented immediately, and all the lost data restored from backups. Experience shows that a detailed disaster-recovery plan may help even a large organization, such as a bank, recover from a terrible disaster (fire, earthquake, flood, terrorism, computer virus) in a short period of time. [Maiwald and Sieglein 02] is one of many references that discuss such a plan and how to implement it.

> An armed society is a polite society. Manners are good when one may have to back up his acts with his life.
>
> —Robert A. Heinlein

■   Hard copy. The media has been touting the paperless office for several decades, but we still use paper. In fact, we use it more and more. Security workers know that crimi-nals often collect papers thrown away carelessly and scru-tinize them for sensitive information such as credit card numbers and passwords to computer accounts. This be-havior is part of the general practice of dumpster diving. The solution is to shred sensitive documents, and even not-so-sensitive papers. See Chapter 10 and especially Section 10.2 for more on shredding and related topics.

■   Spying. Spyware, an important threat, is the topic of Chapter 9, but spying can also be done in the traditional way, by person. You, the reader probably haven't walked around your neighbor's or your ex-spouse's house at night, trying to look in windows and catch a glimpse of a computer screen with passwords, bank statements, or forbidden pictures, but others do that all the time. Industrial espionage and spying conducted by governments are very real. A commercial organization often decides that spying on its competitors is the only way for it to stay active, healthy, and competitive. Spying on computer users can be done by looking over someone's shoulder, peeping through a keyhole, setting a small security camera, planting spyware in a computer, and also in other ways, as described in Section 1.1.

■   Data integrity. Digital data consists of bits. Text, images, sound, and movies can be digitized and converted to strings of zeros and ones. When data is stored, in memory or on a storage device, or when it is transmitted over a communication line, bits may get corrupted. Keeping each bit at its original value is referred to as data integrity and is one aspect of computer security.

Before we look at solutions, it is important to discuss the significance of this problem (see also exercise 2.11). Text is represented in a text file as individual characters, each coded in ASCII (8 bits) or Unicode (16 bits). Thus, each bad bit in a text file changes one character of text to another character. Quite often, this is not a problem. If the file is the text of a book, a personal letter, or someone's homework, one bad character (or even a few bad characters) isn't considered a serious problem. If, however, the file is a legal, medical, or commercial document, the change of even one character may change the meaning of a sentence and may significantly alter the meaning of a paragraph or even the entire document.

> A photo may change its meaning according to who is looking at it.
> —John Berger

An image consists of small dots called pixels (from picture element). Each pixel is represented as a number, the code of the pixel's color. A bad bit therefore changes the color of one pixel. If the bit is one of the least significant (i.e., it is on the right-hand side of the number) the change in color may be insignificant. Even if the color of one pixel is changed significantly, a viewer may not notice it, because the entire image may have millions of pixels. Thus, in general, a few bad bits in an image do not pose a problem, but there are exceptions. An X-ray image or an image taken by a spy satellite may be examined carefully by experts who may draw important conclusions from the color of individual pixels. Such images must therefore keep their integrity when transmitted or stored. A movie is a string of images, so one bad bit affects one pixel in one frame of the movie. It may be noticeable as a momentary flicker and may not be a serious problem. An audio file consists of audio samples, each a number that relates to the intensity of the sound at a certain moment. There are typically about 44,000 audio samples for each second of sound, so one bad sample, caused by one bad bit, may be audible, but may not detract from the enjoyment of listening to music or prevent a listener from understanding spoken text.

The conclusion is that the amount of data integrity that's required depends on the data in question and ranges from no integrity at all (for unimportant data or data that can easily be reacquired) to maximum integrity (for crucial data that cannot be replaced). Data integrity is provided by error-detecting and error-correcting (in general, error-control) codes, and the basic principles of this discipline are described in many texts.

■   The three principles of security management. Three simple principles can significantly reduce the security threats posed by employees in a large computer installation. Perhaps the most important of the three is the separation of duties. This principle, employed by many spy, anti-spy, and secret organizations, says that an employee should be provided only with the knowledge and data that are absolutely necessary for the performance of their duties. What an employee does not know, cannot be disclosed by him or leaked to others. The second principle is to rotate employees periodically. An employee should be assigned from time to time to different shifts, different work partners, and different jobs. Also, regular annual vacations should always be mandatory for those in security-related positions. Every time a person is switched to another job or task, they have to be retrained, which is why this principle adversely affects the overall efficiency of the organization. Also, when an employee is switched from task A to task B, they have to be given the data and knowledge associated with both tasks, which contradicts the principle of separation of duties. In spite of this, it is important to rotate employees because a person left too long in the same position may get bored with it and a bored security worker is a potentially dangerous worker. The third security management principle is to have every security-related task performed by an employee and then checked by another person. This way, no task becomes the sole responsibility of one person. This principle allows one person to find mistakes (and also sabotage) made by another. It slows down the overall work, but improves security.

> Duty is what one expects from others.
> —Oscar Wilde

1.3 Laptop Security

A laptop computer is handy. Those thin, small, lightweight machines are truly portable and can increase a person's productivity. Unfortunately, they also increase the appetite of thieves. You may have asked yourself why so many people eye your laptop when you carry it in public. As many know from their misfortune, one common answer is: people consider a laptop a target. Thus, securing a laptop is a (physical) computer security problem.

Perhaps the most secure solution is to chain the laptop to your wrist, so it becomes your Siamese twin. Although very safe, this solution is uncomfortable, especially during meals and bathroom visits, and may be rejected out of hand (out of wrist?) by most laptop users. The next best thing is to tie the laptop to a large, heavy object, often a desk, with a lock such as a bicycle lock (but if the lock opens with a combination instead of a key, make sure you set it to a random number and not to 123, 666, or another, easy to guess number).

A laptop has a security slot that takes one side of the lock's chain or cable in such a way that breaking the slot causes much damage to the computer and thus renders it useless (or at least less desirable) to a thief. An alternative is to glue an attachment to the computer case, and attach the chain to it. A more sophisticated (or shall we say, more paranoid) owner might consider a motion sensor alarm that chirps or beeps when the computer is moved.

The goal was to bring the world to the students of Miramar High School. The first lesson they got was about crime.

In late October, 2,800 laptops were given to the students at the school—one of four to participate in a pilot program run by the Broward County Public School District (in Florida).

Since then, seven laptops have been stolen from students walking home from school, two by force and five at gunpoint. No students were injured in the robberies.

Another six laptops were stolen from inside the school. On Wednesday, two students were taken into custody.

—From *Sun-Sentinel*, a Florida Newspaper (18 November 2004).

Some software makers offer theft tracking or tracing software combined with a service that can help in tracking any stolen computer, not just a laptop. You purchase the software, install it, and give it an email address to report to. Every time the computer is started or is reset, it sends a stealth message with the computer's current IP number to that address. If the computer is stolen, there is an excellent chance that the thief would connect to the Internet, so its new IP number will be sent to that email address. Both the software maker and the police are then notified and try to locate the computer from its IP number.

◇ **Exercise 1.4:** How is this done?

The whole point about such software is that it somehow has to be embedded "deep" in the hard disk, such that formatting the hard drive (even a low-level formatting) or reinstalling the operating system would not erase the software. Current examples of such security software for both Windows and the Macintosh platforms are [PCPhone-Home 04], [sweetcocoa 05], and [absolute 05]. Because the security software is on the hard drive, replacing the drive removes this protection.

[business.com 04] has a list of various security devices and software for computers. The PDF document at `http://www.rufy.com/laptop.pdf` offers useful information on protecting a Macintosh.

A good idea is to encrypt all sensitive software on a laptop, just in case.

The following simple precautions go a long way in securing your computer so it remains yours:

■ With an electric engraving pen, write your name and either your permanent email or telephone number (but not your social security number or address) on the computer case. For a large computer, write it in several places. The thief knows from experience that selling such a marked machine takes time, so they may try to steal someone else's computer. A car is sometimes stolen for its parts, but computer parts are generally inexpensive enough to deter a thief from the effort of stealing, taking the machine apart, and selling individual parts.

■ A laptop can be hidden when traveling if it is carried in a nonstandard case, especially one with a distinctive color that makes it noticeable.

■ When traveling by car, place the laptop on the floor in the passenger side and throw a rag or a towel over it. This place has the most comfortable temperature in the car, and the rag may camouflage the laptop so it does not attract the attention of passers by. Generally, a computer should not be left in a car for a long period because cars tend to get hot even when the outside temperature is not high.

■ When flying, take the laptop with you. Never check it in as luggage. There is much information on the Internet about airport scams where a team of two or more criminals confuse you at the x-ray checkpoint and end up with your bag(s).

■ Certain versions of the Windows operating system make it possible for the computer owner (administrative user) to prevent starting the computer from a floppy disk or a CD. (This is done with the CMOS setup program). When such a computer is stolen, the thief is forced to replace the hard drive before he can start the computer.

Mac hacking. It has been known that the Macintosh computer suffers much less from hacking and security related problems (except theft) than computers running the Windows or Unix operating systems. One plausible explanation for this is that there are relatively few Macintosh computers (only 3–4% of the total number of personal computers, according to some estimates). One reason for a hacker to spend time and effort on hacking activities is the satisfaction of breaking into many computers and being able to brag about it (if only under a pseudonym). Macintosh hacking can never result in breaking into many computers, thereby giving hackers a disincentive. Another theory for the relative safety of the Macintosh is that its operating system has always been more secure than Windows and Unix. This feature, if ever true, has changed since the introduction of the Macintosh OS X, which is based on Unix. Attacking version X of the Macintosh operating system isn't much different from Unix hacking, and may attract intruders. The following quotation, from [theinquirer 04] in October 2004, may turn out to be true.

"...However according to people in hacking circles it is only a matter of time. One Hamburg hacker told the INQ: 'It would be nice to wipe the smug smiles off the faces of Apple people... you tell a hacker that you are invulnerable and it just makes people want to try that much harder.'

We believe this emotion is known in English as schadenfreude [gloating or malicious glee].

He said that what had kept his group, which is linked to others in Eastern Europe, from going for the Mac was not that it was particularly secure, it was just that people were still having too much 'fun' with Windows." (End of quote.)

Paul Day has a 40-page document [Day 04a] on hardening Macintosh security in OS 10.3. This is accompanied by a 36-page slide presentation [Day 04b]. If you cannot find these documents on the Internet, look for them in this book's Web site.

1.4 Disaster Recovery Planning

A disaster recovery plan is an important part of any organization, whether commercial, charitable, or governmental. It details the steps required to quickly restore technical capabilities and services after a disruption or a disaster. The idea in such a plan is to minimize the impact that a catastrophic event will have on the organization.

The details of such a plan depend on the nature of the organization and are different for different emergencies, but they have to touch upon the following aspects of the organization:

1. Operation. The plan should provide for continuous operation of the organization. In certain emergencies there may be periods where the organization will not function, but they should be minimized.

2. Reputation. The name, brand names, trademarks, products, and image of the organization should be preserved by the plan.

3. Confidence. A well-thought-of plan should increase the confidence of employees, clients, investors, and business partners of the organization.

Developing such a plan consists of the following key steps:

1. The basic components of the organization, such as human resources, equipment, real estate, and data should be identified and assigned monetary values.

2. The basic components thus identified should be ranked according to importance and qualified personnel should be assigned to each element. Those people should develop recovery details for their component of the organization and should carry out the recovery plan in case of a disaster.

3. Once the plan is in place, it should be disseminated to all employees and should be practiced and rehearsed on a regular basis. Several times a year, management should

reserve a day where a certain emergency will be simulated, and the recovery plan carried out as realistically as possible.

The result of a fully developed and rehearsed plan is at least peace of mind and at most, a quick and full recovery from disasters.

> One moment of patience may ward off great disaster.
> One moment of impatience may ruin a whole life.
> —Chinese Proverb

1.5 Privacy Protection

In this age of computers, huge data bases, the Internet, and E-commerce, we are all concerned about losing our privacy. Network and communications experts agree that once an item of information is placed on the Internet, it cannot be deleted because many copies are made almost immediately. Virtually everything found on the Internet, useless or useful, good or bad, big or small, is immediately discovered by search engines and gets copied, mirrored, and preserved by them and by other bodies and organizations.

This section describes two approaches to protecting privacy, the first is based on sophisticated lying and the second is based on perturbing a random variable.

Social researchers and marketers often give away small gifts in return for personal information such as shopping habits. Those tempted by the gift may resort to lying, so the first approach to maintaining privacy is to learn to lie convincingly.

Just lying to a social researcher isn't very useful and may not serve any purpose. It may also sound wrong and may raise suspicion. Why would anyone agree to give out personal information and then invent wrong data about themselves? The answer is, to receive a gift. No one is going to give away their household income level for a song, but many are willing to provide information on their online shopping habits for a free popular song or for large, free disk space on some company's computer. Often, people provide wrong information, a habit which this author does not condone, but if you insist on lying, at least do it properly. Here is how.

Take a sheet of paper and choose a fictitious name, address, income level, year of birth and occupation, then open a free email account. (It will be used as a disposable email address or DEA.) You are now in business and can supply wrong (but consistent) information about your alternate identity in return for a gift. Use this information for a while, then close the email account, discard the fake personal data, and start all over again. One exception is your (fake) income level. This is used by marketers to send you offers of merchandise. If you are interested in high-end, expensive items, declare high income. A low income level will get you offers of cheap, often useless freebies.

Statisticians tell us that people don't lie well. An effective method for deciding on a fake name and address is to use a people search service such as Intelius ([intelius 05], not free). First, search under last name `Smith` and select at random one of the many first names that will be found. Then search under first name `John` or `Jane` and select one of the many last names at random. Finally, search for a street name in a town, and select a nonexistent number. Information obtained in this way looks convincing and will not jeopardize anyone.

Now, for the second approach. When we buy a product, it always includes a registration card that asks for our name, address, age (or age group), family income, and other personal information. People often fill out this card and mail it, or register online, lest they lose the product's warranty. On the other hand, afraid to surrender their privacy, they often lie about their personal data. The point is that the manufacturer doesn't need to know the age of every buyer and user of a product. All that the maker of a product would like to know is the *statistical distribution* of the ages; how many users are 18 years old, how many are 19, and so on. This is the basis of the second approach.

When a user inputs personal data into a program that will send it to a manufacturer, a social researcher, or a government agency, the program adds a random number to it (or subtracts such a number from it). The original data is *perturbed* in this way by the random numbers. Thus, if a data item is 35 (perhaps an age), the program may add 18 and send the sum 53 to the requestor of information.

At the destination, the sum S (53) is received and there is no way to convert it to the original age A (35) and the random number R (18). However, the point is that there is no need to know any specific age. All that the data requestor needs is the distribution of the ages. Thus, this is a statistical problem that can be stated as follows: Given a random variable S that is the sum of another variable A (whose distribution is unknown) and a random variable R (whose distribution is known), find the distribution of A as accurately as possible.

This method is due to Rakesh Agrawal and Ramakrishnan Sirkant who provide detailed algorithms to accurately estimate the original distribution. Unfortunately, these algorithms require a detailed knowledge of statistics and are beyond the scope of this book. The interested reader is referred to [Agrawal and Sirkant 04].

The distribution of the random numbers is important, but knowing this distribution may help a hacker to break this method of privacy protection and to estimate the original data fairly accurately. Suppose that the random numbers are distributed uniformly in an interval $[a, b]$. A hacker may repeatedly ask a person for a data item (say, an age). If the person doesn't lie, they provide the same age, say, 35, again and again, and the hacker receives sums $35 + R$ that are uniformly distributed between $a + 35$ and $b + 35$. Knowledge of a and b and approximate knowledge of $a + 35$ and $b + 35$ makes is easy to compute, or at least estimate, the value 35.

> This is an old technique. I first heard about it many years ago when it was used in a survey about sexual practices. The respondent would mentally answer the Y/N question truthfully and then flip a coin. On heads he would record his answer truthfully but on tails he would reverse his answer. Thus anyone reading the survey would have no idea whether the respondent's Yes answer was true or not but the statistics for all the respondents would accurately match the surveyed population.
> —David Grant (in response to hearing of this method).

⋄ **Exercise 1.5:** Assuming that the random numbers are distributed normally with mean m, explain how a hacker can estimate the original data by repeatedly asking for it.

The solution to this weakness is to ask the individuals being queried to give each item of information only once (or only a small number of times).

> The man who looks for security, even in the mind,
> is like a man who would chop off his limbs in order to
> have artificial ones which will give him no pain or trouble.
>
> —Henry Miller

2
Viruses

Computer viruses are the most familiar type of rogue software. A virus is a computer program that hides *inside another program* in a computer or on a disk, that attempts to propagate itself to other computers, and normally has some destructive function. This chapter discusses the main features of viruses and what makes them different from other types of software.

The dictionary defines the adjective "rogue" as "large, destructive, and anomalous or unpredictable" and also as "operating outside normal or desirable controls." Rogue software generally conforms to these definitions. It is not large, but it is virtually always destructive. It is anomalous because it replicates, and it operates outside of normal controls. This is software specifically designed, implemented, and tested to invade a computer, to replicate and spread to other computers, and to cause harm.

The term *malware* (slang for malicious software) is also commonly used for rogue software. Malware is any type of software designed specifically to disrupt a computer or its operations. This includes viruses, worms, and Trojan horses, but also spyware and adware (Chapter 9), especially those programs that try to reinstall themselves from an invisible copy after the original has been deleted.

This chapter and the four that follow describe the various types of rogue programs, the principles behind these programs, the various types of damage that they inflict, and the tools that have been developed to detect and kill them. Several examples of historically important or especially interesting rogue programs are also included. Table 2.1 lists the seven main types of malware with short descriptions and references to where they are mentioned or discussed in this book. This chapter concentrates on computer viruses, their historical development, their methods of spreading and hiding, and the types of damage they inflict.

Writing a typical software application, such as a word processor, spreadsheet, or a graphics program is normally done in a higher-level programming language and is

Virus	Resides in an executable file and propagates to other executables	Chapter	2
Logic bomb	A virus whose payload is delayed and is triggered by some event in the computer	Section	2.2
Time bomb	A special case of a logic bomb where the trigger is a particular time or date	Section	2.2
Rabbit	A virus whose payload is to annoy and vex the user rather than destroy data	Section	2.17
Backdoor	A hidden feature in software (normally Trojan or spyware) that gives certain people special privileges denied to others	Section	2.24
Worm	Executes independently of other programs, replicates itself, and spreads through a network	Chapter	3
Trojan horse	Hides in the computer as an independent program and has a malicious function	Chapter	4

Table 2.1: Seven Types of Malware.

independent of the operating system to a large degree. Writing a virus, on the other hand, often requires a detailed knowledge of the internals of the operating system, which is why this chapter starts with a short definition and a discussion of operating systems.

2.1 Operating Systems

Designing and implementing computer viruses and other types of malicious software normally requires a good knowledge of the operations, procedures, and internal variables and tables of the operating system the virus is meant to attack. In contrast, those who want only to understand viruses need only a general understanding of what an operating system is and how it works. We therefore provide a definition of this important term and a short discussion of its main functions.

Definition. An operating system is a set of routines that provide services to the users and make it easy for them to use the computer. In a multiuser computer, the operating system also supervises users, protects each user from other users, and protects itself from accidental and intentional damage by users.

⬦ **Exercise 2.1:** Current operating systems for personal computers support separate areas in the computer for different users. Can such an environment be considered a multiuser computer?

The most important services rendered by a modern operating system are (1) booting and resetting, (2) managing volumes and files, (3) managing executable programs (processes), (4) managing memory, and (5) handling interrupts. The following list provides more information on each task:

■   A computer is useful because it executes programs. A computer without a program cannot do anything. When a new computer is purchased, it must have a built-in program so it can start and load other programs. Also, when something goes wrong and the computer has to be reset (or restarted), certain built-in programs are needed. These programs are part of the operating system.

∎   A volume is an input/output device. Typical examples are disk drives (internal, external, or remote), but flash memories, scanners, and card readers are also volumes. A volume can be mounted when needed and later unmounted. Data on a volume is written in files, and a large-capacity volume may store hundreds of thousands of files of different types. Files are often organized in directories and have to be listed, moved, copied, renamed, created, and deleted. The operating system has a file manager that provides routines for all the important operations on volumes and files.

∎   Programs are normally written in a higher-level language, such as C or Java and have to be compiled (translated to machine language), loaded, and executed. The loader and various compilers are part of the operating system. When the user wants to execute a program, the operating system has to find the executable program file, allocate it memory space, append it to the list of active processes, and start its execution by jumping to it. If the operating system can handle several processes simultaneously, it must employ the timer interrupt (Section 2.23) for this purpose.

∎   Memory is a precious resource. Certain programs, especially those that manipulate images and video, need large amounts of memory. The problem of memory allocation and protection is especially important in a multiuser computer, where several user programs reside in memory simultaneously. The operating system has a memory manager that assigns a memory area to each new process, claims the memory when a process completes, keeps track of memory areas assigned to each task, and employs special hardware to protect each user area from other users.

∎   An interrupt is the way the CPU in the computer is notified of urgent or unusual conditions and is able to respond to them immediately. Interrupts are discussed in Section 2.23 and are used to implement a variety of useful features. The following is a list of some of the most important features that are implemented by interrupts: Memory protection, invalid instructions, user requests, terminating a program (normally or abnormally), timer and time slices, input-output operations, errors found by the ALU when performing operations on numbers, and hardware problems such as a voltage drop.

Many textbooks discuss the principles of operating systems and the details of popular operating systems such as Unix, Windows, Linux, and the Macintosh OS.

(The Windows operating system is notorious for its many security flaws. A joke popular with Windows users goes like this. Windows has an error message that reads "Error: Cannot detect any system errors at this time.")

> Get information on the latest software security updates from us.
> —`www.microsoft.com/security/bulletins`
>
> Windows is weak, where's the alternative?
> —`www.cnet.com`, 26 april 2005.

2.2 Computer Viruses

A biological virus (from the Latin for poison) is a shell filled with genetic material that it injects into a living cell, thereby infecting it. The cell then starts manufacturing copies of the virus. A computer virus behaves similarly. It injects its contents, a short computer program, into a host computer, thereby infecting it. When the computer executes the virus code, it replicates the code, and also performs a task, normally damaging files or another software component of the computer.

> In biology, the plural of virus is viruses, but one of the silliest debates in the area of computer viruses has been about the plural of this word. One school of thought, perhaps influenced by the Latin and German plurals, has come up with the terms *viri, virii, vira, virae, viren,* and *virides.* A more original (and funnier) approach is to use *virii* for two viruses, *viriii* for three of them, *viriv* for four viruses, and so on.

The idea of a program that replicates itself may have originated in the early days of computing, when programmers amused themselves by trying to write the shortest program that prints itself. Section 4.3 has more details on this interesting pastime. Such programs have since been written in many programming languages. The example here is in the C language, but see also Figure 4.2.

```
char*a="char*a=%c%s%c;main(){printf(a,34,a,34);}";main(){printf(a,34,a,34);}
```

◇ **Exercise 2.2:** Write a similar program in a programming language of your choice.

The computer virus came of age on 26 September 1988, when it made the front cover of *Time* magazine. The cover story was titled "invasion of the data snatchers" and it described the brain virus (Section 5.2) as an example. The magazine called the virus "small but deadly and only one of a swarm of infectious programs that have descended on U.S. computer users this year." The article ended by predicting that this was just the beginning of the era of computer viruses, and as if especially created to justify this prophecy, the Internet worm (Section 3.4) appeared less than six weeks later. Appendix B is a detailed virus timeline.

When a new scientific field is opened, often the first step is classification. Rogue programs are classified into viruses, Trojan horses, worms, and time (or logic) bombs. The remainder of this chapter discusses viruses, but the other types are defined here, just to give the reader an idea of the differences between the various types.

A virus is a malicious program that resides inside another program (its host). When the host is executed, the virus also executes. It tries to replicate itself by storing copies of itself in other programs. It may also decide to inflict damage.

A Trojan horse is a piece of software (normally malicious) hidden inside an innocuous program. The horse performs its destructive function, then starts its host program. A Trojan horse does not replicate itself and does not infect other programs or files; its damage is localized. Normally, deleting the host program eliminates the Trojan horse and solves the problem.

A *tapeworm* is a parasite that lives inside the body of a bigger creature and sustains itself from its host's resources. A software worm is a program that executes independently of other programs, replicates itself and spreads through a network from computer to computer. The main difference between a worm and a virus is that a virus embeds itself in another file, whereas a worm doesn't hide in another file and resides in the computer as an independent program. Worms are described in Chapter 3.

A logic bomb is generally a virus whose destructive action (its payload) is delayed and is triggered by some event in the computer. A time bomb is a special case of a logic bomb where the trigger is a particular time or date.

"Oh, yeah," Handley agreed dourly. "It's fun to think about, but it was hell to get out of the system. The guy who wrote it had a few little extra goodies tacked onto it—well, I won't go into any detail. I'll just tell you that he also wrote a second program, only this one would cost you—it was called VACCINE."

Auberson laughed again. "I think I get the point."

"Anyway, for a while there, the VIRUS programs were getting out of hand. A lot of computer people never knew about it because their machines might be infected and cured within the space of a week or two, but there were some big companies that needed every moment of on-time—even with time-sharing. After a couple of months, that VIRUS program was costing them real money. It was taking up time that somebody else should have been using. Because it dialed numbers at random, it might stay in one computer for several months and another for only several days."

"But there was only one VIRUS program, wasn't there?"

"At first there was, but there were copies of it floating around, and various other people couldn't resist starting plagues of their own. And somewhere along the line, one of them mutated."

—David Gerrold, *When Harlie Was One*, 1972.

The destructive effects of computer viruses are familiar to computer users all over the world, but the term "computer virus" is familiar to the general public, even to noncomputer users, because those viruses are so prevalent. It seems that the term was first used in 1972 in the novel *When HARLIE Was One* by David Gerrold [Gerrold 88], whereas the practical idea of a computer virus formally originated in late 1983 with Fred Cohen, then a Ph.D. student at the University of Southern California. (The word "formally" implies that there may have been computer viruses before Cohen, but because of the anonymity of their creators we cannot be certain of that.) Cohen implemented a computer virus for the VAX-11 computer and demonstrated its destructive potential to his classmates. Since then, computer viruses have been designed, implemented, and released by many malicious persons, with disastrous results.

Details of this first virus experiment are given in [Cohen 94a]. It took place over several days on 3 November 1983, and was demonstrated to the students of a computer security class a few days later. It took eight hours to write the virus program which consisted of only 200 lines of C code. This size is small for a program, but large for a virus, and most of this code was due to precautions the experimenters took to prevent uncontrolled spread of the virus. To cut down the time of the experiment, the virus had an interesting and original feature. It tried to infect the most-often-used programs first. When results were analyzed later, it was discovered that it took the virus less than half a second to infect a program (and this was on a busy day in a heavily-loaded time-sharing computer).

The experiment was repeated five times and the virus managed to infect all the files on the computer in a minimum of five minutes. The average time for a complete takeover was 30 minutes, and the longest time was one hour. Other experiments followed, on other busy, multiuser computers (there were not many local-area networks available in the early 1980s). Dr Cohen and his team had to ask permission to use such a computer, and had to be very careful not to inflict any damage on the many user programs running during the experiments. One of the most important, and unexpected, results of these experiments was psychological. As soon as the administrators of a large time-sharing computer heard of the success of such an experiment on their computer, they prohibited any more experiments of this type. It is as if they said (or thought) "if your experiment on computer security has failed, then you have demonstrated that there is no problem and you can run more experiments. Once your experiment has been successful, you have discovered a vulnerability, and we cannot let you continue because you may cause damage." The administrators felt that once the security of their computer has been compromised, even in an approved experiment, they have personally been somehow violated.

The first personal computers appeared in the mid 1970s, when the Internet was in its infancy. Those computers were designed for a single user and were not connected to any network, so there didn't seem to be any need for security measures. The first viruses propagated between early personal computers by means of floppy disks. The virus writer would include the virus on a floppy disk with some popular programs, commonly games, and distribute free copies of the disk. When an infected disk was inserted into a disk drive, the virus was executed, infecting the computer and every future floppy disk inserted in it. Over time, the use of large computer labs in industry and education, and the increasing popularity of the Internet have made it much easier to propagate viruses, and have turned viruses into a major security issue.

Being a nonmathematical entity, a computer virus cannot be defined rigorously, but many experts agree that a piece of software that satisfies the following points should be included in the category of computer virus.

- It is capable of propagating between computers on a network. This is the most important attribute of a computer virus and it is what distinguishes a virus from other types of malicious software.

- It installs itself in a host computer without the owner's knowledge or consent.

- It has the potential to damage software on the host by altering or deleting files.

- It can prevent legitimate users from using some or all of the computer's resources.

- It embeds itself in an executable file (its host), such that when the file is executed, the virus is also executed. The virus is hidden inside the host. (But see exception for companion viruses on page 56.)

The last clause in this definition (a virus is hidden in an executable program) raises three interesting points. (1) There are currently many different strains of viruses and not all of them hide in a host file. The companion virus of Section 2.8 is an example of a virus that associates itself with an executable file, but exists as an independent, invisible file. (2) Macro viruses (Section 2.10) embed themselves in data files. (3) This clause illustrates the difference between the three main types of malware. A Trojan horse also hides in a host, but does not replicate. A worm replicates but exists independent of any host files.

(We generally believe that a piece of software cannot damage the actual hardware of the computer, but this is not strictly true. As an example, a malicious program can move the read/write head of a magnetic disk back and forth repeatedly every time the disk is not used by legitimate software, thereby wearing out the disk's high-precision mechanism. Repeated "treatment" of this kind may shorten the life of the disk considerably.)

◇ **Exercise 2.3:** Try to come up with more examples of software capable of damaging hardware.

Recalling the definition of a Trojan horse, it is clear that a virus is a special case of a Trojan horse that can replicate itself and establish copies both inside and outside the computer. In principle, a virus doesn't have to be malicious, but in practice programmers do not tend to write free programs that propagate and install themselves in computers in order to do good.

A typical computer virus consists of two parts of which the first takes care of the virus propagation and the second does the damage. Section 2.12 lists various types of damage inflicted by viruses.

Untraceability is the main feature that distinguishes a virus from other security threats. It is rare for law enforcement or security experts to track down the author of a virus, and it is this virtual guarantee of anonymity that encourages hackers to come up with sophisticated, destructive viruses. An interesting point to realize is that it takes an experienced programmer to write a virus, but less experienced programmers can later "take it from there" and modify an existing virus to perform different tasks and cause new types of damage.

Virus, predator or prey?

Computer users and the general public view viruses as predators that attack computers and prey on their data, but a computer virus has a very different view on the same situation and it regards itself as prey. A virus is designed and implemented not just to attack, but also to survive. Its survival depends on fast reproduction and on avoiding detection. Most viruses are easy to detect and delete. It is also possible to avoid viruses by following simple procedures and using common sense.

The conclusion: It's important to consider both sides of an issue.

Virus kits and polymorphic engines. A virus can be a simple program that can easily be detected and deleted or it can be a complex construction that hides itself in subtle ways. In either case, writing a virus requires some knowledge of the inner workings of the operating system the virus is supposed to attack. Not everyone has such knowledge, which is why anonymous "volunteers" prepare virus kits and make them available in Web sites. Anyone can download such a kit, change the condition that triggers the virus, change the damage that the virus inflicts, and release the virus in the hope to do harm. Thus, a virus kit is a tool for wannabees, those who want to be hackers but don't have the time, the knowledge, or the inclination to learn much about the operation of viruses. The kit automates the process of writing a virus.

A polymorphic engine is sometimes confused with a virus kit, but it is not the same and has a different application. A polymorphic engine is software that can be attached to a virus to make it polymorphic. Polymorphism (Section 2.21) is any technique that enables a virus to appear as different bit strings, thereby confusing anti-virus software.

2.3 Virus Writers

Where do viruses come from and who writes them? After years of research, including interviews with hackers and virus writers, Sarah Gordon, an IBM scientist and virus researcher, has come up with the following categories of virus writers (this author has also contributed to the following list).

- Malicious intent. Such a person simply wants to do damage and cause harm.

- Aggression. An aggressive person needs a way to vent their aggression, and virus writing is as good as any other outlet.

- Contempt for all authority. In science there is no authority, but in other aspects of life we often have to bow to authority for the public good.

- Develop skills. A programmer hears about software vulnerabilities and how they are exploited by viruses. He realizes that writing viruses is a good way to learn about software vulnerabilities, and tries to write a virus (without any intent of releasing it or doing any damage) to see if he can strengthen vulnerable software and make it immune to viruses. Eventually, the virus is released, perhaps as an ultimate test. Such a person may also be fascinated with the miraculous capabilities of self-replicating code.

- Hobby and experiment. A programmer hears about viruses and decides to learn more about this unconventional field of programming. When a virus is finally written and debugged by him, the programmer faces a temptation to release it, and sometimes this temptation proves too great.

- Looking for acceptance in the underground fraternity of virus writers. Someone who wants to become a professional programmer but is rejected by potential employers, may resort to becoming a respected member of the underground.

- The thrill and rush of adrenalin. A youngster who manages to shut down an important commercial server, release a "successful" virus, or break into a secret government computer enjoys a rare feeling of power.

- Enjoying the notoriety. It's not hard to imagine the pride felt by an unknown (and possibly frustrated) person on seeing their virus listed in antivirus software programs.

Such a person may even send the source code of their virus to anti-virus companies, proposing a name for the virus, and claiming to keep these companies in business. It's part of a personality game.

■   Out of frustration. Personal frustration (see profiles below about the lack of girl-friends) often provides a good reason for someone to release malicious software. Seeing others suffer may somehow compensate such a perpetrator for his suffering.

■   Political convictions. Someone living in an occupied or politically repressed country may take out his frustration on others and feel powerful by releasing a virus.

■   Social injustice. Someone who lives in a poor country or neighborhood may likewise feel better when he knows that others suffer too.

■   Let someone else do the dirty job. There are Web sites with virus source codes written by programmers who wait for someone else to copy their code, perhaps modify it, and release it. The site's owner does not disseminate their virus, but claim that it's not their responsibility if someone else does. Such a claim reminds one of the slogan of the American National Rifle Association (NRA) "guns don't kill people, people do."

■   Teach security personnel a lesson. Yes, let them learn once and for all how to protect their precious computers and other equipment. If I don't teach them, who will?

As years pass and more and more viruses appear and then disappear, sometimes on a daily basis, the answers to the questions "where do viruses come from and who writes them" become ever more elusive. Early viruses were a novelty and were often fully analyzed by volunteers, a process that sometimes also yielded clues to their origins. However, with the growing number of viruses and other types of malware (in addition to other security problems such as spam, DoS, and identity theft), detectives and re-searchers simply don't have enough time to disassemble, read, understand, and analyze them.

Factors such as professional and national pride also seem to contribute to this sit-uation. Anti-virus companies and experts sometimes disagree about the origin, trigger, and payload of a virus. When one of them points a finger at a certain country C as the origin of a virus, the government of C, out of misplaced pride, often denies that anything bad can come out of C, and either ignores the problem or declares that it is under investigation.

Another obstacle in the way of virus detectives is the mixed response of the media and the public to news about virus writers. Often, newspaper and television coverage of a suspect's investigation is mostly negative, but also contains a trace of admiration for the clever culprit and fascination at how he managed to defeat the combined talents of many computer professionals. A well-known example is Onel de Guzman who was sus-pect of writing and disseminating the LoveLetter virus. While still under investigation, de Guzman was reported as receiving job offers from computer companies.

As a result of this, very few virus writers have been caught and convicted. Frus-trated security workers sometimes claim that virus writing is a secure, if unpaid, oc-cupation and this claim often leads to the following original idea: What if the virus writers are the anti-virus companies themselves? For an anti-virus company, writing a virus would be a paid occupation. Naturally, all the anti-virus software makers deny this hypothetical claim and point out the following two strong arguments against it: (1) they are professionals, whereas the average virus is obviously written by an amateur and (2) a company consists of the people who work for the company and those people come and go. If a company started writing and transmitting viruses as a commercial policy, it would be just a matter of time before some employee will blow the whistle and leak out information about this activity.

Law enforcement organizations, from small local police departments to the FBI and its equivalent institutions in many countries stress the importance of a profile. They always try to determine the profile of the average criminal and use it to identify suspects. In the case of virus writers, such profiles have been attempted, but they are considered weak because: (1) such a profile is based on the small number of suspects that have been identified and (2) it seems that the profile of virus writers is changing all the time and is moving away from amateurs, youngsters, and computer programmers toward professional and organized criminals.

Profile of a Serial Arsonist

A study involving 83 serial arsonists found that 82 percent were white, 94 percent were male and half were age 27 or younger. Each had set about 31 fires. Most serial arsonists had a history of prior crimes, with 87 percent reporting prior felony arrests.

While two-thirds of the subjects had average or above-average intelligence, 90 percent had only a high school education or less. Most subjects also had difficulties in their personal relationships or with socialization. Among the 83 subjects studied, there were 637 prior placements in institutions ranging from foster homes to jails....

—From `http://www.cbsnews.com/elements/`, 7 July 2003.

The following quotes, culled from various sites on the World Wide Web, illustrate attempts to develop a profile for virus writers.

- Male. Obsessed with computers. Lacking a girlfriend. Aged 14 to 34. Capable of sowing chaos worldwide.

- They [virus writers] have a chronic lack of girlfriends, are usually socially inadequate, and are drawn compulsively to write self-replicating codes. It's a form of digital graffiti to them

(The above two profiles have inspired someone to come up with the following joke: Now I don't know what to do: find a girlfriend or write a new deadly virus.)

- One of the few known virus writers is Marcus Velasco, the 32 year old author of `Lasco.A`, a worm that targets cell phones with the Symbian operating system and Bluetooth functionality (see year 2005 in Appendix B). Here is his profile in his own words (as told in the email interview he granted to the Finnish IT weekly, *ITviikko*)

"I'm a professional programmer. Viruses, hacking and security are my favourites. Viruses are my life....I wanted to demonstrate how the worm works. The reason I published the source code was that the anti-virus researchers at Kaspersky did not believe it was mine."

■ (The following is quoted from the excellent article [Gordon 05].) "Earlier research has empirically demonstrated the cyclic nature of virus writing activity: as virus writers "age out," new virus writers take their places. Enhanced connectivity amplifies the existing problem and various technical factors result in new types of virus writers surfacing as the cycle repeats.

However, a new variable has recently been introduced into the cycle: high profile legal intervention. The virus writing community now has experienced visits by concerned law enforcement personnel; there have been arrests and there will be sentencings. New laws are being considered, enacted, and acted upon. Thus, the virus writing scene is no longer a casual pastime of kids on local Bulletin Board Systems."

What Makes Johnny (and Jane) Write Viruses?

The face of virus writers has shifted since [Sarah] Gordon began interviewing them nearly a decade ago. A writer can be a teenager coding in the family rec room or an undergrad on a university system. Ten years ago, virus writers averaged 14 to 17 years old; today they're 25 to 28. David L. Smith, who was convicted of writing and distributing the Melissa virus, was 30 when he was arrested in 1999.

Usually, older virus writers work as engineers or system administrators in the computing industry. Evul is an engineer; Smith was a network programmer.

And Gordon is in touch with some of the few female writers, such as a 16-year-old European girl who goes by "Gigabyte." Female virus writers like her are generally motivated by an urge to impress boyfriends or male peers, to be accepted in a predominantly male club. But Gordon knows at least one female virus writer in her early 50s. Another, in her 40s, works at a government agency, Gordon says.

It's not simply that teen virus writers are aging. In the past, most lost interest in viruses when they began a profession around age 22. Today, they may still code viruses after entering the workforce. Some don't even start until their mid- to late 20s.

(`http://www.pcworld.com/news/article/0,aid,34405,pg,2,00.asp`), 1/28/05.

Research papers on the psychology and mentality of virus writers can be found at [badguys 05], especially the "papers" section.

2.4 Virus Propagation

A virus can propagate from file to file in a computer and from one computer to another in several ways as follows:

■ Once a virus has infected a program in the computer, it (the virus) is executed every time the program is executed. The virus can start by selecting an executable file at random and infecting it if it hasn't been infected yet. In this way, the virus can propagate inside the computer and eventually infect all the executable files. (When a virus executes, it may also check its trigger and may decide to activate its payload, but this issue, which is treated in Section 2.17, is separate from its propagation.)

- A variation on the previous method is a virus that establishes itself in memory. When the virus executes, it copies itself into memory and remains there until the computer is turned off or is restarted (in addition, the virus may locate a clean file and infect it). Obviously, it is not enough for the virus to reside in memory. It needs a mechanism that will direct the CPU to it and execute it, and the natural candidate for this mechanism is the interrupts that the computer supports. Interrupts (also referred to as traps or hooks) and their use by viruses are discussed in Section 2.23. A favorite of viruses is the interrupt that occurs each time a removable disk is inserted into a disk drive. Once this interrupt occurs, the virus is executed as part of the interrupt-handling routine and it tries to infect the new disk.

- A virus may propagate to other computers through infected software. The virus writer may write a useful program (a calculator, a nice clock, or a program that catalogs files or CDs), embed a virus or a Trojan horse in it, and distribute it, as shareware or freeware, from his Web site. When someone downloads this program and executes it, it may perform its innocuous job (to hide its malicious intent), while also executing the virus (or the Trojan horse) part. That part may replicate malicious code and embed it in another program, or may do its damage in other ways. It is also possible to rig a compiler such that it will infect any program it compiles (or just certain programs) with a virus or a Trojan horse (page 117).

- As an email attachment. An attachment is a useful feature of email. When sending email, we may attach to it an image, some text, a movie, or an executable program. The attachment is a file, and there may be several attachments to one message. A virus writer may send email messages to many recipients, with the virus attached as an executable program purporting to be a useful program or even pretending to be a different type of data, such as an image. When the recipient clicks on the attachment, the virus is executed.

An email message may claim to come from, say, Microsoft and to contain a patch for the operating system to increase security. The message may have a sender address that looks superficially like a Microsoft address.

A typical, real example is an email message where the subject line is drawn randomly from the following list:

```
Re: Details, Re: Approved, Re: Re: My details, Re: Thank you!
Re: That movie, Re: Wicked screensaver, Re: Your application, Thank you!,Your de-
tails.
```

And the content is "Please see the attached file for details." The attached executable file may be called `movie0045.pif` and is a virus (Trojan horse) whose standard designation is `W32.Sobig.F@mm`. Other common names for the attached file are:

```
your_document.pif, document_all.pif, thank_you.pif, your_details.pif
details.pif, document_9446.pif ,application.pif, wicked_scr.scr, movie0045.pif
```

Large providers of email, such as Yahoo, MSN, and AOL, employ their own virus detection software that scans every email attachment and warns the user when a known virus is found in an email message.

The recipient may also be asked to forward an infected email message. Forwarding email is easy and common, so a virus can quickly spread and infect many computers. Sophisticated viruses can start their "job" by scanning the host computer for email addresses and automatically send the infected message to all the addresses they find. Clearly, a person would tend to trust a message coming from someone they know, thereby making it easy for the virus to spread in this way.

Another way of spreading viruses through email is to send email in HTML format. Such email can have several fonts, colors, and backgrounds and may include images. However, a virus can be hidden in such code and be triggered when the message is previewed. Examples of such menace are the KAK Worm (Section 5.9) and the VBS Bubbleboy virus. Users may want to either turn email HTML receiving off or preview only the first few lines of a message.

When receiving email with an attachment, a user should ask the following questions: Is the email sender someone I know? Have I received email from this sender in the past? Do I expect email with an attachment from this sender? Do the sender name, subject line, and message content make sense for an attachment? If the answers to all these are positive, it may make sense to take the risk and open the attachment.

We often hear the following statement "I don't open attachments from people I don't know," but this is similar to saying "I do open email attachments from those I know." Always bear in mind that a person you know and trust may unwittingly send you an infected attachment.

■ A macro virus spreads when users share data files. This type of virus is described in Section 2.10.

In summary, viruses spread through sharing, programming, and modifications. Each time users share a computing resource such as a disk, a file, or a library routine, there is the risk of infection. When a program is written, a virus may be embedded in it by the programmer, and may spread when the program is executed. Similarly, when a file (executable or data) or any other resource is modified or updated, a virus may be installed, that later spreads and infects other files.

> Computer viruses and other malware are so common today that in spite of our best efforts to protect ourselves, we expect our computers to be infected at a certain point. However, no one expects a brand new, just delivered, computer to be infected, yet stories about such cases circulate from time to time. Similarly, when a computer is taken to a shop to be repaired, we expect it to be returned in better shape, and certainly not infected. Along the same lines, when a program is downloaded from a hackers' site and is found to be infected, no one is surprised, but when a newly-purchased program from a reputable software maker arrives on a CD and is found to be infected (a rare, but not unheard of occurrence), we really become aware of the magnitude of the threat posed by rogue software.

2.5 Virus Classification

It is possible to classify computer viruses in several ways as follows:

- By the infection mechanism of the virus. This classification is the topic of this section.

- By the damage the virus inflicts (its payload). This is the topic of Section 2.17.

- By the trigger mechanism. This classification is not very useful.

- By the platform or operating system the virus infects. This classification is often employed by virus (more precisely, anti-virus) workers and is discussed in Section 2.19.

Viruses can be classified by their spreading and hiding mechanisms. A virus can be a boot sector infector (Section 2.6), a file infector (Section 2.7), an email virus, or a macro virus (Section 2.10). Combinations of the above are also possible. A companion virus (Section 2.8) is an example of a combination virus. It borrows the name of another file and becomes its companion. Virus concealment methods are also discussed in Section 2.20.

A File infector virus embeds itself in an executable file and is executed when the file is executed. File infectors can be classified by looking at how they embed themselves into the host program. Several techniques (discussed in detail in Section 2.7) have been observed and are listed here.

- A *shell virus* forms a shell around the original program.

- A *nonoverwriting virus* appends its code to the target program and modifies the program to ensure the virus's execution each time the program is executed. The infected program is slightly modified, but can still be executed and perform its intended task.

- An *overwriting virus* embeds itself inside the infected program, thereby erasing part of its code. When the program is executed, it may perform part of its job, then execute the virus, and finally may crash or do something unexpected.

- An *intrusive virus* replaces some of the original code of the program, typically a procedure (often an interrupt-handling procedure).

- A *simple virus* may arrive in the computer as part of a host program. Each time the host program is executed, the virus selects a candidate for infection and infects it by overwriting part of it. When the candidate is later executed, the virus is executed and a crash or another problem occurs, because the candidate has been damaged. The original virus stays in the host program and infects more candidates.

A boot sector virus (BSI, Section 2.6) embeds itself in the boot sector of a disk (floppy, zip, or hard disk) or a CD, and becomes memory resident when the computer is booted from the disk (if the disk is bootable) or when the disk is inserted into a disk drive and is read. The virus stays in memory while the computer is on, so it can infect any disk mounted in the computer. On the other hand, this type of virus is relatively easy to detect, because it (or at least its first part) is located at the same position on every infected disk. A BSI can infect hard disks, but can propagate only when an infected removable disk (a floppy disk, a zip cartridge, or other removable media) is moved from computer to computer.

A multipartite virus (Section 2.9) combines the advantages of BSIs and file infectors. Such a virus can, in principle, be very effective and spread like lightning. However, this type of virus is rarely seen in practice because it is difficult to design and implement.

A macro virus (Section 2.10) embeds itself in a data file. A macro is a sequence of commands and character strings that's assigned a name. When the name of the macro is found in a document file (such as a text or a spreadsheet file), the macro is expanded. Macros embedded in document files are useful, but can also be viruses.

An operating system virus copies itself into one or more operating system files and gets executed each time any of those files is executed by the operating system. This type is also potent because system files are executed very often and perform important tasks for the user. For example, if the virus embeds itself in the launcher, it will be executed each time the user launches a program. Once the virus is detected, disassembled, and read, experts can determine where (in what operating system files) the virus hides itself. This knowledge makes it easy to check and disinfect a suspect computer.

A general application virus attaches itself to an application (more likely, to several applications) and executes each time the user launches an infected application. Such a virus propagates easily, because users tend to share applications, but its effect is restricted, because it is executed only when an infected application is launched by the user.

A memory resident virus. A virus can reside in memory, but the term "memory resident" does not explain how such a virus operates. We therefore end this section with a short discussion of viruses and interrupts.

For a program A to be executed, it is not enough for it to be memory resident. Some other program has to jump to the start of A. A memory-resident virus can use the interrupt mechanism (see discussion of interrupts in Section 2.22) to direct execution to itself whenever certain interrupts occur. A typical example is the interrupt sent by a removable disk drive every time a disk is inserted. A virus that replaces the handling routine for this interrupt will be invoked every time a disk is inserted and will therefore be able to infect the disk and release any other payload.

The virus can do more than just infecting and damaging. It can exploit interrupts to hide itself. Imagine a virus detective trying to locate the virus on the disk. The detective has to read the boot sectors and examine them, but the (memory resident) virus can (and normally does) defeat that. The virus modifies some of the interrupt routines and also the part of the operating system responsible for disk input/output (in the old DOS operating system this part was called BIOS). If this is done properly, the virus is invoked by the BIOS routines each time a program wants to read a sector. The virus then examines the read command, and if the command wants to read a boot sector (sector 0 of track 0, Figure 2.2a), the virus changes the disk address of the read operation from $(0, 0)$ to where it has hidden the original boot sector (Figure 2.2b).

An associated problem faced by this type of virus is secondary infection. Before infecting a new disk, the virus has to make sure the disk hasn't been infected already. Thus, the virus must contain a unique fingerprint or signature.

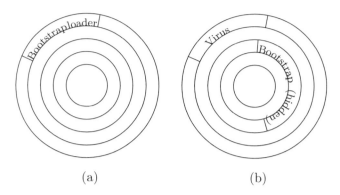

Figure 2.2: A Bootstrap Loader Hidden in a Disk.

◇ **Exercise 2.4:** What's wrong with double infection?

The virus can hide the original boot sector in one of the free sectors (if any) on the disk. The virus uses some of the free sectors, removes them from the chain, and declares them bad. An alternative is to create an extra cylinder on the disk. The capacity of a cylinder is larger than what a virus needs and its presence cannot be detected by the operating system because it receives the number of cylinders from the disk's header. Modern hard drives have large capacities in a small volume, so any added cylinder would be too close to the edge of the disk and would be unreliable. Older disks, both hard and floppy, were more amenable to this technique.

It takes an experienced virus detective to foil such a sophisticated virus.

> We were following the Bucentoro, and seated near the lady I allowed myself a few slight liberties, but she foiled my intentions by changing her seat.
> —Giacomo Casanova, *The Complete Memoirs of Casanova.*

2.6 Boot Sector Viruses

A boot sector infector (BSI) is a computer virus that resides in the boot sector of a disk. Each time the disk is mounted, the boot sector is read and executed, causing the virus to be executed. This section discusses boot sectors and how a BSI operates.

The directory of a disk reflects the file structure of the disk and provides the user with all the information that's normally needed about the files. However, in addition to the files listed in the directory, there is at least one program that's not listed there. It resides in the boot sector of the disk and it is executed each time the disk is mounted. The boot sector of a disk is normally the first sector (sector 0 of track 0) of the disk, and its format depends on the operating system. Often, the boot sector occupies more than one disk sector. It may also include a table with information about the disk itself (such as maker, date of manufacture, model and serial numbers, size and number of tracks) and on the various partitions of the disk.

What's important for our purposes is the fact that the boot sector contains a program that's executed each time the computer is booted. To understand what this program does, we describe the principles of the boot process (see also page 64). The discussion of boot sectors in this section follow the convention used by current PCs. It is simple, easy to understand, and fairly general, but other computers may use boot sectors in different ways.

A computer operates by executing a program. A computer without a program can do nothing. This implies that a newly-bought computer must have a program built into it. This program is called the bootstrap loader and is stored in read-only memory (ROM), which is nonvolatile (it keeps its content when the power is turned off). Each time the computer is booted (started or restarted), it executes the bootstrap loader. This short program reads the first part (the kernel) of the operating system from a disk or a CD and starts it. The kernel then reads the remainder of the operating system and stores it in memory.

The point is that the bootstrap loader is stored in ROM and is difficult and time consuming to replace. It should therefore be general and be able to load any version of any operating system—past, present, and future—from any bootable device. Currently, PCs run Windows, Linux, or Solaris operating systems and each of these goes through newer versions all the time. In the future there may be other operating systems. Currently, bootable volumes are disks, CDs, or DVDs, but in the future there will be other technologies, such as large-capacity flash memories. Another complication arises because a bootable volume may be divided into several partitions, each of which may have a different operating system. Thus, the bootstrap loader should not be limited to loading just one type or one version of the operating system.

The bootstrap loader starts by looking for a bootable volume (disk or CD) and it follows simple rules to determine which bootable volume to select when it finds more than one. The bootstrap loader then reads the volume's master boot sector, loads it in memory, and executes a jump instruction to its beginning. The boot sector contains a short program called the master boot record (MBR). This program knows about the various partitions of the volume and how to read the boot sector of each. It locates all the operating systems in the various partitions of the volume and lists them for the user to select one. Once a specific operating system has been selected on partition P, the MBR reads the partition boot sector (PBS) of P and executes it. The short program of the PBS reads and loads the kernel of the operating system, and it loads the rest.

> There is only one satisfying way to boot a computer.
>
> —J. H. Goldfuss

The ideal place for a virus is in the bootstrap loader, because this program is the very first one to execute. This loader, however, is made in a factory and its content is permanent (modern bootstrap loaders have firmware and can be modified when new versions of the operating system are released). The next best place for a virus is the MBR or one of the PBSs. A virus that's hidden in these locations is called a boot sector infector or BSI.

The precise organization of a disk depends on the operating system. A disk may have one bit in its boot sector informing the bootstrap loader or other operating system routines whether the disk is bootable or not. Alternatively, a nonbootable disk may have a program in its boot sector and the operating system may have to execute this program to find out whether the disk is bootable. In the latter case, a virus can hide in the boot sector of nonbootable disks.

An important point to consider is that the virus doesn't have to be physically located in the boot sector. The boot sector contains a loader program that reads other operating system routines and stores them in memory. It is therefore enough for the virus writer to write the virus as a file on the bootable disk and to modify the loader to load the virus from the disk while it loads other programs. Even though the virus is written on the disk, it may not appear in the disk directory. It may also be written in an extra track, especially formatted on the infected disk. Disk utilities and anti-virus software read the number of tracks from a table in the disk itself, and therefore know how many tracks to read and examine. An extra, undocumented track, either close to the edge of the disk or between existing tracks, may be an ideal place to hide a virus.

Figure 2.3 illustrates two variations on this technique. Part a of the figure shows a bootstrap loader located in track 0 of a disk. Part b shows how a virus may move the original loader to a new, extra track and install itself instead of the loader. Part c shows another bootstrap loader that's going to be disturbed a little (in part d) by the incoming BSI virus. The virus installs itself in the new track. It cuts a small part (x) of the loader, moves it to the end of the virus, and replaces it with a JUMP to the start of the virus. When the virus completes its execution, part x is executed, and then control is transferred to the bootstrap, to finish its execution.

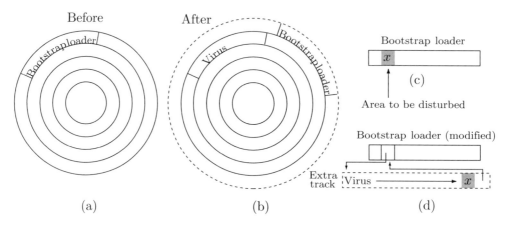

Figure 2.3: A BSI Hidden in a Disk.

◇ **Exercise 2.5:** Suggest another, legitimate use for an extra track on a disk.

Writing a boot sector virus for a certain platform and operating system is only the first step. The next task for the virus writer is to initiate the propagation of the BSI, and this can be done in several ways as follows:

■   The author can prepare a nonbootable removable disk (floppy, zip, or other) with a popular program and infect the disk with the virus. The disk is then given away to a friend or an acquaintance. Once the infected disk is inserted into a computer, the virus is executed. It loads itself into memory, looks for noninfected executable files, and infects them. Each time a disk is mounted, an interrupt occurs and the virus is again executed. If the disk is removable, the virus infects it. (An internal hard disk is mounted when the computer is started or restarted. An external hard disk is mounted when it is plugged into the computer. A removable disk is mounted when it is inserted into a disk drive.)

▪   A similar scenario, but this time the virus writer makes many copies of the disk and sells them to eager computer users who look for inexpensive software. This makes sense for a virus writer living in an unfriendly country, especially someone who owns a store. The brain virus (Section 5.2) is an important historical example of this type of virus.

▪   Similarly, the virus writer may prepare bootable copies of an infected CD with the latest version of the operating system and sell them inexpensively. When such a CD is inserted into a computer, the virus becomes memory resident and it infects executable files and any mounted disks.

▪   The author prepares an infected removable disk or CD. He then goes to a computer lab or an Internet cafe and inserts the disk into a computer. Once some executable files on that computer have been infected, anyone running any of these files will cause the virus to execute, potentially infecting any disks (and even read/write CDs and DVDs) mounted by the user.
    A BSI can infect hard disks, but can propagate only when an infected removable disk (a floppy disk, a zip cartridge, or other removable media) is moved from computer to computer.

2.7 File Infector Viruses

A file infector is a virus that infects an executable file and is executed each time the file is executed. The fact that the virus is executed only when the file is executed implies that it has fewer chances to execute than a boot sector infector. On the other hand, it is easier to write a file infector because this does not require the detailed knowledge of operating system internals needed to implement a BSI. This is why there are more file infector virus strains than boot sector infectors, but fewer computers are infected by them. Experience shows that a typical file infector can infect only one type of file and the common explanation for this is that the average virus writer doesn't want to spend the time needed to learn the structure of several executable files. The writer finds out the detailed format of one executable file, say, Adobe photoshop, and then writes a virus to infect this file and waits for the results. File infectors that can infect two types of executable files are generally much bigger than those that can infect only one type of file, and as a result tend to have more bugs. A file infector embeds itself into an executable file in one of several ways as follows:

■   The virus may form a shell around the original program (this is a shell virus, Figure 2.4a). The virus then becomes the main program and the original program becomes a procedure invoked by the virus.

■   The virus embeds itself into the original code of the program, overwriting part of that code (Figure 2.4b, which illustrates how a virus can fragment itself and hide in "holes" in the program). This is an *overwriting virus*. Such an embedding technique simplifies the virus writer's task, but damages the program, thereby prompting the user to delete the program file and replace it with a clean copy (that may later be reinfected). As a result, an overwriting virus often gets only one chance of executing, and should therefore try to infect as many executable files as possible.

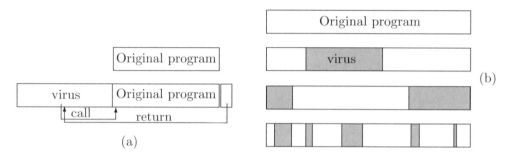

Figure 2.4: (a) Shell Virus. (b) Overwriting Virus.

In order for an overwriting virus to be effective, it shouldn't be embedded at a random location in the program. It must be embedded between two instructions, never in the midst of an instruction, and it should be embedded at a part of the program that has a good chance of executing. Here is what these points mean:

1. Instructions in modern computers have different sizes. Most instructions are 1, 2, or 3 bytes long. Imagine a 2-byte instruction with a virus embedded between its two bytes. When the computer gets to this instruction, it will fetch the first byte of the instruction and the first byte of the virus. The resulting two bytes may or may not be the code of a valid instruction. If the result happens to be the code of an instruction, it will be executed (and will likely do something strange, wrong, and unexpected) and the computer will fetch the next byte or two, which may or may not be a valid instruction. In this case, something will eventually go wrong, but there is a chance that part of the virus will be executed properly. If the result is not the code of an instruction, the execution hardware will issue an (invalid instruction) interrupt, and the operating system will take over. It will abort the program and display an error message which will only confuse the user.

2. Programmers know from long experience that a program tends to spend most of its time in a few loops. Most of the instructions in a program are rarely executed. A good example of such instructions is an error routine which is executed only when an error is discovered. If the virus is embedded in such a routine, it (the virus) will be executed only when the program discovers an error and invokes the routine.

⋄ **Exercise 2.6:** Search the Internet for "Pareto principle."

To ensure that the virus will embed correctly in the program file, the virus writer has to check various locations in the file and find a safe location. This has to be done before the virus is released. Suppose that the virus writer wants the virus to infect files with programs A, B, or C. The virus has to be experimentally embedded by its writer at different locations in program A until a location X is found where executing A causes the virus to execute properly. The pair (A, X) of name and location should now be built into the virus, and similar pairs for programs B and C should be determined experimentally and included in the virus code. Once this testing is complete, the virus will be able to infect these three programs and execute properly when they are executed.

An overwriting virus preserves the size of the infected file, but this doesn't make it harder to discover because modern virus detection software relies on more than the file size to detect viruses. Even a simple checksum will detect a change in the composition of the file, which will immediately raise suspicion.

An overwriting virus that tries to hide its presence may sometimes copy itself close to, but not precisely at, the start of the infected file. This technique is known as entry point obscuring or EPO.

A sophisticated overwriting virus may try to locate a string of nulls in the executable file and embed itself there. Such a string may be space that's reserved by the program for an array or a stack, so occupying it will not damage the executable part of the code. This type of overwriting virus faces two problems: (1) When it is executed, the program may write data into the array (or stack), thereby erasing parts of the virus. (2) Just embedding the virus in an array will not cause it to execute. The virus still has to modify something, at least a `jump` or a `call` instruction, in the program to ensure that it will be executed. The CIH virus (year 1998 in Appendix B) is an example of such an overwriting virus.

An overwriting virus can exploit certain features of the particular operating system it is meant to attack in order to make itself harder to detect. Certain operating systems require that a file size be a multiple of a certain size (perhaps 512 bytes). Sometimes even the size of the header of a file must be a multiple of a certain size. In such a case, there normally is some empty space at the end of the file (or at the end of the header) that can safely be used by the virus to hide itself in.

A variant of the previous type hides itself by corrupting the disk directory. For each file on the disk, the directory contains, in addition to the file name, type, size, and other items, also the start address of the file on the disk (the sector number or sector and track numbers). When the virus is executed for the first time in an infected computer it writes itself on the main hard disk as a file, but does not include itself in the directory (or includes itself as an invisible file). It then scans the directory until it finds a file A it wants to infect. It saves the disk address of A and changes this address in the directory to its own start address. When the user wants to execute file A, the operating system follows the disk address found in the directory, which leads it to the virus. The virus is executed and when done it may decide to execute program A so as not to raise suspicion. Such a virus may be termed a *misdirection virus* and can be implemented such that it will misdirect the execution of several different programs to (different entry points in) itself. Notice that it does not infect any executable files, only their disk addresses in the disk directory.

> Like an illusionist, the virus writer attempts to distract us with smoke and mirrors from the real mechanism at work.
>
> —[Harley et al. 01], *Viruses Revealed.*

■   The virus is add-on (most viruses are of this type). Such a virus appends its code to either the start or the end of the target program. It then modifies the first executable instruction(s) of the program to execute the virus before executing the program itself. Such a file leaves the host program virtually unchanged and only increases its size. Real viruses of this type have been observed to behave in two different ways.

1. The virus increases the size of the target program file, moves the original program code to the end of the file, then installs a copy of itself at the beginning.

2. The virus extends the size of the target program file, so the file has a blank space at the end (Figure 2.5a,b). It then copies a few bytes from the start of the target program, pastes them to the end of the blank space, and precedes them with a copy of itself (Figure 2.5c). The virus then stores a jump instruction at the start of the target program, replacing the bytes that have been moved. When the target program is executed, the jump is executed first, directing the flow of execution to the virus. The virus performs its operation, then restores the moved bytes and jumps to the start of the program (Figure 2.5d). This scheme is termed a *nonoverwriting virus*. A variation on this technique leaves the virus as a separate file and replaces the first few bytes of the target program with a jump to the virus. When done with its task, the virus restores those few bytes and jumps to the first of them, to execute the target program. The virus writer has to be familiar with the file structure of the particular operating system, because an executable file often starts with a header (for the use of the system launcher) and the first executable instruction is not the first byte of the file.

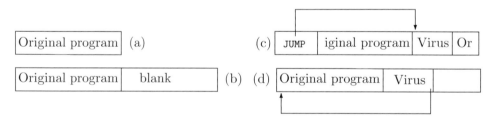

Figure 2.5: Nonoverwriting Virus.

◇ **Exercise 2.7:** Use your programming skills and knowledge of file structure to propose a variant of this technique.

■   An intrusive virus replaces some of the original code of the program. The virus may replace a procedure (a regular procedure or an interrupt-handling procedure) or may replace most of the program. In the latter case, the virus may simulate the operation of the program while adding its destructive function.

■   A simple virus may arrive in the computer as part of a host program. Each time the host program is executed, the virus selects a candidate for infection and infects it by simply replacing the start of the candidate with a copy of the virus. This does not affect the size of the candidate, but renders it useless because it has lost its beginning code. Suppose that the first time the host is executed, the virus infects program A. When A is next executed, the virus is executed first, infecting program B, then A crashes or features strange behavior because its header has been replaced by the virus. When program B is run by the user, it may infect C and also crash or behave erratically. The point is that it is A, B, and C that become suspicious, and not the host program.

■   The virus may replace an entire program with a similar but malicious program. The virus may be written to locate a certain word processor and replace it with the virus. Each time the word processor is executed, it behaves similarly to the original word processor, but has the potential to do damage. The original, trusted word processor becomes a Trojan horse and may infect other programs each time it is executed.

2.8 Companion Viruses

When a file infector embeds itself in a file, it modifies something in the file (the size, modification date, CRC, or the original code) and this modification becomes a telltale sign that can lead to a detection of the virus. The process of infecting a file makes the virus vulnerable. A *companion virus* (sometimes called a spawning virus) does not have this vulnerability. It does not embed itself in any file, but instead exploits some operating system feature or vulnerability to associate itself with a file A in such a way that when the user tries to execute A, the virus is executed. When done, the virus normally executes file A, to avoid raising suspicion.

The first companion viruses were designed to exploit a feature of the old, obsolete DOS operating system. In DOS, when the user types a character string `abc` followed by a `return`, the operating system uses simple precedence rules to interpret `abc`. First, DOS tries to interpret the string as a built-in command. It searches its command interpreter for `abc`, and if it finds such a string, the command interpreter executes it. If the string is not a built-in command, DOS searches the files in the computer for an executable file named `abc`. There are three types of executable files in DOS, `.com`, `.exe`, and `.bat`, so DOS may have to search up to three times for file `abc`. The first search looks for a file `abc.com`, the second search looks for a file `abc.exe`, and the third search looks for a file `abc.bat`.

This rule of precedence gave early virus writers an idea. Write a virus that searches the path directories for any file `xxx.exe` or `xxx.bat` such that there is no file `xxx.com`. When such a file is found, the virus creates a copy of itself as a new (invisible) file and names it `xxx.com`. Next time the user types `xxx`, the virus will be the first executable file found by DOS and will be launched. When done, the virus can find the correct application and launch it.

A variation on this idea is a virus that renames the executable file and assigns its original name to the virus. Suppose that file `abc.com` was found and no file named `abc.exe` or `abc.bat` exists. The virus can rename file `abc.com` to `abc.exe` and call itself `abc.com`.

DOS is now obsolete and has been replaced by Windows. This operating system has complex rules for searching directories when the user types the name of a program, and these rules can also be exploited by a companion virus.

A graphical user interface (GUI) operating system such as the Macintosh OS, associates a data file with an application, such that double-clicking on the data file launches the application. An application and its data files also normally have similar icons. A companion virus can take advantage of this convention as follows. The virus decides to associate itself with an application A. It searches for data files associated with A and changes their association such that double-clicking on any of them will launch the virus. The virus executes and then launches A.

The idea of a companion virus may sound ingenious, but these viruses are easy to detect, simply by searching for executable files (including invisible ones) with identical names and different extensions. A user browsing the list of such files should be able to identify unknown or unfamiliar files with identical names.

A computer virus is commonly defined (on page 38) as a program that hides inside an executable file, but a companion virus exists as an independent file. Some may argue that companion viruses are not really viruses but constitute a separate type of malware. On the other hand, it may be argued that the definition of a virus, like most definitions in the computing field, is not rigorous and allows for programs that do not embed themselves in an executable file, provided that they replicate and satisfy the other clauses of the definition.

2.9 Multipartite Viruses

The advantages of file infectors are as follows: (1) There are more executable files than boot sectors in a given computer, providing the file infectors with more targets for infection. (2) Several different file infector viruses can infect the same executable file. (3) File infectors can propagate through executable files that are sent between computers through Web sites, FTP sites, local area networks, and attached to email messages. On the other hand, a file infector must wait for its host file to execute before it (the virus) can execute.

The advantages of boot sector infectors (BSI) are: (1) They are not limited to executable files. A BSI infects the boot sector of a disk, not any of the files on the disk. (2) Removable disks that are exchanged between computer users tend to have more data files than executable files, which is why removable disks are responsible for the spread of many BSIs but not many file infectors.

A virus writer who understands the advantages of both infector types can combine them in a new type of virus, a *multipartite* (or dual-infection) virus. This type of virus can infect both boot sectors and executable files, so it can propagate either (1) on removable disks that are manually taken from computer to computer, or (2) inside executable files that are transferred between computers on any type of network.

The advantage of this type of virus is obvious, but not many of them have been seen, because a multipartite virus has a downside, it is complex to design and implement. It requires a deep knowledge of the operating system internals in two areas, booting and executable files. Also, the final virus is large, which makes it harder to hide and may result in more programming bugs (generally, the bigger a program, the longer it takes to debug).

In order to propagate itself effectively, a multipartite virus has to be efficient. When it is executed, it should perform the following tasks:

■   It should establish itself in memory (if it is not located there already), like a BSI, by modifying one or more interrupt-handling routines, especially the routine that's invoked when a removable disk is inserted. This way the virus will be able to infect the boot sectors of new disks inserted into the computer.

■   Once this is done, the virus should look for executable files that it recognizes and should try to infect as many of them as possible.

This short list of tasks is easy to read and understand, but difficult to program, which is why some multipartite viruses adopt a simple (but much less effective) spreading policy. If the virus is embedded in an executable file (i.e., if it is currently a file infector) it tries to infect the boot sector of new removable disks, whereas if the virus is a BSI (i.e., it came from a boot sector and is now located in memory), it tries to infect executable files.

◇ **Exercise 2.8:** Show why this policy for spreading the virus is bad.

It is also possible to combine the features of a virus and a worm in one piece of malware. The MTX malware (Section 5.12), for example, propagates both as a worm and as a file infector.

2.10 Macro and Script Viruses

In the computer world, the term *macro* refers to a name or a symbol that stands for a list of commands or a string of characters. When using a word processor to write a letter, the heading with the date and our name, address, and telephone number is always the same. It makes sense to define a macro called `header`, such that typing the single word `header` typesets this information in the format we like (it expands or plays back the macro). If we want two headers in different styles, perhaps for personal and professional letters, we can either define two macros or write a single macro that depends on a parameter, such that the expansion `header pers` will execute the commands for typesetting the header of a personal letter and `header pro` will do the same for a professional letter. The popular word processor Microsoft Word supports extensive macros (see, for example, [Roman 99]) that can, among other things, create, rename, save, and delete files, and typeset headers, footers, and section titles.

⋄ **Exercise 2.9:** The date is different each day, so how can we say that a header with the date is always the same?

Macro: A set of keystrokes and instructions that are recorded, saved, and assigned to a short key code. When the key code is typed, the recorded keystrokes and instructions execute (play back). Macros can simplify day-to-day operations, which otherwise become tedious. For example, a single macro keystroke can set up a connection using pcAnywhere.

—From `securityresponse.symantec.com/avcenter/refa.html`.

A macro is useful, but it also introduces a security weakness; it may be a virus. A macro virus for Microsoft Word is a `.doc` file whose header section consists of the virus commands. When Microsoft Word opens such a file, it innocently executes the commands, which can insert unwanted text at certain points, change the current font or style, and also infect other `.doc` files found in the computer. In principle, a macro virus is not limited to `.doc` files and has the potential to cause any type of damage. Most of the macro viruses that have been detected and analyzed were specifically written for Microsoft Word and Excel. A typical trigger for a Word macro virus uses the document's version count. Microsoft Word keeps in the document file a counter that counts the version of the document. This counter is used by many macro viruses to trigger the virus's payload when it equals the current date or time or when it is divisible by a certain prime number. A macro may be useful either in a certain document or in general. General macros for Microsoft Word are stored by the Windows operating system in the global template file `NORMAL.DOT`, thereby making it easy for a macro virus to copy itself from an infected Word document to this file. Once there, the macro is always available. If the user accidentally types the macro's name, it is expanded into the current document and infects it.

Some macros have a predetermined name, identical to the name of a command. Thus, if a macro `FileSaveAs` exists in Microsoft Word, it will be expanded every time the user selects the menu item `Save as` from the `File` menu.

A macro virus often spreads as an email virus. A well-known example is the Melissa virus of March 1999 (Section 5.5).

Virus detection software can identify macro viruses, but as a cautious user you should be familiar with the macros you use with any program, and check often for new, unfamiliar macros.

In principle, macro viruses can be eliminated (or at least greatly limited) by allowing only special-purpose macros. A word processor with restricted macros may allow one macro to enter text, another macro to analyze it, a third macro to print the result in a special format, but will not allow one macro to do the entire job. Such restrictions limit what a macro virus can do and thereby discourage virus authors. However, because of competition, software makers tend to implement powerful features in their programs and this trend, while helping the users, also makes the virus writer's "job" easier.

Modern operating systems often support scripts. Microsoft VBA (visual Basic for applications) also supports powerful scripts. A script is a list of commands that's assigned a name. When the name is typed, the commands are executed. A miscreant may write a malicious sequence of commands, assign it the name of a common, useful script, and try to distribute it to unsuspecting users. When a user types the name of the script, the commands are executed and may release their harmful payload.

In principle, macro and script viruses are the same. The only difference between them is that a macro virus is hidden in a data file whereas a script virus is not associated with any file and resides in the computer as a script, part of the operating system.

2.11 Infected Images

In the past, several viruses and worms carrying an infected attachment have tried to disguise it as an image simply by changing its extension from executable (normally .exe) to an image (commonly .jpg). However, in September 2004, several Web sites that monitor the birth of new viruses started warning the public about a new type of infected jpeg image file that can carry malicious code.

A raw, uncompressed image file contains only image information (colors of pixels, most often in compressed form). Such a file doesn't have any executable instructions and cannot be executed. It can only be decompressed and displayed. It is possible to embed a virus (or for that matter any other type of data) in an image file, but the virus will not be executed. For an image file to become a security threat, its format has to be modified so it forces whatever program decompresses it to execute instructions embedded in it by a hacker. It turns out that Microsoft had a security vulnerability in one of its products that made it execute code embedded in jpeg image files if the files were tampered with in a subtle way.

Image files tend to be large, so they are normally stored and transmitted in compressed form. Jpeg is a common algorithm used to compress image files, and a Web site may include several images in the jpeg format. When a Web browser downloads a Web site, it also downloads the images found in the site and has to decompress (or decode) each image before it can be displayed.

The security hole that allows this threat was discovered by an anonymous hacker in the decoder employed by several Microsoft operating systems, most notably Windows XP, 2000 and NT, to render jpeg images. When a file with a .jpg extension arrives by email, Windows recognizes its header and invokes a special decoder to render it. The programmer who years ago wrote the original version of this decoder did not think in terms of security weaknesses and hackers. He simply wrote a program that reads a jpeg file, decompresses it, and renders it pixel by pixel.

An infected image may arrive in a computer as an email attachment (most likely attached to spam or chat message). An alternative is to receive a junk message with a link to a Web site that displays an infected image. When the browser downloads the image and starts decompressing and displaying it, the malicious code in the image is executed and may infect files and/or release a destructive payload. An example of such payload is to search for images in the victim's computer and infect them.

Security experts immediately issued warnings and expected a wave of photo viruses to be unleashed. True to form, two malicious programs that take advantage of this flaw appeared almost immediately. They are dubbed JPGDownloader and JPGTrojan.

In response, Microsoft has very quickly issued a critical alert [MS04-028] announcing a new security flaw in the form of a buffer overrun in software it uses to display jpeg images. A security patch to fix this buffer overrun was also released. Unfortunately, past experience shows that there will always be users who neglect to download and install the patch and they will needlessly become victims of this new, short-lived threat.

For the technically-inclined readers, here are the details of this vulnerability. Certain Microsoft products, most notably "Microsoft Visual Studio .NET Enterprise Architect" employ a jpeg decoder or parser, part of library file `gdiplus.dll`, to render jpeg images. This decoder has a subtle buffer overflow weakness that can be exploited by an especially-constructed jpeg file to introduce rogue software and run it. Over the years, `gdiplus.dll` went through several versions, so other unknown vulnerabilities may be lurking in it.

Jpeg is a compression algorithm especially designed for continuous-tone images. It has a nonlossy option, but is virtually always used as a lossy algorithm. The jpeg algorithm shows how to start with a (large) image and produce a smaller stream of bits that represents it. In addition, there is something called JFIF (jpeg file interchange format [Salomon 04]). This is a set of specifications that show how to organize the bit stream output by jpeg in a file that can be sent between computers, saved, and displayed. JFIF introduces the concept of a marker, to include various useful features in the compressed jpeg image file. Such features include image resolution, aspect ratio, horizontal and vertical pixel densities, and most importantly for our purposes, comments.

It is useful to have comments, such as image title, date, image owner, and copyright, in an image. JFIF specifies a comment segment that starts with the `COM` marker, the two bytes `FFFE`. These bytes are followed by a 16-bit (two bytes) unsigned integer specifying the length of the comment in bytes. Anyone familiar with the representation of information in bits and bytes knows that an unsigned 16-bit integer can represent unsigned integers from 0 to $2^{16} - 1 = 65,535$. (Readers unversed in the mysteries of binary numbers should consider the storage capacity of three decimal digits. They can similarly represent integers from 0 to $10^3 - 1 = 999$.) Thus, the maximum length of a comment is 65,535 bytes, enough for all reasonable comments. The two bytes occupied by this 16-bit length integer are included in the length of the comment, which is why the value of the length integer must be at least 2. Figure 2.6 shows an example of a comment where the length field is 11.

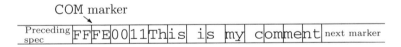

Figure 2.6: A JFIF Comment.

The decoder in `gdiplus.dll` knows about this subtle point. When it finds the marker `FFFE` it starts by reading the two bytes that follow the marker as an unsigned integer and subtracting 2 from it, to obtain the actual length of the comment (the comment itself is skipped by the decoder because it is not an integral part of the image). Now imagine a JFIF file with a comment marker followed by a 16-bit unsigned integer whose value is a nasty and invalid 0 (or 1). When 2 is subtracted from the unsigned 16-bit number 0000000000000000 the result is 1111111111111110 or hexadecimal FFFE. This value is converted by the decoder to the unsigned 32 bits $FFFFFFFE_{16} = 2^{32} - 1 = 4,294,967,295$. The decoder (whose intelligence is only artificial) has to read and skip a comment whose length is about 4.25 billion bytes, so it is no wonder it (the decoder) gets in trouble. This is the buffer overflow vulnerability of jpeg. The hacker who first thought of this exploit has analysed the behavior of the decoder in this (never before considered) case and discovered that reading and skipping such a long comment leaves the decoder in a state where it tries to execute certain instructions to unlink data pointed to by a certain pointer. Once this was discovered, it was easy for the hacker to exploit this behavior in order to force the decoder to execute code hidden in the JFIF file.

After the problem was identified, analyzed, and understood, it was easy to patch it. The presence of malicious code in a jpeg file can easily be detected by the decoder by looking for the byte sequences FFFE0000 or FFFE0001. Once any of these is found, the decoder stops and raises the alarm.

Buffer Overflow: A Security Flaw.

Many security weaknesses, vulnerabilities, and flaws have been discovered in operating system routines, in network software, and in popular, everyday application programs. Most of these vulnerabilities are highly technical and their details are outside the scope of this book, but this inset discusses one of the most common such weaknesses, namely the dreaded buffer overflow. Figure 2.7a shows a fragment of code (in a simple, hypothetical assembler language) that illustrates the source of this problem. The program starts with an ADD instruction, at a certain point it calls a procedure P, and it ends when it executes the STOP instruction. However, the STOP is followed by a data item A, by an array B of 24 bytes, and by procedure P. While the program executes, it may store data items in B and the point is that many programs don't check for buffer overflow.

A hacker who is familiar with the program may realize that the array is followed by executable code, and may send special data to the program to overflow the array and thereby rewrite the first instruction of the procedure. This instruction (a LOD in the figure) is replaced with a jump to executable code placed by the hacker in the computer, perhaps as a virus or a Trojan. This is the essence of the buffer overflow vulnerability.

Here is an actual example of a buffer overflow vulnerability. A Web browser is a program that reads HTML code (text and commands) from a Web site or from a local file in the computer and displays text and images at the right positions on the screen to construct a viewable Web page. IFRAME is a typical HTML command. It has to do with floating frames, frames that can be positioned anywhere on the page, much like an image. The two tags IFRAME and /IFRAME specify the start and end of such a frame.

The IFRAME tag has parameters, two of which are NAME and SRC. The former is followed by the name of the frame, normally a short string. The latter is followed by a URL to the Web page that should be read and placed in the frame. Both the name and the URL are strings of characters and are stored in short, internal buffers inside the

```
        ADD ..            ADD ..
          .                 .
          .                 .
        CALL P            CALL P
          .                 .
          .                 .
        STOP              STOP
     A: DATA 123       P: LOD ..
     B: ARRAY 24          STO ..
     P: LOD ..             .
        STO ..             .
          .               RET
          .            A: DATA 123
        RET            B: ARRAY 24

         (a)              (b)
```

Figure 2.7: Source Code for Buffer Overflow.

browser. Someone discovered that version 6 of the well-known Web browser Internet Explorer for Windows 2000 and XP stored these items in short buffers without testing for buffer overflow. A specially-contrived long frame name or long URL overflows these buffers and rewrites executable code as described above. These vulnerabilities have since been patched.

A buffer overflow vulnerability can be eliminated in two ways. The simpler fix adds code to check the index to the buffer. The program maintains an index to the array, it increments the index each time it stores another data item in the array, and it decrements the index when an item is deleted. It is simple for the programmer to include instructions to check the index before it is incremented, to make sure the index hasn't reached the end of the buffer, but this has to be done every time the index is incremented, which slows down the program somewhat. A more complex patch is to move all the executable code of the program together and follow it with all the data items and arrays, as illustrated in Figure 2.7b. Any buffer overflow will, in such a case, rewrite a memory area outside the program, and this area is normally protected by the operating system.

2.12 Virus Life Cycle

Figure 2.8, following [Cohen 94a], is pseudo-code that illustrates the main components of a typical virus. It is surprisingly easy to read.

Remember that the virus code is already stored at the beginning of an executable program and is executed each time the program is launched by the current user (who may or may not own the program). The string SigNature is a unique identification

```
Program Virus
{"SigNature";

Procedure infect
 {loop: exec:=select random writable executable file;
 if (first line of exec = "SigNature")
     then goto loop; else prepend Virus to exec;}

Procedure damage
 {code to do the actual damage}

Boolean Procedure trigger
 {Code to check trigger condition}

Main program
 {infect;
 if (trigger) then damage;
 goto continue;}
continue:
}
```

Figure 2.8: Pseudo-Code of a Virus.

of the virus, used by it to prevent multiple infections. Notice that this string is the first thing in the executable program's file, but is not itself executed or printed by the virus because when the virus's main program starts, it invokes procedure infect. That procedure randomly selects an executable program file F (but it has to be writable by the current user), verifies that it is not already infected (by checking for the signature), then infects it by prepending its code to F. The virus program then executes the trigger to find out whether to release its payload (destructive task), and ends by going to the label continue. This label marks the start of the executable program that follows the virus, and this program now executes. (Depending on the damage done by the virus, this program may execute correctly, execute badly, or not execute at all.)

It doesn't take much programming experience to see that this pseudo-code needs much work. If all the executable files have already been infected, then procedure infect goes into an infinite loop. Also, this pseudo-code does not try to propagate itself outside the computer; it is satisfied with infecting all the local files one by one.

The figure illustrates the life cycle of a typical virus. The cycle consists of three stages, activation, replication, and operation. The virus is activated in the host computer, it replicates itself and then performs its main "task" if the triggering condition is satisfied.

Activation. The virus embeds itself in a program and is activated when the program is executed. Many viruses are designed to activate when the computer is started and also each time it is reset (each time the computer is "booted"). To do this, the virus must embed itself in that part of the operating system that's executed when the computer is booted. We follow with a short discussion of the bootup process (see also page 49). A computer can only operate by executing a program, which means that a new computer must have a program built into it. This program is called the bootstrap loader and is stored in read-only memory (ROM). When the computer is started or is reset, it starts executing the bootstrap loader. This short program loads (from a CD or a hard disk, but in the old days, from a floppy disk) an operating system executive program that in turn loads those parts of the operating system that should reside in memory (often referred to as the kernel of the operating system) and executes certain operating system utilities (autoexec programs).

The ideal place for a virus is in the bootstrap loader, but this loader is made in a factory and its content is permanent (modern bootstrap loaders are made as firmware and can be modified when new versions of the operating system are released). The next best place for a virus is the operating system executive program. This program is a file written at a special location on the hard disk (normally called the boot sector) and it can be modified. Many of the older viruses embedded themselves in this executive program. The next ideal place for a virus is any program executed by the executive program (any autoexec program).

Other viruses embed themselves in various applications and utilities used from time to time. Such a virus is executed only when its host program is launched by the user.

A sophisticated virus may, once activated, copy itself to memory and reside there (until the computer is turned off) as an interrupt-handling routine (interrupts and their handling routines are discussed in Section 2.22). Such a virus is referred to as memory resident and is activated each time the interrupt occurs.

A virus may embed itself in interrupt routines that handle common interrupts. Examples of such interrupts are timer (invoked several times each second to update the clock displayed on the screen), keyboard (invoked each time a key is pressed on the keyboard), removable disk (invoked each time a disk is inserted into a removable drive), and printer (invoked when the printer runs out of paper, is jammed, or senses another problem). A modern computer can handle many other interrupts.

A large mainframe (a multiuser computer) normally has compilers for several high-level programming languages. Each compiler includes a library of commonly-used procedures and functions. A typical example is a square-root routine. When the compiler compiles a program for user A and it comes across a statement such as `var:=sqrt(y+1.5)`, it generates machine instructions that (1) prepare the value `y+1.5`, (2) copy the square-root routine from a library, append the copy to the program being compiled, and call it with this value, and (3) store the result in variable `var`. If the square-root routine is infected, then running it causes other files, programs, or routines in the user's private library (located in A's private directory on the large, shared disk) to be infected. When any of those infected routines is executed, it infects other routines in A's directory on the disk. It cannot infect files in other directories because the operating system protects the disk directory and memory area of each user from any other users. Eventually, all of A's files may become infected.

The infection doesn't have to come from the compiler's routines. User A may be the culprit who writes the virus and embeds it in a private program, utility, or routine that he hopes to loan to other users.

At a certain point, a user B borrows a file from A. This can be a useful program, a library routine, or a data file. If this object is infected, then each time it is executed by B, it infects files in B's area. The administrator can prohibit users from borrowing from each other, but some users will always find ways of breaking such a rule, because borrowing saves time. This is another example of the trade-off between convenience and security. If the infection starts with one of the compiler's library routines, then the infection can spread very quickly throughout the users of the computer, regardless of what user A does.

2.13 Viruses and UNIX

A similar situation exists in Unix. If user A brings an infected file into his area, the virus in this file will activate each time the file is executed (if the file is an executable program) or is interpreted (if it is a data file that has commands embedded in the data). When user B borrows an infected file from A, that file acquires privileges in B's area and can infect files in that area. If a virus is inserted into a file belonging to a root user, infection can spread far and fast.

2.14 Viruses and the Macintosh

The Macintosh operating system has traditionally suffered less than others in terms of viruses (see the discussion on page 27), but is not immune to attacks. A handy feature introduced by the Macintosh operating system since its beginning in 1984 is that a data file can be associated with an application and it has the same (or a very similar) icon as the application. When a file is created, say by an editor program titled `abEdit`, the file gets an icon (and a flag) that identifies it as an `abEdit` file. Double-clicking on the file opens it in `abEdit`.

A virus can take advantage of this feature. The virus may search for `abEdit` files and change their flag, so they will open, when double-clicked, in another, infected, editor. If that editor resembles `abEdit`, the user may process the file for a while before realizing that the current program is not `abEdit`, and is doing something bad, perhaps sending the current text file to an address on the Internet.

The new version X of the Macintosh operating system is based on Unix, so Unix viruses and other types of attack may easily affect a Macintosh.

The "debate" continues to rage on about UNIX and Linux viruses. Much of what you may have read is simply uninformed and inaccurate. More and more "virus experts" are crawling out of the woodwork and many seem to have little "real world" knowledge of UNIX. This is probably because most viruses and anti-virus software is written for Windows-based systems. However, that is no excuse for disseminating misinformation. . .

—`www.claymania.com/unix-viruses.html`

2.15 Viruses and the Amiga

The Amiga computer, made by Commodore, was a popular personal computer in the 1980s, and still has a large user base. This computer had two features that made it very easy for a virus to propagate. The first feature was the way its operating system read a floppy disk inserted into the drive. An Amiga floppy disk had a special program, a driver, that was located and input by the operating system before the rest of the disk could be located and input. A virus hiding in this driver was, of course, executed each time the disk was inserted into a disk drive. The second feature was the popularity of Amiga users' groups. Such groups still exist [Amiga 04] and serve as swap meets where users exchange disks with popular programs, such as games. Needless to say, this kind of sharing warms the hearts of virus writers.

2.16 Virus Replication

The virus is a sequence of machine instructions (computer instructions stored as binary numbers). It is a simple matter to write a loop that copies any sequence of instructions. An active virus in memory can therefore easily generate a copy of itself, write it on the hard disk as a small file, then execute instructions to prepend this file to any other file or to send it, as an attachment in an email message. The file can then be deleted. Once a disk is inserted into a removable disk drive, the virus can activate itself by the interrupt from the drive and write a copy of itself on the disk, for fast propagation to other computers.

2.17 Virus Payload

The payload is the main, malicious "task" of a virus. It is performed when the triggering condition is satisfied. Following are several types of damage that computer viruses typically inflict.

■   The virus may do nothing; its sole purpose is to stay alive. This happens in practice if the virus was written for a different type of computer or a different version of the operating system. A Macintosh computer contracting a virus for Windows may not suffer any damage (unless it starts executing a program, such as Virtual PC, that simulates Windows). When a virus detection program is next run, it may discover the virus, which can then be deleted.

⋄ **Exercise 2.10:** Propose other reasons for the existence of viruses that do nothing.

■   It may display a message, such as "Gotcha," a political slogan, or a commercial advertisement. Again, virus detection software can be executed to identify the infected file and disinfect it (delete the virus part).

■ It may want to read a certain sensitive or private file. The virus propagates, and each time it is executed it checks whether the current user (the one who is executing the infected program) has "read access" to the desired file. Such a virus is in fact spyware (Chapter 9), and may be planted by a competitor, a spy, a curious employee, a suspicious lover, or even a child who wants to read his parents' correspondence or discover their secret passwords.

■ It may slow the computer down by monopolizing and exhausting limited resources. Such a denial-of-service (DoS) virus may use large quantities of CPU time by executing loops that do nothing. It may replicate itself and occupy large portions of memory or the disk. It may occupy a network connection by endlessly sending messages. It may cause crashes and printing problems, and in general annoy and vex the user rather than destroy data. A virus of this type does not attach itself to other software and is sometimes referred to as a rabbit.

■ It may completely deny any services to the user. It may infect every executable file on the disk, then go into an infinite loop. When the user restarts the computer, any program launched will be infected. The program will execute the virus, which will then go into an infinite loop. To remove such a virus, the computer will have to be started from a write-protected disk or from a CD.

■ It may erase all the files on the host computer. This is serious damage, but the kind of damage that a prepared user can recover from in reasonable time. The user can completely erase the disk and restore its contents from a backup. A variant of such a virus may change file names, either randomly or systematically.

■ The virus may quietly replicate itself and transmit copies outside the host until a certain date, when it makes itself known by inflicting some damage. Such a time-bomb virus is more serious, because by that date there may be many millions of copies, lying dormant in host computers, waiting to release their payload simultaneously. The Michaelangelo virus (Section 5.3) is a well-known example of this type.

■ It may select some files at random and change several bits in each file, also at random. This type of damage, referred to as *data diddling*, may be more serious, because it results in problems that seem to be caused by hardware failures, not by a virus. (For an example of such a virus, see year 1989 in Appendix B.) A computer, even a personal computer, may have hundreds of thousands of files on a single hard disk, and the damaged files may not be discovered by the user immediately. In such a case they may be written on the backup disk, corrupting it and thereby making a full recovery slow and tedious. What makes this and similar attacks so nasty is that there is no direct link between the cause (the virus) and the symptom (the damage).

◇ **Exercise 2.11:** Modern computers have several types of files, such as text, image, video, sound, and executable. Discuss the potential effect of modifying one bit in each type of file.

■ A sophisticated, nonrandom data diddling virus may inflict more damage. Such a virus may look for a list of postal codes (such as the zip codes in the United States) and modify one or two digits in each. It may interfere with the operation of a word processor by changing a text file each time it is saved by the word processor, then restoring it and making other changes. Imagine a virus that makes random changes when a document is saved and remembers the changes. When the document is again saved, the virus restores the changed characters (some of which may in the meantime have been corrected by the user), randomly changes others, and remembers the new changes. Such a virus may drive the user crazy, but its constant interference will also make it easier to identify.

⋄ **Exercise 2.12:** Come up with other ideas of sophisticated data diddling viruses.

■   One step beyond data diddling is random deletion of files. A modern operating system maintains the last date of modification for every file. A virus may search for files that haven't been used for a while (i.e., with old modification dates) and delete them. There is a good chance that it'll be a while before the user needs one of those files, and when that happens, the user may contribute the nonexistence of the file to an accidental deletion (my memory is getting bad) or the carelessness of another user (I keep telling her not to touch my files). A sophisticated user who knows how to program, may write a program that scans all the files on the computer periodically, identifies old files (with, for example, modification dates that are six months old) and backs them up on another disk or on a recordable DVD. A hacker who is familiar with the habits of this user may write a virus that also runs periodically and deletes 10% of all the files with modification dates close to six months. The result is that the automatic backups are incomplete, but this fact takes time to discover. When the problem is discovered, it takes a security-conscious user to attribute the problem to a virus, then it takes time and effort to locate the virus. The missing files, rarely used but nevertheless important, remain missing.

■   A virus may quietly propagate from computer to computer, doing no damage, but checking each infected host, looking for a computer that can easily be taken over. Once such a computer is found, the virus takes it over, effectively converting it to a zombie machine. Such a virus is particularly useful to those who want to inflict damage and remain anonymous. A common example is a spammer. Someone who sends millions of email messages hawking fraudulent or useless products is interested in responses, but wishes to remain out of reach of any potential victims. A perpetrator of a DoS attack can also benefit from zombie computers.

■   A virus may be written by an organization or an individual to weaken a competitor. Imagine a print shop A that provides printing, binding, copying, and Internet services to customers. One day, a competitor opens up a similar shop B nearby, and tries to siphon off business by dropping prices temporarily. The owner of business A may decide to fight in an original fashion. The idea is for A to write a virus, go to business B, rent time on a computer, and install the virus, which then propagates from computer to computer in B. When the virus arrives at the computer that handles the accounts, it randomly selects and deletes a certain percentage of the accounts payable. Once B's income drops mysteriously and steadily, she may decide to close shop.

A more sophisticated version may interfere with the automated, computer-controlled production or manufacturing of a competitor. Imagine a plant that makes tractors, where computer-controlled machines perform some of the manufacturing steps, such as automatic welding and tightening of bolts. A competitor manages to install a virus that propagates to the computer that controls part of the manufacturing. The effect of the virus may be to reduce the torque applied when tightening certain bolts. The result—breakdowns followed by accidents with the tractors, law suits, and bankruptcy. Pretty serious stuff!

- Many operating systems maintain a protection code or access permission for all files. In Unix, each file has a 9-bit permission code that specifies permissions for reading (r), writing (w), and executing (x) the file for the file's owner, the local group of users, and the rest of the world. Thus, permission code 111101000 (or, alternatively `rwxr-x---`) allows the owner complete access, lets the group members read and execute access, but not write privilege, and prohibits anyone else from using the file in any way. The Unix command for changing file permissions is `chmod mode filename`. It can be executed only by the file's owner or by the administrator (root user), but a virus can use low-level commands to achieve the same result. Those who have read the preceding examples carefully should have got the idea already. A virus may change permissions randomly, semirandomly, or nonrandomly.

A random change of permissions is annoying, but temporary, because users are certain to notice it very quickly. A bad user will take advantage of suddenly being able to read a confidential file, but a good user will alert the administrator. A semirandom change of permissions may involve the following steps: The virus changes permissions randomly and remembers the changes. User A notices a permission change in a file. A is suddenly either able to read a secret file or unable to write into his private file. A alerts the administrator. The virus restores the permissions. The administrator checks and finds no problem. Result: User A is (wrongly) accused of a false alarm. No one wants to be blamed for crying wolf, so next time A notices wrong permissions, he may decide not to report it. A nonrandom change of permission may make a top secret file available to anyone. The hacker and his group of users/accomplices are ready and they copy the file immediately. By the time the problem is noted and is corrected, it may be too late.

> File access permissions are implemented by the operating system and provide pretty good protection against unauthorized file access. However, an operating system is not all powerful and there are ways to circumvent its protection. The following quotation shows how "firewire target disk mode," a feature found on the Macintosh OS X (which is based on Unix) can be exploited to fully access all files on a hard disk.
>
> "FireWire target disk mode allows a Macintosh computer with a FireWire port (the target computer) to be used as an external hard disk connected to another computer (the host). Once a target computer is started up as a FireWire hard disk and is available to the host computer, you can copy files to or from that volume."
>
> —From `http://docs.info.apple.com/article.html?artnum=58583`

- The virus may replicate itself very fast in a network, thereby consuming network resources and denying network services to legitimate users. The Internet worm of Section 3.4 is an example of such a virus (actually, a worm), but there are many other known examples of viruses that deny other users all kinds of services.

■   Competition between individuals in the same office is common. When an office manager retires, moves up, or is fired, the powers to be have to select a replacement. If the new manager is to come from the same office, the employee with the best productivity record stands a better chance, while someone who was caught making mistakes in the past will certainly not be offered any promotion. Place yourself in the position of an old, capable employee A, who stands to receive better pension if he retires as a manager, slowly realizing that a new, much younger recruit B is performing excellently. What would you do in such a case? After much thought and soul searching, A (sometimes) decides to sabotage B's projects. A macro virus is written and is installed in B's computer to affect spreadsheet data files. The virus performs a very simple task. Each time a spreadsheet file is opened, the virus randomly changes one number in it. After the virus has spread into all of B's spreadsheet files, B's productivity declines at an alarming rate. Based on wrong data fed by the virus, he constantly makes wrong decisions, is reprimanded, and loses his chance of promotion.

◇ **Exercise 2.13:** Come up with other scenarios where someone may decide to create a virus to sabotage someone else's work.

■   This is a complex example of a virus employed together with a covert channel to leak highly-secret information from well-protected files. What makes this example of a virus important is that the technique of combining a virus with a covert channel may be applied to many real-life situations and cause serious damage to a large organization with important secrets, such as a large bank, a government agency, or an army. We start by describing the so-called Bell-LaPadula model [Bell and LaPadula 74], one of the earliest computer security theoretical models.

Imagine an organization with users (subjects) and information files (objects). Each file has a security level specifying its degree of sensitivity, for example, unclassified, confidential, secret, and top secret. Each user also has a similar security clearance. Users want to access (read) files, to append information to existing files, and sometimes also to create files and add them to the collection. The organization has sensitive information that should not leak to unauthorized persons, so it has to come up with a security policy, restricting the access of users to files. In the Bell-LaPadula model, a user with security clearance A is allowed to read files on security levels less than or equal A and is allowed to write to files on levels greater than or equal A.

In more detail, there is a set of access rights that restrict what a user can do with a file as follows:

■   Read-Only. The user can only read the file.

■   Append. The user can only write to the file and cannot read it.

■   Execute. The user can execute the file but can neither read nor write.

■   Read-Write. The user has read and write permissions to the file.

The main Bell-LaPadula security rule is: A user with security clearance A can read, write, append, and execute files at security level A. The user can read and execute files at levels less than A (reading down) and append files at levels greater than A (writing up). Figure 2.9 illustrates this rule for a file system with five levels and two users with security clearances 2 and 4.

There is also a secondary rule dealing with something called a control attribute. When a user creates a file, the user becomes the controller of the file and is allowed to pass any of the four access rights of the file to any user (except that no other user can be the controller of that file).

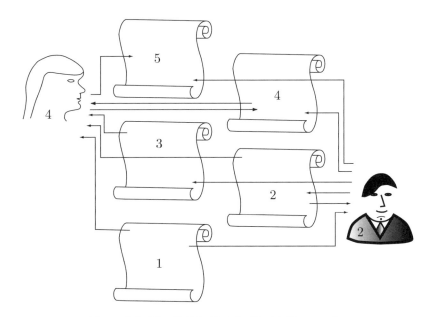

Figure 2.9: The Bell-LaPadula Model Illustrated.

The reason for the reading down restriction is to guarantee that highly-sensitive information would not be leaked to a low-level user, and the reason for the writing up restriction is to make sure a high-clearance user cannot leak sensitive information to unauthorized, low-clearance users.

This model seems secure and has proved itself over the years when it was implemented in an operating system. However, it is vulnerable to a virus attack because it allows a low clearance user to infect high-level files. A user with low clearance A can write, and therefore can infect, a file at security level A with a virus. When the file is later executed by a user with higher-clearance B, the virus may infect another file at level B. When any of the two infected files is executed by a user with higher-clearance C, the virus may infect another file at level C, and so on. This vulnerability implies that the lowest-level (least trusted) user can infect the highest-level (top secret) files. The vulnerability has nothing to do with any bugs in the implementation of the security software; it is a weakness of the Bell-LaPadula model, which was designed to protect secrets, not to protect from the menace of computer viruses.

Such a virus, created and injected by a low-clearance user, can subject high-clearance users to the usual damage of a virus, such as denial-of-service, data diddling, and change of permissions. This, however, is only the beginning. It turns out that such a virus can, if combined with a covert channel, leak data from high-level, secret files, to low-clearance users.

Imagine two executable files S (a high-level, sender process) and R (a low-level, receiver process). Any covert channel used by S to send data to R must involve some synchronization from R to S, a straightforward process, because S can read data prepared by R. Thus, S and R can use a small file that R can write and S can read. To synchronize itself with S, R writes a special symbol in the file, and erases it later. This is similar to a global variable, with the difference that information can only go from R to S. With this in mind, here are some examples of covert channels.

Example 1. S can send secret data bit by bit to R by varying its memory requirements. To send a 0, process S waits for a synchronization signal from R, then requests a large amount of memory from the operating system, then releases it after one second. To send a 1, S again waits for a synchronization from R, releases most of its memory, then requests it back from the operating system after one second. R can receive the bits by sending a synchronization signal and then checking the amount of memory available. This is a slow process that's also subject to errors, because other processes may request memory from the operating system. We therefore say that this covert channel is noisy. Nevertheless, reliable covert communication is possible if the communicating processes use an error-correcting code with the secret data. Notice that this covert channel uses a shared resource, namely the clock.

Example 2. Secret data can be sent from S to R by creating a contention for a shared resource, such as a printer. To send a 1, S waits for a synchronization from R, checks to see if the printer is attached, and attaches it if it is not. To send a 0, S similarly waits for a synchronization, checks to see if the printer is attached, and detaches it if it is. R sends a synchronization, then attempts to attach the printer. If this is successful, R interprets it as a 0, otherwise as a 1. R then detaches the printer if the attach operation was successful and sends another synchronization signal for the next secret bit.

Example 3. This example exploits the details of a specific I/O scheduling algorithm, but can be varied to use other I/O scheduling algorithms. Imagine a hard disk with a set of read/write heads that moves radially from cylinder to cylinder. The movement of the heads is very slow compared to the CPU speed, so it has to be organized efficiently. There is a head scheduling algorithm called the "elevator algorithm" that works as follows: I/O requests for data on the disk are queued by ascending cylinder number. Requests are then dequeued in order of ascending cylinder number until no greater cylinder number remains (i.e., the upper end of the cylinder is reached) and then are dequeued in descending order until no lower numbered cylinders remain (i.e., the lower end of the cylinder is reached). This process is repeated indefinitely.

Suppose that R has data in cylinders 31 through 39 of the disk and S had read access to the disk. R issues a request for cylinder 35, waits until it is notified of its completion, then relinquishes the CPU. S then issues a request for either cylinder 33 (to send a 0) or 37 (to send a 1), then relinquishes the CPU. R then issues requests for cylinders 38 and 32, thereby receiving a 1 or 0 depending on which request completes first. (End of example 3.)

⬦ **Exercise 2.14:** Describe in general a few more mechanisms for covert channels.

In general, in a computer with an operating system that supports flexible shared resources, there always exist covert channels. This example shows how the combination (or synergistic relation) of a virus and a covert channel can be more powerful than just having a virus and a covert channel. A virus can penetrate to high-security places but cannot send back secret information to low security levels. A covert channel can leak information down security levels, but cannot propagate to highly secret files. Their combination, however, is powerful because it can do something neither of them can do by itself, namely it can leak secret information even in an environment specifically designed to protect secrets.

From the dictionary
Synergism: The whole is greater than the sum of its parts.

Such a synergistic relation can be created in many ways. The Internet worm (Section 3.4) combined a virus and an algorithm (fortunately, not very sophisticated) to find passwords in computers it penetrated. The combination of virus (to spread) and algorithm (to find potential victims) became very powerful and helped the worm to spread very quickly through the Internet. It is virtually certain that a future super virus will combine an ability to spread with a powerful, flexible algorithm that can locate vulnerable computers while learning from the mistakes and successes of past viruses.

■ A virus can also be benevolent, but examples of such viruses are normally more complex (see year 1988 in Appendix B). A detailed discussion of the potential of such viruses can be found in [Cohen 94b]. A hypothetical example of a benign virus is an antibody. This is anti-virus software specifically designed to eradicate one virus V. The antibody propagates like a virus. Before it "infects" a program, the antibody examines it for infection by V and cleans it if needed. The antibody then infects the program by attaching itself to it, such that every time the program is launched, the antibody is the first task to execute and it examines the program again for infection by V. Once all occurrences of V have been removed from the computer, the antibody removes itself from all the executable files it had "infected."

To verify complete eradication of V, the antibody has to make sure that all the executable files in the computer have modification dates that are later than the date the antibody itself has started its operations (a little thinking shows that this does not provide complete verification). Once the antibody verifies this, it may create a special file to act as a flag. When any copy of the antibody finds that the flag file exists, it deletes itself.

Such an antibody sounds like an ingenious solution, but once the virus creator hears of the antibody, he may produce a slightly different strain of V that will be unrecognizable by the antibody. Virus writers don't like their virus to be killed by another virus.

$\diamond$ **Exercise 2.15:** Try to forward a simple argument showing why good viruses are harder to design and implement than bad ones.

Many computer programs have hidden, undocumented, and surprising features that are referred to as easter eggs. An easter egg is normally placed in the code of the program by the original programmer or team of programmers, and is often meant to be funny.

A typical easter egg is hidden in the popular program *Adobe Acrobat Reader*. Version 4 of this program plays a dog bark when a certain key combination is pressed. One Web site that collects easter eggs is [eeggs 05]. In mid 2005 this site had more than 7800 of them. Easter eggs can also be found in movies, music, television shows and commercials, books, and art.

2.18 Virus Organization

The thousands of computer viruses that have been detected, identified and analysed in the last two decades feature a large variety of approaches to the problems of propagation, triggering, and manipulation. It is infeasible to describe all the solutions used by viruses, so this section discusses the four main components found in the majority of viruses.

Infection marker. A virus infects a program by installing itself (or a modified copy of itself) in the program. It is unnecessary to infect a program more than once, and multiple infections are also dangerous for the virus because each infection increases the size of the program file, thereby making it easier to detect the virus. Once a virus infects a program, it signals its presence by an infection marker, a special code stored by the virus at a point where it can be found by the virus. Before infecting a program, the virus checks for the presence of this marker.

Infector. This is the code that actually does the infection. It creates a copy (identical or modified) of the virus and stores it in the program being infected.

Trigger check. This piece of code checks the conditions for triggering the damage (the payload, also termed warhead or manipulation part). The conditions may depend on the date, the number of times the virus has replicated itself, or on the content of the program the virus has infected. If the conditions are right, the virus releases its payload (i.e., executes the manipulation part that does the damage). A good trigger (good from the point of view of the virus writer) should wait a while (even weeks or months) before inflicting the damage, because this makes it more difficult for the victim and for security experts to identify the source of the virus. Such a delay mimics methods for self-preservation that have evolved in living organisms and are described in, for example, [Dawkins 90], except that nature's schemes for self preservation are much more subtle than those of computer viruses.

Manipulation. This is the code that executes the payload (the damaging task) of the virus. It is invoked by the trigger check and may delete files, corrupt files, display a message, make random modifications to the operating system, or perform other destructive operations.

2.19 Virus Naming

Because of the importance of computer viruses and because of their large numbers, it is important to have a standard for naming them. No standard has never been formally agreed upon by industry (makers of anti-virus software) but an informal standard exists and is used by virus experts to refer to viruses and to warn the public about them. This standard, however, is not binding, and many virus names deviate from it. Macro viruses, the most common type of virus, often have complex names that consist of several parts.

Many new viruses are derived from existing viruses and are not completely new. This divides the world of viruses into families. Each family of viruses receives a name. When a new virus appears that's not derived from any family, it becomes the founder of a new family and a new family name is assigned. The name is coined from some important feature of the virus, such as some text it may display, the platform or the operating system it infects, or its damaging effect. The name may also include a number that indicates the size (in bytes) of the virus.

Within a family, names have a short (up to three letters) suffix. Thus, the first 26 strains of family `SHAME` have designations `SHAME.A` through `SHAME.Z`. When more viruses are added to a family, they get a two-letter suffix that runs from `AA`, `AB`, through `AZ` to `BA`, `BB`, through `BZ`, and so on. If more than $26 + 26^2 = 702$ similar strains appear, a three-letter suffix can be used.

A suffix may also include strings that provide additional information about the particular strain of virus. Examples are the following:

`@MM` (Mass mailing distribution). This virus normally uses email to spread.

`.APP` (Appended viruses). Such a virus appends its code to the file it infects, but fails to provide for correct replication.

`.CAV` (Cavity virus). This type of virus copies itself into "cavities" (regions of all zeros) in an executable program file.

`.DR` (Dropper file). A file that introduces the virus into the host program.

Over time, the standard evolved to also include a prefix that indicates the type of file or the specific platform infected by the virus. Examples are the following:

`A97M/` A macro virus that infects Microsoft Access 97 files.

`BV/` A Batch-file virus. This type looks like a batch or script file and affects any program that interprets the commands included in the virus. (A batch file has a `.BAT` extension.)

`CSC/` A Corel Script virus or Trojan horse that infects Corel Draw document files, template files, and scripts.

`PP97M/` A macro virus that infects Microsoft PowerPoint 97 files.

`W32/` A file-infector or boot-sector virus. This type infects various versions of the 32-bit Windows operating system.

Thus, for example, the standard name `W32.Blaster.T.Worm` refers to a worm that attacks certain vulnerabilities in Windows 2000 and Windows XP. It has a suffix `T` and the extra indicator `Worm` because it is not a virus. The name `Concept.Fr.B` indicates a macro virus that originated in France and is a version of the virus `WM.Concept` that's been modified to work with French-language versions of Microsoft Word.

See [Encyc1 04] and [Encyc2 04] for two detailed virus encyclopedias with names and descriptions of thousands of computer viruses.

2.20 Virus Hiding Methods

Once a virus has released its payload, complete recovery from its destructive effects may be slow, complex, and agonizing. However, it is often easy to get rid of the virus itself once it has been identified. If the virus hides in a file, the file can be deleted and replaced with an original. If the virus hides in the boot sector, the operating system can reinstall the boot sector on the infected disk. There are some exceptions, most notably the MTX virus/worm (Section 5.12), where deleting the virus is a multistep process and should be done manually, not by a program (the interested reader should consult [pchell 05] for the detailed removal instructions). This section discusses ways and means used by viruses to hide themselves in the computer.

A boot sector virus (BSI, Section 2.6) hides in the boot sector of a disk. It seems that identifying such a virus should be easy. The computer owner (or a security worker) can prepare in advance a copy of the boot sector, and later compare it to the boot sector of a suspicious disk. However, a well-designed virus can often defeat this simple check because of the way disks are read and checked. Binary information recorded on a disk cannot be read with the naked eye. In order to read the boot sector and print it, display it, or compare it to a list of instructions (in fact, to read anything from a disk), a program is needed. The program works by invoking operating system routines (sometimes called basic input/output system or BIOS) and the point is that the virus can modify these routines. Specifically, the routines can be modified such that when they are asked to read the boot sector, they will provide a copy of the original, non-infected sector that had been hidden on the disk by the virus.

The security expert can take the suspect disk to another computer and try to read the boot sector there, but the virus may be executed from the boot sector (and modify the BIOS routines) as soon as the disk is inserted into the new computer. The disk should therefore be read in a different type of computer or in the same platform but under an operating system that the virus doesn't recognize. An alternative is for a security expert to write low-level disk routines, similar to the ones used by BIOS, and read the disk with these routines.

The virus itself doesn't have to be located in the boot sector. It can be hidden elsewhere on the disk and be loaded by the loader in the boot sector when the disk is mounted. Such a virus modifies the boot sector, but only in an insignificant way, by adding a few instructions that load the virus. The virus itself may be hidden in an extra track or in unused disk space (but in this case the virus may be erased when a new file is written on the disk).

The Macintosh operating system organizes a file in two forks, a data fork, with the content of the file (instructions or data) and a resource fork, with character strings, parameters, icons, and extra code segments. It is possible to hide a virus in the resource fork of a file as a code resource. The virus still has to be executed, which means that some executable program (most likely the one in the data fork of the same file) must be modified to read the virus, store it in memory, and execute it.

A file infector virus (Section 2.7) embeds itself in an executable file and therefore has to modify the file in some way. Such a virus can be detected by detecting the modifications to the infected file. The modifications may affect (1) the file size, (2) its most recent modification date, (3) the code inside the file, and (4) the file's access permissions.

An overwriting virus writes itself over the code of the original file and therefore preserves the size of the infected file. A nonoverwriting virus modifies the size of the file but may be able to fake this modification and thereby fool anti-virus software. (The virus may save the original size, embed itself in the file, then restore the size. Stealth techniques are discussed in Section 2.22.) The obvious conclusion is that virus detection software should not rely only on the size of a file to detect infection.

The header of a file may also contain a simple checksum of the rest of the file. (In its simplest form, the checksum is a byte that's the exclusive-or of all the bytes of the file.) Almost any change in the composition of the file affects the checksum, and this may be an indicator of file corruption, a better indicator than just the size of the file. However, a clever virus may fake the checksum (it may copy the original checksum from the header and restore it later, a common stealth technique).

Even a simple virus that modifies the file size may avoid detection because anti-virus software cannot tell why the size of an executable file has changed. When anti-virus software is executed, it may scan the disk and save the sizes of all the executable files it finds. The next time it is executed, it may discover that the size of an executable file A has changed, but this may be the result of updating A. After all, programs go through new versions all the time, and many new versions update the original program file instead of creating a new file.

Some viruses infect only large files, because a virus embedded in a small file may significantly modify the size of the file, thereby raising suspicion. This behavior may be termed a *psychological factor* and it illustrates the great lengths to which virus writers may go in their attempts to foil detection.

A program consists of instructions and data. The data part consists of constants and variables, and some of the variables are arrays. An array is a set of consecutive memory locations reserved by the program. When the program starts executing, the array is normally empty (more precisely, undefined). During its execution, the program may store data in the array. A virus author who is very familiar with a particular program may write an overwriting virus that embeds itself in an array in the executable file of the program. (The author has to know precisely where the array is located in the file, because everything in an executable file, instructions, data, and arrays, consists of bits and therefore looks the same.) A virus located in an array does not change the size of the file and does not affect its executable code. However, once the program starts executing, it may write data in the array, thereby erasing the virus' code. There is also the question of how the virus can get executed, because a program does not execute arrays of data.

An operating system may impose restrictions on files and such restrictions may be exploited by viruses. An operating system may require, for example, that a file size be always a multiple of 512 or some other number of bytes. A virus writer who plans to attack a certain computer and is familiar with the popular programs on that computer, may know that a certain program file has a long, empty "tail" where a virus can be hidden. There is still the question of the virus being executed. The original code of the program must be modified to include at least a jump or a procedure call to the virus.

Detailed knowledge of the operating system and the files and tables it uses may lead to sophisticated viruses that hide themselves in a variety of ways. A favorite of some virus authors is a virus that modifies the disk directory instead of modifying the infected files.

For each file on a disk, the disk directory contains, in addition to the file name, type, size, and other items, also the start address of the file on the disk (the sector number or sector and track numbers). When the virus is executed for the first time in an infected computer it writes itself on the main hard disk as a file, but does not include itself in the directory (or includes itself as an invisible file). It then scans the directory until it finds a file A it wants to infect. It saves the disk address of A and changes this address in the directory to its own start address. When the user wants to execute file A, the operating system follows the disk address found in the directory, which leads it to the virus. The virus is executed, and when done it may decide to execute program A to avoid raising suspicion. The term *misdirection virus* is sometimes applied to this type of virus. It can be implemented such that it will misdirect the execution of several different programs to (different entry points in) the virus. This is only one of many examples that illustrate the ingenious ways in which viruses and other malicious software can be hidden in a computer.

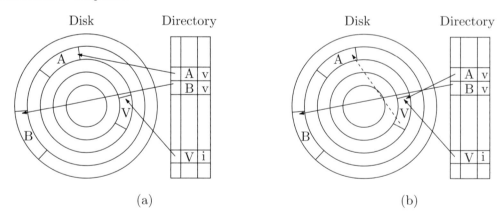

Figure 2.10: (a) Original Directory. (b) Modified Directory.

Figure 2.10 illustrates how this technique works. Part a of the figure shows a disk with three files A, B, and V and a file directory with three items per file, disk address (the pointers), name, and a visibility flag. Note that file V (the virus) is invisible. In part b we see how the directory entry for file A is pointing to the virus, and how the virus has the disk address of A (the dashed arrow). The directory entries for the other files haven't changed.

Next, we discuss the use of a CRC in locating viruses and how a virus can protect itself from such detection.

Most programs (executable files) never change their content. The program does not modify itself when executed. The same is true for the boot sectors on disk drives. Such sectors contain programs that load files from the disk, and those programs are always the same (they change only when new versions of the operating system are installed). It is therefore relatively easy to write an anti-virus program that will scan all the executable files on a disk, store their sizes in a table, and use this table in future executions to locate those executable files whose sizes have changed. This anti-virus program should be run periodically, to notify the user of any changes.

Unfortunately, it is relatively easy for a sophisticated virus writer to defeat the protection offered by this type of anti-virus software. Once the virus decides which file to infect, it can obtain the size of the file from the operating system, compress the file, prepend or append itself to the file, then pad the file with zeros to bring it to its former size. A typical executable file may compress to about half its original size, leaving plenty of room for the virus, which is normally a small program. When the executable file is launched, the virus (which is not compressed) executes first. It performs its tasks, then decompresses the executable program, so it can also run. The only effect that may be observed by the user and cause suspicion is the short delay caused by decompressing the executable file. The cruncher virus (Section 5.10) is an example of a compression virus.

◇ **Exercise 2.16:** Can it happen that compressing an executable file will not leave enough room for a virus?

A more sophisticated version of such anti-virus software can try to detect the presence of a virus by means of a checksum or a CRC. The operating system should compute a checksum or a CRC (cyclic redundancy code) for each new executable file stored on the disk and save the CRCs in a table. The anti-virus software checks, in such a case, every executable file by computing its CRC and comparing it to the CRC in the table. Any differences indicate changes to the file, even if its size hasn't changed.

A little thinking shows that even the use of CRC to detect viruses is not foolproof, because a sophisticated virus writer may learn how the operating system computes the CRC and use this knowledge to embed the virus in an executable file without modifying its original CRC. To do this, the virus (1) computes the CRC of the executable file, (2) compresses the file, (3) prepends itself to the file, (4) pads the file with zeros to bring it back to its original size, then (5) changes some of the zero bytes to restore the file's CRC to its original value.

If the CRC computation is kept secret, the virus writer may buy the anti-virus software (more likely, locate a copy in underground hacker sites), disassemble it, and read and understand the part that computes the CRC. A sophisticated virus may even locate the table with all the file lengths and CRCs and store in it the new length and CRC of the file it has modified. The table should therefore be saved in encrypted form, using a password supplied by the user.

A more sophisticated application of a CRC is to compute the CRC of a clean (uninfected) file, then sign it with the private key of (1) the program's author, (2) the owner of the computer, or (3) the person who is cleaning the computer. Digital signatures are discussed on page 280. The signed CRC then becomes an authenticator of the file. In order to check a file for infection, the CRC of the file has to be computed, the authenticator has to be unlocked, and the original CRC in the unlocked authenticator compared with the new CRC just computed. The point is that unlocking the authenticator requires only the public key, not the private key, of the person who locked the authenticator. The virus may have access to the authenticator, but it cannot unlock it in order to modify the CRC. The best the virus can do is to corrupt the authenticator, which will confuse the user.

This scheme makes sense for commercial software purchased from a trusted source. The software can be locked at the source, and sold on a CD that will also have the authenticator (a small file) and the necessary public key.

An interesting but impractical idea is to have the operating system ask the user for permission each time a program wants to write to a file. In principle, the user should know what files the program is supposed to modify, but in practice, users generally don't know much about the details of program behavior and the way it writes to files, especially operating system files and temporary files that the program may create.

The person most familiar with what files a given program should be allowed to write to is the creator of the program. In principle, the creator may construct a list of file names that the program should be permitted to write to. Such a list should be stored in the same directory as the program and be accessed by the operating system each time the program tries to write to a file. However, a clever virus may modify this list and add the names of files the virus plans to attack. The list may be encrypted by the user, but then the operating system may have to ask the user for the encryption key each time the program wants to write to a different file. The user then enters the key, but the virus may monitor the keyboard and record the keystrokes. Despair!

> Action is the antidote to despair.
> —Joan Baez

2.21 Polymorphism

Unfortunately, the basic features of a computer virus are so powerful that (at least in principle) it may be possible to write a virus that mutates and infects each new file as a different string of bits. This feature is often referred to as polymorphism. Such a virus may be virtually impossible to locate by anti-virus software. Here is one such scenario. Suppose we have identified a program V (a string of bits) as a virus. When infection starts, V has infected a program P_1, and it resides in P_1 (Figure 2.11a) as an encrypted file E_1 plus a small decryption routine D_1. When P_1 is executed, the virus is also executed. Routine D_1 decrypts E_1 into the original virus V. The virus is then executed, it selects a different encryption algorithm and encrypts itself into E_2. It then

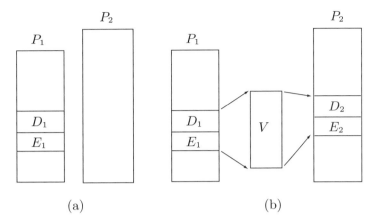

Figure 2.11: A Mutating Virus.

prepares a suitable decryption routine D_2, and it infects program P_2 by storing E_2 and D_2 in it (Figure 2.11b).

There are now two infected programs, P_1 and P_2, and the point is that the viruses located in them are the same, but constitute different bit strings. The virus has mutated. Such a virus may be virtually impossible to detect, but there is more! This concept of a mutating virus can be extended in frightening ways.

To scare the reader even more (actually, to educate the reader), we describe a virus designed to mutate at random into many strains. The original virus contains m encryption algorithms, it is triggered by one of n conditions T_i, it infects a file in one of n ways I_i, and it has n options M_i to damage the computer. This virus spends its life switching between two modes, mutate and replace. It starts in the mutate mode, where it spreads m mutations of itself by using its m encryption methods as shown earlier. This infects m files with different copies of the virus, all with the same infection, triggering, and damage mechanisms, but all looking different. When done, the virus switches to the replace mode, where it selects different infection, trigger, and damage mechanisms. It then switches to its mutate mode, and infects another set of m programs. This can be repeated n times, with the result that up to $m \times n$ files have been infected with different bit strings, making it impossible for anti-virus software to locate the various instances of the virus. Moreover, because of the n different triggering conditions and damage mechanisms, this single, compound (confound?) virus appears to the victim like n different viruses.

⋄ **Exercise 2.17:** Have you been frightened enough (see also exercise 9.2)?

In addition to mutating, a virus may hide itself in a compressed file in such a way that the bits with the virus part depend on the rest of the infected file and are therefore always different. Such a file has to be completely decompressed in order to identify the virus. The cruncher virus (Section 5.10) is such an example.

Polymorphism can also be achieved in other ways and a few techniques are listed here.

■   Programmers know that there normally are several ways to implement a given task in a computer program. Thus, it is common to have in a program two sections of code A and B whose order of execution is immaterial. They can be executed as either AB or BA, which implies that the same program can be written in two different ways (it can become two different bit strings). If there are three sections of code that can be executed in any order, then the program can be written in $3! = 6$ different ways. Thus, a virus can create versions of itself that differ in the order of certain sections of code.

⋄ **Exercise 2.18:** (For programmers.) A program works with registers and memory locations. Suggest several ways to clear register 4 (set it to all zeros).

■   A virus can modify itself and become a different string of bits simply by inserting several `nop` instructions in its code. A `nop` (no operation) is an instruction that does nothing.

■   A virus that propagates as an email attachment can use one of many prepared names for the attachment. An example of this behavior is the MTX malware (Section 5.12)

The next point to consider, when trying to locate and eradicate viruses, is the so-called "tail-chasing" effect. Suppose there are three programs P_1, P_2, and P_3 in a computer, and the first two are infected. While anti-virus software cleans P_1, program P_2 may be run by the user (or by one of the users) and it infects P_3. When P_2 is later cleaned by the software, program P_3 is run by someone and it infects P_1 or another program (Figure 2.12). It is clear that cleaning a file system must be done in a quiet environment, but this is getting more and more difficult as operating systems become more sophisticated. Even a personal computer with one user has a number of active programs that are invoked by the operating system (either when the computer starts or at other times), are executed in the background, and are transparent to the user. Typical examples are: (1) A routine that connects periodically to a standard clock on the Internet to readjust the computer's clock. (2) A routine to perform periodic maintenance tasks to get rid of unused logs and cache files and to automatically backup certain important operating system files. (3) A utility to periodically defragment disks. If any of those programs is infected, it will infect others each time it is run.

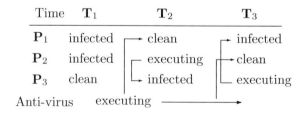

Figure 2.12: A Tail Chasing Effect.

⋄ **Exercise 2.19:** Look at the activity monitor of your computer to locate other routines that are currently active, especially those that are not part of the operating system.

The conclusion is that as many active processes as possible should be stopped before any attempt is made to clean viruses from a computer.

2.22 Virus Stealth Techniques

Stealth techniques are mentioned on page 77 in connection with a virus faking the size or the checksum of a file. This section discusses the concept of virus stealth and how stealth techniques work. Consider the example of a virus that embeds itself in a file. The process of writing the virus code in the file may modify the size of the file. If the operating system maintains a checksum for the file, the checksum will also be modified. A cleverly-designed virus may attempt to avoid detection by restoring the original size and checksum of the file. This is an example of a virus stealth technique.

A file has a header with fields for the file size, creation date, latest date of modification, and other data items. These fields are updated by the operating system each time the file is accessed, but a virus can update them back to their original values. The trick is for the virus to read these fields before it embeds itself in the file and save this information. After the virus has hidden itself in the file, it restores the fields in the file header to their original values, but it does that *without* invoking the operating system. Recall that an operating system is a set of routines that provide services to the users and make it easy for them to use the computer. Programmers normally use the operating system services to access files, but a good programmer who is familiar with the details of the input/output on the computer can write a program to read and write files directly, bypassing the operating system services. When the operating system is not asked to access a file, it doesn't update the fields in the file's header.

Any kind of operation where a virus "lies" to the user, modifies interrupt handling routines, or bypasses standard procedures may be termed a *stealth technique*.

⬦ **Exercise 2.20:** Try to come up with an extreme stealth technique.

Most stealth methods are based on modifying various interrupt handling routines. Interrupts and their exploitation by viruses are discussed in Section 2.23. Stealth techniques can be classified in five categories as follows:

▪ No stealth. An overwriting virus often damages its host file irreparably and calls attention to itself this way. Such a virus employs no stealth techniques and is easy to detect and destroy. This category includes only viruses that don't care about being discovered. Often, a virus is detected because of a bug in its code or because its author did not anticipate an unusual condition that affects the host file only rarely. Such viruses are not included in this category.

▪ Stealth neutral. This category includes viruses that embed themselves in an executable file without damaging it but do not otherwise attempt to hide. Such a virus is designed to release its payload once, and then be detected and deleted.

▪ Elementary stealth. Viruses that take only elementary steps to hide themselves in the infected file belong in this category. Examples of elementary steps are restoring the size, modification date, and checksum of the infected file. Figure 2.13 illustrates how this approach works. Part a of the figure shows a file with some data and a header with three fields, size, date, and checksum. In part b, a virus saves the three fields in memory, and in part c it attaches itself to the file, changing the three header fields in the process. Finally, part d shows how the virus has restored the three header fields from memory using low-level input/output commands that bypass the normal operating system routines.

■   Intermediate stealth. The virus prepares a copy of the infected file or boot sector and modifies certain interrupt handling routines to present the copy to any nosy software. When anti-virus software tries to detect the virus by looking for modification in files, it is defeated by such stealth techniques.

■   Advanced stealth. A virus writer who wants to be original may study several common anti-virus programs, find weaknesses or loopholes in them, and design a virus that hides itself based on this knowledge.

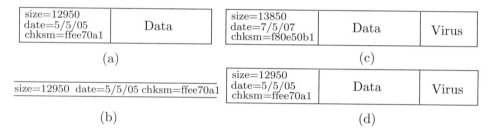

Figure 2.13: Elementary Stealth Virus.

2.23 Interrupts and Viruses

An interrupt is a simple mechanism, utilizing both hardware and software, that enables a computer to respond quickly and efficiently to urgent and unusual conditions. When an urgent or unusual condition occurs, an interrupt-request signal is sent to the CPU by the circuit that detected the condition. The CPU looks for interrupt-request signals before it executes the next instruction. If it finds such a signal, the CPU interrupts the execution of the current program and invokes a special interrupt-handling routine that handles the condition. The various interrupt-handling routines constitute the software part of the interrupt mechanism. The routines are part of the operating system, which is why an interrupt always transfers control to the operating system. The sensors, interrupt-request signals, and the CPU sensor mechanism make up the hardware part. The terms *traps* and *hooks* are often used for interrupts.

The CPU of a computer has three main components, the control unit, the ALU, and the registers. The registers are storage units for intermediate, temporary results. The ALU (arithmetic and logic unit) is a set of circuits that perform all the operations on numbers specified by the instructions in the program. The control unit is the main part of the CPU. It is the part that reads (fetches) the instructions from memory and executes them one by one in a seemingly endless loop. The control unit knows how to execute each instruction in the instruction set of the computer and has an execution circuit for each instruction. It employs a special register called the *program counter* or PC. This register always points to the next instruction and is incremented by the control unit each time an instruction is executed.

In addition to executing instructions, the control unit also implements the hardware part of the interrupt mechanism of the computer. Every source of interrupt (i.e., every circuit that can identify unusual or urgent conditions) is connected with a wire to the control unit and it can send an interrupt-request signal on that wire. On sensing such a signal, the control unit performs several extra steps to initiate an interrupt, and then resumes its normal operation.

Figure 2.14a lists the main steps in the loop of the control unit. In each iteration of its loop, the control unit (1) fetches the next instruction from memory, (2) increments the PC, (3) decodes the instruction to find out what it is, (4) executes the instruction, and then (5) examines all the interrupt request lines, looking for pending interrupts. If it finds any, it executes several extra steps, two of which are listed in the figure. Part b of the figure shows how interrupt-request lines (IRQs) from various parts of the computer arrive at the control unit.

```
1. Fetch next instruction.
2. Increment the PC.
3. Decode the instruction.
4. Execute the instruction.
5. Check all IRQs. If IRA i is high, then
   5.1 Save the PC.
   5.2 PC ← start address of int. routine i.
6. Go to step 1.
```

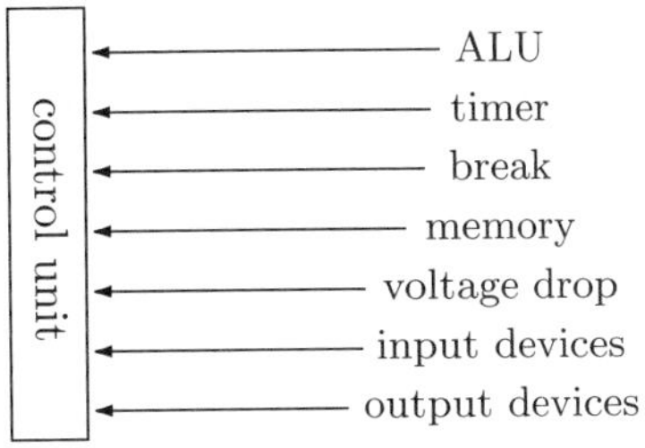

control unit —— ALU
—— timer
—— break
—— memory
—— voltage drop
—— input devices
—— output devices

(a)   (b)

Figure 2.14: The Control Unit and Interrupts.

A simple example of an interrupt is a divide by zero. Mathematically, a division by zero is undefined and should be avoided. In a computer, the hardware circuit that divides numbers is part of the arithmetic and logic unit (ALU). When this circuit identifies a zero divisor, it sends an interrupt signal to the control unit (the CPU component that executes instructions). The control unit then interrupts the normal execution of the program and invokes a special interrupt-handling routine to handle a divide-by-zero interrupt. The routine normally displays an error message and may either terminate the program or give the user a chance to modify the divisor. Other examples of common interrupts are the following:

■   Memory protection violation. In a multiuser computer, several user programs reside simultaneously in different areas of memory. At any given time, only one program executes. If a program tries (intentionally or accidentally) to access memory outside its area (even if it only tries to read data, not to write), the memory protection hardware in the computer senses it and creates an interrupt signal. Before the next instruction is executed, the control unit senses the interrupt and invokes the routine associated with this type of interrupt.

■   A timer. A modern computer has special hardware to keep and update the current time and date. In addition, there is a timer that's used by the operating system to switch between processes. To the software, the timer appears as a memory location whose content is decremented automatically all the time. When the timer reaches zero, a timer interrupt occurs, the current program is interrupted and control is transferred to the timer handling routine. The operating system sets the timer location to a certain number n of time units and starts a program by jumping to it. After n time units have elapsed, the timer reaches zero and the timer routine is invoked, selects another process, and starts it or resumes it. This way, the CPU can be switched to a different process every n time units. The formal term for this type of operation is *multitasking by time slices*.

■   An invalid instruction. When the control unit comes across an invalid instruction (a bit pattern that's not the code of any instruction) it issues an interrupt. The handling routine for invalid instructions is invoked and simply prints an error message and terminates the program.

■   Resetting (or rebooting) a computer is done by an interrupt. This is discussed in the answer to exercise 2.21.

■   A break. One of the more interesting applications of interrupts is to respond to users' requests. When a program wants to print the time or the date, it creates an artificial interrupt that invokes a special handling routine, part of the operating system. The routine finds out that the interrupted program needs the time or date, it resumes the interrupted program and sends it the requested data. The artificial interrupt is created by a special instruction, often called **break**. Before executing this instruction, the program must store information about the request in memory. The **break** instruction accepts one parameter, an address that points to where the request information is stored.

Input/output (I/O) is an especially important and common example of the use of the **break** interrupt. A typical I/O process is initiated by the user program as a request (in the form of an interrupt) to the operating system. The operating system sends low-level commands to the I/O device (keyboard, printer, disk, or anything else), it either sends the output to or waits to receive the input from the device, then resumes the user program. We examine this process in detail on several levels as follows:

- Suppose that a user program U wants to read a file named abc from the disk into an array buf. The programmer writes a statement such as read(abc,buf,1000) where 1000 is the length of array buf.
- The compiler (part of the operating system) reads the statement and compiles it into a **break** instruction whose single parameter points to memory to where a special code is stored. The code tells the operating system that the program is

requesting input and it includes the string abc, the address buf, and the constant 1000.

- When the break is executed at run time, it creates an interrupt that transfers control to its handling routine, also part of the operating system. The routine follows the pointer (the parameter of break) to where the request information is stored. Once the routine understands the request, it performs the following steps:

  1. It changes the state of user program U to "inactive." The program will have to wait until the input data is sent from the input device to array buf. In the meantime, other processes (either background processes or programs of other users) will be executed by the CPU. The operating system maintains a list of all the processes in memory and assigns each process a state of "active" or "inactive." Active processes execute and inactive ones wait.

  2. It converts the file name (string abc) to the start address (track and sector) of the file on the disk. The association of name to disk address of all the files is stored in the disk directory.

  3. It sends the appropriate commands to the input device.

  4. Finally, the routine selects the next process to execute and jumps to it.

- When the input data is ready, the input device itself sends it to array buf in memory. This process is known as direct memory access or DMA. When done, the device issues an interrupt.

- We denote by P the program the CPU happens to be executing at the time this interrupt is created (P can be any program). When the CPU is ready to execute the next instruction of P, it checks the status of all the interrupt request lines. When it finds an interrupt request signal, it invokes the corresponding handling routine. Program P has been interrupted.

- This routine finds out that the data requested by U is ready. It changes the state of user program U to "active" and selects the next process to execute. This process can be program P, the original user program U, of any other waiting process.

> If your work speaks for itself, don't interrupt.
> —Henry J. Kaiser

Once the important mechanism of interrupts is understood, it is easy to see how interrupts can be exploited by computer viruses. A file infector is executed when its host program is executed. A macro virus is executed when its host file is processed by an application. A boot sector infector (BSI) is executed when the disk it has infected is inserted into a disk drive and the program in the boot sector is executed. The BSI copies itself from the boot sector to memory, but it still has to ensure that it will be executed from time to time. The best way to do this is to invade and modify an interrupt handling routine. Each interrupt has a handling routine associated with it, and that routine is invoked when the interrupt occurs. When the BSI copies itself from the boot sector to memory, it modifies certain interrupt handling routines by storing in each of them a jump or a call instruction to the virus. The virus is now memory resident and is activated each time an interrupt invokes one of the modified handling routines.

Certain interrupt routines are natural candidates for infection by a BSI. The timer routine is an example. It is invoked each time the timer is decremented to zero, and it is used to switch the CPU between processes. Imagine a virus that stores a `jump` instruction to itself at the end of this routine. This virus will be invoked after the operating system has selected the next process to be started or resumed, but before it (the OS) has actually started or resumed the process. A clever virus can find out from the timer routine which process will be the next to execute, thereby having a chance to modify or infect that process. Admittedly, implementing such a virus requires detailed knowledge of the internals of the operating system process scheduling.

Another candidate for a modified handling routine is the keyboard routine, which is invoked each time a key is pressed on the keyboard. A virus infecting this routine will be invoked each time the user presses a key on the keyboard and will therefore be able to save all the keystrokes and send them periodically outside the computer. Keystroke loggers are discussed in Chapter 9.

What about removable disks? When a removable disk is inserted into a disk drive, a sensor in the drive issues an interrupt signal. The current program is interrupted and the interrupt handling routine is invoked. It mounts the disk and resumes the current program. A virus that modifies that routine will be invoked each time a removable disk is inserted into a drive and will therefore be able to infect clean disks.

Once a virus has modified some interrupt handling routines, it becomes memory resident. It will be invoked when any of those routines is called, and will be able to do its "job." However, most memories of today's computers are RAM, which is volatile. When the computer is turned off or when it is restarted, the operating system, including all the interrupt handling routines, is reloaded from a disk. Both the memory resident virus and the infected handling routines are gone. Thus, the next task of a virus writer is to find ways for the virus to survive a reboot of the computer. The following exercise sheds some light on this interesting problem (but see also exercise 6.7).

⋄ **Exercise 2.21:** Most of the memories used in current computers are volatile; they are erased when the computer is turned off or is restarted (rebooted). Suggest a way to use interrupts to implement a resident virus that survives rebooting.

2.24 Trapdoors

A program is a finite set of instructions. It starts at its first executable instruction and is executed until a `STOP` instruction is encountered or until an error is discovered. The first executable instruction of a program is normally the first thing in the program, but a program may also start with an array or with bytes of predefined data and this may be followed by the first executable instruction. Thus, it is not enough to write, compile, and load a program in memory. The programmer also has to specify the *entry point* into the program.

The source code fragment of Figure 2.15a starts with an array A and its main entry point is labeled S; this is the address of the first executable instruction. Another entry point in this program is P, the start address of a procedure that the main program calls. Label S has to be explicitly declared as an entry point by the programmer. If procedure P is to called by another program, then its name P also has to be declared an entry point. The names and locations of all entry points are saved in the executable program file, in contrast with the names of other labels, such as B, that disappear once the program has been compiled.

In Figure 2.15b, a section of code has been appended to our program, with a new entry point Q. This section performs some operations, calls procedure P, and stops. If Q is declared an entry point but is not documented by the programmer, then Q is a trapdoor (often also referred to as a *backdoor*). Anyone who knows that Q is an entry point into the program, can enter at that point, while others cannot. (This is similar to saying that anyone who knows the name of a program can execute it, or that anyone who knows a URL can surf to it.) Thus, a trapdoor is an undocumented entry point in a program.

```
A: ARRAY 100        A: ARRAY 100
S: ADD ..           S: ADD ..
   LOD                 LOD
B: NEG              B: NEG
   CALL P              CALL P
   .                   .

   .                   .
   STOP                STOP
P: INP ..           P: INP ..
   STO ..              STO ..
   .                   .

   .                   .
   RET                 RET
                    Q: INP ..
                       CMPR ..
                       .

                       .
                       CALL P
                       STOP

    (a)                (b)
```

Figure 2.15: Source Code for a Trapdoor.

A trapdoor is not necessarily bad. Trapdoors serve useful and legitimate purposes such as testing, debugging, and maintaining the program. Sometimes an entry point that was included temporarily in a program during its development phase is accidentally left. However, a trapdoor can be a powerful tool in the hands of a wrongdoer and are commonly found in viruses, worms, Trojans, and other types of malware.

In God we trust, all others we virus scan.
—Anonymous

3
Worms

A *tapeworm* is a parasite that lives inside the body of a bigger creature and sustains itself from its host's resources. A software worm is a program that executes independently of other programs, replicates itself, and spreads through a network from computer to computer. A worm is a type of rogue software that resides in a host computer, but it is not a virus because it is not embedded in a host program. A  worm propagates from host to host by exploiting a security hole or a vulnerability discovered by its creator. Section 3.4 shows how the Internet worm exploited security weaknesses in the `finger` and `sendmail` UNIX utilities. Section 2.11 describes a vulnerability in a decoder for jpeg images.

It seems that the idea of a software worm was first proposed by John Brunner in his novel *The Shockwave Rider*, where these programs are referred to as *tapeworms*. Inspired by this story, researchers at the Xerox Palo Alto Research Center (PARC) tried to implement and experiment with programs that propagated from computer to computer and perform useful tasks. They reported on their results in 1982 [Shoch and Hupp 82] and it took until 1988 for the first widely-spread worm to appear and create havoc. In the years since that attack, this particular malicious software became known as the Internet worm. It is a classic example of a worm and is described in Section 3.4.

The discussion here follows the work, ideas, and recommendations of [Staniford et al. 02]. It examines the mechanisms used by known worms, and considers ways to create worms that are extremely sophisticated and dangerous because they can spread and embed themselves in a matter of hours or even minutes in millions of computers and remain a threat for months. An important part of the discussion concentrates on worm communications. We list several reasons for why a worm's author should be able to command the worm during its spread (i.e., send commands, signals, or even executable code to the large number of copies of the worm). Techniques for doing that are also presented. Finally, we present the idea of an international cyber center for disease control (CCDC) dedicated to the unending war against worms and other types of rogue software.

The main feature of worms, a feature that distinguishes them from viruses and Trojan horses is their speed of propagation. A virus propagates when users send email, launch programs, or carry disks between computers. A worm propagates itself throughout the Internet by exploiting security weaknesses in applications and protocols we all use. Thus, a perpetrator interested in deep penetration of the Internet may try to implement a sophisticated worm. Because of this attribute, future worms may pose a threat to the Internet, to E-commerce, and to computer communications and this threat may be much greater and much more dangerous than that posed by other types of rogue software. A worm that has infected several million computers on the Internet may have the potential for a global catastrophe. Here are just three possible scenarios:

▪ Such a worm could launch vast DoS attacks that are out of the reach of current protection technologies. Such powerful attacks can bring down not only E-commerce sites, but sensitive military sites or the root domain name servers of the Internet. Such an attack may be an ideal tool in the hands of terrorists or may be perpetrated intentionally by a rogue nation to serve as a prelude to a large-scale war.

▪ It is well known that rogue software often searches for sensitive information such as passwords and credit card numbers, but a wide-spread worm may blindly search for any kind of information based on a set of keywords. This type of a "needle in a haystack" search is inefficient, but with millions of worms searching simultaneously, it may produce quick results.

▪ A well-known adage says "you can't fool all the people all the time," but when the same false message arrives from millions of computers it may fool all the people some of the time. A wide-spread worm may cause much confusion and disrupt the lives of many by sending misinformation from millions of computers or just by making public the sensitive data it had discovered.

It's easy to come up with other, no less frightening "applications" of a global worm, because we depend on the Internet more and more, and not just we as individuals, but the infrastructure of entire nations. Past experience with fast-spreading worms should serve as a warning to what the future may have in store for us in this corner of the discipline of computer security.

> In general, the speed of a worm's spread is dictated by the efficiency of finding new targets. Apart from optimizing the scanning code, a couple of minor variations in scan sequence can result in significant improvements in speed.
>
> —Stuart Staniford, Vern Paxson, and Nicholas C. Weaver,
>
> *Warhol Worms: The Potential for Very Fast Internet Plagues*, Feb 2002.

3.1 Code Red I

Among the many software products produced and marketed by Microsoft Inc. there is a Web server known as the Microsoft internet information services (or IIS, see [IIS 04]). In June 2001, a vulnerability that exposed IIS to attack because of a remote buffer overflow was discovered and published in [CVE 01]. Just one month later, in July 2001, a new worm, designated Code-Red (later Code Red I or CRv1) appeared and started spreading by exploiting this weakness.

Once Code-Red has infected a host computer, it spread by generating 99 random IP addresses and trying to infect any IIS servers found at these locations by exploiting the same vulnerability. In some cases, another random IP was generated and the worm tried to deface the Web site (if any) at that address.

The first version of this worm had a serious bug. It always used the same seed for the pseudo-random numbers it generated. This meant that all the copies of the worm generated the same random numbers and tried to infect the same computers. The anonymous perpetrator has also noticed this error and has quickly come up with a second version that became known as Code Red I v2 or CRv2 (not to be confused with Code Red II). This was identical to the first version, with three differences (1) the bug in the random number generator had been corrected, (2) the new worm did not deface any Web sites, and (3) it targeted the White House Web site (http://www.whitehouse.gov) for a DoS attack.

In just a few days, this second version had spread to virtually all the computers running Microsoft IIS servers. It then turned itself off intentionally and later started resurfacing once a month.

The worm propagation analysis presented here follows the mathematical model developed in [Staniford et al. 02]. The model makes some simplifying assumptions. It assumes that the worm behaves perfectly, in particular that its random number generator generates good pseudo-random numbers. It also assumes that there are N computers running IIS on the Internet, and that this is the maximum number of computers that can be infected. (In reality, some of those computers will have installed security patches before being attacked or may be off when the worm tried to attack them.) The initial infection rate (the number of vulnerable computers the worm can find and infect in one time unit at the beginning of its operations, when relatively few computers had been infected) is denoted by K and is assumed to be constant (in reality K varies because data packets sent by the worm take different times to arrive at their targets and because potential victims have different speeds). The time when the attack has started (day, hour, and minute) is denoted by T, and the current time is the variable t. The important quantity is the percentage of vulnerable computers that have been infected at time t. This is denoted by $a(t)$

At time t, the percentage of computers that have been infected (out of the N available hosts) is $a(t)$. In the next time interval dt, the number of machines $N\,da(t)$ that will be infected is given by

$$N\,da(t) = [Na(t)]K[1 - a(t)]\,dt. \tag{3.1}$$

This is because the number of computers infected in the next dt seconds is the product of (1) the number $N\,da(t)$ of infected hosts, (2) the number $K[1 - a(t)]$ of computers each of those infected hosts can infect in a unit time, and (3) the time interval dt.

Equation (3.1) yields the differential equation

$$\frac{da(t)}{dt} = Ka(t)[1 - a(t)],$$

that no longer depends on N and whose solution is

$$a(t) = \frac{e^{K(t-T)}}{1 + e^{K(t-T)}}, \tag{3.2}$$

where T is the constant of integration. Equation (3.2) is well known from the study of the growth of epidemics. It is easy to see that when the worm starts (i.e., when $t = T$), the equation yields $a(T) = 1/2$. Later, as t grows, the difference $t - T$ is positive, so $e^{K(t-T)}$ grows without limit, causing $a(t)$ to approach the value 1. Recall that $a(t)$ is the percentage of computers infected at time t. Thus, Equation (3.2) implies that this percentage approaches 1, regardless of the number N of potential victims, and depending only on the initial infection rate K.

The conclusion from this simple analysis is that a well-debugged worm that operates like Code-Red can infect virtually every vulnerable computer on the Internet within a reasonably short time period provided that K is large enough. Fitting the number of computers infected by the first wave of CRv2 to Equation (3.2) shows that this worm had an initial infection rate K of about 1.8 per hour. Its second wave of activity had a smaller rate of about 0.7.

Following the success of Code Red I, A similar worm, designated Code Red II (after a string found in a comment inside the worm) appeared in early August 2001 [Code Red II 01]. It was a rewritten version of Code Red I and exploited the same IIS vulnerability. Once infecting a computer, Code Red II installed a backdoor allowing its controller unrestricted access to the infected computer. Evidently, the worm had been tested by its creator only on Windows 2000, because when it infected computers running IIS under Windows NT, it crashed the operating system.

Like its predecessor, Code Red II generated pseudo-random IP numbers, but these were not uniformly distributed. A random IP number was generated with probability $1/2$ from its own class A, with probability $3/8$ from class B, and with probability $1/8$ from the entire IP address space. This type of localized spreading makes sense for a worm, because computers with IP addresses close to address X tend to be geographically close to the computer whose IP is X. Often, such computers are part of the same local area network, and it has been noticed that the worm spread rapidly within such a network, once it has infected one computer in it.

The nimda worm (nimda is the reverse of admin) first appeared in mid September 2001 and was likely written by the same person responsible for the two Code Red versions. Nimda was a multi-vector (or a multi-mode) worm because it tried to spread itself in several ways. This approach to worm propagation has proved useful and nimda spread quickly and extensively even behind firewalls. It remained as a menace on the Internet for months. Nimda spread in several ways as follows:

■   The main technique for nimda propagation is by exploiting the IIS vulnerability.

■   Nimda also searches address books in an infected computer and emails itself to all the addresses found there.

■   It copies itself across open network shares.

■   It installs code on Web sites in infected computers such that anyone browsing the site gets infected.

■   It scans for the backdoors left by Code Red II and the sadmind worms. This is why it's likely that all three were implemented by the same person.

At the Lawrence Berkeley National Laboratory, special software was used to count the frequency of nimda trying to connect to computers on that site from many infected computers. The counts of nimda probes rose in 30 minutes from zero to nearly 100 per second.

3.2 Worming Techniques

There is an ongoing debate about whether it is proper to openly discuss ideas and techniques for rogue software. After all, such information can be tremendously useful to someone intending to do harm. Regardless of the arguments on both sides, such techniques have been presented, discussed, and analyzed in the open literature, and the discussion in this section presents only information that has already appeared elsewhere.

It is obvious from the examples of worms so far that a powerful worm should try to spread by exploiting known and new weaknesses and also by employing several methods, as done by nimda. Probing a potential computer for accessibility is done by sending it a 40-byte SYN packet (this is part of the TCP protocol). If a target is accessible, it takes only a few hundred bytes to exploit its vulnerability and send it a copy of the worm. An efficient worm should therefore be able to probe hundreds of computers per second.

A key feature for a successful worm is finding a new, unknown, and widespread security hole in popular software. A worm that exploits such a hole can expect a high infection rate in a short period of time. An example of such a hole is described in detail in Section 2.11.

The following is a description of four other approaches to rapid worm propagation, approaches that may cause a worm to spread to millions of computers before any human experts can intervene and try to stop the infection.

Hit-list Scanning. It is known, both from observing worms spreading "in the wild" and from theoretical analysis that the initial rate of infection of a worm is low. It takes a certain critical mass for the infection to take off and become widespread. A well-designed worm can overcome the low initial infection rate through the use of hit-list scanning.

The idea is for the hacker to start by preparing a list of potentially vulnerable machines, ideally ones with good network connections. The list should be fairly long, perhaps at least 10,000 IP numbers and preferably up to 50,000 numbers. Preparing such a list takes some work, so we propose a few ideas as follows:

■   Scan the entire Internet in order of IP number. Such a scan may be detected, but the perpetrator may get away with it if he has access to a fast Internet connection (such as an optical cable, OC). Each probe consists of sending a single SYN data packet to a computer and waiting for a response. If the scan can be completed in a few hours, the hacker may walk away, especially if the perpetrator is a large entity (a government) or if he uses someone else's connection.

■   Scan the entire Internet (by trying every IP number, but not in order) over a long period, say a few months, so as not to attract attention. Such scans are performed all the time, so a slow scan may not raise suspicion. A slow scan implies that some of its results would be out of date when it is complete, but the list doesn't have to be perfect.

■   The hacker starts by acquiring a few hundred zombies and let them do the scanning for him. This can be termed distributed scanning.

■   Compile a list of domain names, then use a whois service such as [Network solutions 04] to obtain the IP of each domain. The domain names themselves can be obtained by a network crawler similar to the ones used by the various search engines.

■   A survey innocuously conducted by a network researcher may contain a list of domain names or IP numbers of owners of a vulnerable server.

■   It may even make sense for the hacker to write and release another worm, just for the purpose of assembling such a list.

◇ **Exercise 3.1:** Suggest another way of compiling such a list.

Once the list is ready, it is built into the worm. The worm is then released into one of the computers on the hit-list and starts scanning the list, probing computers. When it finds a vulnerable host, ready to be infected, the worm divides the list in two, sends a copy of itself with one half of the list, and keeps the other half.

As new copies of the worm spread throughout the Internet, they carry shorter lists. When a worm is generated with a list of length 1, it switches from the hit-list mode to its normal mode of scanning and propagation. The point is that the hit list enables the worm to achieve deep initial penetration of the Internet in a very short time. It has been estimated that an efficient use of this technique can infect tens of thousands of computers in just a few seconds. Such fast operation may make it extremely difficult for human experts to intervene on time. The result is a deeply embedded worm that may take months to completely eradicate.

Permutation Scanning. Just generating random IP numbers and probing each is an inefficient process. Many numbers may be generated twice, thereby wasting precious worm time (precious, because initial infection is critical to the success of a worm). Also, the worm has no way to measure its success, to estimate its own penetration. The permutation scanning method presented here solves these problems, but it depends on the ability of the worm to find out whether a potential target is already infected.

Permutation scan requires the worm to generate all the IP numbers (i.e., all the 32-bit integers) but not in their natural order. The worm should be able to generate a permutation of the IP numbers. Such a permutation can be generated by an encryption algorithm. A block encryption method takes a block and encrypts it to another block in a unique way, such that if block A is encrypted to X, then no other block is encrypted to X. The worm has to implement such an encryption algorithm and use a key to encrypt each 32-bit IP number to another 32-bit number. The same key can also be used to decrypt, if needed. When the algorithm is applied to encrypting all the IP numbers in their natural order, the result is a sequence of the same numbers, but in a different order, a permutation.

A worm employing permutation scanning encrypts IP numbers and probes the computer at each encrypted IP number, looking for a vulnerable computer. When such a machine is found, the worm infects it with a copy of itself. The copy then performs the same permutation scanning as its parent, but starting from its own IP number. When a worm finds an already-infected host, it selects a random IP number and continues with the permutation scan from that number.

The result is that each copy of the worm appears to be scanning IP numbers at random, but the permutation minimizes any duplication of effort. Imagine a worm W that finds an infected machine M. W knows that the worm that infected M is now working its way through the permuted IP numbers starting from M, so W should not continue its permutation scan from M, but instead switch to another IP number N and continue from there. Thus, a permutation scan helps the worms coordinate their effort.

A true implementation (i.e., free of bugs) of permutation scan is efficient and causes widespread infection in a short time. It has another advantage. When a copy of the worm generates several permuted IP numbers and all prove to be infected, the worm may decide that the infection is comprehensive and it can stop the scanning.

For an even better performance, a sophisticated worm may check the timer of its host and wake up at a predetermined time (for example on the first day of every month). When fully awake, the worm may select another encryption key (predetermined and the same for all the copies of the worm) and begin another permutation scan starting from its own IP number and continuing until an infected host is discovered. Such scanning policy virtually guarantees that any new computers with the same vulnerability that came on the Internet after the latest scan will be discovered and infected by the worm. Also, any infected computer that was cleared of the worm but not patched will quickly be reinfected. With such deep penetration, the worm may inflict severe damage when its trigger is eventually pressed and it releases its payload.

A slightly more complex version of permutation scan is partitioned permutation scan. The worm is initially "responsible" for an interval $[a, b]$ of IP numbers. When it infects a vulnerable computer, it sends half its interval to its newly-created child and retains the other half. When the interval become sufficiently small, the worm switches to the original permutation scan. This scheme is an example of a divide-and-conquer algorithm.

An interesting twist on permutation scan can be added to multi-mode worms. Such a worm exploits several security holes, so it has to scan the Internet for computers that have the first hole, then for those that have the second hole, and so on. It may employ permutation scan looking for machines with the first vulnerability. When it senses saturation of infection, it can (1) reset the initial IP number to its current IP address, (2) select the next encryption key, and (3) start another permutation scan where it looks for machines that have the second vulnerability. The point is that when the worm switches to the second vulnerability there will have been many worms established (i.e., many copies of the worm will be active), so all the machines with the second vulnerability will quickly be located and infected.

When a worm is discovered, one way to protect machines from it is spoofing. The computer may be programmed to respond to a probe as if it were infected. In the case of permutation scan, a spoofing computer will protect all those that follow it in the IP permutation, but this protection is only temporary. Once the copies of the worm switch to a different encryption key, the permutation will change. When the spoofing machine is probed, it will again protect those computers that follow it in the new permutation, but those that were originally protected will now be exposed to infection. If the human defenders are quick and organized, they may spoof a large number of machines (perhaps by releasing a good worm), and this may offer good protection. However, it takes time to design, implement, test, and release a good worm, so this approach to worm protection may not be practical.

Topological Scanning. Recall that many viruses look for an address book with email addresses in a newly-infected computer, then send messages to all the addresses on the list, trying to infect more computers. Such an address book is an easily-obtained hit-list and can also be used by a worm. We can think of the email address in the address book as a security hole that exists in practically every computer. Topological scanning is any method that employs information found inside a computer (such as email addresses in a book and URLs in lists of favorites) in order to infect other computers. Once the worm exhausts this local information, it can switch to permutation scan.

Flash Worms. An attacker with access to a fast Internet connection can scan the entire Internet (the entire 32-bit IP address space, consisting of $2^{32} \approx 4.3$ billion numbers) for computers with a certain weakness in a few hours. This scan is done before any worm is released. The resulting hit-list of addresses may be large, but the work of searching through it and actually infecting machines is divided between the copies of the worm (and there will be a growing number of copies).

Once the first worm is embedded in a computer, it divides the list into blocks, then goes over the addresses of a block, trying to infect computers. When a vulnerable computer is found and is infected, the worm sends a copy of itself with that block. The copy divides this block into subblocks and proceeds in the same way. At the same time, the original worm scans the second block, trying to infect another computer. When a child worm receives a block smaller than a certain size, it simply scans it, trying to infect all the computers listed on that block, and sending them copies of itself, but with no blocks of addresses.

Recall that the hit-list method calls for dividing the hit list in two. If we compare the hit-list scheme to a binary decision tree, then the current method, which can be termed a flash worm, is comparable to the B-trees that are used to implement disk directories because they are so much more efficient than a simple binary decision tree.

It may happen that a copy of the worm finds itself in a machine where it cannot reach any other computers. A copy may also be killed quickly if it happens to be discovered immediately. In such a case, an entire block of IP numbers is lost, so a variation of this method creates overlapping blocks. If block 1 has addresses a_1 through a_n and block 3 has addresses a_{n+1} through a_m, then block 2 will consist of addresses from the middle of the interval $[a_1, a_n]$ to the middle of the interval $[a_{n+1}, a_m]$. Each IP will be scanned twice, but the worm will be robust and its penetration will be deeper.

A variation on this approach may be attractive to a hacker who controls several high-speed servers (most likely as zombies). A typical worm is a small program, perhaps just a few hundred bytes long. In contrast, an extensive list of IP addresses may be tens of megabytes long. The version proposed here starts with an initial worm that carries only a few IP addresses "on its back." When a fresh copy of the worm is generated, it receives only a few IP addresses from its parent. To receive more addresses, the copy gets in touch with one of the hacker's servers. The server decides what part of the total list of addresses to send each copy. The first few copies may receive large chunks of the list, while each subsequent copy may receive a smaller sublist.

The point is that the servers are under the control of the worm's creator, who may modify their behavior depending on how the collective worm is doing. The servers can also report back to the hacker, in real time, the current number of copies of the worm and how many addresses have been sent to those copies. The servers are needed only for the initial spread of the worm. Once the number of copies grows above a certain threshold, the servers stop sending addresses to the copies and instead respond to requests from the copies with a code that instructs the copies of the worm to send their lists of addresses to any new child they create.

It is possible to include in every worm a large list of IP addresses in compressed form. This has the advantage that the worm is independent of any outside servers and each of its copies may carry a large number of addresses. The disadvantage is the time it takes the worm to decompress the list (this may slow down the worm's propagation and may render it vulnerable to early discovery) and the memory space the decompressed list requires in the host's memory (which may attract the victim's attention).

The worm designs presented here lead to the conclusion that a well-designed, well-prepared worm that has access to a list of potential vulnerable sites may be able to infect many thousands, and perhaps even millions of computers in a matter of minutes. This is scary, because there isn't much that human defenders can do in a few minutes. Such a worm may find itself well embedded in the Internet, and may be able to carry out a devastating attack "in plain site" (i.e., while everyone is helplessly looking and before anyone can kill any of the worm copies).

Contagion. The preceding text concentrated on fast-spreading worms. Such a worm is actively looking for potential victims to invade and infect and can therefore generate a vast number of copies in a few minutes, then start releasing its (possibly deadly) payload. Such a worm may be practically impossible to detect while it is propagating, but it has one weak feature. Its rapid spread leaves one telltale sign, each infected server suddenly switches into high gear and starts generating much more Internet traffic than normal. Such behavior may indicate to the server's owner or administrator the presence of a worm trying to multiply, and may lead to an effective early discovery and killing of the worm. A hacker worried about this effect may choose the opposite strategy for spreading his worm. This strategy, termed *contagion*, is based on slow, passive worm propagation, which does not generate any abnormal Internet traffic or leave any other suspicious traces. Such a worm can slowly embed itself in a huge number of computers, waiting for its trigger to be pressed.

As an example of such worm strategy, imagine a hacker who had discovered two security holes, H_s, which can enslave a particular type of Web server, and H_c, which can do the same to a popular Web client (perhaps a browser). The first copy of the worm is installed on either a server or a client and it waits for an opportunity to propagate. When such a worm resides in a server, it waits until a client happens to visit. The worm probes the client for security hole H_c, and if it finds such a hole, the worm propagates to the client, sending it copies of both H_s and H_c together with the normal data (a Web site, an image, an audio file, etc.) sent by the server. When an infected client surfs the Web, visiting various sites, the worm checks the server at each site for weakness H_s. On finding H_s, the worm propagates to that server, again sending copies of both H_s and H_c.

This type of worm spread is passive. The worm waits for a visit, instead of continually trying many IP numbers. When such a worm resides on a server, it can be a bit more active by trying to attract clients. It may embed in the server special html tags that are read and used by search engines to find and rank Web sites. Such tags are not visible to an occasional visitor, and are rarely observed by the server's owner. The example shown here includes three tags, description, keywords, and abstract, taken from the Web page of a book,

```
<META NAME="description" CONTENT="Data Compression: The Complete Reference, is described">
<META NAME="keywords" CONTENT="data compression, text compression, image compression">
<META NAME="abstract" CONTENT="Data Compression: The Complete Ref., ISBN 0-387-98280-9,
published Dec. 1997. The book covers the main methods and techniques for compressing
digital data. It includes many exercises with solutions, a glossary, and an index.">
```

but a worm may bait clients by advertising pornography, inexpensive products, or free software. Thus, a contagion worm spreads from a server to clients, and from each client to many other servers, much as a contagious disease spreads among persons who happen to come in contact with each other.

Because of the passive, slow nature of this type of worm propagation, it may be virtually impossible to detect it by looking for abnormal, or higher than normal, patterns of communication. There may be exceptions, but they are rare. An exception may be a server that sends only small quantities of data. When the worm sends a copy of itself, the amount of data sent may be double the normal and may be detectable.

⋄ **Exercise 3.2:** What kind of server may send only small quantities of information in response to a request from a client?

When a copy of the worm starts its operations, it may send a signal (that includes its IP address) to the worm's author. The count of the signals provides the author with the total number of worms in place and the IP addresses make it possible for him to command the individual copies. When the worm's creator feels that there are enough copies of the worm, he may trigger them to release their payload. Alternatively, the worm copies may be instructed to start a fast, active spread, followed by releasing the payload after a while. Instead of the hacker sending commands to the worm, the individual copies may be instructed to periodically look at a certain address where they will eventually find their instructions.

The weak point of this scheme is the need to find a pair of security weaknesses in a server and a client. This may limit the choices of a worm creator, especially because security weaknesses are discovered all the time and are constantly being patched. A scheme based on a single security hole is more appropriate for a contagion worm and such a scheme may be based on the properties of peer-to-peer networks. The inset below discusses the peer-to-peer paradigm of computer communications.

Peer-to-Peer Networks

We are familiar with Web browsers. A browser is an example of a client, a program that asks another program to send it information. The sender is known as a server. The client-server model (or paradigm) is very useful and is used in many areas of computer communications, such as FTP (file transfer) and email. An email server is a computer that runs all the time and is dedicated to sending and receiving mail. It receives email messages for users and keeps them. A user may connect to the server at any time with a client program and retrieve, read, and delete the messages.

The peer-to-peer model of communications is radically different. It was developed in 1984 at IBM. (The acronym P2P is often used, but is confusing because this acronym also stands for point-to-point.) There are no dedicated servers and no clients. Instead, there are users (peers or nodes) who are all equal. Each node is a computer running a program that serves as both a client and a server. A node may be turned off by its owner (a user) at any time. A node can initiate and complete a transaction with another node when both are on.

The term peer-to-peer is general and refers to any protocol that employs the peer-to-peer model of communications. An important example is the Network News Transport Protocol (NNTP) used to transfer Usenet news. In practice, though, the term peer-to-peer is normally used to refer to file sharing networks. These are protocols that allow users to chat and transfer files between personal computers. Familiar names such as Gnutella, FastTrack, and Napster, are examples of file sharing networks.

The main advantage of a peer-to-peer network is obvious. There is no need to have someone purchase, run, and maintain a central, fast server. We know from long experience that even the fastest server slows down when the number of users grows. In contrast, the speed (more precisely, the total bandwidth) of a peer-to-peer network grows with the number of nodes.

The first generation of peer-to-peer networks differed from the concept described here because it had a centralized file list, as in Napster. The second generation of peer-to-peer networks, such as Gnutella and FastTrack, used decentralized file lists; they were pure peer-to-peer. The third generation of peer-to-peer networks added anonymity features. Examples of anonymous networks are Freenet, I2P, and GNUnet.

It is important to understand the difference between a protocol and an application. The BitTorrent network, for example, started as a protocol, a set of rules that specify the details of file transfers [bittorrent 04]. Once this protocol became popular, several people wrote programs that implemented it. The point is that users on different platforms with different programs can connect and communicate if the programs implement the same protocol. The BitTorrent protocol, for example, has attracted so much attention recently, that currently it has the following implementations: ABC, Azureus, BitAnarch, BitComet, BitSpirit, BitTornado, BitTorrent, BitTorrent++, BitTorrent.Net, G3

Torrent, mlMac, MLDonkey, QTorrent, SimpleBT, Shareaza, TorrentStorm, Bits on Wheels, and TomatoTorrent.

An attacker wanting to spread a worm to all the nodes of a peer-to-peer network needs to find only one vulnerability in the protocol or in the programs used by the nodes. In addition, the use of a peer-to-peer network for worm propagation has the following advantages:

■   The users tend to vary all the time. In a network such as BitTorrent, a new user may join, chat, transfer some files for a while, then get tired of this and switch to other activities. New users join all the time, so there are always new, fresh users, whose computers are "crying out" to be infected.

■   A peer-to-peer network is often used to transfer large files, because its users may illegally swap new, large applications and movies.

■   The peer-to-peer protocols are often designed by individuals and therefore tend to pay less attention to security than client-server protocols. The latter are mainstream protocols and are exposed to public scrutiny (by means of RFCs, requests for comments) all the time, even before they are implemented.

■   Peer-to-peer programs are more likely than servers to execute on personal computers, where a worm can find much personal information.

■   Peer-to-peer network users tend to swap "gray" (pornography) or illegal material (pirated music or movies) and therefore tend to be reluctant to draw public attention to strange or suspicious behavior they may detect.

■   Peer-to-peer networks may be immense. Some estimates of the size of Kazaa, for example, go as high as 5–10 million connections per day. The number of users is clearly in the millions and may be in the tens of millions.

It seems that an attacker may find an organization, such as a university (Kazaa users often use computers located at a lab in a university) with weak security, infect one computer with a worm that exploits a vulnerability in the Kazaa protocol, and let it spread silently through Kazaa file sharing until it infects most of the organization's computers and many computers outside. Within a few weeks, millions of Kazaa users' computers may be infected by copies of the worm, quietly waiting for a trigger to dump their payload. All this can be achieved without significantly disturbing the normal patterns of communications.

◇ **Exercise 3.3:** It is difficult to predict how deep and how fast a worm can spread in a client-server or in a peer-to-peer network. It seems that the best way to obtain such information is to release such a worm (a good worm, that only calls home, and does nothing else) and measure its penetration. The public will be notified and instructed on how to kill the worm at the end of the experiment. Comment on this scheme.

Worm communication. The discussion above has mentioned several mechanisms for worm communication with its creator. A different, distributed-control technique is presented here, where such communication involves the individual copies of the worm.

When a worm creates a copy, it sends the copy to a known location (it knows the IP address of the copy). It is clear that each parent knows where each of its children is located. In addition, the parent can embed its own IP address in the copies (children) that it creates and sends out. Thus, each worm can tell where its parent is located. A natural extension of this idea is for a worm to embed an entire list of IP addresses of other worms (its ancestors) when it creates a child. The child appends its own IP number to the list and embeds the augmented list in each of its children. If this is done starting from the first copy of the worm, then each copy will have a complete list of its ancestors (parents, grandparents, and so on, but not uncles and cousins) and a list of its immediate children. These lists organize the entire worm colony in a tree (Figure 3.1a).

This way, a copy W of the worm can send a message to its children and they can forward it to their children. Such a forward message will eventually reach every copy of the worm in the subtree whose root is W. A worm can also send messages backward to all its ancestors. Such wide-spread communications involves a certain amount of risk because some copies may have been "captured" (i.e., discovered and disassembled) and their captors will receive and interpret messages sent to them. Capturing node x of Figure 3.1a, for example, will isolate the entire subtree shown in dashed. Encrypting the commands would not help, because each worm would have to carry the encryption key, which would then become known to any disassembler. The disassembler (a captor of the worm) could then not only read messages sent to the worm, but also send fake messages to possibly diffuse all the worm copies. The technique of digital signatures (Section 12.10), however, offers better security. Any captor who disassembles a worm and reads its code would still be able to decrypt and read messages sent to the worm. However, the captor would not be able to send fake messages to other copies of the worm because this requires the private key of the sender. In particular, the SSL protocol may be useful to a worm, and public-domain implementations of this protocol such as OpenSSL [OpenSSL 04], are becoming easier to obtain.

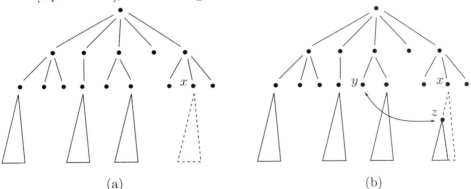

(a)   (b)

Figure 3.1: A Tree of Worm Communications.

In addition, each time a copy of the worm probes a node and finds it already infected, it can exchange (a copy of) its list with (a copy of) the list of the newly-discovered neighbor. This can help restore parts of the worm tree that have been lost due to a killed or captured worm. Figure 3.1b shows how part of the tree that was lost because of the capture of worm x has been restored because of a newly-established cross-connection between y and z.

⋄ **Exercise 3.4:** Show how to extend this method so that the communications lines between worms will form a graph, not just a tree.

The worm's author can now send a single command, signal, or even new executable code to the original worm (the root of the tree) and have this information trickle down the tree to every worm in the colony. It is clear that the loss of the root would completely defeat this type of communication, so a worm employing this technique should contain extra code to send the creator the IP addresses of all the nodes in the two or three tree levels directly below the root.

Recall that the worm is a small program in machine language, so how can its creator send it new code to change its behavior? One solution is to embed many procedure calls in the worm program. Every few instructions there should be a call to another procedure. When the worm is originally written, the procedures do nothing. Each procedure simply returns immediately. When the worm is compiled, the object file starts with the main program, followed by useful procedures, followed by the empty procedures. When the author wants to modify the worm's operation, he may rewrite several procedures, compile the entire worm program with the new procedures, and send only the end of the object file (the newly-compiled, no-longer-empty procedures) to the worm, to replace the last part of the worm's code.

Another technique is to write the entire worm in a high-level language that's interpreted. Any modification involves sending new versions of some of the original statements, deleting some statements, or adding new ones. This is similar to word processing. When the worm rearranges itself with the new statements, it executes its code by interpreting it. Such a worm must have two parts, the main body of the worm, made up of the high-level statements, and an interpreter, a small program in machine code that will not be modified.

The worm's author may have several reasons to modify the worm. Imagine a successful worm that's slowly being discovered and eradicated. At a certain point in time, only a few thousand undiscovered copies remain in the Internet, then the author discovers a new security hole. He can quickly modify the existing copies to serve as a base to exploit the newly-discovered weakness and invade a large number of computers.

⋄ **Exercise 3.5:** Come up with some other reasons for modifying a worm in mid-stream.

3.3 Proposing a CCDC

It is now obvious that worms pose a serious threat to individual computers, to computer communications, to the Internet in general, and even to the infrastructure of entire nations. What can the world do to bring this threat under control or at least to reduce its magnitude? The authors of the excellent paper [Staniford et al. 02], to which this discussion owes much, argue in favor of establishing a cyber center for disease control (CCDC), similar to the centers for disease control and prevention (CDC [CDC 04]) of the United States government. The CDC's mission is to promote health and quality of life by preventing and controlling disease, injury, and disability. Similarly, the mission of the CCDC should include the following points:

- To quickly identify any outbreak of rogue software.

- To isolate, disassemble, and understand any newly-discovered threat.

- To actively fight new infections.

- To anticipate new types of viruses and worms and to educate the computer security community about these future threats.

- To plan methods and tools to detect any anticipated threats.

- To educate the public about computer security and safe ways of using computers.

Identifying outbreaks. Currently, new attacks of rogue software are identified, isolated, disassembled, and read by volunteers who then propose ways to neutralize an attack. There is no central organization dedicated to these tasks. It normally takes at least hours for news about a new attack to reach the millions of Internet users. It also takes at least a day or two for volunteer experts (often located at universities) to understand the threat and develop countermeasures. This type of response is too slow for the worm techniques discussed in this section. Moreover, a clever worm creator may combine the worm attack with a separate DoS attack designed to slow communications between the various volunteers working on the worm and between them and the suffering public. It may come as a surprise to most readers to learn that the volunteer experts concerned with identifying and fighting rogue software communicate by means of a few mailing lists. A perpetrator who knows about those lists and who specifically targets them in a DoS attack, can greatly delay any response to the main attack.

The proposed CCDC can develop several mechanisms for communications between those responsible for a defense. Such mechanisms should not be limited to the Internet and may include fax, telephone, and wireless. The CCDC should also launch organized research into ways to quickly and automatically detect a worm attack. This can be achieved by, for example, software that listens to traffic on the Internet, analyzes its patterns, and discovers anomalies. Another option is hardware sensors placed at several strategic locations in the Internet, again listening to traffic and analyzing it. Such work cannot be done by private individuals or organizations. It has to be planned and coordinated by a government-sponsored agency.

Analyzing new worms. When a worm is discovered, its spreading mechanism (or at least its principle of spreading) is known from the way it is discovered. Experts

are then called in to disassemble the worm and understand its trigger and payload. In
the past, worms and viruses were small and fairly simple to read and understand, but
we may not always be that lucky. A clever fraudster may write a program with lots of
extra, unneeded and unused (chaff) instructions. Given the original source code, with
labels and comments, such instructions can easily be identified and ignored. Trying
to read and understand disassembled code, with no labels, no comments, and no real
way to distinguish instructions from data, may complicate the process of reading and
understanding the code, as illustrated by Figure 3.2.

```
   ADD R4,#500          100 ADD R4,590
   SUB R0,D             101 SUB R0,280
L: MULT E,F             102 MULT E,F
   .                        .
   .                        .
   .                        .
M: DIV S,R1             110 DIV S,R1
   .                        .
   .                        .
   LOD J                223 LOD 278
   STO L                224 STO 102
   .                        .
   .                        .
J: JMP M                278 JMP 110
   .                        .
   .                        .
D: DATA 23              280 ??? 23
   .                        .
   .                   590 CMP 0,0 % literal 500

        (a)                        (b)
```

Figure 3.2: Source Code And Disassembled Code.

Part (a) of the figure is easy to read, but part (b) suffers from the lack of labels
and from the inability of the disassembler to distinguish between instructions and data.
Thus, the literal 500 is disassembled in part (b) as an instruction (whose code happens
to be 500) while the data item 23 at label D is disassembled into ??? because 23 doesn't
happen to be the code of any instruction.

Even having full access to the source code of a program does not always make it
easy to read and understand it. Any reader who doubts this statement should look
at the programming "pearls" submitted to the international obfuscated C code contest
[IOCCC 04].

The CCDC should therefore develop tools for program analysis. Many worm writers use routines copied from publicly-available software libraries that have the codes of
past worms. The ability to recognize such routines in a disassembled code can greatly
enhance its readability. The CCDC should also have laboratories with different plat-

forms, operating systems, and communications software, to help in analyzing worms and viruses by executing their codes slowly, instruction by instruction and examining its effects.

> I am often asked if virus writers are good programmers. This is a little like asking if Jack the Ripper was a good surgeon—for the most part, such a question is not only irrelevant, but offensive. Any skill displayed in executing a malicious act can only make that act more abominable.
> —Jim Bates (Pimpernel software) in [Virus bulletin 05] May 1994.

Fighting new infections. It is clear that the proposed CCDC should educate the public in topics such as analyzing data traffic, that can lead to early detection of worms. It may also be useful to place special software agents at the largest Internet gateways, where much of the Internet traffic passes. Such agents are normally passive, but when a new worm is discovered, they can be quickly trained by CCDC personnel to recognize data packets that contain the worm or parts of it and delete them.

Anticipating new threats. New worms may either be based on old ones or use new principles. The CCDC should have researchers think of ways to revive and extend old worms. Once someone comes up with an idea for a future worm, the CCDC may want to anticipate it and reprogram its agents to fight it if and when it is observed. Whenever someone discovers a security hole, CCDC personnel should think of how it could be exploited by a new worm (a new security hole will be patched, but this takes time, perhaps even weeks). When new communications software is released, the CCDC should work closely with its maker to scrutinize the software for security weaknesses.

The CCDC could also issue a set of recommendations to software makers, in much the same way as the International Telecommunications Union (ITU) issues recommendations to makers of telecommunications equipment. The recommendations should be directed toward developing secure software, software that will not have security holes to begin with.

Public involvement. No one lives in a vacuum. We compete with each other all the time, we try to develop new ideas, approaches, and points of view that help us compete, but by doing so we also cooperate. This observation implies that the CCDC should be open to the public. Anyone should be allowed to contribute ideas and everything (well, almost everything) that the CCDC does should be public knowledge.

Operating in an open environment has its cost. The perpetrators would learn all about the strategy and tools developed by the CCDC, but judging from past experience, the advantage to CCDC from news, ideas, and suggestions coming from the public will far outweigh any danger stemming from having this knowledge in the hands of wrongdoers.

A final basic issue regarding the CCDC is to what degree it should operate in an open fashion. For example, during an outbreak the CCDC could maintain a Web site for use by the research community. Such an approach would allow many different people to contribute to the analysis of the outbreak and of the pathogen, perhaps adding invaluable insight and empirical data. This sort of coordination happens informally today, in part; but it is also the case that currently a variety of anti-viral and security companies analyze outbreaks independently, essentially competing to come out with a complete analysis first. This makes for potentially very inefficient use of a scarce resource, namely the highly specialized skill of analyzing pathogens.

Rogue software is a global problem, so the CCDC should ideally be an international organization, perhaps a new United Nations agency. An international agency would make foreign governments more cooperative. Also, having skilled watchers in all time zones may help all of us sleep better. It feels different when you know that someone (a brother, but not big brother) is watching while you are asleep.

3.4 The Internet Worm

The Internet worm first appeared on 2 November 1988 and spread quickly, infecting Sun 3 and VAX computers running UNIX by exploiting security weaknesses in the version of UNIX used by those computers. Rogue programs were rare in 1988, so the effects of the worm mystified computer users. The most noticeable effect of the worm was to load infected computers with so much work (to replicate the worm) that they slowed down and in many cases completely stopped because certain UNIX resources were exhausted. An account of the isolation and analysis of the worm can be found in [Rochlis and Eichin 89].

The following day, groups of system programmers at The University of California, Berkeley and MIT had managed to isolate the worm and started studying its code. Less than 12 hours after the first infection, the Berkeley group had issued a set of instructions to stop the spread of the worm, including a patch to the UNIX *sendmail* utility. A few hours later, a group at Purdue University issued a simpler set of instructions, and these efforts managed to stop the spread of the worm within a few days. In the weeks that followed, the worm had two predictable results (1) other rogue programs appeared and (2) computer users became aware that the security of their computers was an illusion. *The New York Times* called the worm "the largest assault ever on the nation's systems" (notice the use of the vague term "systems"). The worm gave a tremendous boost to the field of computer security and resulted in updated security policies and in modifications to UNIX that prevented similar attacks, although attackers always seem to be one step ahead of security people.

The worm took advantage of certain UNIX features that were designed to simplify the sharing of resources in UNIX networks. Those features caused security weaknesses and have since been eliminated, but they are discussed here because they contribute to our understanding of how the virus worked.

UNIX has a *finger* utility that allows a user to obtain information about other users, such as full name, login name, telephone number, and whether the user is currently logged in. This utility uses a daemon (a background process) named *fingerd* that performs the input/output for *finger*. The daemon senses a request coming from a remote program, opens a connection, reads one line of input, then sends back a response to the input. The worm exploited the fact that *fingerd* was written in the C language, and used the input command *gets*. This command receives a string of input characters and stores them in an input buffer *without* checking for buffer overflow. The worm sent a long input string that overran the buffer and overflowed into the code of the daemon, thereby altering it for the purpose of the worm.

UNIX also offers a *sendmail* utility for sending mail. This program has several modes, one of which operates as a background process (daemon) where *sendmail* continuously checks a certain port for incoming SMTP email. When such email is sensed, the daemon performs the handshaking SMTP protocol in order to receive the email message and identify its recipient. The *sendmail* security weakness exploited by the virus had to do with debugging. Normally, the recipient of an email message is a user address, but the debugging feature allows testers to specify a set of instructions as the recipient. The worm used this feature and specified a special set of instructions that served its purpose.

Section 8.3 discusses passwords and how they are handled in UNIX. The section also discusses guidelines for selecting secure passwords and shows why a password should not be a word found in dictionaries. The worm used lists of words, including the standard UNIX online dictionary, in an attempt to decrypt passwords in the password file of the host computer. The UNIX password file has since become privileged, so only system administrators can read it. In addition, each password verification in UNIX is followed by a short delay (about a second) to prevent what is now termed "phishing" of passwords (Section 10.4). Modern operating systems try to check every new password selected by a user and reject it if it is found in a dictionary or if it is based on the user's name or the account's login name.

Specifically, the worm tried to guess the passwords of the accounts in the password file of each computer it invaded. The process was carried out in three steps. In the first step, the worm tried the following six strings for each account in the password file: (1) the null string (no password), (2) the account name, (3) the account name concatenated with itself, (4) the first name of the user (this is available in the user information field in the password file) with the first letter translated to lower case, (5) the last name of the user, and (6) the account name reversed. In the second step, the worm compared each encrypted password in its list of favorite passwords to all the encrypted passwords in the hijacked password file. (The worm had a list of 432 favorite passwords, most of which were valid English words or proper names. It seems that the worm's creator stole passwords and copied words and names from dictionaries, then encrypted them to form his list of favorites.) In the third and last step, the worm opened the UNIX online dictionary located in `/usr/dict/words`, encrypted it word by word, and tried each word against all the encrypted passwords in the password file. Upon finding a capitalized word, the worm also tried its lowercase version. Performing the three steps in their entirety can take an extremely long time (perhaps up to several weeks on 1980s computers), so the worm stopped the search after a few minutes. It also paused from time to time during the search and tried to spread itself to more computers.

Researchers that dissected the worm and read and understood its code were impressed by the worm's password encryption routine. Naturally, this routine had to produce the same encryption as the standard UNIX `crypt()` routine (page 198), but it used shortcuts that made it nine times faster.

The worm also exploited the use of trusted logins. This is a convenient UNIX feature (that has since been (ab)used by other malicious software) that allows a user to access remote computers without having to enter passwords repeatedly. The worm exploited this feature by trying to locate computers that would trust the account invaded by the worm. The worm did that by examining files for lists of remote computers and accounts trusted by the host computer. On finding a trusting computer, the worm tried to copy itself to it as if it (the worm) were a remote user trying to perform a remote operation.

With these weaknesses in mind, it is easy to understand the operation of the worm. It consists of two parts, a main program and a bootstrap routine. Once the worm has propagated to a new computer, the main program would search for information on other computers in the local network. This was done by reading local configuration files and executing UNIX utilities that collect information on current network connections. The worm would use the knowledge collected in this way to propagate its bootstrap to each computer connected to the local network.

The bootstrap program was transferred to a different computer as a C program and would be compiled on the new machine and invoked there with three arguments, the network address of the computer it came from (the infecting machine), a port number on the infecting machine, and a special number that served as a one-time password. The idea was for the bootstrap to connect to the specified port on the infecting machine, send it the temporary password, and wait for it to send a copy of the main program. If the main program on the infecting machine did not receive the temporary password from the bootstrap, it disconnected itself from the bootstrap.

If communications between the bootstrap on the new host and the main program on the original infected computer was established, the main program transferred to the bootstrap several binary files, followed by a copy of the bootstrap itself. The binary files were compiled versions of the main program, written to run on different computers and on a different version of UNIX. The bootstrap loaded these binary files, linked them with the standard libraries, then tried to invoke them one by one. If none of them executed, then the command file or the infecting worm deleted all the files, including the bootstrap, leaving a clean, uninfected computer. If any of the binary files ran successfully, it stored in the infected computer's memory all the binary files and the bootstrap, deleted the files from the disk, then tried to break into another computer.

Contrary to most cases of rogue software, the author of the Internet worm was identified within a few weeks on the pages of *The New York Times*. It was Robert T. Morris, a 23-year-old Ph.D. student at Cornell University and son of the chief scientist of the NSA (national security agency). Evidence against him was easily collected because he talked to friends about the worm, copies of the code were found in his computer account at the university, and computer usage records showed that he used university computers to test the virus before releasing it to the Internet. It is not clear why he spent time and effort to inflict damage. Reasons range from wanting to get at his father, to trying to demonstrate the weak security of the Internet, to trying to impress a girl. He was arrested, tried, and sentenced to three years of probation, 400 hours of community service, and $10,050 in fines.

[Cohen 94a] has interesting details (on page 103) on how audit and analysis of network statistics were used to identify this individual.

[Creators of viruses are] stealing a car for the purpose of joyriding.
—Robert Tappan Morris in 1983 Capitol Hill testimony, cited in
The New York Times 11 November 1988.

He found on Examination, that the Worm was produc'd from a
small Egg deposited in the little Roughnesses on the Surface of
the Wood, by a particular kind of Fly or Beetle; from whence
the Worm, as soon as it was hatch'd, began to eat into the
Substance of the Wood, and after some time came out again
a Fly of the Parent kind, and so the Species increas'd.

—Benjamin Franklin, *London 1757–1775*

4
Trojan Horses

A Trojan horse is a common type of rogue software. Such a program hides in a computer and has some malicious function. In contrast to viruses and worms, Trojans do not replicate. This chapter summarizes the main features of Trojans and also discusses how to modify a compiler in a devious way, to make it plant Trojans in programs that it compiles.

The Trojan war, described by Homer (Greek $O\mu\eta\rho o\varsigma$) in the *Iliad* and the *Odyssey*, took place about 3200 years ago, in the beginning of the 12th century B.C.. We don't know whether the war actually took place or even if Homer existed, but throughout history (and even today) this chapter of Greek history has fascinated readers and writers alike and has inspired countless stories, poems, plays, and archaeological excavations. The *Iliad* describes how, having failed to capture Troy after 10 years of siege and war, the Greeks, on the advice of Odysseus, made a giant wooden horse, left it at the gates of Troy, ostensibly as a peace offering, and pretended to sail away. The Trojans, intentionally confused by the Gods, dragged the horse inside the city walls and celebrated their "victory." At night, Greek soldiers emerged from the horse's hollow belly and opened the city gates, allowing their compatriots to pour in and capture and destroy Troy.

Over time, the term "Trojan horse" became a synonym for a trap. In the nomenclature of rogue software, a Trojan horse is a malicious program that masquerades as a benign, useful application or an operating system routine. Unlike viruses, Trojan horses do not replicate and spread themselves. The horse stays where it is but can nevertheless be malicious and destructive. An example of an insidious type of Trojan horse is an anti-virus program whose execution intentionally introduces viruses onto the computer. Some experts even claim that Trojan horses are responsible for the initial installation of most viruses.

Another common example is a Trojan horse that replaces the login procedure. When logging into a multiuser computer (and today many personal computers have multiuser operating systems), a user is asked to input a login name and a password. A login Trojan horse attaches itself to the start of the login procedure, to become the first piece of code to be executed. It asks the user to enter a login name and a password, which the Trojan horse then saves and may also transmit to its owner. The horse then displays a message "wrong login, please try again" and invokes the original login routine. The user, being human, tends to trust the message (not suspecting that it came, so to speak, from the horse's mouth) and tries again, this time successfully. A similar trick is described in Section 10.5.

⋄ **Exercise 4.1:** What's the advantage of placing a Trojan horse in a user's word processor or editor?

The following are ten of the most common Trojans identified in 2003. Some have since disappeared, but there is still much information on the Internet about them. KeySnatch, Dropper, MoneyTree, Unknown Trojan, MoneyTree.DyFuCA System Soap Pro, Spyster 1.0.19, Trojan.Win32.Revop.c, Coulomb Dialer, Unknown Dialer

4.1 Applications of Trojans

Many Trojan horses have been discovered over the years on various platforms. They were designed to perform all kinds of tasks, a few of which are described in this section.

Example: The SSH Trojan horse. SSH (secure shell) is a protocol defining a set of network connectivity tools that are used by increasing numbers of people on the Internet. Many users of `telnet`, `rlogin`, `ftp`, and other communications programs do not realize that their password is transmitted across the Internet unencrypted. SSH encrypts all traffic (including passwords) to effectively eliminate eavesdropping, connection hijacking, and other network-level attacks. In addition, SSH provides a myriad of secure tunneling capabilities, as well as a variety of authentication methods. OpenSSH is a free version of the SSH protocol, available from `http://www.openssh.com/`.

On or about 30 July 2002, someone managed to replace several crucial source code files in the SSH directory at `ftp.openssh.com` and `ftp.openbsd.org`. The bad files were identified and restored from the original, uncompromised versions on 1 August 2002, but some infected files may have propagated to sites that mirror the main OpenSSH site. The bad files contained a Trojan horse that, when compiled and executed, allowed a user at a certain IP address to gain unauthorized remote access to any computer running the infected files. The level of access would be that of the user who compiled the source code.

A CERT advisory was immediately issued, encouraging all who downloaded a copy of the OpenSSH distribution to verify the authenticity of their distribution, regardless of how it was obtained. Users were also advised to inspect any other software that had been downloaded from the compromised site.

Example: A keystroke logger (or a keystroke grabber) is a Trojan horse that runs in the background, recording the user's keystrokes. (This is also an example of spyware or rat, Chapter 9.) The keystrokes are written onto a hidden file and are later transmitted to the Trojan's owner or even retrieved personally. The latter option makes sense in cases where the culprit has physical access to the infected computer, such as in an office or a lab.

Every computer user knows the importance of keystrokes. Every password is entered through the keyboard, so the perpetrator of a keystroke logger can easily obtain all the passwords of the computer user/owner. Even bank account numbers often have to be typed, making the financial resources of the computer owner vulnerable to the hacker.

One solution is to minimize the number of keystrokes by using copy and paste. A computer owner may keep all sensitive information, such as passwords, account numbers, and credit card numbers in an encrypted text file. Whenever any sensitive information is needed, the owner decrypts this file (its password has to be typed, and is intercepted by the hacker, but the hacker may not have access to the file), copies the data, then pastes it into a login program, an ftp program, or an Internet browser. The copy and paste are done by typing special keystrokes (such as a function key or a command key) that are always the same and don't provide any useful information to the hacker.

Some Swiss banks hit on a different solution. The bank provides its customers with a special minicalculator that's synchronized with the bank's main computer. A customer wanting to transact business with the bank from their computer type their password into the minicalculator, which generates a second, random password good for just one transaction. The customer then types the second password into their computer (Figure 4.1) and it is recognized by the bank's computer for one transaction only. Intercepting such a one-time password is futile, making this two-step authentication scheme highly secure.

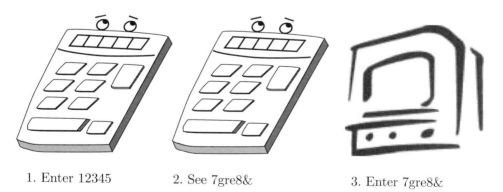

1. Enter 12345 2. See 7gre8& 3. Enter 7gre8&

Figure 4.1: A Secondary Password.

> Trojan horses, which open back doors on computers for hackers to enter through, have become easy to develop and are being used to steal banking details. Such Trojans wait for a user to browse a Web site with the word *bank* in it. At that point, the Trojan records the user's key strokes, capturing their user name, password and account numbers.
>
> —Eugene Kaspersky, Kaspersky Labs, `http://www.kaspersky.com`.

Example: A screen capturing program. Anything typed by a user is echoed and displayed on the monitor screen, for visual verification. Thus, when a password is pasted into a browser, it is shown on the screen for a short time. A hidden program that captures the screen (periodically or each time the user presses "return") can therefore be useful to a hacker. The `Theef 2.0` Trojan horse is known to capture the computer screen continuously, as well as performing other destructive operations. A common solution is to display the password as a string of asterisks.

⋄ **Exercise 4.2:** Search the Internet for more examples of common trojans.

4.2 Installing a Trojan

A simple way of installing a program with a Trojan horse on many computers is to write a useful application or utility and sell it (perhaps as shareware) for a very low price. This should be a program that the user will execute often, or at least on a regular basis, so here are some ideas:

■ Anti-virus software. Someone who buys such software is supposed to execute it often or at least as soon as a new virus update appears.

■ A cleanser. A modern operating system is complex and may require periodic house cleaning. The following list may look familiar to many personal computer owners.

1. Applications and utilities may create temporary files and forget (if written by an inexperienced programmer) to delete them.

2. Log files, cache files, and automatic messages created by the operating system should be deleted from time to time.

3. Access permissions of important operating system files may be modified accidentally by imperfectly-written programs or when the computer crashes or hangs. A sudden power failure may also damage the permissions. Thus, someone (or something) should periodically check and restore the original permissions.

4. Programs often have a help facility, and a program may have lots of small files with help text in many languages. A user who speaks only Armenian, for example, may want to delete all the help files in other languages.

5. The file directory may become slightly damaged over time. Running a disk repair utility once a week may be a good idea, as this can locate and repair small problems before they turn serious.

6. Certain operating systems recommend that files should be defragmented periodically.

7. The operating system may automatically backup certain crucial files.

The conclusion is that a modern operating system requires a lot of maintenance. The operating system may do this work automatically, but it tends to do it late at night. If the computer is off at that time, the maintenance work is skipped. This may give a hacker the idea to write a utility that will do all the maintenance tasks for a certain operating system and will do them better than the operating system itself. Such a utility can be very handy. To be really useful, it should not be launched by the user, but decide by itself when to run. Obviously, such a utility has full control over the computer and may be an ideal place to store a Trojan horse. Here is what one user has to say about this type of utility (Macaroni for the Macintosh OS X):

"Though it's just an impression, I can say that my system is running much snappier than pre-Macaroni days. That's even with me running some of the other very good utilities out there manually. Not having to worry at all about when to run different scripts is well worth the nominal fee charged here. Highly recommended."

In the 1970s, when the UNIX operating system and the C programming language were developed, the developers (Dennis Ritchie and Ken Thompson) discovered that a compiler can be rigged (or bugged) to embed a Trojan horse into any program it compiles, or only into certain routines or statements. For example, a C compiler (which is itself written in C) can be rigged to insert a Trojan horse into the login routine of UNIX. The point is that the Trojan horse does not exist in the source code of the program being compiled, so an examination of the source code will not yield anything suspicious.

Once the compiler has been rigged, an examination of the source code of the compiler itself will naturally disclose the bug, but an insider fraudster can proceed in three steps that leave virtually no traces:

■ Rig the compiler (since this is done intentionally, it is by itself a Trojan horse and not a bug; a bug happens accidentally).

■ Compile the compiler itself. This creates an executable compiler with a Trojan horse.

■ Remove the Trojan horse from the source code of the compiler. This leaves the original, clean compiler whose examination will yield nothing suspicious.

> The act of breaking into a computer system has to have the same social stigma as breaking into a neighbor's house. It should not matter that the neighbor's door is unlocked.
>
> —Ken Thompson

The result is a Trojan horse embedded in an executable file that's a C compiler. When the compiler is run to compile a program, it executes the Trojan horse, which may decide to embed malicious code (another Trojan horse) in the program being compiled. Both the source code of the program and that of the compiler are clean, but the object codes (the executable files) are infected. This scheme opens up a entire spectrum of possibilities for a hacker, because executable files, especially large ones, are notoriously difficult to disassemble, read, and understand. This kind of Trojan horse is dangerous because it survives reading, rereading, checking, recompiling, or even rewriting of the program. In some sense it is the ultimate parasite.

More details of this technique and examples of C code can be found in [Thompson 84], which is also reprinted in [Denning 90].

This technique has only a limited application for a fraudster, because any malicious code installed by it in the object code of a compiler disappears when the clean source code of the compiler is recompiled. Unfortunately, this technique can be extended to produce an infected compiler where the infection survives recompilation! The Trojan horse literally *lives* in the compiler. For those exegetes who must have the complete story, Section 4.3 may prove useful.

exegete \EK-suh-jeet\, noun: A person who explains or interprets difficult parts of written works. <div align="right">—A dictionary definition.</div>

The fact that a compiler (and by implication, other operating system programs, such as software libraries) can be compromised in such a subtle, nasty way implies that such programs should be kept under strict control by administrators. System programmers (those who update and maintain the operating system itself) are highly-respected professionals, but even they don't last forever. They come and go and even one unreliable programmer in a thousand can do untold harm.

Another way to propagate a Trojan horse is by means of Java applets. The Java programming language has features that make it a natural candidate for use in network applications. One of those features is the Java applets. Unfortunately, this handy feature also introduces a vulnerability. Java applets can be loaded into a computer without the owner's explicit consent, and such an applet can be a Trojan horse. It can collect keystrokes, periodically capture the screen, and send this information to its creator, by simulating the operations of an Internet browser. To the computer owner, this activity looks like innocent E-commerce application, which makes it difficult to detect.

There are software products such as Omniware, Telescript, and Dyad that offer remote execution mechanisms. They also provide opportunities for wrongdoers to load rogue programs into personal computers.

4.3 Rigging a Compiler

This section presents the details of the technique mentioned earlier where a Trojan horse can be planted in a compiler such that the source code of the compiler remains clean and the Trojan survives multiple compilations of the compiler itself.

We start with the concept of a program that prints itself. The problem is to write a program (preferably, the shortest program) that prints itself and does nothing else (this has also been mentioned at the beginning of Chapter 2). A program can, of course, print any strings of characters and the content of any variables. Thus, the following C program prints the string `hello world`.

```
main() {
print("hello world");
       }
```

It is easy to write a program that will print the above program

```
main() {
print("main() {print(\"hello world\");}");
       }
```

(where the notation \" is used to include quotation marks in a character string), but this program doesn't print itself, it prints the first program, which is simpler. At first it seems that our task is hopeless. Any program that prints itself will have to have two parts, a command that prints and a string to be printed. The two parts will always be greater than the string to be printed, (or equivalently, the string printed cannot be as big as the entire program) resulting in an impossible task.

The key to solving this problem is to realize that we can have something in the program perform a double task. A string of characters, for example, can be printed twice. This way, the result printed by the program can be as long as the program itself and can be adjusted to become identical to the program. An example is shown here, in Exercise 2.2, and in Figure 4.2, but anyone with even minimal programming experience is urged to try this independently. The revelation experienced when you finally discover how to do this task far surpasses any benefits you can obtain from me showing you how. But if you really want it, here is an (admittedly hard to read) example.

```
char*a="char*a=%c%s%c;main(){printf(a,34,a,34);}";main(){printf(a,34,a,34);}
```

Figure 4.2 may be easier to read. For those inexperienced in programming, here is an explanation of this program. Line 1 declares a character variable `t[]`. Lines 2–11 place the bulk of the program (lines 13–22) in `t`. The syntax rules of the C language regarding strings have been relaxed to improve readability. The main program (lines 14–22) declares an integer variable `i` and prints three strings. Line 18 prints line 1 as a string, lines 19–20 print lines 2–11 (the content of `t`, each character individually), and line 21 prints lines 13–22 (again from `t`, but this time as a string). Clever!

Now consider a hacker who wants to penetrate a certain UNIX installation and be able to use its computers at will. One approach is to plant a Trojan horse in a sensitive, powerful UNIX routine, that will let the hacker in through a back door. An example of a powerful system program is the `login` routine. This routine is charged with identifying valid users and rejecting illegitimate ones. It is powerful because it decides who will be allowed into the computer. A simplified version of this routine may look like this:

```
main() {
 print("login:"); read(username);
 print("password:"); read(password);
 if(check(username,password)==true)
  {... admit the user...};
 else
  {... reject the user...};
       }
```

```
1  char t[]= {
2  '0 };
3  main()
4  {
5   int i;
6
7   printf("char t[] = {");
8   for(i=0; t[i]!=0; i=i+1)
9    printf("%d, ", t[i]);
10   printf("%s", t);
11  }'
12
13  0 };
14  main()
15  {
16   int i;
17
18   printf("char t[] = {");
19   for(i=0; t[i]!=0; i=i+1)
20    printf("%d, ", t[i]);
21   printf("%s", t);
22  }
```

Figure 4.2: A Self-Printing C Program.

```
check(username,password) {
  ... code to encrypt and check the password...
                    }
```

A Trojan horse can be inserted into the check routine as follows (match is a procedure that compares two character strings):

```
check(username,password) {
 if(match(password,"hacker")) return true;
 else
 ... code to encrypt and check the password...
 endif;                    }
```

The infected routine will admit anyone who enters the password hacker, regardless of the user's name. Other passwords will be checked as before.

◇ **Exercise 4.3:** (For UNIX users.) Name other UNIX routines that are powerful.

In principle, it is easy to modify the login routine to let the hacker in, but in practice, a hacker may have to be an experienced C programmer, to apply for a job at the computer center, to actually get the job, to spend some time becoming a trusted employee, and to find a few minutes alone with the source files, away from any prying eyes and security cameras. Once done, the hacker should stay on the job for a while, to allay any suspicion. Even after all this, a routine check of the `login` procedure will disclose the Trojan horse. A clever hacker will understand all this and may look for a better approach.

A better scheme is to rig a compiler in a simple way, as shown earlier. An insider with access to the source code of a C compiler could plant a Trojan horse in the object code of the compiler by the following three steps:

- Plant a Trojan horse in the source code of the compiler.

- Compile the compiler. This creates an executable (object code) compiler with a Trojan horse.

- Remove the Trojan horse from the source code of the compiler. This leaves the original, clean compiler whose examination will yield nothing suspicious.

The result is a Trojan horse embedded in an executable file that's a C compiler. When the compiler is run to compile a program, it executes the Trojan horse, which may decide to embed malicious code (another Trojan horse) in the program being compiled. Both the source code of the program and that of the compiler are clean, but the object codes (the executable files) are infected. This scheme opens up an entire spectrum of possibilities for a hacker, because (1) executable files, especially large ones, are notoriously difficult to disassemble, read, and understand and (2) the C compiler is used to compile all kinds of programs, among them operating system programs that have full access to all the files. Planting a Trojan horse or a virus in a powerful system program such as `login` can make the perpetrator as powerful as the chief administrator.

The critical part of the C compiler, from our point of view, is the `compile(s)` procedure. It accepts a string `s` of characters (the next line of source code) that it compiles. The following is a simplified picture of `compile`:

```
compile(s) {
   ... instructions to compile...
   ... a line of C code...;
            }
```

This procedure is invoked for each line of source code. It creates object code and appends it to the object file that's being generated. This, of course, is a highly-simplified picture, but it is enough for conveying the basic ideas of bugging the compiler. (In reality, a compiler has to perform several passes over the source code to collect information before it generates any object code.) Procedure `compile` can be rigged in a simple way to plant a Trojan horse in the `login` routine.

```
1 compile(s) {
2  ... (unmodified) instructions to compile...
3  ... a line of C code...
4  if(match(s,"check(username, password) {"))
5   compile("if(match(password, \"hacker\")) return true;");
6            }
```

Line 4 compares the string in s to the string "check(username, password) {". A match indicates that the program currently being compiled is indeed login. In such a case, the compiler is instructed (in line 5) to compile the short Trojan horse code "if(match(password, \"hacker\")) return true;" that becomes part of the object code of the login routine (even though it does not appear in its source code). After rigging the compiler in this way, the perpetrator tries the login routine every day, until he finds the Trojan horse (i.e., he finds he can log into any account by means of his secret password). He then cleans up the compiler source code by removing lines 4–5 above.

In practice, this process is more complex, because the simple test of line 4 may not be enough to identify the login routine, because the Trojan horse is more complex than shown here, and because the hacker may want to bug several operating system routines at the same time (in case his access to the compiler source code may soon be curtailed or completely cut off).

This clever scheme for bugging the compiler leaves the source code of the compiler clean. It therefore can easily be defeated by recompiling the (clean source code of the) compiler. However, this scheme can be extended to plant a Trojan horse that stays in the object code of the compiler even after several recompilations! The extension (as well as the original scheme) depends on a software feature called *self-referencing*. As far as the compiler is concerned, self-referencing means that the compiler is written in the language it compiles. The most-important example of a self-referencing compiler, as far as this author is aware, is the C compiler which became such an important part of the UNIX operating system, but the practice of writing a compiler in its "own" language is now common. When we hear of such practice, it seems impossible. We can write the first C compiler in C, but it will be impossible to compile this compiler.

Because of this problem, self-referencing must be a multistep process, where the first step is to write a minimal C compiler in assembler language and assemble it. We call this first compiler version 0, and we denote its source code and executable file by S_0 and E_0, respectively. Version 0 is a primitive compiler that's both slow and produces inefficient machine code, but it is only a first step. (We assume that an assembler and a loader exist already, but someone has to write and debug them before our multistep process can be carried out.)

The next step is to write a better compiler, version 1, that produces efficient machine code. The source code of this version is written in C and is designated S_1. It is compiled by compiler E_0 to produce compiler E_1. E_1 is a C compiler that produces optimized code, but is slow, because it was compiled by E_0.

The next and final step is obvious, use E_1 to recompile S_1, resulting in E_2 (there is no S_2). E_1 is slow to compile, so it takes a while to produce E_2, but once produced, E_2 is both fast (because E_1 produces optimized code) and produces optimized code (because it is a translation of S_1 and S_1 was written to produce optimized code).

The entire process, summarized in Figure 4.3, reminds one of the adage about pulling yourself up by your own bootstraps, but it works!

We are now ready to describe what may be termed the ultimate parasite. This is a Trojan horse that can live in the compiler's object file for a long time and survive any number of recompilations. The idea behind such a terrible threat is really very simple.

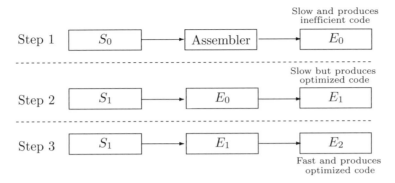

Figure 4.3: Bootstrapping A Compiler.

We have seen how the compiler can be rigged to insert a Trojan horse in the login routine when compiling it. In the same way, the compiler can be bugged to insert a Trojan horse in itself (i.e., in its own new object code) every time *it* is recompiled. In addition to executing its payload, such a Trojan horse must replicate itself every time it is executed, but we already know, from the examples of programs that print themselves, that such a thing is possible.

We assume that the object code of the compiler already has a Trojan horse, but the source code has been cleaned. The Trojan horse has to identify the case where the compiler compiles itself, and has to plant a copy of itself (i.e., of the Trojan horse) in the newly-produced object code. Figure 4.4 shows a simplified picture of how the compiler can be rigged to bug itself when recompiled. Notice that the code of this figure is very similar to that of Figure 4.2, except that instead of printing string variable t, this variable is passed as a parameter to routine compile().

```
1  compile(s) {... compile the current line...
2  char t[] = {... a character string...};
3  if(match(s, "compile(s) {")) {
4   compile("char t[] = {");
5   for(i=0, t[i]!=0, i=i+1)
6    compile(t[i]);
7   compile(t);
8   compile("print(\"hello world\")");
9                            }
10            }
```

Figure 4.4: A Rigged Compiler.

Line 2 places the Trojan horse's code as a character string in variable t in much the same way as in Figure 4.2. On line 3, the compiler identifies the fact that it is compiling itself. Once this is ascertained, lines 4–7 compile the Trojan horse (they prepare the object code of the horse and insert it into the newly-created object code of the compiler) exactly as done by the three print commands in Figure 4.2. Finally, line 8 compiles the payload, in our example, simply the harmless declaration "hello world."

This fragment of the rigged compiler source code is greatly simplified. The experienced reader will notice that the copy of the horse and the payload are inserted into the object code of the new compiler right after the header "`compile(s) {`" i.e., at the beginning of the `compile()` routine instead of at the end, but this, as well as other minor points, can be taken care of by a clever hacker.

◇ **Exercise 4.4:** Try to identify another weak point of this simple code.

Once the rigged compiler of Figure 4.4 has compiled itself, the extra code can be removed from it, leaving a clean source code of a C compiler. (The modification date of the compiler source file will have changed, which may serve as a clue to the administrators, but that's all. If this date change isn't discovered quickly, it may lose its significance after a while.) Every time this clean source code is compiled, the (bugged object code of the) compiler produces a new bugged object code.

Now that we have seen how a bug (more precisely, a Trojan horse) can live indefinitely in a compiler, we consider the next natural question. How can an unscrupulous wrongdoer infiltrate a highly-secure computer center staffed by professionals and gain enough trust to be allowed to mess up with the compiler (especially considering that the center's administrators may have read this section and know all about planting Trojan horses in a compiler)? The obvious answer is, by planting a virus. A virus planted by a low-level employee or even a complete outsider can propagate in the computer center from program to program until it gets a chance to locate and infect the compiler (whose name, perhaps `cc.exe` or `cc.c`, is public knowledge).

In order to infect the compiler, the virus has to reside in a program that belongs to a user who has permission to write to the compiler, but in a large computer center several trusted system programmers may have this permission. The hacker may even copy the compiler source code, rename the copy and rig it at his leisure, check the bugged compiler by recompiling it several times, then store the rigged compiler object code in the computer as one of his files. Upon gaining the right access permission, the virus simply replaces the original (object) compiler with this file. Once the virus writer has noticed that the Trojan horse is in place, he can plant another virus that will kill the original virus from all the infected programs.

◇ **Exercise 4.5:** There is a simpler way to eliminate the original virus without writing and distributing a new virus. Any ideas?

See the excellent article [Witten 87] for more details on this and similar topics.

> You know horses are smarter than people. You never
> heard of a horse going broke betting on people.
> —Will Rogers

5
Examples of Malware

The history and main features of several computer viruses and worms are described in this section. More examples can be found in Appendix B. Due to the prevalence of rogue software, there are many similar descriptions on the Internet.

5.1 The Lehigh Virus

The Lehigh virus appeared at Lehigh university in Bethlehem, Pennsylvania in the fall of 1987. Thus, this was an early virus. It attacked the now-obsolete DOS operating system that was then very popular. The perpetrator was never identified, but was likely a student with PC programming experience and knowledge of DOS. The virus located itself in the stack segment of the COMMAND.COM file, an important part of DOS. Because of this special location, the virus didn't change the size of the file, which initially made this virus difficult to locate. However, the infection did change the last modification date of this file, which helped security consultants at Lehigh in identifying and locating the problem. The virus infected the first four floppy disks inserted in the drive, then damaged the hard drive itself by overwriting the file allocation table, a data structure where file names are associated with disk addresses.

The existence of the virus was suspected once its massive damage was discovered. To understand this process, it helps to know how the computing environment operated at Lehigh at that time. The university purchased certain programs that its students were allowed to use. A student could walk into a computer lab, check out a floppy disk, insert it into a computer in the lab, and run the software. Students were also allowed to take a disk home and copy it, so as to have a private copy of the software.

Floppy disks are not very reliable, and in such an environment, where a disk is used heavily by many students, disks tended to go bad. On an average day, five disks were returned as bad and had to be replaced, but when the virus started its operations, 500 disks were returned by students as bad. It was clear to Lehigh programmers that something was wrong, and fortunately they had been trained in computer viruses, and knew what to suspect. They started examining the bad disks and found out that file COMMAND.COM, which should always be the same, had a recent modification date. The file was then carefully examined and compared with an original file on a brand new disk. This was how the virus was discovered.

The following morning, the employees had a program to examine floppy disks for the virus and delete it. They sent email messages to everyone on campus and placed messages in every mailbox, asking people to let their disks be examined and cleaned. A trained person with a PC was sent to every building on campus, and asked everyone in sight to submit their floppy disks for a check and also bring any disks they had at home.

Such a process is not always successful, because people move in and out of such a campus, but at Lehigh it succeeded because the people in charge took immediate and decisive action and because the spread of the virus was limited. Within two days the campus was clean of the virus and no other copy of the virus has been seen again outside of virus labs.

The calendar played an interesting role in this episode. The problem started two days before the start of the fall break at Lehigh. Had the consultants failed to eradicate the virus in two days, students going on vacation would have spread the virus to their home computers and to other environments, thereby turning its eradication into a slow and difficult process.

5.2 The Brain Virus

The brain virus (so called because it labeled any floppy disk that it infected "brain") was first discovered on 22 October 1987. It was the first virus to be discovered in the United States and was designed to damage the directory of floppy disks used in the (now obsolete) DOS operating system. After a tedious process of isolation and analysis, the two names Basit and Amjad were found in the virus, together with their address in Lahore, Pakistan. As a result, this virus is also known as the Pakistani virus. It seems that the two brothers spread the virus by selling certain expensive and popular software titles very cheaply on infected floppy disks to tourists.

The brain virus infects only floppy disks. Part of it replaces the boot sector of the disk and the remainder is located in three clusters (a cluster is two sectors) in the disk directory (called the file allocation table, or FAT), which is damaged as a result. A copy of the original boot sector is also stored by the virus in those clusters. The clusters themselves are declared bad by the virus. When the disk is inserted into the drive, the boot sector is read and the virus is executed. It copies itself to memory and modifies the interrupt addresses of several interrupts.

When software tries to read the disk, the drive generates an interrupt signal which causes the brain virus to be executed. If the software tries to read the boot sector, the virus redirects the input request to the area in the corrupted directory where it had hidden the original sector. If the read operation is for another sector, the virus infects the disk. The virus looks, in such a case, for its own signature, which is the numbers 34 and 12 in the fourth and fifth bytes of the boot sector. If the signature is found or if the disk is write protected, the virus assumes that the disk is already infected and it simply reads the requested data from the disk. Otherwise, the virus stores itself in the boot sector and three sectors of the disk directory, then proceeds with the read request.

The main damage inflicted by the brain virus is the destruction of the disk directory, but files on the disk are sometimes also damaged. The disk directory can, in principle, be reconstructed, but this requires considerable effort.

5.3 The Michaelangelo Virus

The well-known Renaissance painter and sculptor Michelangelo (Miguel Angel) Buonarroti was born on 6 March 1475 (he died on 18 February 1564). In early 1991, a computer virus that was triggered to activate on 6 March was discovered in Europe and was quickly dubbed the Michaelangelo virus (but see joke below).

Back in the early 1990s, floppy disks were common, and the Michaelangelo virus was designed (like many other viruses of the time) to propagate by booting from an infected floppy disk. The Michaelangelo virus hides in the boot sector and partition areas of MS-DOS disks. The boot sector is the first sector read when the computer starts or is reset. Thus, the virus installs itself in memory each time an infected disk (bootable or not) is inserted in the disk drive and is read. Once the Michaelangelo virus is memory resident, it infects the boot sectors of any new disks inserted into the drive. The propagation mechanism of this virus is therefore simple, straightforward, and is shared by many old viruses.

Each time the virus is executed, it checks the date, and on the 6th of March it erases the system area of the hard disk. The hard disk will no longer boot and has to be reformatted. The virus is hidden in the boot sectors, which makes it easy to detect the virus. It was in fact detected before its first activation date, which saved many users the annoyance of being its victims.

With all the fuss over the Michaelangelo Virus, I noticed that March 6 was also Ed McMahon's birthday. I can just see it now, on March 6, 1993 millions of PC users will be greeted with the message:

* Congratulations! Your computer may already be infected! *
—Doug Krause in the RHF Joke Archives `netfunny.com/rhf/jokes/`.

5.4 The SirCAM Virus

The standard name of the SirCAM virus is `Win32.SirCam.137216`. Strictly speaking, it is a worm that was discovered on 17 July 2001. It arrives at a computer as an email attachment. The subject line of the email message has the name of the attached file. That file is randomly taken from the sending computer and is given one of the extensions `.bat`, `.com`, `.lnk` and `.pif` (in addition, it has its original extension, so it has two extensions).

The email message itself is pseudo-random and may be in English or Spanish. The English messages have the format:

```
Hi! How are you?
I send you this file in order to have your advice
See you later. Thanks
```

The middle line was to be randomly selected from the following list. However, because of a bug in the worm's random number initialization, the first choice is always used:

```
I send you this file in order to have your advice
I hope you can help me with this file that I send
I hope you like the file that I sendo you
This is the file with the information that you ask for
```

The Spanish message looks like:

```
Hola como estas ?
Te mando este archivo para que me des tu punto de vista
Nos vemos pronto, gracias.
```

Because of the same bug, the middle line is always the first line of the following list:

```
Te mando este archivo para que me Des tu punto de vista
Espero me puedas ayudar con el archivo que te mando
Espero te guste este archivo que te mando
Este es El archivo con la informacion que me pediste
```

When executed, the virus copies itself as file `C:\RECYCLED\SirC32.exe` to disk drive C as well as `SCam32.exe` in the Windows System directory. It also modifies the two registry keys

```
HKEY_LOCAL_MACHINE\Software\Microsoft\Windows\CurrentVersion\RunServices\Driver32="\SCam32.exe"
   HKEY_CLASSES_ROOT\exefile\shell\open\command=""C:\recycled\SirC32.exe""%1" %*"
```

and creates the new key `HKEY_LOCAL_MACHINE\Software\SirCam`.

The first key causes the virus to be executed when Windows starts. The second key causes it to execute whenever any `.exe` program is executed. The virus gets a list of `.DOC`, `.XLS` and `.ZIP` files in the "`My Documents`" folder. It appends one of these files to the end of itself and saves the result to the "Recycled" folder, adding a (second) extension to the file name. This file is later attached to the email messages that the virus sends.

The virus is activated to damage the computer in one of two cases: (1) The date is 16th October and the computer is set to display dates in the format `dd/mm/yy`. (2) The attached file contains "FA2" that's not followed by "sc". In either of these cases the virus deletes all the files on drive `C`. It then follows with the space filler operation, where it fills the remaining space on drive `C` by appending text to file `c:\recycled\sircam.sys`. The space filler operation also occurs after 8000 executions of the virus, even if no files are deleted.

The virus appends a random document from the infected computer to itself and emails this new file.

The virus infects Windows versions 95, 98, and Me. Due to a bug in the virus, it does not replicate under Windows NT, 2000, or XP.

5.5 The Melissa Virus

The Melissa virus (official name `W97M_Melissa`) was first detected on Friday, 26 March 1999. It originated in an Internet `alt.sex` newsgroup. Melissa is a macro virus that attacks the Microsoft Word 97 and Word 2000 applications and propagates via email attachments. The initial attack was widespread, affecting many sites. The virus infects MS Word documents and in order for it to propagate, a user has to open an infected document.

If the Microsoft Outlook email program is present in the infected computer, the virus sends infected messages to the first 50 addresses in the owner's address book. The main damage inflicted by Melissa is the extra load it places on mail servers. On the day it first appeared, Microsoft had to shut down its incoming email, and Intel and other corporations reported adverse effects.

Melissa arrives an an attachment to an email message whose subject line is "Important Message from `<name>`," and whose body text is "Here is that document you asked for... don't show anyone else ;-)". The attachment is often named `LIST.DOC`. If the recipient opens the attachment, the infecting file is written on the disk. The file itself contains a list of passwords (since disabled) for several pornographic Web sites. The file also contains a Visual Basic script that copies the virus-infected file into the `normal.dot` template used by MS Word for custom settings and default macros. It also creates the following entry in the Windows registry:

`HKEY_CURRENT_USERSoftwareMicrosoftOffice"Melissa?"="...by Kwyjibo"`

Melissa's Visual Basic code then creates an Outlook object, reads the first 50 names in each Outlook Global Address Book, and sends each addressee the same email message with the attachment that caused this particular infection. The virus works only with Outlook, not Outlook Express.

In those rare cases where the minute value at the moment of virus activation equals the day of the month, the following text is displayed "Twenty-two points, plus triple-word score, plus fifty points for using all my letters. Game's over. I'm outta here." (This text is taken from a Bart Simpson cartoon and refers to the game of Scrabble.)

A user can avoid Melissa by carefully examining each email message and all email attachments. Melissa is identified by its subject line and the fact that it has a small attachment (about 40Kb) named `LIST.DOC`. As a courtesy to the Internet community, any recipient of Melissa should inform the sender that their computer has been infected and has become a source of infection. In addition, many email servers already know the signature of this virus and identify any email message containing it.

David L. Smith, a 31-year-old programmer and the author of Melissa (which he so named as a "tribute" to a Florida lap dancer he had fallen for), was identified, tried, and sentenced to 20 months imprisonment and a fine of $5,000.

5.6 Scores Virus

The Scores virus (actually, a Trojan horse) was designed, in early 1988, to attack applications on the Macintosh computer. In general, the number of Macintosh viruses has always been much smaller than the number of PC viruses (even in the past when DOS, the predecessor of Windows, was the chief operating system for PCs). The reasons for this may be the relatively small number of Macintosh computers (around 3–4% of the entire computer market) and the resistance of the Mac OS to viruses. It may also be that it is harder to write a virus for the Macintosh because the operating system is more complex (but version X of this operating system is based on UNIX, which makes it vulnerable to UNIX viruses).

The effect of the Scores virus starts when a floppy disk with an infected application is inserted into the disk drive and the infected application is executed (or is first copied to the hard drive and then executed). The virus executes first. It examines the system file for a previous infection. If the system file is clean, the virus infects the computer by adding certain resources to the system, note pad, and scrapbook files, and creating two invisible files (one of which is called `Scores`, hence the name of the virus) in the system folder. Most of the added resources are of type `init`, which is an executable resource. Thus, the executable part of this virus consists of three inits.

The inits in the system file are loaded into memory and executed each time the computer is booted. On the second day, those inits go into action. Every few minutes, they start looking for an uninfected application. If one is found, it is infected by adding a resource of type `code` and setting the application to execute this resource, followed by a normal execution of the application, each time the application is launched.

Four days after the initial infection, the Scores virus starts looking for applications called *ERIC* and *VULT*. These were two programs written by EDS (electronic data systems) for in-house use. If a user launches one of those programs, the virus stops it after 25 minutes.

Seven days after infection, the virus crashes any of the two applications when they execute and try to write to disk.

Apparently this virus was written by a disgruntled employee. It also first appeared in EDS's Dallas, Texas office, causing users there to experience slow execution, random crashes, and printing problems. Even though it was targeted at the *ERIC* and *VULT* applications, it spread to computers outside EDS, causing minor damage, but major headaches.

5.7 Swiss Amiga Virus

The case of the Swiss Amiga virus (that first appeared in November 1987) is particularly interesting because of the response of the person in Commodore (the maker of Amiga) responsible for defending against viruses. The Amiga personal computer (still used today) was very popular in the 1980s and had large, well-organized users' groups. As might be expected, software was shared in meetings (copy parties) of those groups, on floppy disks. It's no wonder that someone wrote a virus that propagated on those disks. The technical description of the virus is easy to find on the Internet and is boring, so this section concentrates on the war of nerves between the Commodore anti-virus expert and the anonymous virus writer. We start with a short description of the virus.

"The virus copies itself to $7EC00 and patches the Cool-Vector to stay resident in memory. After a reset the virus uses the `DoIO()`-Vector to infect other disks."

The virus was not destructive. Every 15th reboot of the computer it displayed the message

```
Something wonderful has happened
Your AMIGA is alive !!! and, even better...
Some of your disks are infected by a VIRUS !!!
Another masterpiece of The Mega-Mighty SCA !!
```

Today it is known that SCA was an acronym for the Swiss Cracking Association, a group working to remove software protection. Presumably the virus was written by someone in this group.

The virus embedded itself in one of the operating system files on the disk, so the response of Commodore was to write a program that looked for the first byte of the virus in that file and alert the user if the specific byte was found. A week later the anonymous virus writer responded by modifying the first byte of the virus. The second disinfectant program looked for one of those two initial bytes, with the result that the virus writer modified the virus to start with one of ten different bytes. The third version of the disinfectant software checked to see that the first byte of the virus was not the legitimate byte of the Amiga file. The next mutation of the virus had as its first byte a byte that was legitimate as the first byte of an Amiga program, but its second byte was not a legitimate Amiga program byte. It is not clear how this cycle ended, but we hope that the virus writer had better things to do with his time.

5.8 Christmas Card Virus

The Christmas card virus appeared in late 1987 and propagated through mainframe computers. It was intended as a Christmas greetings, one of many such greetings sent, even as early as 1987, by computers as email. Computer users were used to receiving such greetings, so when you saw a greeting email message from someone you knew, you opened it and read it immediately. The perpetrator created this virus and sent it to two recipients that he knew. The first one refused to open it, but the second recipient opened it. All he saw was a greeting on his screen, but the hidden virus searched his address book and sent a copy of the greeting to all the addresses in this book in the name of the second recipient. From then on, things started snowballing. Experts estimate that at the height of its activity, this virus, that didn't actually infect any computers, managed to spread half a million cards all over the world. It took months to convince people to delete this message without opening it, which slowly stopped the spread of this virus.

As a result of this virus, it is common to find on the Internet, every year around December, messages such as the one here, warning recipients of the danger of opening greeting email messages.

"Sophisticated computer viruses are hiding behind some Christmas e-cards, wrecking the season of goodwill, analysts warn."

The Christmas card virus is important because it was one of those rare cases where the perpetrator was quickly and easily identified. This virus didn't do any infection, so it always propagated with the same file name, which made it easy to identify all the files by that name that have been sent and to locate the earliest one, sent by the original writer, a student in Germany. This is a rare example of the use of audit in tracking down an attacker.

> NOTE: Our cards are virus free. However, viruses on your computer can be transmitted via e-mail attachments.
>
> —From `http://powerpres.com/xmas.html`

5.9 VBS.KAK Worm

The Wscript KAK worm appeared in September 2000 and attacked PC computers running Outlook Express. It uses a known security vulnerability to attach itself to every email sent from an infected computer. It is written in Javascript and it attacks both the English and French versions of Windows 95/98, if Outlook Express 5 is installed.

What makes this worm unique is its ability to infect a computer by simply reading or previewing an email message. The worm hides in the HTML code of the email itself. When the message is previewed or opened by the recipient, the worm automatically takes control and infects the computer.

If neither Outlook Express nor MS Internet Explorer 5.0 are installed, the worm is unable to infect the machine. The worm has another time-triggered payload. On the first day of each month at 5 pm, a message is displayed and Windows is sent a command to shut down. When Windows is restarted, the message "driver memory error" is sometimes displayed.

Upon infection, the worm places a file called `KAK.HTM` in the `C:\Windows` directory and a temporary file with an `.HTA` extension in the `C:\Windows\SYSTEM` directory. It also places a file `KAK.HTA` in the Startup directory. Then the worm adds the following lines into the `AUTOEXEC.BAT` file and renames the original autoexec file `AE.KAK`.

```
@echo off>C:\Windows\STARTM~1\Programs\StartUp\kak.hta del
C:\Windows\STARTM~1\Programs\StartUp\kak.hta
```

Next, the worm adds the following changes into the Windows Registry
`HKEY_LOCAL_MACHINE\SOFTWARE\Microsoft\Windows \Currentversion\Run\cAgOu`
This `cAgOu` file points to the temporary `.HTA` file dropped into the `Windows\System`
directory earlier. The worm also adds the following line to the Windows Registry.
`HKEY_CURRENT_USER\Identities\Software\Microsoft\Outlook Express`
  `\5.0\signatures\Default Signature`
This default signature points to the `KAK.HTM` file loaded into the Windows directory.
Every email that is sent after infection has this `KAK.HTM` embedded in the HTML of the
email which spreads the worm to others.

5.10 The Cruncher Virus

The cruncher virus originated in The Netherlands in June, 1993. It infected `.COM`
executable files in the old DOS operating system, but did not appear to do any damage.
This virus is memory resident. It compresses the files it infects but doesn't bother
to append zeros to bring an infected file to its original size, as discussed on page 79.
When the first cruncher-infected `.COM` program is executed, the virus installs itself in
memory such that it will be invoked when interrupt 21 occurs. It then infects `.COM` files
(executable programs), except `COMMAND.COM` and very small `.COM` files. The modification
date and time of the infected files in the disk directory are not changed. Once the
infected `.COM` file is decompressed and the virus is identified, the strings `MK/Trident`
and `Cruncher V1.0a` are found in the virus code, which makes it easy, albeit time
consuming, to identify the virus.

The interesting feature of the cruncher virus is that the entire `.COM` file has to be
decompressed before the presence of the virus can be detected. This is because the
virus compresses the file with an adaptive algorithm. The details of such an algorithm
are outside the scope of this book, but are covered in any text on data compression.
In brief, an adaptive compression algorithm modifies the compression process continuously in response to the frequency of symbols that have been read so far from the file
being compressed. The virus appends itself to the end of the `.COM` file, so it exists in
compressed form at the end of the compressed file. However, because of the adaptive
nature of the compression, the precise bit pattern of the compressed virus depends on
the `.COM` file and is always different. This is why anti-virus software has to completely
decompress any compressed `.COM` file to detect the presence of the cruncher virus.

> For the last 24 years, NCSS has been fine-tuning the art of number crunching.
> Today, NCSS offers you the latest technology in statistical analysis....
> —From `www.ncss.com`

5.11 Opener Virus

Discovered in late October 2004, the Opener virus, originally titled renepo, infects the Macintosh computer. It disables Mac OS X's built-in firewall, creates a back door so its author can control the computer remotely, locates any passwords stored on the hard drive, and downloads a password cracker program called John- TheRipper. Opener is designed to spread and infect any Macintosh OS X drives connected to the infected Macintosh and it leaves infected computers vulnerable to further hacker attack.

Macintosh owners with infected computers reported an unknown startup item called "opener" in /Library/StartupItems/. The executable file is a well-commented bash (terminal) program. It scans for passwords for every user, processes the hashed information on the infected computer, turns on file sharing, and puts all this stuff into an invisible folder called .info in each user's public folder. More detailed analysis of the virus's code has resulted in the following technical details:

■ Opener tries to install ohphoneX, a teleconferencing program, for spying on the Macintosh user through the user's own webcam.

■ It kills the useful utility LittleSnitch (that reports software that tries to call home) before every Internet connection it makes.

■ It installs a keystroke recorder.

■ Allows backdoor access in case someone deletes the hidden account.

■ Grabs the open-firmware password.

■ It installs OSXvnc.

■ Grabs the PID (serial number) of Microsoft Office 2004, as well as serial numbers for Mac OS XServer, Adobe registrations, VirtualPC 6, Final Cut Pro, LittleSnitch, Apple Pro Applications, any existing DynDNS account, Timbuktu, and other software.

■ It tries to decrypt all the MD5 encrypted user passwords.

■ It decrypts all users' keychains.

■ Grabs the AIM logs, and many other personal settings and preferences with info. It even looks into the bash (terminal) history.

■ Grabs data from the computer's classic (OS 9) preferences.

■ Changes the Limewire settings to increase the upload of files from the infected computer.

■ The hidden user account set by opener was named "hacker" by earlier versions of this virus, but is now called LDAP-daemon, a technical, innocuous name.

■ It uses the daily cron task to try to get the Macintosh owner's password from the virtual memory swapfile.

- It installs an application called `JohnTheRipper`, a password cracker that uses a dictionary method to crack passwords.

- It installs `dsniff` to sniff for passwords.

Even those unfamiliar with the terms and details above may agree that this much activity is frightening.

In early November 2004, a week after the discovery of opener, Apple, the maker of the Macintosh and of its operating system, released the following statement:

"Opener is not a virus, Trojan horse, or worm. It does not propagate itself across a network, through email, or over the Web. Opener can only be installed by someone who already has access to your system and provides proper administrator authentication. Apple advises users to only install software from vendors and Web sites that they know and trust."

In response, antivirus experts said that while opener was not an immediate threat, it is a worm because it attempts to copy itself, and is therefore a virus as well, because worms are a special type of virus.

5.12 MTX Worm/Virus

The MTX malware (formal designation `W95.MTX` or `W32/Apology`) is a combination of three nasty parts, a virus, a worm, and a Trojan horse (the latter provides a backdoor that downloads certain pieces of code and installs them). It first appeared in August/September 2000 and was designed to attack computers running the Windows 95 operating system. The name MTX stands for "matrix" because this word was found inside the virus part of MTX. It propagates by email and infects certain executable files in specific directories. The virus also tries to block access to certain Web sites and block email access to other sites in an attempt to prevent the user from locating information and downloading new virus definitions.

MTX is well known for the "trouble" it takes to prevent the user from getting help. It actually modifies an operating system file to make it impossible for the user to visit certain Web sites and to send email to others. More information about this menace is available at [MTX 05].

When MTX invades a computer, it decompresses itself, installs the worm and backdoor parts in the computer, then infects many files. The virus part infects a file by installing itself close to the start of the file but not at the very start. This technique, which makes it difficult for anti-virus software to locate MTX, is referred to as entry point obscuring or EPO.

The worm part of MTX prepares a copy of library file `Wsock32.dll` and names it `Wsock32.mtx`. The "send export" function of the copy is then modified to point to its own code. The effect of this is to send MTX, as an attachment, to a special email message that is sent, without the user's knowledge, after each legitimate message.

The MTX attachment may have one of many potentially misleading names, some of which are listed below. Many of these have a `.pif` extension, which stands for program information files. Such files are used by Windows to execute old DOS programs, but the attachments always include executable code of type .exe, so when the receiver clicks on an attachment, it is executed by Windows and MTX infects the receiving computer.

```
I_wanna_see_you.txt.pif
Matrix_screen_saver.scr
Love_letter_for_you.txt.pif
New_playboy_screen_saver.scr
Bill_gates_piece.jpg.pif
```

Names of attachments.

To entice the receiver to click on the attachment, it often has two extensions, the first of which is .jpg, suggesting an image. However, the second extension is often .pif.

The worm also prepares an auxiliary file named Wininit.ini that's executed when the computer is restarted and whose function is to delete Wsock32.dll and rename Wsock32.mtx Wsock32.dll. After creating Wininit.ini, the worm executes the virus part of MTX.

The virus part looks for specific antivirus programs. If the virus finds any of them executing, it does nothing. Otherwise, it decompresses the worm part, places a copy of it, named Ie_pack.exe, in the user's Windows directory (typically C:\Windows), and executes it. After Ie_pack.exe is executed, it is renamed Win32.dll.

The virus also creates the Trojan backdoor as executable file Mtx_.Exe and executes it. This is a downloader program that goes to Web site i.am/[MATRIX] where plug-ins for the virus are downloaded and executed. The virus part then searches for Windows executable files in the current directory, in the Windows directory, and in the Temp directory. Files that satisfy the following conditions are infected: (1) File size that is not divisible by 101, (2) file size is greater than 8 Kbyte, and (3) file has at least 20 import call instructions.

The virus also adds a registry entry that executes the Mtx_.Exe downloader automatically every time Windows is started. The downloader is invisible in the Task List.

MTX spreads by modifying file WSOCK32.DLL. This file controls the connection of the computer to the Internet, and MTX modifies it such that it sends a copy of the worm, as an attachment, in a second message that follows (unknown to the sender) each email message. The modification also prevents the computer user from visiting certain Web sites that belong to anti-virus software makers and information providers. These are sites whose URLs contain the 4-character strings nii., nai., avp., f-se, mapl, pand, soph, ndmi, afee, yenn, lywa, tbav, and yman.

In addition, this modification prevents the user from sending email to the following URLs wildlist.o*, il.esafe.c*, perfectsup*, complex.is*, HiServ.com*, hiserv.com*, metro.ch*, beyond.com*, mcafee.com*, pandasoftw*, earthlink.*, inexar.com*, comkom.co.*, meditrade.*, mabex.com, *, cellco.com*, symantec.c*, successful*, inforamp.n*, newell.com*, singnet.co*, bmcd.com.a*, bca.com.nz*, trendmicro*, sophos.com*, maple.com.*, netsales.n*, and f-secure.c*.

These techniques make it difficult for the victim to receive information, ask for help, or download anti-virus software and instructions, thereby turning this malware into a persistent infection that requires much time and effort to get rid of.

Epilogue. For a while, a Web site popped up that proposed ways to get around the blocking of sites by MTX. The main idea was to use IP addresses instead of domain names in URLs. It seems that the originator of this malware (or perhaps one of its authors) felt temporary remorse. However, that Web site was short lived and quickly disappeared.

> Old men are fond of giving good advice, to console themselves
> for being no longer in a position to give bad examples.
> —François de La Rochefoucauld

6
Prevention and Defenses

The discussion of rogue software in the preceding chapters illustrates how dangerous this menace is. A worm can appear out of nowhere and infect all the computers of an organization within minutes. Once deeply embedded, it starts sending tentacles outside, looking for more computers to infect, and may also look inside for sensitive information to send back to its creator. Thus, discovering this type of software early, preventing its appearance in the first place, and defending against it are important goals of any computer user, whether an individual or part of an organization. Methods and ideas for preventing malware and defending against it are the topic of this chapter.

6.1 Understanding Vulnerabilities

The first step in the fight against computer viruses is an understanding of vulnerabilities that viruses exploit in order to propagate and inflict damage. The following is a list of such weaknesses:

- User apathy. Even though every computer user is aware of the threat of viruses, people always feel that "it's not going to happen to me." Computer users share software without checking for infection, they ignore suspicious behavior that may indicate the presence of a virus, and they don't spend the time to learn and apply basic security measures.

- Insufficient security control. Many computers, especially personal computers, are not equipped with hardware and software features that help in detecting and isolating viruses and other security threats. Large, multiuser computers generally perform much better in this area.

■   Misuse of available security features. Anti-virus software should always have the latest virus update. Running such software with old virus updates is an ineffective use of an effective security feature. Other examples are misuse of permissions and passwords. Permissions (to use computing resources) are an effective tool that can prevent accidental damage to the file system. An administrative user who allows free access to anyone is misusing this tool. Passwords are also a powerful instrument, but they should be chosen carefully (Section 8.3). Users often choose an easy-to-remember password, but such passwords tend to be easy to guess.

■   Weaknesses in the operating system. Modern operating systems are extremely complex and are implemented and maintained by large teams of programmers. Vulnerabilities and weak points are discovered all the time in this type of software. Quite often a discovery is made by a security expert or a clever user who then notifies the manufacturer of the operating system. Sometimes, a weakness is discovered by a virus writer who immediately sets up to exploit it.

■   Unauthorized use. There are those who regard breaking into a computer as a challenge, and the more secure and secret the computer, the greater the challenge. Once a hacker manages to break into a computer, the temptation to cause havoc is great, often too great.

■   Anonymity of networks. Before the era of computer networks, a malicious person had to actually walk into a computer center in order to do damage. Nowadays, with the prevalence of networks, attackers have the advantage of anonymity.

These points illustrate the need for a comprehensive security program that includes (1) identifying vulnerabilities to viruses, (2) correcting them and plugging up security holes, and (3) monitoring the results. In the home, individual users should constantly train themselves in security issues. This is done mostly by reading security literature, which is freely available on the Internet. Such literature lists recently-discovered viruses and other security hazards, it recommends tools and techniques for user protection, and it keeps the user on his toes. In the workplace, management should provide resources for virus prevention, resources that should include at least the following points:

■   Training seminars. From time to time, an employee should be sent to a seminar where the basics of security are covered and security policies and procedures are described and rehearsed. Experience shows that training is important. A group of well-trained users who are aware of security threats and are willing to cooperate is ultimately the best weapon an organization can have in the war on viruses. User education is expensive for a company, but pays for itself in the long run. Training should be mandatory, should be done periodically, and should include the following topics:

1. A background on viruses, how they are planted, how they propagate, the types of damage they inflict, and how to detect their presence. Users have to be aware of the risk of bringing private software into their work computers and of sharing software.

2. Software vulnerabilities exploited by viruses in the past. This may help a user to detect current weaknesses.

3. Company security policies and contingency procedures.

■   Any decisions pertaining to the acquisition of new software and hardware should involve security experts.

■   Monitoring user and network activity. Special software can monitor the activities of the various user computers and report any suspicious activity to a central monitoring facility. Examples of abnormal activities are an increase in CPU activity during lunch break or at night, and an unusually large number of email messages coming in or going out. Network activity is especially easy to monitor automatically and it is an important tool in fighting viruses. The activity should be monitored all the time and the number of packets per second coming in and going out should be saved. At any time, this number should be compared with the corresponding numbers in the past few days. Any large deviation may signal the presence of a virus.

■   Emergency policies must exist and users should be trained in them, so they know what to do and who to turn to in emergency situations where a virus or other type of attack is discovered.

■   Limited sharing. An organization should try to limit the sharing of computing resources among its members, and the sharing of data between itself and the outside world. In practice, there should be only one gateway between an organization's local-area network and the Internet, and this gateway should be protected by security experts. A common security break in such an environment is someone who brings in a modem and uses it to hook up his office computer to the Internet directly, not through the gateway.

■   One aspect of limited sharing is a "no external storage" policy, adopted by some organizations, that prohibits employees from bringing laptop computers, disks, or other storage devices such as flash memories to work. When external storage has to be brought in, it has first to be checked and approved by a special clearinghouse (see next point). Unfortunately, there is a temptation to bring external storage into a work environment. An employee may want to play a computer game or work on their taxes during lunch break, so they bring a program from home on a (possibly infected) disk or CD. Similarly, an employee may want to copy a useful piece of software from work to their home computer, so they take it out on a company disk, then return the disk. Past experience has indicated that this policy is sound, so it should be adopted, carefully explained to all employees, and enforced (even by having guards at the doors if necessary).

■   A company clearinghouse. Sharing should be limited, but from time to time it is necessary. An organization, especially a large one, needs new programs and data files all the time, and it is a sensible policy to first install any new object in a special computer, a clearinghouse, where it can be used, examined, and tested for a while, before it is moved to production computers. This policy detects known viruses, as well as programs that aren't very useful to the organization and should be rejected regardless of any security considerations. A clearinghouse may help even in the case of a new, unknown virus. If a program stays in the clearinghouse for a while, the new virus may be discovered elsewhere, and new tests in the clearinghouse may locate and eradicate it from the program before it is used for production.

⋄ **Exercise 6.1:** Show an example of a small organization that can operate for years without any new software or data from the outside.

■   It seems reasonable that programs distributed by discussion groups, private servers, hackers' "warez" servers, and friends should be suspect and should be included in the "no external storage" policy. Many organizations also feel that shareware and freeware should also be treated similarly. Large software makers like to add to their advertisements a disclaimer that says: "Don't fall for cheap shareware, it may have viruses. Buy from us and buy with confidence." The interesting fact is that viruses in commercial software are more common than viruses in shareware. The latter category is in fact very rare. Once this fact is recognized, hindsight makes it easy to explain. Shareware is normally written by one person or by a small team of partners. It is easy for the shareware writer to control the security in his office or home. It is also important for the writer to distribute clean software. After all, his name is on the software and he hopes to boost his reputation and also make money. It is much harder for a large software maker, with hundreds or thousands of programmers, to control security. An employee may be able to include a new virus in fresh software, with the result that thousands of CDs are shipped and bought, only to cause a new infection that takes time and effort to clean up. Testing new software before it is "burned" on commercial CDs may not help, because it may contain a new, never before seen, virus. An employee in a huge software place may not care about causing a big problem and may even be happy to be the anonymous source of trouble. This is why infected new software, even new operating systems, have been released in the past.

The conclusion is unavoidable. Do not ban shareware and freeware, just make sure it is downloaded from the original maker and not from a shareware depository or a friend.

■   Self isolation in an attack. When an organization senses an attack, it often tries to isolate its network from the outside world. A familiar term is "to pull the plug." This is definitely good practice. If an attack is fast or is not subtle, pulling the plug immediately is going to limit the damage. If a virus has been spreading throughout the organization for months and started its damage today, then pulling the plug isn't going to help, but will not contribute to the problem. The conclusion is that an organization should have several key members who know how to pull the plug and at least one of them should always be ready and available. There should also be an emergency policy that tells those employees specifically, in much detail, how to perform this operation and how and when to return things to normal. Many large companies depend on the Internet for their business and cannot afford to be isolated from the Internet (and thus deny service to their customers) for long.

■   Audit. The originators of the Christmas card virus and the Internet worm were identified as a result of audit. Details about the movement of data packets on the Internet were saved and analyzed, leading searchers to certain networks and geographical areas. Generally, audit isn't useful in tracking down attackers because operating systems do not save enough information that can later be used to trace the progress of a virus and thus serve as an audit trail. Even if such tools become part of common operating systems in the future, they would not prevent viruses, only help to locate their authors.

- **Backups.** It is important to have complete and recent backups, regardless of viruses or any other security concerns. At the time of writing (late 2004) hard disk prices have dropped to such a level that most computer owners, individuals as well as organizations, can afford to have a backup disk for each disk used in the computer. Backup programs are fast and perform incremental backup; they copy only files that have been modified since the last backup. Backups also help repair virus damage, once the backup itself has been tested for the presence of viruses. Backups may have their problems, and two of them are mentioned here. One problem with backups is that certain old operating systems require that certain of their files be written on the disk in a certain order. This was true for older versions of DOS and for the early versions of the Macintosh OS X. When such an operating system is restored from the backup, this condition may not be satisfied, leading to a nonfunctional operating system. (Normally, the operating system can be reinstalled from the original CD that came with the computer, so this may not be a big problem.) Another, more important problem, is how long to keep a backup. A typical personal computer may have two large internal disks, kept identical by the user, so one can always be used as a backup of the other. In addition, there may be an external disk, mounted and updated perhaps once a week to serve as another backup. Thus, the oldest backup is about a week old. A virus may damage or delete important data files, and if it takes the user more than a week to discover the damage, the files are gone, because the copies on the backup are also damaged. A partial solution is to backup important data files on a DVD-R once a week, and keep the DVDs permanently, or backup the files on a DVD-RW and rotate several such DVDs. However, a DVD has a capacity of 4.7 Gb, which may be too small for a business with large data bases.

> [Backup] utilities are great but will never replace paranoia and the discipline of daily updates to multiple sites.
>
> —Robert Campbell, January 2005.

Case study. A backup disk may be held by a disgruntled employee for ransom. An old (1977), little-known case in point involved data stolen from Imperial Chemical Industries (ICI). A computer-operations supervisor (we'll call him John) for ICI in Holland was reading a book on computer security that stressed the importance of backup tapes (this was in the 1970s, when tapes were more common than disks) and warned of potential theft of such tapes. A while later John was passed over for a promotion, an event (or rather, a nonevent) that made him vengeful. Recalling what the book said about the ransom potential of sensitive data, he decided to put theory into practice. As a supervisor, he was authorized to check out disks and tapes, and one weekend in 1977 he and an accomplice went to two company locations and took possession of about 100 original and backup disks and tapes. The data thus taken was sensitive and consisted of payroll records and pension-fund investments. John demanded a ransom of £275,000 and the company, realizing it would cost much more than that to restore the data, agreed to pay. Fortunately, British police managed to apprehend and arrest John and his accomplice when they tried to collect the ransom.

6.2 Defenses Against Malware

Virus defense should involve (1) technical means, some of which are described here, (2) common sense in using your computer, and (3) legal means. Applying all three approaches can keep a user out of trouble for a long while, although perhaps not forever.

In principle, it is possible to have perfect virus protection simply by isolating the computer from any communications with the outside world. Imagine a dentist's office using a computer to generate billings and update patient's records. The necessary programs already exist and can be safely used. As long as input comes only from a keyboard or from an internal disk drive, output is sent to a monitor or a printer, and no new programs are installed, the computer is secure. However, the reason computers are so popular is that they can be used for communications and entertainment. Few would willingly disconnect their computers from the Internet, and this basic fact implies that virus protection is imperfect.

One of the best practical defenses (at least in the opinion of this author) is to simply use common sense and be careful in using the computer. Just as you wouldn't consider purchasing foods or medicines from untrusted sources, don't purchase or accept software from untrusted sources. Don't borrow software from friends or colleagues. If you want to purchase shareware, wait at least a few days before using it, to make sure no one else has discovered a virus in that software. When you list a folder or a directory, take a quick look at the modification dates of the files. You may notice a suspicious date (such as a recent date for an old executable file). Most importantly, don't open email attachments from unknown senders or even from known senders if the email message appears meaningless, unfamiliar, unnecessary, or misspelled or if it is in an unfamiliar style. In the workplace, make sure employees know they are not supposed to bring software from home.

Another good (although not perfect) protection is to limit transitivity. When computer A in a network gets infected, it infects another computer B, which in turn infects C and so on. Limited transitivity is a mechanism (implemented by a policy, an algorithm, an operating system, or a piece of hardware) that guarantees that anything sent from A to B will not be sent from B. Computer B is free to send anything to other computers, except what it has received from A. Such a mechanism would severely limit the spread of a virus and would also discourage virus writers. Attempts to implement such mechanisms have always proved too restrictive and were therefore impractical.

In certain applications, viruses can be kept out because of the special way the data is interpreted. If you could see inside the computer memory or the physical data written on a disk, you would simply see strings of bits. The bits themselves are meaningless, but the programs we write tell the computer how to interpret certain strings of bits. If a program tells the computer to interpret a certain string as a name, an address, or a telephone number, then the computer will not spread copies of that string; the string will not be a virus. Now imagine a very sensitive application of computers, namely electronic fund transfer (EFT) networks used by banks to transfer (sometimes very large amounts of) money. This application should be protected from viruses and this is achieved by the way it interprets the data being transferred. Each transfer (a string of bits) is interpreted as a *from* account, a *to* account, an *amount*, and a *check* digit.

The check digit provides a checksum to guarantee the reliability of the entire string. If a virus is sent as a transfer, its first couple of bytes would be interpreted as a *from* account, the next couple of bytes would be interpreted as a *to* account, and so on. Even though the virus is a program, it would not be executed by the computers dealing with the transaction, because they don't execute the transfers, only interpret them. Such a method protects from viruses, but can be implemented only in special-purpose applications, not in general.

6.3 Anti-Virus Software

The first part of this section is a general discussion of anti-virus software. It is followed by a description of the three main types of such software, namely virus-specific software, generic anti-virus software, and preventive measures.

Anti-virus software is currently very popular and several commercial programs are made and are regularly updated by software makers. Computer users looking to purchase such software should search the Internet for "antivirus software." Anyone who already has such software is urged to update it and run it regularly. The updates (normally monthly, but sometimes issued when a fast spreading virus is discovered) are most important, because new viruses appear all the time. Currently, such software is fast and can search 100,000 files in about 20–30 minutes, depending on the speed of the computer. One factor that can slow down such software is searching inside compressed files. If the anti-virus software is told to decompress all the compressed files on the computer and search each for viruses, it can double its execution time. In spite of its usefulness, anti-virus software has a few problems that users should be aware of. Following is a short list based on the author's long, personal experience.

■ The main problem with anti-virus software, in the opinion of this author, is that a new virus may spread quickly and infect thousands of computers worldwide before any anti-virus software makers can isolate and analyze it and issue an update, and certainly before most users can download, install, and run this update. Issuing virus updates requires more and more work on the part of software makers (in October 2004, for example, one of the major players in this field has issued three updates), and they may eventually ask for annual subscriptions for the updates, which would reduce even more the number of users with up-to-date virus information.

■ It takes only about 20–30 minutes to scan and search an entire disk for viruses, but certain users consider this time period too long. As a result, some anti-virus programs have an automatic scheduling feature, where the user can set the software to launch at a certain time (perhaps late night) and run automatically. Such a feature is useful, but only if the user verifies (perhaps the following morning) that the software was really launched, ran, and did its job. The user also has to check the log, to find out whether anything suspicious had been discovered.

■ The reason anti-virus software is fast is that it knows where in a file each virus is hidden and it checks only those locations. The discussion of mutating viruses In

Section 2.21 shows that a virus may locate itself in different places in each file it infects, thereby making it infeasible for anti-virus software to find the virus. The cruncher virus (Section 5.10) is time-consuming to detect because it resides in a `.COM` file which it compresses with an adaptive compression method. To detect this virus, the anti-virus software has to completely decompress all the compressed `.COM` files it finds in the computer.

■   A user may use anti-virus software improperly. The software should be set to scan every disk, CD, and DVD inserted into the computer, but it should also be executed on a regular basis to scan the hard drive and all backup disks. In addition, the software itself, not just the periodic virus updates, should be updated from time to time, to reflect new approaches to virus detection and the powerful features of new operating systems. Such updates are not free, and users often neglect to purchase them.

■   A file may contain a bit pattern identical or very close to that of a known virus. This is rare, but it causes a false alarm and may confuse a user.

■   Finally, anti-virus software is effective only against known viruses. If your computer is one of the first to be infected by a new virus, it may take a few weeks, even a month, until your anti-virus software will be updated and will detect it.

◇ **Exercise 6.2:** Is it possible to scan files for new, as yet unknown, viruses?

A different type of anti-virus software is an *integrity checker*. This type of software does not scan a disk, but instead tries to identify changes to files (both applications and operating system files) as a result of virus activity. Once such changes are found, the user has to decide whether they are normal or due to a virus. In the latter case, the virus still has to be identified and located. The obvious downside of this approach is that a virus can be found only after it has infected a file or has inflicted some damage. On the other hand, an integrity checker can discover the effects of a mutating virus. Traditional anti-virus software which scans a disk can, in principle, discover a virus before it can do any harm, but in practice users tend to run this software only when they notice something wrong.

> In theory, there is no difference between theory and practice. But, in practice, there is.
>
> —Jan L. A. van de Snepscheut

A continuous integrity checker checks a file each time the file is opened. The integrity checker has saved the time T the file was last opened and checked by the integrity checker (the file size was also saved). If the file has a modification time different from T (or if its size differs from what it was at time T), the integrity checker raises an alarm. It is then the user's task to decide whether the change in the file was caused by a virus or by an innocent action of the operating system.

A *behavior blocker* illustrates a different approach to anti-virus software. Such a utility looks for potentially destructive commands sent to the operating system, and notifies the user before a command is executed. Examples of destructive commands are an attempt to format an entire disk, an attempt to delete all the files or many files, a command to delete a large part of a file, or several commands that write to files that seem unrelated and reside in different directories. A false alarm is always possible, but an integrity checker may sometimes block a virus before it manages to do any harm.

Much time and effort is continually spent by many researchers into anti-virus study and research. One research group dedicated to just this topic is [IbmAntiVirus 05], a Web site that also has many downloadable research papers on viruses, virus writers, and anti-virus techniques.

The remainder of this section discusses three types of anti-virus software in some detail. Ideally, we expect anti-virus software to accomplish the following goals:

■ To detect all known viruses and malware that already exist in the computer, advise the user on each occurrence of rogue software discovered, and help the user to delete them. Such anti-virus software has to be executed on a regular basis by the computer owner (in the case of a personal computer) or by the person in charge of computer security (in the case of a computer in an organization).

■ To detect unknown viruses. This sounds impossible but it makes sense because many new viruses are created from kits and therefore resemble existing viruses. All the new viruses created from the same kit may modify certain interrupt handling routines in the same way and have many identical bit strings. (See also exercise 6.2.)

■ To scan incoming email, all downloaded files, and any removable storage devices inserted into the computer, and detect all known viruses and malware in them. It is not enough to run this type of anti-virus software only from time to time. Instead, it has to be a startup item; it has to be launched automatically (i.e., by the operating system) each time the computer is started or is reset, and it has to reside in memory and be invoked by an interrupt each time any of the following actions takes place: (1) email is examined, (2) a file arrives from the outside, and (3) a new storage device is mounted.

■ To record all its activities in a log file. Such a file should be examined by a person, because anti-virus software may accidentally suspect a clean file of harboring a virus and may delete or disinfect it. Also, when a virus is found in an incoming email message, the sender has to be notified. Imagine a virus infecting a computer owned by A. The virus searches the computer for email addresses (most personal computers have an address book with names and email addresses) and sends email messages to every addressee found, with an attachment and some text enticing the receiver to open the attachment. When anti-virus software on another computer receives a message from A and discovers a virus in it, A should be notified. Thus, anti-virus operations should not be transparent to the user/owner.

These are ambitious goals that are not fully achieved by any of the current antivirus software products. However, the list above shows that the task of anti-virus software is complex. There are many hundreds of known viruses and new ones appear all the time. Current computers have huge-capacity disk drives and it is common to have hundreds of thousands of files on a single disk. Anti-virus software must therefore contain large tables with information on many viruses and has to employ clever algorithms and shortcuts in order to scan and disinfect an entire disk in a reasonable period of time. It is therefore no wonder that the makers of such software keep the details of their programs secret. The secrets are kept not just from competitors (and from this author) but also from writers of future viruses. Those who have read the material about viruses in this book and know how viruses operate would doubtless agree that a clever virus writer who knows how a certain anti-virus program P works, can design a virus that will completely avoid detection by P. Such a virus is sometimes called a retrovirus.

In addition to anti-virus software (which mostly discovers viruses after they have entered a computer), steps can be taken to prevent the entry of viruses into a computer in the first place. This is why the discussion here distinguishes three types of anti-virus measures, virus-specific detection methods, generic techniques, and preventive techniques. We start with a short description of each of the three types.

■   Virus-specific detection methods, as their name implies, look for and identify specific viruses. Most anti-virus software operates this way. The anti-virus program scans files in the disk (or only in certain directories), looking for bit strings that signal the presence of (that are the signature of) known viruses. When a virus is located, the program gives the user a choice of deleting the virus automatically, placing the infected file in quarantine for detailed inspection later, or ignoring it. The third option makes sense for viruses whose deletion is complex and should be done manually, by the user, rather than automatically by the anti-virus software. Generally, it is easy to disinfect boot sectors and macro viruses, but much harder to repair infected executable files.

■   Generic virus detection techniques don't look for specific viruses but instead examine the computer (files on the disk and programs in memory) for anything suspicious, unusual, or anomalous. An example of such activity is an attempt to modify the size of an executable file by a user program. A generic technique cannot identify the presence of a specific virus, but can warn the user that something suspicious has taken place (or is about to take place) in a certain file or in a certain memory-resident program.

■   A virus preventive technique creates an environment in the computer where viruses hesitate before they enter, or cannot thrive (i.e., execute) once they have entered. Preventive techniques are mostly commonsense measures such as having up-to-date backups of files, being careful in Internet surfing, and generally being suspicious and not trusting.

The following discussion provides more information and details on these three types of anti-virus measures.

Virus specific detection. (This topic is also mentioned early in this section.) Once a virus is discovered, experts isolate it, disassemble its code, read and understand it, and decide how to identify future occurrences of the virus and how best to delete it. This may be a long, tedious process that may require help from experts on the particular operating system attacked by the virus. A typical isolation and identification process is described in [Rochlis and Eichin 89] which is appropriately titled *With Microscope and Tweezers*. The main factors that complicate the analysis of a virus are the following:

■   Disassembling a program is much more complex and error-prone than assembling it. The discussion here is for the benefit of readers who insist on the entire story, but it can safely be skipped by others. An assembler reads the source code of a program and translates each assembler instruction into a machine instruction. A disassembler performs the opposite task. It is given a long binary string, and it has to identify the individual machine instructions in it and translate them back to assembler instructions. A program in assembler language has at least three features that complicate this process (see also Section 3.3).

1. Machine instructions have different sizes. Even worse, the same instruction may have different sizes depending on its operands or addressing modes. This complicates the first task of a disassembler, namely to take a long bit string and break it up into individual machine instructions. A typical example is an ADD instruction. In its simplest form, this instruction adds two registers and may be written as ADD R2,R4. Such an instruction often fits in one byte. When a constant has to added to a register, the same instruction is written as ADD R5,#1234 and may occupy perhaps two bytes. When the content of a memory location is to be added to a register, the instruction may be written ADD R6,ABC where ABC is a label. When this instruction is assembled, it may occupy (depending on the size of addresses in the computer and on the addressing mode used) three bytes or even more.

2. A program is a mixture of instructions and data, but the assembler translates everything into bits. An instruction such as ADD R5,ABC may be assembled into the three bytes 3D, A9, and 70 (in hexadecimal), but these bytes may also be the result of a directive (sometimes also called pseudo-instruction) of the form DATA H3DA970 (where the H stands for hexadecimal). Thus, a disassembler has to disassemble each byte both as an instruction and as data, and the human reader may have a difficult time trying to decide whether the byte is an instruction or data.

3. When a program is written in assembler language, certain instructions are labeled, which makes it easy to refer to them from other places in the program. Thus, an instruction may be written as ADD R6,ABC where ABC is a label. Such a label must be defined elsewhere in the program, perhaps in a line ABC: DATA 0. When the ADD instruction is assembled, symbol ABC is replaced with its numeric value which is the distance from the start of the program to the line where ABC is defined. The instruction may end up being assembled into the string 34|6|180 where 34 is the opcode of ADD, 6 is the register number, and 180 is the value of symbol ABC (a relative address). When the ADD instruction is executed, it adds the constant 0 found in location ABC to register 6. The disassembler, however, is presented with a string of bits, so it doesn't have access to the original labels.

▪   The virus author may include several sections of unnecessary and unused code in the original program, some of it consisting of random numbers, in an attempt to confuse detectives and throw them off the right track. Even worse, those extra code sections may include code copied from past viruses. Such code would look familiar to experienced detectives who are trying to understand the new virus, with the result that they may concentrate on these sections while neglecting the really important parts of the virus.

▪   The virus may make decisions based on random numbers, it may mutate as discussed in Section 2.21, and it may compress and encrypt itself in different ways, depending on different keys. All this means that the same virus may infect different computers and reside in them as different bit patterns. Anti-virus software that employs virus-specific bit strings may not be able to locate such a virus or may have to spend inordinate amounts of time searching each file for many different bit strings.

Once the virus code is understood, experts identify certain bit strings that constitute the "signature" of the virus. Anti-virus software that looks for specific viruses will
have to look for those strings in executable files. (If this is a macro virus, anti-virus
software looks for its signature only in certain data files.) One factor that may slow
down the search is the presence of compressed files. A personal computer may have
many compressed files on a disk, and they may be infected. It turns out that computer
users tend to compress data files more than they compress executable files. A data
file may be huge and it may be needed only several times a year. Executable files, on
the other hand, are only rarely very large. Even a large program, such as an image
processor, may require much space in memory, but its executable code on the disk isn't
particularly big.

◇ **Exercise 6.3:** Show examples of very large data files and of data files that are rarely
used.

Thus, anti-virus software should scan compressed files as an option. If a frequently-
used disk has many compressed files and they slow down the anti-virus scan considerably,
the owner may consider encrypting them. An encrypted file (especially if it is also
compressed) may present an insurmountable challenge to a virus (it will at least look
unfamiliar) and may be left uninfected.

Often, anti-virus software has an option of disinfecting files. It is the opinion of
this author that disinfecting a file is a questionable step and that it is always better to
replace an infected file with a clean one whenever possible. An infected file may contain
the main body of a virus, but may also have small amounts of data (perhaps in the form
of counters or flags) left by the virus in other parts. Disinfecting a file by removing the
main body of the virus may not leave an absolutely clean file.

Another problem with disinfecting a file is that the file may contain a bit pattern
identical or very close to that of a known virus. Disinfecting such a file (which is clean)
leaves a damaged and unusable file. On the other hand, replacing the file with a clean
version causes no damage.

Generic virus detection. Generic anti-virus software does not look for the signature of any particular virus. Instead, it looks for suspicious activities and unauthorized
modifications of operating system routines. This kind of software consists of two general
types, activity monitors and behavior (or integrity) checkers.

When the user tries to format a disk, the operating system routine that actually
performs this operation (we'll call it F) verifies the request with the user before doing
anything. Thus, if a virus wants to format a disk (an especially damaging payload, since
no data rescue software can reconstruct files from a reformatted disk) it has two options,
(1) modify F to skip the user verification and (2) issue the low-level commands that F
normally issues to the disk. Generic anti-virus software tries to defeat both alternatives,
but can never achieve absolute success.

In order to defeat alternative 1, a clean copy of F may be prepared in advance
in ROM (where a virus cannot erase or modify it) and the activity monitor has to
compare F to this copy every time it (F) is invoked. This more or less ensures that
a clean, unmodified copy of F will do the job. A sophisticated virus may, of course,
find ways to defeat this protection, but it has to be sophisticated indeed. However,

when the operating system is updated to a new version, routine F may change, and it is impractical to require the user to unplug the ROM with the clean copy of F (and other routines) and plug-in a new ROM.

In order to defeat alternative 2, the activity monitor must have a way to discover who has issued the low-level commands to the disk. The activity monitor can do this (again, not with absolute certainty) either by tracing the address where the low-level command was issued from or by checking the processor status at the moment the low-level command was issued. The details of these two actions may interest advanced readers and are presented here.

A computer has a special register called the program counter (PC). This register contains the address of the next instruction and is incremented by the control unit each time an instruction is fetched from memory and before it is executed. The activity monitor knows where F is located in memory, so it makes sense for it to check the PC each time a low-level command is issued. If it finds an address within F, it assumes that F and not a virus has issued the command. Unfortunately, by the time the activity monitor can check the PC, it (the PC) has already been modified several times. There is therefore a need for special hardware that will save the PC when a low-level command is issued, and such hardware already exists in the form of the interrupt facility of the computer.

When an interrupt occurs (interrupts are discussed in Section 2.23), the PC is saved (normally in a stack), so that the interrupt-handling routine could return to the interrupted program and resume it. Thus, the idea is for F to follow each low-level command by a **break** (page 86) with a special code that asks the **break** handling routine to invoke the activity monitor. The activity monitor checks the second item in the stack. If this item is an address inside the memory area of F, the activity monitor is satisfied and it returns to the **break** routine which in turn returns to F.

⬦ **Exercise 6.4:** Why does the activity monitor check the second item in the stack and not the item at the top of the stack?

An activity monitor also wants to make sure that any sensitive operation in the computer is being carried out by the operating system and not by a virus mimicking operating system routines. Again, special hardware already exists in the CPU in the form of the *processor state*. Any CPU has a special register with several status flags that indicate the status of the most recent result generated by the CPU. The flags are updated by the hardware all the time (a flag is a 1-bit register). One of the flags, the processor status flag, indicates the type of program, user or operating system, that the CPU is currently executing. This book cannot go into details on how this flag is updated, but the important feature, from the point of view of fighting viruses, is that the processor status (as well as the other status flags) is saved on the stack each time the PC is saved. Thus, when the activity monitor retrieves the second item from the top of the stack and checks it, it also retrieves the processor status and checks it too. If the status flag indicates that the CPU was executing an operating system routine when the break interrupt was issued, the activity monitor is satisfied.

An activity monitor is complex, yet it does not provide absolute security. A determined virus writer may find ways to circumvent the checks performed by the activity monitor. Nevertheless, added security is obtained by an activity monitor because designing and implementing such a virus requires detailed knowledge of both the operating system internals and the way the activity monitor works. It also requires a long implementation and testing period. Such knowledge isn't common, and most viruses are not tested well.

Other aspects of generic anti-virus software are discussed in the first part of this section.

Preventive techniques. The list of preventive measures proposed here is not completely new. Several of these measures can be found elsewhere in this book as warnings, advice, and suggestions on how to avoid viruses, but they are listed here specifically as *preventive measures.*

■ Anti-malware organizations maintain useful online information on recent viruses and other malware (see list of resources on page 10). Microsoft, whose many software products are common targets of malware, also maintains Web sites [MSsecurity 05] and [MStechnet 05]. These and others like them should be consulted by careful users, because information, as is well known, is power.

■ All removable disks and cartridges, and most flash memories have a write-protect option. This is often a tab on the disk, but may also be activated by special software. This option is a preventive measure and should be used whenever possible.

■ Operating systems can greatly help in implementing preventive measures. When an operating system is first installed in a computer, it should disable network access by default. When a user wants to connect to a network, access should be turned on manually. Virtually all current operating systems start with network access turned on, which makes it possible for a virus to enter or for spyware to transmit information. A similar feature is for the operating system to turn off any resource sharing. Many users don't use resource sharing and don't even know that such a feature exists and that it is on by default, and this ignorance provides great help to viruses and other types of malware.

■ An open-source operating system has several advantages, but it also constitutes a preventive measure because it enables programmers to peruse the source code and find security weaknesses.

■ The Windows operating system by Microsoft has close ties to several applications, such as Outlook Express and Internet Explorer, also by Microsoft. These ties constitute a security weakness because any updates and modifications to the operating system can introduce security holes in those applications. Moreover, a patch issued to repair such a hole in one application may introduce a different vulnerability in another application. Such cases have happened, which is why having applications that are independent of the operating system is considered a preventive measure. (Unfortunately, a close relation between an application and the operating system often makes the application graphically more attractive and easier to use. Software makers know that software users generally prefer ease of use of software to security, which is why so much vulnerable software is made all the time and not just by Microsoft.)

■   Computers can perform complex tasks, but such tasks require complex programs. Without a program, a computer can do nothing. Programs are steadily becoming more complex and powerful, but are still no substitute for human intelligence. Computer users know from experience that programs that feature complex behavior and that perform complex tasks automatically tend to have more bugs (and bugs that are more mysterious) than simple programs. We are now aware that complex, automatic programs also have more security holes than simple programs. Thus, a simple program that doesn't try to perform complex tasks automatically but stops from time to time and asks for guidance from the user is a preventive measure.

◇ **Exercise 6.5:** Use your experience to show an example of an automated program or process that fails under certain conditions.

■   Those who are part of an organization sometimes get news, rumors, and warnings about viruses from buddies in the office or elsewhere. Those should be forwarded to the person in charge of security for confirmation. This is a security measure that prevents the spread of hoaxes (Section 6.5).

■   Email attachments constitute a security risk and are discussed in Section 2.4. Obviously, an attachment in an email message from an unknown person should not be opened, but what about an attachment in a message from a familiar, trusted person? It is common to find that your best friend has sent you an email message with a poisoned attachment, but it is always (almost always?) done unwittingly. A virus invading a computer may look for an address book and use it to mail copies of itself as attachments to all the addressees in that book. Therefore, if you don't expect an attachment, if the message itself doesn't explain the attachment, and if the attachment doesn't seem necessary, don't open it. Be alert. A message may also pretend to come from a bank or a merchant, asking to click on a URL to verify an account or personal information. Again, this may be a trick for malware to penetrate your computer. This advice is mentioned elsewhere in the book, but is repeated here because it is a preventive measure.

■   A similar point is to be suspicious of files (mostly executable files, but also data files that can have macros) downloaded from newsgroups, from hacking/cracking Web servers, or from new, unfamiliar Web sites that offer useful and inexpensive software. Even a file that seems unexecutable, such as an image in JPEG format or an audio file in mp3 format, may turn out to be an infected executable program disguised as innocuous data. Even a real JPEG image may contain executable parts (Section 2.11) and may therefore be infected by a virus.

■   Even a program sent by a trusted source may be infected. Recall that a virus may lay dormant for a long time before it releases its payload. This raises the chance of the virus being discovered before it does any damage, but some virus writers may take this "risk" in the hope that a quite virus may penetrate into many computers and may therefore prove very lethal when it finally wakes up. A friend may send you a free and beautiful screen saver that works fine for a few months, then turns out to be a time bomb and inflicts much damage to both yours and your friend's computers.

⋄ **Exercise 6.6:** What is the most popular type of software?

■   Many applications may benefit from a macro facility, but virtually all known macro viruses (Section 2.10) infect data files for Microsoft Word and Microsoft Excel, two components of the well-known Microsoft Office suite. Such files should be considered potentially dangerous, especially when received in email. Whenever possible, a macro facility should be turned off. A somewhat safer alternative is to use `.rtf` format instead of `.doc` and `.csv` instead of `.xls`, because these formats don't use macros.

■   Anti-virus software can scan mounted disks and flash memories, so it should be used as a preventive measure. Needless to say (but nevertheless it is said here and also early in this section), such software has to have the latest update, and this should be checked each time the software is run. In an organization, there is one person in charge of updating anti-virus software, but the final responsibility for this lies with the end user.

■   A firewall (Section 7.6) can stop viruses and is therefore a preventive measure. Large organizations tend to have a hardware-based firewall, whereas a home user may only afford a personal firewall. The latter type is software based and may, in principle, be compromised by malware. In either case, a firewall complements anti-virus software and both should be used as preventive measures.

■   Older personal computers had to be booted from floppy disks. Later models had hard disks with the operating system installed, so booting from a floppy became an option. Newer versions of operating systems did not fit on a floppy, but it was still possible to include them on a zip disk and boot from it. Current operating systems are too big for floppies and zip disks, so they are installed from CDs or DVDs. Anyone using an older computer (and an old operating system) should consider disabling booting from a floppy disk as a preventive measure. Any removable storage devices with operating system software should be write protected whenever possible.

■   Two advanced and popular email programs, Outlook and Outlook Express, are particularly vulnerable to email infection by malware and are known to be the source of many infections. One reason for this is their use of the Windows script host (WSH). A possible preventive measure is to use a different application or even a different platform, such as a Macintosh or UNIX, to communicate by email. Those who need the sophisticated features offered by the two applications above should check periodically for security updates and patches from Microsoft, available at [MSoffice 05].

■   Most operating systems support file names with extensions. The extension (often three letters) associates the file with an application and serves as handy identification. Sometimes, the operating system hides the extension in the assumption that users know their files and prefer to deal with short names, but as a security measure, users should ask to see these extensions. A conflict between a file's extension and its icon can serve as a red flag to raise suspicion, as are files with two extensions or with many spaces preceding the extension.

■   Another important preventive measure is to have regular backups of all important files. Backups are discussed on page 143 and are also the topic of the next section.

Strictly speaking, backing up files is not a preventive measure, but it is related to preventive measures because it makes it so much easier to recover from an attack.

6.4 Backups and Such

At home, the owner of a personal computer should make sure that the main disk is backed up periodically (Figure 6.1) and that virus-detection software is installed, has the latest virus update, and is executed on a regular basis. An important point to keep in mind is that a dormant virus may lie in the backup disk. Once a virus is discovered, the backup disk should be scanned and disinfected before it is used for data recovery. Because of the destructive power of viruses, there are companies (such as [Symantec 04], Computer Associates [CA 04], and [McAfee 04]) and organizations such as [Wild List 04], [NIST 04], [CERT 04], and [EICAR 04] that specialize in virus information, detection, and elimination. Those bodies put out information on any new virus within hours of its detection. A computer user should therefore keep a watchful eye on virus news (on television, in newspapers, or in announcements on the Internet). Just knowing that a new virus has appeared and how it propagates can help users avoid contamination.

Figure 6.1: Backing Up a Computer To Disks.

(A word about the importance of early virus detection. A typical virus propagates exponentially. Once a virus has installed itself in a host computer, it may send many copies of itself to other computers before being detected and deleted. Each of those copies may in turn infect many computers before it is discovered. The case of binary propagation is especially simple and easy to analyse. Suppose that a virus starts from one computer and sends out just two copies of itself. The first generation of this virus infects two computers, the second generation infects four computers, and the nth generation infects 2^n computers. For $n = 10$, there will be $2^0 + 2^1 + \cdots + 2^{10} \approx 2050$ infected computers, although some of them may be infected more than once, and for $n = 20$ there will be more than two million infected computers.)

In a place of work, where data destroyed by a virus may cripple a company, there should be an experienced person or group (a virus czar, a crisis team, or a help desk) always available for emergencies. This person, who can be an employee or an outside consultant, should visit the computer facility periodically and make sure that (1) all the computers have up-to-date virus-protection software and (2) all the employees know where to turn to when a virus is discovered or its presence suspected. Versions of the following story circulate in many offices:

John discovered a virus in his office computer. The virus expert was called and took half a day to clean the computer and recover the data. The following day, the same virus came back. After spending several days fighting this virus, it was discovered that John himself unknowingly infected his computer immediately after each cleaning. He had a game that he liked to play during lunch break. His wife, a student, brought the game from college on an infected disk. Every time john inserted the disk into his office computer, the virus installed itself afresh. (No word as to what happened to John's career.)

An approach to virus control that makes sense in some situations is to write-protect the sensitive parts of the hard disk. A good operating system should make it possible to write-protect individual folders (subdirectories) on the hard disk. All the folders with system files, applications, utilities, and permanent data should be write-protected with a password. Users can generate and save programs and data files outside these folders, to limit the destructive effects of a virus. Such a scheme makes sense in, for example, a university, where there must be large labs with computers for students' use. A careless or malicious student can infect only certain parts of the disk, making it easy for technicians to disinfect the computer. Another example is a post office, where the users are employees that use preinstalled software and don't have to write or install any programs. Limiting the access of those employees does not adversely affect the way they work, but serves to increase security.

A similar approach is to equip each individual computer with a small disk that has only a minimal operating system and the temporary data. The programs and permanent data that the users need are downloaded from a central server. The server can be maintained and secured by experienced technicians, which reduces its chance of infection, but this approach may be too slow for places where many computers are used all the time and speed is essential.

Fighting computer viruses must start with a policy for detecting them. A computer user should be aware that any odd behavior of the computer may indicate a virus (although experience shows that most cases of odd computer behavior are due to software bugs, human errors, or hardware failures). A home user noticing unusual behavior may not have much choice and may have to resort to virus-protection software, but at work, users should be trained to call for help immediately. A security expert may be able to decide in a short time whether a problem is due to a virus and solve it with a minimum of interruption to normal work. Here are examples of odd, unusual computer behavior that should raise suspicion (but bear in mind that future viruses may be written by people who have read this list, and so may feature completely different types of behavior).

■   A file has a "time stamp" indicating the last time it has been modified. If an old file turns out to have a recent modification date, it should be cause for suspicion. The length of a program (executable) file should normally stay the same. Any unexplainable change in the length of such a file is also a reason to suspect that a virus attached itself to the file.

■   A familiar program suddenly slows down or takes longer than usual to start.

■   Simple tasks require excessive disk access.

■   A program tries to write to a CD (which is normally read only).

■   Programs suddenly indicate less available memory than in the past.

■   The computer restarts itself suddenly, for no apparent reason, or requests permission to restart, citing an official-looking but unfamiliar reason.

■   Unusual or irrelevant messages are displayed on the monitor screen.

■   There is suddenly an unusual amount of network traffic. This is easy to detect when a modem (telephone or cable) is used. The lights on the modem flicker quickly, indicating heavy network traffic, while legitimate programs run slow.

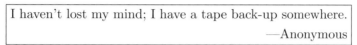

I haven't lost my mind; I have a tape back-up somewhere.
—Anonymous

Vaccines. Someone thinking about virus eradication may come up with the following idea. A virus normally checks a file before infecting it, looking for its (the virus's) signature to avoid secondary infection (Section 2.12). If the signature of a virus is known, we may embed it in all the files in our computer, which will fool the virus. This is the concept of a vaccine. It's a simple concept, but it fails in practice for the following reasons:

■   There are many known viruses and new ones appear all the time. It is practically impossible to embed so many signatures in a file, and the signatures may even conflict and destroy each other. It is also infeasible to embed the signatures of new viruses in all the executable files in a given computer and still hope for all the programs to execute correctly.

■   Some viruses don't leave a signature and simply reinfect any given file again and again.

■   In extreme cases, vaccination may do more damage than the virus itself. Imagine a virus that infects only small programs and doesn't inflict serious damage. Small programs can be vaccinated against this virus simply by making them large, but this occupies disk space and may interfere with any automatic updates to the programs in question. Before such vaccination is done, its bad side effects should be compared with the potential damage done by the virus.

■   The signatures of different viruses may conflict, so vaccinating against one virus may expose a file up to infection by another virus. For example, the signature of virus A may be to set the byte at position x in the infected file to 12_{16}. When A is discovered and is analysed, the vaccination expert updates the vaccination software by changing this byte to 12_{16} in order to fool virus A. A while later, a new virus, B is discovered, whose signature is to set the byte at position x to 00_{16}. The expert, who has already forgotten about virus A, modifies the vaccination software by changing byte x to 00_{16}, thereby rendering all files open to infection by A.

Self repair. Error-detecting and error-correcting codes are currently very common and can be very powerful. They are included in many digital devices, not just computers and disk files, and their use is often transparent to the user. A common example is CDs and DVDs. These storage devices have a small physical size and large capacities, so the bits recorded on them must be physically extremely small. Both CDs and DVDs are read by reflecting laser light, and it is obvious that even the smallest scratch on the plastic surface of the device affects the reflection of light. A sophisticated error-correcting code is therefore a must for such devices, and the codes used on CDs and DVDs can automatically correct errors in thousands of consecutive bits. The details of such codes are outside the scope of this book, but they are based on a simple principle, namely *increased redundancy*. When a channel code is added to data, it always increases the number of bits. Stated another way, reliable data always has more bits than strictly necessary.

The principle of correcting errors through increased redundancy can be carried out to virus detection and elimination. Imagine a program that has redundant bits, so it can check itself every time it is launched and even correct many errors in itself. When such a program gets infected by a virus, the next check will detect a problem. If the problem cannot be corrected automatically, the program will notify the user and will quit.

Such a self-correcting program seems a good weapon in the war against viruses, and it is, but only up to a point. Once virus writers learn of this trend, they may counter it in various ways, some of which are listed here:

- The obvious problem is that the virus writer will discover how the redundancy was generated (the formula or the algorithm to compute the redundant bits). Once this is known, the virus can embed itself in a program and recreate the redundancy. An example of adding redundancy is a CRC and the discussion on page 79 shows how knowledge of the CRC formula can defeat this simple protection.

- A virus may be written specifically to modify the redundant part of a program in a way that will infect the program. Instead of being defeated by the redundancy, such a virus exploits it. An example is the `mirror` utility for the PC that creates a copy of any file with reversed bits. The idea is to check the integrity of a program by comparing it to its mirror. If the program file and its mirror are not exact complements, the operating system corrects the program by replacing it with the mirror of its mirror. A virus writer noticed this technique and wrote a virus that infected the mirror by embedding a mirror image of the virus in the mirror file. When the program was checked, it was different from its mirror, and when it was recreated from the mirror, the result was an infected program.

- Even in cases where the virus knows (or suspects) only that redundancy is used to protect a program, the virus can defeat this protection. It can defeat the protection even if it doesn't know the precise way redundancy is included in the program. Before the virus embeds itself in a program A, it copies A and saves the copy. The copy can be saved either as a separate file (perhaps invisible) or by appending it to the infected A. The virus then infects A. When the infected A is launched, the virus is the first to execute and it does the following: (1) It infects some other programs. (2) It performs its damage (payload). (3) It replaces the infected copy of A with the saved copy and deletes the saved copy. (4) It launches A. When A is launched, it checks itself, but it detects no problem, because this is the clean copy of A. When A completes, it is clean, but the virus (which has already infected some other programs) can infect it again in the future.

◇ **Exercise 6.7:** How can the virus reinfect A as soon as A finishes? (See also exercise 2.21.)

Limit permissions. Most viruses infect executable programs, so it seems that it should be enough to limit the permissions of executable programs. Most executable programs don't modify themselves, so if file A is an executable program, it should have only execute permission but no read or write permissions. If a file has no write permission, the operating system won't allow anyone, even the file's owner, to modify it in any way. This simple precaution can defeat many viruses, but can itself be defeated by a virus that has system (or owner) privileges, since they are able to change the file's access permissions.

Software fault-tolerance. The concept of fault tolerance is to have several copies of the same hardware circuit or the same software program. When one copy fails, another copy is immediately used instead. It is normally easy to tell when a piece of hardware doesn't work, but when a computer program fails, it often simply generates a wrong result. Thus, fault tolerance in software requires at least three copies of a program. A special voting circuit compares the three copies, and if one copy differs, it is rejected. Imagine three computers executing three copies of the same program. If one program is infected, the voting circuit will reject its output. This is good protection against viruses, but it is expensive because it requires three computers and the voting circuit. Thus, it can be used only in cases where lives depend on the results produced by the programs.

In principle, a virus can infect all three copies of the program, so this technique does not provide perfect protection, but basic security steps that limit sharing can reduce the chance of such multiple infection significantly.

◇ **Exercise 6.8:** What if all three copies produce different results?

A cryptographic checksum. Normally, a checksum or a CRC is enough to guarantee the integrity of a data file. If the file is modified as a result of data corruption, its new CRC will differ from the original CRC. The discussion on page 79, however, shows that a virus can embed itself in a file and change bytes of data until the new CRC of the infected file equals the original CRC. A cryptographic checksum (or CCS, [Cohen 87]) is an improvement over a simple checksum or CRC. The idea is to encrypt file F with an encryption key k and compute a checksum S on the encrypted file. The encrypted file can then be deleted, but the triplet (F, k, S) should be saved and the key k should be kept secret.

Now imagine a hacker who has discovered F and S and wants to infect F without modifying its CCS. The hacker has first to find the key k, then construct an infected file F' whose CCS under k will be the same S. If the encryption is strong, the only way for the hacker to find k is to encrypt the original file F under every possible key, compute the checksum, and compare it to S. If the number of possible keys (the key space) is very large, this process is too slow. It will tie up the entire computer and will raise suspicion. Even under ideal conditions, such a brute-force approach may take many thousands of years.

In the unlikely case where the hacker has found the correct key k, he still faces the problem of modifying file F in such a way that its new CCS under key k will be the original S. This problem doesn't seem to have any efficient solution. A brute force approach where many tests are run is again too slow to be time effective.

6.5 Hoaxes

The standard dictionary definition of a hoax stresses its humorous or mocking aspects and may go like this: "A hoax is an attempt to deceive, especially with a joke or by mockery or mischief. It's a humorous or mischievous deception."

Virus hoaxes are reports of nonexistent viruses. They are propagated as email messages that include some of the following:

■   Announce the discovery of an undetectable, highly-destructive new virus.

■   Warn users not to read emails with a particular subject line such as "Join the Crew" or "Budweiser Frogs."

■   Pretend that the warning was issued by a well-known security organization, ISP, or government agency, most often IBM, Microsoft, AOL, or the federal communications commission (FCC) in the United States.

■   Make a fantastic claim about the payload of a new virus. For example, a hoax called "a moment of silence" claims "no program needs to be exchanged for a new computer to be infected by this virus."

■   Employ nonsensical technical jargon to describe the effects of the virus. For example, a hoax called "good times" says that the virus can put the CPU into "an nth-complexity infinite binary loop;" a nonexistent condition.

■   Urge readers to forward the warning to others (such a hoax is known as a chain letter).

We already know that viruses can be destructive, but even a hoax about a nonexistent virus can do harm. A full treatment of hoaxes and their effects can be found in [vmyths 05] (make sure you read at least [Rosenberger 05]), but here are the main reasons why hoaxes are bad.

■   Hoaxes can be as disruptive and costly as a genuine virus.

■   Users tend to believe a hoax, overreact to it, and forward hoax messages to everyone on their mailing list. This can create a temporary deluge of email which overloads mail servers and causes delays in delivering mail and even crashes. The damage may be equivalent to that done by a real virus, with the difference that the hoaxer doesn't have to design, implement, and test any code.

■   An organization that receives a hoax may also overreact and take drastic action, such as temporarily closing down a mail server or shutting down its entire network. This cripples communications and adversely affects normal business at least as effectively as a real virus, again with very little effort on the part of the hoaxer.

■   Virus experts who deal with real viruses and other threats may get distracted by a hoax and waste precious time and effort trying to track it.

■   A hoax, like other rumors, can persist for a long time before it dies off, and its cumulative effect (wasting users' time and causing pain and suffering) may be out of proportion to the work needed to start it.

■   A hoax can inspire new viruses (the opposite is also true). The "good time" hoax, for example, was followed by a real "good time" virus (also called GT-Spoof).

■   A hoax may turn out to be real. This causes psychological damage followed by real physical damage. An example is the email messages with the subject line "Rush-Killer virus alert" that started circulating on 1 April 2000. They warned of viruses that dial 911 (the United States emergency telephone number) and urged readers to forward the warning to others. The messages seemed like a hoax, but it later turned out that the virus was real.

Most people who claim to speak with authority about computer viruses have little or no genuine expertise. Some virus experts describe it as "False Authority Syndrome"— the person feels competent to discuss viruses because of his job title, or because of his expertise in another computer field, or simply because he knows how to use a computer.

—From [vmyths 05]

Chain letters. An electronic chain letter is an email message that urges readers to forward it to others. There are four main types of chain letters as follows:

■   Hoaxes. A chain letter may warn readers about a terrorist attack, a scam, or a new computer security threat. Some of these hoaxes can be classified as myths, but all should be ignored by conscientious readers.

■   Fake freebies. A chain letter may promise gifts (such as free flights, free cell phones, or cash awards) to those who forward it. Again, the best policy is to delete such email.

■   Petitions. A chain letter may ask the reader to sign a petition (often of a political nature or against proposed legislation) and forward the letter. Some of these letters may refer to genuine causes, but many are for or against old topics that have expired. If you want to become an activist, please be considerate and don't do it by sending a chain letter email.

■   Jokes and pranks. It seems that some people have nothing better to do than waste others' time. An example of a joke letter is the "Internet cleaning" chain message which claimed that the Internet would be closed for maintenance on 1 April (and asked to be forwarded).

Chain letters are more a nuisance than a security threat, but they waste our time, spread misinformation, and distract us from more important activities, while also generating much junk email traffic that slows down mail servers.

Hoaxes and chain letters are nasty and may cause damage, which is why this section concludes with a short list of points that can help avoid hoaxes and nip chain letters in the bud.

■   An organization should have a clear policy on virus hoaxes. The policy should be distributed to all employees and should state (among other things) that all virus warnings received by email (even those that came from a legitimate source such as an anti-virus vendor or from a trusted party) should be forwarded to the person responsible for computer security (typically the chief security officer, or CSO) and to no one else. This person will check all virus warnings and decide which ones are real.

■   Any security-conscious computer user should be kept informed about hoaxes. Information is available in many Web sites of organizations that are active in the security area. An example of such a site is [sophos 05].

■   Don't forward chain email letters even if they offer money, fame, gifts, or useful information. This obvious point is unfortunately disregarded by some receivers, to the detriment of us all.

■   When receiving unsolicited email don't trust any links in it, even if they seem familiar and legitimate. If you want to take advantage of offers from an organization, find its URL, type it manually, and send a message (instead of responding to the offer) to verify the offer.

Back up my hard drive? How do I put it in reverse?
—Anonymous

7
Network Security

7.1 Internet Vulnerabilities

A network vulnerability is an inherent weakness in the design, implementation, or use of a hardware component or a software routine. A vulnerability invites attacks and makes the network susceptible to threats.

A threat is anything that can disrupt the operation of the network. A threat can even be accidental or an act of nature, but threats are mostly intentional. A threat can damage the network, slow it down, or make it unavailable. Any type of rogue software represents a threat.

An attack is a specific approach employed to exploit a known vulnerability. A passive attack is designed to monitor and record network activity in an attempt to collect information to be used later in an active attack. Examples of passive attacks are packet sniffing (page 205) and traffic analysis. Passive attacks are difficult to detect.

An active attack tries to damage a network or its operation. Such attacks are easier to detect, but are also more damaging.

The following sections describe the most important threats and attacks that actually occurred on the Internet. They do not include viruses, Trojan horses, and the other types of rogue software that were described in earlier chapters.

> Give a person a fish and you feed them for a day; teach that person to use the Internet and they won't bother you for weeks.
>
> —Anonymous

7.2 Port Scanning

When two programs on different computers exchange data, all the data packets sent between the programs have (among other specifications) the same port number. Accessing a network opens a port and is similar to opening a door. This makes ports especially important for network security. When data packets arrive at a computer from different sources, each stream of packets uses a port number. A port is identified by a 16-bit integer and there can be up to $2^{16} - 1 = 65,535$ ports.

There are three classes of ports, well known (0 through 1023), registered (1024 through 49151), and dynamic/private (49152 through 65535). The well-known ports are assigned by [IANA port 04] and are normally used by operating system processes. Some examples are FTP (port 21), TELNET (port 23), SMTP (port 25), and HTTP (port 80). Registered ports are typically used by user applications (as opposed to operating system processes) when they have to contact a server, but such ports can also identify named services that have been registered by a third party. Dynamic/private ports are used by user applications, but their use is rare. Such ports do not have any meaning outside of any particular TCP connection.

A port scanner is a program that listens to data arriving at and departing from certain ports on a computer. Port scanning has legitimate uses in managing networks, but is also used heavily by hackers to gather information that identifies open doors to the computer. Information collected by port scanners is used to identify operating system utilities installed in the computer, and exploit known vulnerabilities in those utilities in order to break into the computer. Port scanners are implemented by sophisticated hackers who make them available on the Internet.

In many cases, it is easy to detect the activity of a port scanner simply by checking the log files that are continuously updated by the operating system. Once a port scanner is detected, its transmissions can be traced back to their origin and sometimes stopped. However, the mere activity of port scanning is not illegal. Newer port scanners exploit a vulnerability associated with SYN packets and half-open connections. Those are much harder to detect, because half-open connections are logged by the operating system.

There are several types of port scanners as follows:

- Vanilla: The scanner attempts to connect to all I/O ports.

- Strobe: A specialized scan looking only for certain services to exploit.

- Fragmented packets: The scanner sends fragments of packets. Such fragments can sometimes get through certain packet filters in a firewall.

- UDP: The scanner looks for open UDP ports.

- Sweep: The scanner connects to the same port on several (even many) computers.

- FTP bounce: The scanner goes through an FTP server (to appear legitimate).

- Stealth scan: The scanner partly disables the log service of the operating system, so it (the operating system) can no longer record the scanner's activities.

Web site [dslreports 04] offers a free service looking for port scanners.

Nmap (Network Mapper) from [insecure 04] is a free open source utility for network exploration and security auditing. Among other checks, it looks for port scanners.

7.3 Spoofs

The term spoof means to pretend to be someone else, to falsify one's identity, or to cover tracks. It is no wonder that various spoofing methods are used by hackers to gain access or to obtain information. This section describes various techniques for spoofing over a network.

IP spoofing. A computer may be protected from attack by restricting the IP addresses that may send it data. A router may have a list of IP numbers and it allows only data from these numbers to enter the computer. A hacker who has this list may spoof the router by sending data that appears to have come from a legitimate IP address. Someone who doesn't have the list may discover an allowed IP number by sending the computer data packets with consecutive IP numbers until a packet gains entry to the computer.

Defending against spoofing is never perfect, because it involves built-in weaknesses in the TCP protocol. However, a full understanding of the problem, combined with a few simple precautions, can reduce this threat. The defense involves two main techniques as follows:

- Filtering. If the computer is part of a local area network, the network has a range of IP addresses. When data is sent outside a local network (uploading), the filter software at the router should block any source IP outside the range of the local network. This prevents someone in the local network from sending spoofed data outside the local network. When data is received (download), the filter should block any packets with source IPs that are within the range of the local network.

- Encryption and Authentication. There are Internet protocols that specify the details of data encryption and how to authenticate messages. While imperfect, such protocols may help to eliminate simple IP spoofing attacks.

Sequence number spoofing. The TCP protocol specifies the use of sequence numbers within data packets. Each data byte has a sequence number, and the receiver must acknowledge the sequence number of the last contiguous byte it has received. When TCP connection between two computers (server and client) is established, the server selects an initial sequence number (ISN) and communicates it to the client by means of the three-step protocol. The ISN becomes the sequence number of the first byte of the first packet. If the packet contains N data bytes, then the last byte has sequence number $ISN + N - 1$. Thus, the first data byte of the next packet has sequence number $ISN + N$ and this number is included by the server in the packet's TCP header. For each packet received, the client sends an acknowledge where, among other items of information, it indicates the sequence number of the last *contiguous* byte it has received. This tells the server how much of the data has been received by the client as one contiguous block.

As an example, suppose that the ISN selected by the server is 1000 and each packet is 100 bytes long. The sequence numbers of the packets sent by the server would therefore be 1000, 1100, 1200, 1300, and so on. Assume that packet 1300 is taking a different route and is delayed or even lost on its way to the client (Figure reffg:SNspoofa). The client has received up to byte 1299, so all its acknowledge packets from now on, until it receives packet 1300, are going to contain sequence number 1299 (Figure reffg:SNspoofb). After the server has received several acknowledgements with 1299, it resends packet 1300, followed by 1400, 1500, and so on (Figure reffg:SNspoofc). If the server has resent packets of data several times and it still receives incomplete acknowledgements, it stops sending, closes the connection, and signals to the user application that the connection had broken.

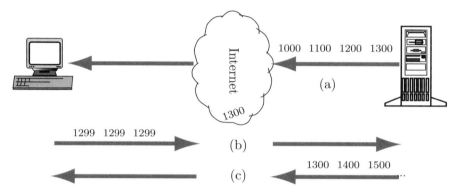

Figure 7.1: ISNs and Acknowledgments.

Sequence number spoofing is the case where a hacker can compute or guess the next set of sequence numbers in a data transmission. The hacker can, in such a case, send false packets of data and they will be received with full trust by the client program in the receiving computer. Good defense against this kind of attack is to encrypt the data. If the hacker doesn't know the encryption key, any false data inserted will not decrypt properly and will therefore be useless to the owner (who can request a retransmission) as well as to the hacker (who can try to corrupt the next transmission).

It's hard to believe that someone will go to such trouble just to break into someone else's computer, but many cases of IP spoofing are known and it is easy to locate detailed descriptions of some on the Internet. Perhaps the most famous case is that of Kevin Mitnick.

On Christmas Day 1994, a hacker first probed a set of computers owned by Tsutomu Shimomura, a scientist and computer security professional in the San Diego area. Once vulnerability was discovered, an attack was launched employing IP spoofing. The hacker managed to break into the computers and steal files. True to being a security expert, Shimomura kept detailed logs on the use of his computers in his absence. Once back from his vacation, the logs told him of the attack. The stolen files were tracked by the FBI to `toad.com`, to computers in Marin county, north of San Francisco, to Denver, San Jose, and finally to Kevin Mitnick, a hacker in Raleigh, North Carolina. After spending five years in jail, Mitnick was released on January 21, 2000. The details, as told by Shimomura, can be found at [takedown 04].

Session hijacking. This type of attack occurs when a hacker gains privileged access to a network device, such as a router, that serves as a gateway between the server and client. The hacker can, in such a case, use IP spoofing to take over the entire session of data transmission and send any information, rogue programs, and corrupt data to the client's computer.

Most authentication in the TCP/IP protocol takes place at the time the connection is established, and this can be exploited by a hacker to gain access to a machine by, for example, using source-routed IP packets. This allows a hacker at node A on the network to participate in a data exchange between B and C by placing himself in the middle and routing the IP packets to pass through his machine.

An alternative is to use "blind" hijacking, where the hacker guesses the responses of the computers at B and C. The hacker can, in such a case, send a command and cannot see the response, but can guess the response to many commands. A typical command is to set a password allowing access to B and C from somewhere else on the network.

DNS. A domain name server (DNS) is a computer used specifically for networking. It has a dictionary with IP addresses and the corresponding URLs. When a computer wants to send data, it has to prepare packets with the IP address of the receiving computer. The human user normally knows the URL (a meaningful string), so the sending application has to connect to the DNS first, send it the URL, and receive the corresponding IP address. Only then can the application send data with the proper IP and TCP headers. This is why, when we want to browse a certain URL, the browser sometimes displays the message "looking for..." for a few seconds.

◇ **Exercise 7.1:** Each of us has certain URLs that we browse often, yet the browser has to look up the IP address of a site each time. explain why.

One threat related to DNS is man in the middle (MIM). A hacker may register a domain name, such as `aple.com`, that is similar to an existing popular URL. When a user mistypes `aple` instead of `apple`, the browser receives from the DNS computer the IP address of the hacker's site, and connects to that site. Now the hacker is in control. His site can display information similar to that displayed by the real site, while also sending its own malicious software. The hacker can even retrieve from `apple.com` the web pages the user wants, then forward them, perhaps modified, to the user (Figure 7.2).

Another option is for the hacker to insert himself "inline" between a user and a Web site using a sniffing program to intercept the exchange of data between them.

A common MIM attack involves denial-of-service (DoS) against a network node by flooding it with messages and so preventing it from responding to legitimate users and visitors. This attack can be directed either against a server computer to force it to crash, or against the network connection to cause heavy packet loss.

Another threat related to DNS is DNS poisoning. In the past, the most common DNS software was the Berkeley Internet name daemon (BIND). Early versions of this software had weaknesses that made it easy for a hacker to modify the IP addresses associated with any URLs. Once a hacker changes the IP associated with, say `apple.com`. Anyone trying to connect to that URL will be connected to the hacker's site, with potentially disastrous results.

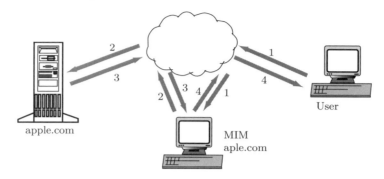

Figure 7.2: Illustrating Man in the Middle.

A well-known example of DNS poisoning is the defacing, in 2001, of the Web site of RSA Security [RSAsecurity 04]. The anonymous hijacker rerouted visitors from RSAsecurity.com to a fake site that looked like the RSA site but was different in significant ways. Anyone who noticed the differences in the Web site, assumed that RSA Security, an important developer of encryption techniques and products, had been compromised. In fact, only the DNS was attacked and corrupted.

A hacker preparing a fake site to lure unsuspecting visitors can make his site look identical to the original site, but with modified, redirected links. Anyone following a link may find themselves redirected to a pornographic site, or unintentionally loading a virus disguised as an image.

Imagine a customer trying to buy a piece of equipment online. The online merchant uses the secure socket layer (SSL, Section 12.10) protocol to encrypt the transaction. A hacker places himself, as a man in the middle, between the customer and the merchant, intercepting all communications. The hacker cannot decrypt the messages, but can record them and replay the customer's messages to the merchant once a day over the next ten days. The hacker does not modify the customer's messages (he does not behave as an impostor), not does he pretend to be the customer, yet the customer may receive ten identical pieces of the equipment with ten bills (or with one large bill). This kind of hassle is referred to as a replay attack.

The following is a typical case of spoofing that exploits a vulnerability in the popular Safari Web browser. It was discovered and published in late 2004 by Secunia [secunia 04], a company that monitors vulnerabilities in thousands of software products

---

```
Safari Window Injection Vulnerability
Secunia Advisory:  SA13252
Release Date:  2004-12-08
Critical:  Moderately critical
Impact:  Spoofing
Where:  From remote
Solution Status:  Unpatched
Software:  Safari 1.x
Select a product and view a complete list of all Patched/Unpatched Secunia
advisories affecting it.

Description: Secunia Research has reported a vulnerability in Safari, which can
be exploited by malicious people to spoof the content of websites.
```

The problem is that a website can inject content into another site's window if
the target name of the window is known. This can e.g. be exploited by a malicious
website to spoof the content of a pop-up window opened on a trusted website.

This is related to: SA11978

Secunia has constructed a test, which can be used to check if your browser is
affected by this issue:

http://secunia.com/multiple_browsers_window_injection_vulnerability_test/

The vulnerability has been confirmed in Safari version 1.2.4. Other versions may
also be affected.

Solution: Do not browse untrusted sites while browsing trusted sites.
Provided and/or discovered by: Secunia Research
Original Advisory:
http://secunia.com/secunia_research/2004-13/advisory/
Other References: SA11978:
http://secunia.com/advisories/11978/

7.4 Spam

We are all familiar with spam. Spam is unwanted, unsolicited email sent in bulk to
many unwilling recipients. Most of it is commercial advertising for dubious products,
get-rich-quick schemes, or quasi-legal or health services. Current spam levels (in early
2005) are estimated at 75% of all email and are growing.

Spam is named after the 12-oz cans of spicy ham made by the Hormel company
since 1937 [spam 04]. By itself, spam is nuisance, not a security concern, but it can
be exploited for a DoS attack. A central computer dedicated to sending and receiving email for a large organization can be attacked by sending its many users massive
quantities of identical email messages. This consumes valuable network bandwidth, it
overloads the CPU, eats up disk space on the email server, and can cause it to crash (by
overflowing some data structure) or freeze (by keeping the CPU permanently occupied
with receiving, logging, sending, and forwarding the spam messages).

⋄ **Exercise 7.2:** Use your experience with spam to list products often offered in spam
messages.

> Use of the term "spam" was adopted as a result of the Monty Python skit in which
> our SPAM meat product was featured. In this skit, a group of Vikings sang a chorus
> of "spam, spam, spam. . ." in an increasing crescendo, drowning out other conversa-
> tion. Hence, the analogy applied because UCE (unsolicited commercial email) was
> drowning out normal discourse on the Internet.
>
> —From http://www.spam.com/ci/ci_in.htm

It may come as a surprise to many that most spam messages are sent from computers (mostly private personal computers on high-speed cable or DSL networks) that have
been infected by special strains of viruses. Such a virus hijacks the infected computer

and turns it into a *spam proxie* (a special case of zombie). A major spammer may at any time control thousands of spam proxies that serve him obediently and send millions of spam messages anonymously (Figure 7.3). The sobig virus (technically a worm, see year 2003 in Appendix B) was the first specimen of malicious software designed to create spam proxies, but similar viruses (mostly variants of the original sobig) are implemented and released all the time and manage to infect tens of thousands of computers worldwide every week. The virus installs special software known as spamware that takes over the computer (essentially hijacking it) and handles the distribution of spam.

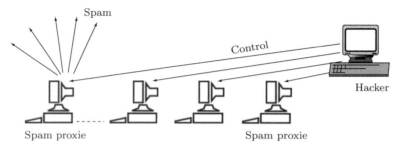

Figure 7.3: An Army of Spam Proxies.

Once a hacker has released such a virus and has obtained a fresh army of spam proxies, he may try to sell them to spammers through special online forums that are often closed to the general public. URLs such as `Specialham.com` and `Spamforum.biz`, which are hosted mostly in Russia and China (but also in Florida), may not look very useful or interesting to a casual visitor or even to security-conscious persons such as readers of this book, but are familiar and very useful to spammers. These sites also carry advertisements for bullet-proof hosting (ISPs, most of them Chinese, that allow spam) and allow spammers to exchange news and information. The news is mostly about steps taken by ISPs and law makers and enforcers in various countries to make the lives of spammers more difficult. Much information is offered on ISPs and networks that close their eyes to spam in return for the high revenues obtained from spammers.

Security workers and experts also visit these sites often and make certain items of information available to the public to illustrate the seriousness of the spam menace. For example, [spamhauslasso 05] has a list of the top 10 spam-friendly ISPs and shows that most of them are American.

◇ **Exercise 7.3:** Browse the [spamhauslasso 05] site to locate the latest list.

Much of the spamware currently in use is written by the Russian programmers and spammers Ruslan Ibragimov and Alexey Panov. The former is known for his **Send-Safe** proxy spamware and the latter is the creator of **direct mail sender** (DMS), a spamware package. It is known that new waves of a sobig-like viruses are normally followed by many discoveries of these spamware packages in hijacked personal computers.

The **Send-Safe** program has a feature that speeds up the sending of spam and makes it harder to identify its source. This feature, proudly titled "use proxy MX" by its creator, makes the spam messages appear as if they came directly from the ISP's mail server instead of from the sending (spam proxy) PC. This troubling behavior has been noticed by major ISPs such as AOL, Time Warner Cable, and Earthlink, yet `Send-Safe` is still available for sale (for \$50–500, depending on the number of messages sent) at [send-safe 05], thereby exacerbating the already-serious spam threat.

> Send-Safe is a bulk email software program based on a unique know-how sending technology. It provides real anonymous instant delivery—you can use your regular Internet connection because your IP address will never be shown in the email headers. Send-Safe performs email validation and displays delivery statistics in real time, which gives you the ability to evaluate the quality of your mailing lists. Send-Safe mailing software is free of charge. Our pricing is based on the number of emails you send over a given period of time.
>
> —From `http://www.send-safe.com/`.

An article at [Spamhous 05] titled *should MCI be profiting from knowingly hosting spam gangs?* claims that hosting spam-friendly sites such as [send-safe 05] is routinely practiced by certain communications companies (again, mostly outside the United States) because of the higher premiums paid by spammers.

Is this a case of putting money before morality? This author doesn't have the answer. Do you?

More and more computer installations use spam filters and it is common to hear from a network administrator that his filters identify as spam more than half of all the email received and either delete it or return it. The problem with returning spam email is that the sender may use a fake return address, the address of a third, innocent party, that ends up getting flooded with the spam.

Many Web sites that help users in the fight against spam are listed at [spam abuse 04] (actively engaged in fighting spam since 1996). Another site that accepts spam reports and checks them is [spamcop 05]. Spamhaus is an organization that tracks the Internet's spammers, spam gangs and spam services. It is located at [Spamhaus 05], it provides dependable realtime anti-spam protection for Internet networks, and it works with law enforcement to identify and pursue spammers worldwide.

Spamhaus maintains a register of known spam operations (ROKSO) database with names, addresses, and much information on the top 200 spammers. In early June 2005, the top 10 were the following:

- Alan Ralsky. Operating mostly in Michigan, United States. One of his companies is Additional Benefits, LLC.

- Michael Lindsay. Mostly in California, United States. Companies are iMedia Networks, InterNetco Communications, and GalaxyNET Telecom.

- Andrew Westmoreland with partner Kai Bannon. In Florida and Texas, United States. Operate under Internet Access Group, Inc.

- Jeffrey A. Peters, CEO of JTel.net (or CPU Solutions) Corp. Located in St Petersburg, Florida, Mr. Peters disappeared from the spamming business long enough for his spamhous ROKSO records to expire during 2004, but has reappeared in early 2005.

■ Alexey Panov. Claims to live in Russia. Company is Trendlogic GMBH located in Germany. Email `ckync@ckync.com`.

■ Ivo Ottavio Reali Camargo, operating from his office in Florianopolis, Santa Carina, Brazil.

■ Ruslan Ibragimov. Moscow, Russia. Web address `send-safe.com`.

■ Robert Soloway. Oregon, United States. Aka NIM Corporation and Newport Internet Marketing.

■ Ryan Pitylak, Steve Goudreault, and Mark Trotter. Michigan, United States. Associated with Alan Ralsky.

■ Yambo Financials. The Ukraine. It attempts to look legitimate by renting postal addresses at American and British remailing services and forwarding-phone services.

Table 7.4, based on information compiled by [Spamhaus 05], lists the top ten spam countries and top ten spam service ISPs as of late May 2005. For each country and ISP, the table lists the number of current spam issues.

	Countries		ISPs	
1	United States	2497	mci.com	230
2	China	553	sbc.com	133
3	South Korea	325	crc.net.cn	92
4	Brazil	202	comcast.net	72
5	Russia	182	kornet.net	71
6	Taiwan	169	interbusiness.it	68
7	Canada	161	xo.com	66
8	Japan	139	cncgroup-hl	59
9	Argentina	107	brasiltelecom.net.br	56
10	Italy	103	level3.net	51

Table 7.4: Top Ten Spam Countries and ISPs.

The four main reasons why spam is so bad are as follows:

■ It is easy to send. All that a spammer needs is spam software and a fast Internet connection. Such a connection may send a flood of millions of identical messages a day, while costing only about $100 a day. On the other hand, if any of the millions of receivers spends just 10 seconds on deleting a spam message, the total effort may add up to thousands of hours wasted each day by the receivers. In addition, spam sent as email to cell telephones may cost its receiver money, not just time.

■ Many spam messages ask the user to click on a link to be removed from the mailing list. As many of us have found, clicking to be removed from such a list at best verifies to the spammer that the email address exists and at worst may result in a virus infection. There is also the ethical question of why I should have to get off a mailing list I never asked to be placed on.

■   Spammers tend to use computing resources illegally or even to steal them outright. A spammer may employ an Internet attack to get hold of a PC, then use that PC to forward its spam messages. The receivers see messages coming from the PC, and complain to its owner, often a clueless individual who has no idea of the many security pitfalls lurking in the Internet.

■   Spam is trash. We have all seen messages advertising worthless merchandise and deceptive or fraudulent services.

Case study. Convicted fraudster Alan Ralsky has been spamming for many years. He has grown from a small time operator, under the "Additional Benefits" moniker, to one of the bigger spam houses on the Internet with a gang of fellow morally challenged types working with him to pump out every type of sleazy deal and scam offer into millions of internet users' mailboxes.

Ralsky does both mailings and hosting for people who want to spam. Using dial-up accounts that he buys under aliases or leases from large modem dial-up providers like UUNet, Genuity, etc. He sets up a dummy ISP pretending to have "users" that need dial-up access. This serves his purposes well, as complaints are directed from the large providers to this dummy ISP and are of course thrown away. Due to the big bandwidth purchase, large networks often close an eye to the spamming so as not to lose the revenue.

Nowadays Ralsky hosts "offshore" in China to evade US authorities. But the off-shore hosts are soon blocked and terminated so he's forced to hop from one Chinese provider to the next like most of the spam gangs. One of his tricks in the USA is to host the websites on the same dial-up connections he uses to spam out of. He then uses an auto-updating DNS server to point to a new IP address whenever one of the dial-ups drops carrier or gets cut off. Behind the times as usual, the companies who provide the connection for his DNS servers state that "our Acceptable Use Policy doesn't cover this... we need to talk to our lawyers, etc. etc.," which gives the Ralsky gang several weeks of use.

—From `http://www.spamhaus.org/rokso/evidence.lasso?rokso\_id=ROK1290`.

It helps to know how spammers obtain so many valid email addresses. The main technique is called coregistration and works as follows:

You surf to a Web site that seems interesting, even useful. It offers something, a product or a service, for free or almost free. There are also several checkboxes, some already filled, that promise more information or free membership. When any of these boxes is checked, your email address is sent to the Web site owner who may sell it to a spammer. In the marketing world, this is known as coregistration. Spammers pay for valid email addresses depending on where they came from. Addresses provided by a site promising freebies may be sold for a few pennies each, while those collected by an established business, with many repeat customers whose buying habits are known, may be worth a few dollars each to a spammer. Remind yourself that such a Web site was set and is run for one purpose, to make money. The owner is not trying to help you.

As a simple precaution, try to uncheck all the prechecked boxes before you ask for more information or subscribe to a free service or newsletter. Be selective; don't ask for more free information than you really need. Remember, there is no such thing as a free lunch. If there is a box labeled "check all," don't use it. A simple trick is to display a "submit" checkbox in a prominent place on the monitor, where the user can easily see it, and hide all the prechecked buttons in the unseen area of the Web page, where the viewer has to scroll to see them. This technique is known as "below the fold." Don't fall for such a trick. Before you click on any "submit" button, scroll slowly and examine the rest of the page! Look especially for checkboxes that promise to share your information with partners. Another nasty habit is to automatically enroll a user for a subscription or another service, and forcing them to disenroll explicitly, often at much trouble and waste of time. This is known as a "negative action offer."

A Web site that collects names and addresses has to have a privacy policy where it states whether it shares this information with other parties. If a site does not display such a policy, or if it has no policy at all, avoid it. Naturally, the worst sites promise privacy and break this promise all the time.

It is also a good idea (practiced by this author) to leave immediately when you see the words "free gift." These words are a sure sign of something wrong, because a gift, by its very nature, is free. (A quick Internet search for "free gift" has returned more than two million results.) The phrase "free gift" is a redundancy (exercise 11.2), so it should be suspect. Many free gifts also turn out, upon close scrutiny, to have strings attached or to demand excessive shipping and handling fees. Free offers (freebies) are similar. Most offers of free stuff are leads designed to generate names and addresses that are eventually sold to spammers. To cure you of the desire to receive freebies, search the Internet for the keyword "freebie" and examine some of the more than a million sites you will find.

⋄ **Exercise 7.4:** Yes, go ahead and do this. What are the first three sites?

A similar scam to avoid is contests. Contests are very often used as bait to lure unsuspecting users to submit their names, physical addresses, telephone numbers, and email addresses. Your chance of winning in a real contest are so small, and the number of fake contests is so large, that it's not worth it to participate in them. The same is true for sites offering prizes.

Another important technique of collecting email addresses is harvesting them (some prefer the term scavenging) from the Whois data base at [arin 04]. For example, a search for IP 130.166.2.76 results in information that includes email addresses domainad-min@csun.edu, abuse@csun.edu, and helpdesk@csun.edu. The spammer can simply try all the 2^{32} IP numbers in order, and examine each result automatically, by special software, looking for strings that may be email addresses.

Internet search engines are common and very useful. Such an engine works by crawling the Internet, locating Web pages, and saving and indexing them. Along the same lines, spammers use spambots, software that crawls the Web, examining Web pages looking for email addresses, and harvesting them for future abuse or for sale. An obvious (but alas, not ideal) protection is to obfuscate all email addresses in a Web page. Instead of writing an email address in your Web site in a form such as `leopold.bloom@ulysses.name`, it is better to have something like `leopold bloom at ulysses dot name`.

There are commercial services that provide relief from spam for their members by blocking it. A typical spam-relief service maintains a list of approved senders and asks each of its members to provide their own list of approved senders. The service "sits" between the member and the member's mail server, and the member uses the same email software to send and receive messages. However, the software connects to the service which, in turn, connects to the member's email server. Messages whose senders are in the service's list of approved senders (or in the individual member's list) are let through to the member. For any other messages, the service sends the sender a short challenge message, like the one of Figure 7.5, asking the sender to click (just once) on a certain link. If the sender clicks on the link, he is added to the service's list of approved senders. The idea is that a spammer would not be able or willing to respond to many challenges.

Thus, the member receives email only from approved senders, but also has access to a list of unapproved (blocked) messages. The member can read messages from this list, delete messages, and also remove any sender from the approved list.

Examples of such services are [Knowspam 04], [SpamArrest 04], [MailFrontier 04], and [Mailblocks 04]. Here is how Mailblocks works.

1. Alice opens an account at mailblocks. She copies the address book of her current email software and sends it to mailblocks. This book becomes the kernel of her new protection. All the addresses in this book are whitelisted.

2. Bob sends Alice an email message. If Bob is in Alice's address book, she receives his message. Otherwise, the mailblocks service blocks the message temporarily and sends Bob a challenge message. Figure 7.5 (where the misspellings haven't been corrected) is a real message that this author received on 31 December 2004.

3. If Bob is a bona fide user, he elects to return the challenge to mailblocks, which then forwards his message, as well as any other message, to Alice. (Submitting the challenge requires a click, typing a seven-digit code, and hitting "submit.") If Bob's message was automatically generated, or if he is a spammer who doesn't have the time to answer challenges, his future email to Alice will be automatically deleted until Alice adds him explicitly as a recognized user.

Mailblocks is another obvious example of a trade-off between security and convenience of use. There are similar free services, but they are supported by advertisement, which partly defeats their purpose. (Mailblocks itself has three levels of service where the lowest one is free and is supported by advertising.)

A simple technique to reduce spam is to open several alternate email address. When one gets flooded with spam, tell your correspondents to use another one. There are several large companies, such as Yahoo and Hotmail, that provide free email addresses, but they are frequently targets of massive spam and various attacks.

A common sense idea is to avoid giving out your email address as much as possible. If you have a Web site with your address, try to write it in the form `john at abc dot com` or a similar format. If you set up a message board or a discussion group, try to display just part of any email address.

Date:Fri, 31 Dec 2004 00:18:58 -0800
From:Chad Hurwitz <churritz@mail.com> Add To Address Book
Subject:Re: Re: Is that your document? [Authorize]
To:david.salomon@csun.edu

Hi,

You just sent an email to my churritz@aaa.com account, which is now being managed
by my Mailblocks spam-free email service. (If you didnt recently send a message to me,
please see the Note below*.)

Because this is the first time you have sent to this email account, please confirm
yourself so you'll be recognized when you send to me in the future.

It's simple.To prove your message comes from a human and not a computer, go to:
http://app21.mailblocks.com/confirm2.aspx?ck=CGNodXJyaXR6C21haWwybWUuY29tFm...

This is the email message you have sent that is in my Pending folder waiting for your
quick authentication:

Subject: Re: Is that your document?
Sent: Dec 31, 12:18 AM

If you have not confirmed within several days, your message will automatically be deleted.
Personal Message:
!!!!!!!
Hi! Since I, Chad from DRO INC. m_a_r_p, get way too much spam,
I've opted for the Challenege/Response system provided by mailblocks.
So, if you are seeing this message, then you have sent me a message
to me (churritz@aaa.com or churritz@mail.com) but you haven't yet
proved you're a real person and not a spamer. Please follow the
directions and click the link ABOVE and then enter the number shown
on that page. You will only have to do that ONCE. HOWEVER: WARNING:
You only get this challenge once. So, if you delete this message
before clicking on the above link, any message you send to me in the
future will be trashed and i'll never know you are a real person.
After your verification, i will reply with any M_A_R_P, t_s_p_solve or
v_r_p_solve issues. P.S. Mailblocks deletes all challeneged messages
over 10k, so if your message was larger than that you may have to
send it again aft! ! er verification. I apologize for this inconvenience.
Thank you for sending me email!
!!!!!!!

*Note: If you did not send the above message to me, and you would like to report this
email as unwanted, please notify Mailblocks by clicking here, and we will ensure that you
do not receive any further notification regarding the above message. Mailblocks
investigates all reports made using this link.

Email for Humans... Mailblocks
Try Mailblocks web-based personal email -- faster, cleaner interface, more storage,
bigger attachments, and 100% spam-free. About Mailblocks

(c) 2003-2004 Mailblocks Inc. All rights reserved.

Figure 7.5: A Typical Mailblocks Confirmation Request.

Zombies. Certain types of malware are used to capture control of a computer and command it remotely. Such a captured machine is known as a zombie and is an ideal means of hiding the identity of a perpetrator. It is known that DoS attacks are often carried out after the attacker has gained control of many computers and turned them into zombies. A targeted Web site is flooded with a vast number of meaningless messages sent by computers whose innocent users know nothing about the attack. The attack keeps legitimate users from using the site, causing inconvenience to users and monetary losses to the site's owners. Such an attack is referred to as distributed denial of service (DDoS). Zombies are also used by spammers to hide their identities. A spammer who controls a zombie computer, sends this slave a (normally stolen) list of email addresses and instructs it to send a message (or several messages) hawking useless merchandise, fraudulent schemes, or unwanted services to all the addresses. Zombies are less destructive than viruses or other types of rogue software because they rarely damage data.

⋄ **Exercise 7.5:** The term zombie is also used in UNIX. Find out what it indicates?

The following incident illustrates the power that a hacker can gain by taking over and enslaving a large number of computers. We all spend time (some of us perhaps too much time) surfing the Internet. We do this by typing a URL, such as `www.ibm.com`, but the communications software has to use a numeric IP address such 123.098.321.0. There is therefore a need for address translation from the convenient, easy-to-remember URLs to the numeric IP addresses, and this service is provided by many dedicated computers called domain name servers (DNS).

Notice that the IP address associated with a given URL may change, because the owner of the URL may move and change his Internet service provider (ISP), or because the ISP assigns dynamic IP addresses to its clients. Thus, every time we try to browse a Web site or perform a file transfer, our computer has to connect to a DNS to resolve the URL. An ISP has at least two DNS computers, and their information has to be updated every day from the central DNS computers operated by Akamai, a company that specializes in distributed computing solutions and services. Each time a new URL is registered and is assigned an IP address by an ISP, the ISP reports the pair (URL, IP) to Akamai. Also, each time the association between a URL and an IP is changed, the ISP has to report the new association.

The use of URLs is convenient, because it is easier for a person to memorize a character string than to remember a long number, but it makes the central DNS computers a natural target for wrongdoers and a weak point in the Internet (the Internet was originally designed to be survivable in the sense that it should have no single point of failure).

It therefore came as no surprise to security workers that the central DNS computers were attacked for two hours on Tuesday, 15 June 2004. This was a distributed denial-of-service (DDoS) attack, where a vast number of requests is directed toward the victim, making it impossible for the attacked computer to respond to all the requests. As a result, legitimate requests cannot be satisfied, which denies this service to users.

It was quickly discovered that the attack came from a large number of compromised computers; zombies. A hacker can locate and collect a set of zombies by unleashing a special Trojan horse. The horse manages to find its way into a computer, where it runs silently in the background, continually looking for a command from its owner. Such a rogue program is often referred to as a remote-access Trojan or RAT, although the term bot is also sometimes used.

An experienced hacker can create such a bot, set it loose in the Internet, and wait for it to multiply and occupy a large number of computers. The hacker then sends a command to all the bots, directing them to send a legitimate request to the same computer, resulting in a flood of requests that can block access to the attacked computer for at least a few hours and perhaps even days.

What was new and special in the attack described here is that it somehow managed to block access to four specific sites, the main Yahoo, Google, Microsoft and Apple sites.

Case study. A report in [Information Week 04] on 15 November 2004 tells the story of Jeremy Jaynes, a 30-year-old major spammer who was caught, tried, and convicted after an eight-day trial in late 2004. This is an important example that illustrates how simple it is to become a major spammer, bother millions of people, and make a lot of money, because there is always a small percentage of recipients who respond to any offer.

The almost unbelievable facts of this case can be summarized in just two numbers. At least 10 million email messages sent each day, bringing a monthly income of $400,000 to $750,000. If you have an email address (and most of us have several addresses) chances are you received at least several messages from Mr Jaynes.

The operation was based in a house in Raleigh, North Carolina (in the United States) that had 16 high-speed Internet lines installed. Experts say that this kind of Internet access is an overkill for a residence and is normally found in organizations with hundreds of employees. The spam messages aimed to sell software, pornography, and work-at-home schemes. Specifically, this spammer "specialized" in software that promises to clean computers of private information, pornography, a service for selecting penny stocks as investments, and a fraudulent scheme that promised $75 an hour for work done at home on delinquent FedEx accounts. In addition, Jaynes (who is also known as Gaven Stubberfield and has other aliases) was always adding, changing, and rotating products.

Investigators found that Jaynes, who operated under the alias Gaven Stubberfield, received 10,000 to 17,000 responses a month, about one response to every 30,000 email messages sent, but this minute percentage was translated to $40 a response, which turned this spamming operation into a lucrative business. Prosecutors believe that, when arrested, the net worth of Jaynes was about $24 million.

The key to Jaynes' commercial success was the sheer number of email addresses he had collected. He had millions of addresses in lists illegally obtained from AOL and eBay. These sites are among the chief targets of spammers, because their customers are people who have shown an interest in e-commerce and should therefore be natural targets of spamming. It is known that an AOL programmer was charged with stealing a list of 92 million addresses, and investigators suspect that Jayne somehow obtained this list.

(Jason Smathers, a former software engineer at America Online (AOL) was arrested in early February 2005 and charged with using his inside knowledge to steal a list with names and accounts of 92 million AOL members. He then allegedly sold it to a friend, Sean Dunaway, who in turn sold it to a spammer. Each of the two men is facing a maximum sentence of five years in prison and a fine of $250,000. AOL stated that no passwords or credit card numbers were involved and that Smathers had been fired.)

E-commerce by itself isn't spam and shouldn't be unnecessarily discouraged by laws. Therefore, laws against spam cannot outlaw the practice of sending, even on a massive scale, email messages promoting products and services. An antispam law should concentrate on what distinguishes spam from legitimate e-commerce, namely sending unsolicited email and email with false information as to its origin or transmission.

In the trial, prosecutors proved to the satisfaction of the jurors that Jaynes had registered Web sites under false company names, which made it impossible for his victims to trace him. He also sent email with false routing information and used special software to generate phony domain names and paste them as the source addresses of his messages, a trick many spammers employ to confuse spam filters.

During the trial it became known that Jaynes had the "right" background for his operations, because he worked as a distributor of old-fashioned junk mail in the past decade. With him were charged his sister and another helper.

We don't know the precise techniques employed by law enforcement to locate him and collect the evidence, but it seems that other spammers are much more sophisticated. They reside in countries that are indifferent or hostile to the United States and they operate by taking over computers of innocent Internet users and converting them to zombie servers, thereby making it impossible to track the origin of their email.

The jury has recommended a nine-year prison sentence in this, the first felony trial of a spammer in the United states. On 8 April 2005 the judge concurred, sentenced Jaynes to nine years in prison, and then set him free on a one million dollar bond until the appeals process concludes.

Zombie networks of computers, known as bot nets, are available to buy over the Internet. There was a Web page with one for sale—an Internet shop for zombie networks, with 5,000 machines for $300.

—Eugene Kaspersky, Kaspersky Labs, `http://www.kaspersky.com`.

More Spam Advice

Most of the ideas and advice offered in this inset appear elsewhere in this chapter, but read and follow them anyway, because this list is important, it is based on long experience, and may improve your Internet experience.

Spammers want to know who is receiving their messages, so that they can focus their next campaign on willing or vulnerable victims (popularly known as suckers). Even if you don't reply to spam, there are ways for the spammer to verify that you have received and opened it. Some examples are:

■ If you have your email program set to preview messages (i.e., to show you the contents of the message in a window below the list of email), the spammer may be able to verify that the email has been received.

■   If you click on a link to unsubscribe from a mailing list, you have confirmed to the spammer that your email address is active. The spammer can then sell your address to others.

■   Spammers can include a "web bug" in an email. This is a link that connects to the spammer's Web site as soon as the email is read or previewed. If you want to avoid letting spammers know that their mail got through, follow the advice given here.

How to avoid spam.

■   Use anti-spam software, update and run it regularly. This software can significantly reduce unwanted email, especially if it is programmed to receive feedback from the user/reader and employ it to learn (from the subject line or sender's address) which messages are spam.

■   Never buy anything advertised by unsolicited email because this only encourages future spam. Once your email address becomes known to the seller, it will be added to the huge address lists that are sold to other spammers, with the result that you'll receive even more junk email. Worse still, responding to spam advertises you as a sucker and opens you to further fraud and identity theft attempts.

■   If the sender's name sounds unfamiliar, delete the email without any hesitation. Most spam is just a nuisance, but often it includes viruses and other nasty software.

■   Never respond to spam messages or click on any links in them. Replying to spam—even to unsubscribe from it—confirms to the spammer that your email address is a valid one, thereby encouraging more spam.

■   Opt out of any further information or free or attractive offers. When you fill out forms on the Web, uncheck any checkboxes that offer further information or offers.

■   Don't use the preview mode in your email viewer. Spammers can verify that a message has been previewed, even if it hasn't been opened, because the preview effectively opens the email.) Knowing that you have read their messages encourages the spammers.

■   Try to decide whether an email message is spam based only on the subject line and sender's name and address. Use the bcc field if you email many people at once. The bcc (blind carbon copy) field hides the list of recipients from any individual recipient. If you include the addresses in the To field, spammers may harvest them and add them to mailing lists.

■   Restrict the use of your email address on the internet. Don't publish it on Web sites, newsgroup lists or other online public forums. Spammers have software that crawls the internet to find addresses in such places, harvest them, and add them to mailing lists.

■   Give your main address only to those you trust (and even then be ready for your address to be discovered and abused by spammers).

■ Always have several secondary email addresses ready. (Those are easy to open at sites such as Yahoo, Hotmail, and `emailaddresses.com`) When you fill out Web registration forms or surveys on sites with which you don't want further contact, use a secondary email address. If the secondary address is flooded by spam, simply close it. This protects your main address from spam.

7.5 Denial of Service

Many Internet attacks try to obtain private data or to damage data. In contrast, a denial-of-service attack aims to shut down an entire network, a single server, or a particular Web site. The attack tries to prevent legitimate users of a service from using that service. This can be done by one of the following methods:

■ Flood a network with traffic. This makes it hard or impossible for legitimate users to send or receive data.

■ Disrupt connections between two computers. This prevents remote access to the machines.

■ Attempt to prevent a particular user from accessing a service.

■ Disrupt or prevent network access to a particular computer or network. A hacker may open an account at an ftp site, then store data and retrieve it repeatedly, thereby consuming disk space and monopolizing network services at the site.

A denial-of-service may be part of a bigger attack, but it disables a useful resource such as a computer or a network. If the resource is private, its owner may be inconvenienced. If the resource is public, its users may suffer loss of service. If the resource is commercial, its owner suffers monetary losses. A denial-of-service is considered an easy type of attack. Even a single hacker, using an old, slow computer and a slow modem may be able to disable (or at least slow down) faster servers or even whole networks.

There are three types of denial-of-service, (1) consumption of scarce or nonrenewable resources, (2) destruction or alteration of network information, and (3) physical destruction or alteration of network components.

The first type, consumption of scarce resources, relies on the fact that computers and networks need resources such as electrical power, CPU time, memory space, disk space, and network connections. The easiest resource for a hacker to consume is network connectivity. It is possible to tie up the network connections of a computer, such that it waits for some data that never arrives, so it remains hung up. All that the hacker has to do is start opening a connection to a network server but never complete this process. The victim server has reserved a port and a data structure for the connection, but the port remains half open. The hacker (or a group of coordinated attackers) can very quickly tie up all the available ports of a server. In the meantime, other users, legitimate or not, who try to establish connections are denied access.

Such an attack is called a SYN flood. Even someone with only a slow computer and slow modem can stop a large server very quickly. Here is a detailed description of this threat.

A typical client/server network consists of a server (a computer with files that are useful to a group of users) and many clients (users who want access to those files). When a client tries to connect to the server, both the client and the server have to execute a connection protocol. They have to exchange certain messages that establish the connection. This is true for all the TCP connections, such as email, telnet, and http.

In its simplest form, the protocol starts when the client sends a SYN message to the server. If the server is ready to open a connection, it sends back a SYN-ACK message, expecting to receive an ACK message from the client. When this is accomplished, the connection is open and communication can start.

In a SYN flood attack, the client simply does not send back the ACK message (Figure 7.6. This leaves the server waiting, and creates the half-open connection. The server maintains a data structure in memory with information on all the half-open connections and this data structure may overflow and damage other data in memory. The operating system may check for overflow and simply ignore any SYN messages in such a case. The half-open connections then start expiring, creating space in the structure, but the attacker can continue sending SYN requests that keep the structure full for a few hours or longer.

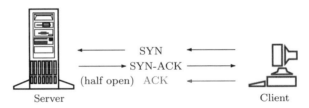

Figure 7.6: A SYN Flood Attack.

In practice, a hacker uses IP spoofing to perpetrate a DoS attack. The attacking computer sends the attacked server SYN messages that appear to come from a legitimate client. The hacker, however, selects a client that's unable to respond to the SYN-ACK from the server, which leaves the server hung up and draws attention to the client.

Any incoming connections established before the attack are still functioning. Also, the server can send data out while this type of attack is going on. The attack affects only new clients trying to connect to the server.

Consumption of scarce resources can also take the form of the hacker using the victim's resources against the victim. An example is an abuse of the Chargen and Echo services associated with UDP data packets. A detailed description of these services is beyond the scope of this book, but the following paragraphs provide the main facts.

Data packets are sent over computer networks all the time, and sometimes are lost (dropped). Chargen (character generator, defined in [RFC-864 04]) was developed to locate the cause for dropped packets. It is a service that generates random characters either in one UDP packet or in a TCP session. The UDP chargen server looks for a UDP packet on port 19 and responds with the random character packet.

With TCP chargen, once a connection is established, the server sends a continuous stream of TCP packets until the connection closes. The data itself is random and is ignored.

Echo (defined in [RFC-862 04]) uses UDP and TCP port 7 and is employed as a debugging tool. It sends any data packets received from a source back to that source.

An infiltrator can create a DoS attack by spoofing an IP address and causing two computers to send packets with random data to each other. In more detail, by connecting a host's chargen service to the echo service on the same or on a different computer, all affected computers may be effectively choked because of the huge number of packets produced and sent. In addition, if several computers are connected in this way, the network connecting them may also become congested and deny service to any other computers whose network traffic needs to be forwarded by that network.

An attacker may also generate a huge number of data packets and send them to a target computer. This is a bandwidth consumption attack that may involve a group of intruders.

Even resources that are not related to network services may be consumed. A hacker may write a program (a virus or a Trojan horse) that only creates copies of itself and starts executing them. Very quickly, the CPU will have thousands, then millions of copies to execute. This not only slows down the CPU, but may overflow operating system resources. The operating system switches the CPU from program to program, allocating each program a time slot. It therefore must have a table of all the programs (processes) currently active in the computer. When new processes are created by the virus, the table fills up quickly and the operating system must take appropriate steps to handle the new processes being created all the time. They have to be placed in a queue, and when this queue overflows, it may corrupt data in memory.

An attackers may also consume massive amounts of disk space by, for example, generating many email messages, generating errors that have to be logged, and reading huge files from anonymous ftp servers and writing them on the disk. When the disk is full, this attack stops, but when the user needs more disk space later, the operating system issues an error message (disk full).

An intruder may be able to cause an operating system to crash or to become unstable by sending unexpected data over the network. A well-known example of such an attack is called the ping of death.

The TCP/IP protocol specifies data packets that can range in size from 20 bytes (only a short header with no data bytes) up to 65,536 bytes. The protocol does not specify how to handle bigger packets, because no one envisioned an attack based on large data packets. As a result, some operating systems feature unpredictable behavior when a packet larger than 65,536 bytes is received. The operating system may crash, freeze, or reboot itself.

Hackers have discovered that such an attack is particularly "successful" when the large data packets are sent as part of the Internet control message protocol (ICMP). ICMP is a component of the TCP/IP protocol that transmits error and control messages between computers. Two specific data packets specified by ICMP are `ECHO_REQUEST` and `ECHO_RESPONSE`. These are commonly sent by a computer to determine whether a remote computer is reachable via the network and are commonly known as "ping," which gave this particular attack its name (the name "smurf attack" is also used sometimes).

The original ping program was written as part of UNIX by Mike Muuss [ping 04] and generated so much interest that the ping concept became part of the Internet protocol.

If your operating system is experiencing frequent crashes with no apparent cause, it could be the result of this type of attack.

The obvious defense against the ping of death is to patch the low-level routine that sends data packets to never send large packets, and patch the routine that receives packets to ignore packets that are too large. In practice, this should be done by the makers of the operating system and issued as a security patch.

The second type of DoS threat involves destruction or alteration of network information. An attacker may be able to change the IP number of a victim's personal computer, change the registration of the operating system, or change prerecorded telephone numbers used by the modem to call outside servers.

The third type of DoS threat involves physical destruction or alteration of network components. This can be done by an intruder physically appearing in a computer center and disabling, breaking, or disconnecting cables and other hardware devices. A hacker may also climb a utility pole and disconnect telephone lines or television cables, thereby disrupting service to users in the neighborhood.

Once the DoS threat is understood, there are certain things a security expert can do to reduce the effect of DoS attacks, but most require modifications of the operating system, which can normally be done only by its manufacturer. Any half-open port should close automatically after a fraction of a second (unfortunately, this may affect legitimate users with a slow communications line). When the number of active processes in memory reaches a certain limit, the operating system simply ignores any new processes (but this may backfire when an administrator wants to run a program to monitor the state of the computer). The size of disk files may be limited to, say 2 Gb (but this may prevent users form having legitimate large files, perhaps with movies).

7.6 Firewall Basics

A firewall is a combination of software and hardware that decides what kinds of requests and what specific data packets can pass to and from a computer or a local network. Figure 7.7 illustrates a typical hardware firewall that protects an entire local-area network. A firewall for a personal computer is normally fully implemented by software, whereas a small network of computers often found in a home (typically consisting of 2–3 computers and a printer) may use a hardware firewall that's built into the network's router.

The main task of a firewall is to block certain requests for data transfer, and the firewall makes these decisions based on rules. A firewall starts with some built-in (default) rules, and its user/owner can add, delete, and modify rules. We can say that a firewall enforces an access policy through the rules, and a rule tells the firewall what

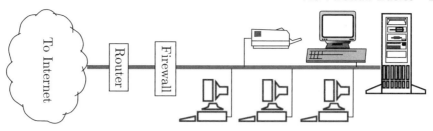

Figure 7.7: A Firewall in a LAN.

properties of a data packet to examine and how to decide whether to let the packet through or not.

An effective firewall must be easy to adapt to the needs of any user. Such a firewall should be able to check any property of a data packet, should be able to take various actions depending on what it finds, and should do all this fast, so as not to slow down the flow of data to and from its host computer or network.

A typical firewall performs the following tasks: (1) limit incoming data, so that data coming from certain senders (or that has certain properties) will be blocked, (2) limit outgoing data, so a program will not be able to send data outside (to call home) without the owner's knowledge, (3) generate and save a log of all its activities, especially on data packets it has blocked, and (4) do all this fast and be transparent to the user.

Examples of properties of data packets are the various fields in the header of a packet, such as device, direction, source and destination addresses, and source and destination ports. A rule may specify that all packets arriving at, say, port 5500 should be blocked, or that packets arriving from IP 192.168.1.50 should always be let in.

A firewall rule specifies a set of conditions and what action to take when a condition occurs. A complex rule can check several conditions, while a simple rule is limited to just one condition. Rules can also be hierarchical. In such a case, each rule is simple and checks one condition, but a rule can have several child rules, each checking one condition. This way, each rule is simple, but the overall performance can be complex.

In general, a rule consists of a condition and an action. A condition is a property, a relationship, and a value. For example, a condition may be destination port = 5500. If a condition is satisfied, the corresponding action is taken. Otherwise, the firewall proceeds to the next rule. In a hierarchical firewall, each condition also specifies its parent and its children (if any). In such a firewall, if a condition of a rule is met, the children of that rule will be tested one by one. If the condition is not met, then the sibling rule (the next rule on the same level) is checked. If none of the conditions of the sibling rules are met, the next rule on the previous level is checked. Figure 7.8 shows an example of a hierarchical tree of rules and the order in which they are checked.

Certain useful conditions may be unrelated to the content of any data packets. These include properties such as date, day of the week, time, parent idle time, and parent byte count. Experience gained by network administrators suggests that limiting access to certain Web sites or certain services during peak times of the day may improve overall network performance. Similarly, many restrictions on network usage may be relaxed or lifted on weekends.

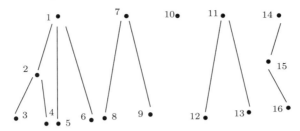

Figure 7.8: Hierarchical Firewall Rules.

A sophisticated firewall may maintain simple statistics on the data packets that satisfy each rule. When a packet satisfies a rule, its idle time is set to zero, its match count is incremented by 1, and its byte count is incremented by the size of the packet. Such statistics can be useful to the computer owner and to the network administrator, and can also be used in rules. For example, if a rule hasn't detected data from a certain sender within a specified idle time, the action of the rule is executed (even though no data packet has been received) and may send a probe to the sender or may alert the user that the sender isn't responding fast enough.

Examples of actions are "delete," to delete a data packet, "pass," to let it through (into or out of the computer), "drop," to drop the connection (in case of a DoS attack that tries to hang up the connection), and "log," to log the data packet and then apply the next rule to it. (For incoming data packets, the "drop" action sends a TCP RESET command to the sender, while for an outgoing packet the same action sends a small TCP FIN packet.)

The two main components of a firewall are the gate and the choke (there can be several such pairs in a large firewall). The gate transfers or blocks the data and the choke is the filter that decides which data to block. Those familiar with firewalls like to compare the gate to a security checkpoint and the choke to a security guard.

In addition to its main task of checking conditions and executing actions, a modern firewall can perform more sophisticated operations as described below.

■   A modern firewall may also include rules for checking the data of a data packet, not just the fields of its header. This useful feature is referred to as *content filtering*. The user may instruct the firewall to block all incoming (and perhaps all outgoing) data packets that contain a certain string of characters. This can block common viruses and worms that have already been detected and analyzed. An advanced firewall should also be able to recognize ethernet hardware addresses (the so-called MAC addresses), so that the rules would be able to distinguish between outside traffic and local traffic.

■   Another advanced task is to limit the amount of data (the bandwidth) allocated to certain users or to certain applications. This way, a firewall can help in *bandwidth management*. Consider an ISP that offers cable Internet access to private users. A private user normally has one or two computers and generates a small amount of traffic, perhaps browsing, sending email, and transferring files. Also, most of this traffic should be incoming. As long as each user conforms to this pattern, the ISP can support many users with one cable and can remain competitive. If one user suddenly starts consuming large amounts of bandwidth (perhaps because the user generates spam or has other commercial activities), other users may notice low speeds and may start complaining. The ISP may decide to limit the amount of data each user can send, and this task (bandwidth management) should best be performed by the ISP's firewall.

■ *Bandwidth accounting* is another important task performed by modern firewalls. The owner/operator of a local network needs to know how the network is used over time. Network usage varies between day and night, weekdays and weekends, and from month to month. A firewall can provide information about the amount of traffic flowing to and from (and the amount being blocked at) each computer on the network. When such information is presented graphically, it can tell an important story. It can tell the network manager that certain computers are active on weekends, and that the total network bandwidth is insufficient, say, right before lunch time on Fridays.

■ Another important picture that a good firewall can paint is the pattern of *connection logging*. The firewall can keep a record of every connection opened between a computer in the network and an outside address. The date, time, and amount of data transferred in each direction can also be logged. Such information can provide an audit trail which may be invaluable when something out of the ordinary, such as an attack, occurs. Connection logging provides a bird's eye view of the usage of an entire local network, and may suggest ways to improve its behavior.

> Call it a clan, call it a network, call it a tribe, call it a family.
> Whatever you call it, whoever you are, you need one.
> —Jane Howard

8
Authentication

Billy left home when he was in his teens and went to seek his fortune in Australia. When he returned home thirty years later as a mature, successful man, his relatives came to meet him at the dock in Southampton. He later remarked on this meeting to a friend "after not having seen my mother for 30 years, I have recognized her instantly among my many aunts, uncles, and other family." This short (and usually true) story illustrates the use of identification and authentication in real life. We authenticate a person by looking at them and listening to them, and we can do this even after a long interval during which the person has greatly changed. A computer, unfortunately, cannot see its owner/user and has to rely on other means for authentication, which is the topic of this chapter.

The term *authentication* signifies the process of verifying someone's identity. The discussion in this chapter concentrates on local authentication, authentication by biometric means, and password authentication. There is additional material on consumer authentication and protection on page 243.

Local authentication is verification done when the person is located nearby and is available for questioning and scrutiny. Local authentication of a person is achieved by something that the person has, knows, or is.

A key is something a person *has*, so it is a means of authentication. A key authenticates a person to a lock. A password is something that a person *knows*, and it authenticates the person to a computer or an ATM machine in a bank. A fingerprint or a DNA is part of a person. It is something a person *is*, and it also serves as (biometric) authentication.

8.1 Local Authentication

Thus, local identification, where a person tries to use a local computer, is easy and reliable. It may use attributes such as a key (to open the door to a protected facility), personal knowledge (a guard at the door may personally know the user), paper or plastic identification (examined by a guard), fingerprints (verified by touching a special pad), voice prints (verified by talking to a special circuit), or facial identification (currently not very reliable).

In contrast, remote authentication is more complex and is never absolutely secure. You can send your picture remotely to authenticate yourself to a person who knows you, but this requires a person who knows you, and it isn't completely secure, because a determined perpetrator pretending to be you can get hold of your picture, or wear a latex mask resembling you and attempt to fool someone watching him on a remote screen. You can place your finger in a device that reads your fingerprints and sends them to a remote location for authentication, but such a device can be fooled by a glove with your fingerprints or by an eavesdropper who intercepts the fingerprint data on its way and modifies it. Currently, remote authentication is normally done by passwords (Section 8.3), which is why fraudsters are always after passwords.

⋄ **Exercise 8.1:** Try to come up with a scheme of remote authentication based on knowing someone personally.

An expensive alternative to the use of passwords is a machine that scans your retina (Section 8.2) and sends a pattern of the blood vessels. This is not absolutely secure because the pattern data can be intercepted on its way, but encryption can make it virtually secure. A cheap alternative, for cases where high security is not needed, is a video camera mounted on your computer, identifying you to a friend. It's difficult to imagine a hacker who will go to much trouble trying to impersonate both your image and your voice.

8.2 Biometric Techniques

The term biometric (from the Greek for bio=life, metric=degree) refers to authentication by means of biological (more accurately, physiological or behavioral) features.

The first effective biometric technique was the anthropometric test (anthropometry means literally "measurement of humans") designed by Alphonse Bertillon in 1883. It was the first scientific method widely used to identify criminals. It was based on precise measurements of certain lengths and widths of the head and body. It was later shown to be inferior to fingerprinting and was supplanted by it.

At the time of writing (early 2005) the use of biometric techniques for remote authentication and identification is coming of age. Technologies, devices, and algorithms are becoming more sophisticated, costs are coming down, and usage is getting easier and less intrusive. What was until recently the domain of science fiction and spy novels is fast becoming a hard reality. Biometric techniques use various human characteristics to identify a person, but such characteristics are difficult to measure, they vary all the time, and some may be faked. Fingerprinting is an illustrative example. Each person has unique fingerprints, which is why this attribute has been used for decades to identify criminals and link them with crimes. Even more, we use the term "fingerprint" in many contexts, such as "fingerprinting by DNA analysis" or "CRC is the fingerprint of a file." However, a person's fingerprints vary during the day with changes in temperature, humidity, skin moisture and oiliness, and cuts and bruises. The precise image of fingerprints therefore varies, which is why fingerprint identification should be based on invariant features of the fingerprints, not on their actual image. In addition to fingerprints, biometric identification devices employ other biological features found in the face, eyes, voice, gait, body temperature, and even signature (yes, physical signature on paper) and typing habits.

The term *identification* refers to the first time a person is presented to a security device. Once the device registers the biometric parameters of the person, every subsequent visit of that person is for the purpose of authentication. A simple example is biometric identification and authentication of the owner of a personal computer. The first time a PC is turned on, it considers whoever is at the keyboard its owner. It asks for a name, a password, for other personal items such as an address, telephone number, and email address, and finally, for a fingerprint, an iris scan, or other biometric data (assuming that the proper sensing devices are hooked up to the computer). From then on, the computer associates this data with its owner and uses it to authenticate the owner on subsequent sessions.

An important feature of any security procedures and devices, but especially of techniques for biometric authentication, is scalability. Employees come to work every day (at least, they should come), while a visitor shows up only sporadically. Authenticating an employee should therefore be quicker, simpler, and less intrusive than authenticating an outside visitor.

The following is a short description of a few popular biometric technologies.

Fingerprints. The print of even one finger is a complex image and it is known that several prints of the same finger produce slightly different images. However, the image of a fingerprint has certain features that either don't vary or change only rarely from image to image. Figure 8.1 shows two examples of fingerprints and four such features, ridges (one is marked in part b), furrows (the valleys between ridges), minutiae points (marked by circles, mostly in part a), and sweat pores (the triangles in part b). Minutiae are the points at the end of ridges, the intersection of two ridges, and where a ridge splits.

One approach to comparing two images of fingerprints is to find the minutiae points and then map their relative placement on the finger. If two such maps are sufficiently similar, the fingerprints are deemed identical. The downside of this approach is that many fingerprint images are of low quality, which makes it difficult to locate enough minutiae points with high precision. Also, in rare cases two completely different fingerprints may have very close maps of minutiae points. The final decision should therefore be made by a person. This is fine in forensic cases, but cannot be used by a computer trying to authenticate someone automatically.

Another approach to comparing two fingerprint images is to use statistical correlations. An origin point is selected and the line segments connecting it to each minutiae

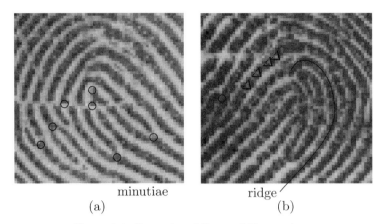

minutiae   ridge
(a)   (b)

Figure 8.1: Examples of Scanned Fingerprints.

point are measured and become vectors. Statistical correlation is then computed between the two sets of vectors in the two images. This approach produces accurate results, but is very sensitive to the orientations of the two fingerprint images being compared. Even the smallest rotation changes all the vectors and corrupts the result of the test.

(Privacy advocates and activists object to fingerprints being collected and saved for authentication purposes, even by governments, on grounds of privacy. See, for example, [networkusa 05].)

Iris scans. The iris of the human eye (Figure 8.2, plural is irides) is the colored ring that surrounds the pupil. It is a muscle (more accurately, a muscular structure) that varies the pupil's size, thereby controlling the amount of light that enters the eye. Note that the iris is not the retina.

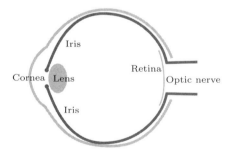

Figure 8.2: The Main Parts of the Eye.

An iris scan records features such as striations, pits, rings, furrows, and freckles in the iris. The scan results in more than 200 such features that can be used for comparison of two images and thus for authentication. This is much more information than is provided by fingerprints. An iris scan is unique not just for a person but for the eye. The scans of the left and right eyes of a person are different. An iris scan does not require special equipment and is done with a video camera. The camera doesn't even have to be close to the eye, as is the case with retinal scan, and works fine even with eye glasses. The scan itself is a quick and simple procedure. The person being scanned has to be placed such that he sees his eye reflection in the camera from a comfortable distance, and a video image is taken. The only problem with this method is unwilling individuals. Also, there is no effective algorithm to compress the resulting images efficiently, which is why iris scan has large storage requirements.

◇ **Exercise 8.2:** A fraudster A obtains access to the iris scan of B. In order to fool the camera and get authenticated as B, A prepares an artificial eye with B's iris scan and hires C, a person with a glass eye, to replace his eye and get authenticated. How can we sense and defeat such an attempt?

> The first glass eye was made in 1832 by the glassblower Ludwig Müller-Uri in Lauscha, Germany. Although artificial eyes can be manufactured from plastic today, no other material is said to be equal to a glass eye created from a special blend of Cryolite glass.

It may come as a surprise to most that the basic idea of using patterns in the eye for personal identification and authentication is not new. It was originally proposed in 1936 by Frank Burch, an ophthalmologist. Lacking computer technology, this idea was impractical and was way ahead of its time. Several of the James Bond movies in the 1980s "used" this technology, but it wasn't until 1994 that practical algorithms for comparing iris scans were developed by John Daugman. It has been shown that the chance of false authentication by these algorithms is extremely low.

The first application of iris scan was as part of the booking procedure to identify prisoners. Currently, iris scan is used in several airports to authenticate frequent passengers and speed up their pre-boarding check. In the future, this technique may be used by banks to authenticate ATM transactions.

Iridian technologies [iridiantech 05] is one of the companies that promote iris scans and make equipment for scanning and authenticating.

Retina scan. The retina is a thin layer of cells at the back of the eyeball of vertebrates and some cephalopods (Figure 8.2). The cells (rods and cones) in the retina are photoreceptors; they convert light to neural signals. The retina is rich in blood vessels and it is the structure of these blood vessels that is unique to the person and can serve as biometric identification and authentication.

A scan of the retina is done in low light and requires a special optical coupler that can read the patterns in the retina at high resolution. Eye glasses have to be removed, the head has to be kept still, and the eyes must be focused on the light for a few seconds.

The high reliability of this technique is due to the fact that current technology cannot duplicate the retinal pattern in another eye, even in a glass eye.

At present, this authentication technique is perhaps the most secure of all the biometric methods. It is also too expensive for anything but the highest security applications. Retinal scans are used for identification and authentication in highly-secure rooms and facilities of the military, nuclear power plants, and any organization willing to pay the price in money and resources.

As can be expected, many view this type of scan as potentially harmful to the eye and object to it on this basis.

Face recognition. Wouldn't it be nice if you could stand before a door to a secure room and let a camera scan your face. A computer would then recognize it and unlock the door. Face recognition is still at its infancy because the human face is so complex and there are no simple tests to distinguish between faces. Our brain is very different from a computer in this respect. When John Doe moves to the antipodes and comes back for a visit after an absence of 20 years, he instantly recognizes his old mother, even though her face has changed so much during his absence (partly from getting older but mostly from missing John, who rarely wrote). Computers, however, are notoriously unreliable in tasks that require this kind of intelligence.

Consumer and privacy advocates object to any large-scale implementation of face recognition because of the ways this immature technology has been used so far. In several instances, local governments placed cameras in crowded places (such as a stadium during a crucial ball game) in an attempt to match faces in the crowd to faces in databases of criminals, terrorists, or just plain suspects. Regardless of the legal or ethical considerations involved, these experiments failed technically. Technology simply isn't up to such a task yet.

Smart cards. In the 1950s and 1960s, input was fed to computers from punched cards. Then came terminals, followed by smart terminals. In a similar development, credit cards first appeared in the 1950s and were followed by smart cards in the 1970s (but mostly since the mid 1980s). A traditional credit card has a narrow magnetic stripe with a little information recorded. A smart card (Figure 8.3) is a plastic card that looks like a credit card, but has an integrated circuit (a chip) embedded that gives it its smartness. The chip is either a microprocessor (with some internal memory) or just a memory unit with non-programmable logic.

Figure 8.3: A Smart Card.

A microprocessor chip in a smart card operates on 8, 16, or 32-bit words and has memory capacity in the range of 300 bytes to 32 Kbytes. It has a primitive operating system and can download programs and run them. A memory-only chip is less expensive than a microprocessor, but is less secure (lacking the execution logic of a microprocessor, a memory chip depends on the card reader for its security). Its capacity typically ranges from about 100 to about 16,000 bits.

The chip has tabs or connectors on its surface, through which a special device (a card reader) can read its data and status and send it commands and new data. Such a card has to be inserted into the device to achieve a connection. Many newer chips are contactless; they can be accessed remotely, without any physical touch, by electromagnetic waves. Such a card has an antenna and can communicate when brought into the range of the reader (typically a few inches). Some contactless cards may have batteries but most get their power from the reader's antenna. A contactless card is handy in applications where speed is important, such as in a subway.

A hybrid card has two chips, one with contacts and the other contactless. The two are not connected and each can serve a different purpose. A combi card has one chip with both contact and contactless interfaces. This type is supposed to have high security and is expected to be adopted mostly by financial institutions.

Smart cards are made by several manufacturers, so there is a need for a standard. The basic smart card standard is titled the ISO 7816 series, parts 1–10. This standard is derived from the financial ID card standards and details the physical, electrical, mechanical, and application programming interface to a contact-chip smart card.

Currently, smart cards are especially popular in Europe where they are used as credit and debit cards, telephone cards, bank cards, and as passes for mass transportation. One of the many companies that make smart cards and associated equipment is [gemplus 05]. The smart card government handbook [smartcardalliance 05] is a comprehensive reference on smart cards and includes an overview of smart card and related technologies and implementation guidance for government organizations planning smart card applications.

Smart cards have many applications, the most important of which are listed here.

■   Controlling a mobile telephone. A smart card contains a telephone number, password, and account information. Without a card, the telephone is not assigned a number and is unusable. Once the card is inserted into the telephone, it (the telephone) knows its own number and recognizes the user. The telephone stores billing information and frequently-used numbers on the card.

■   A satellite dish television uses a smart card to store account and security data. The account information tells the card what channels the user subscribes to.

■   More and more credit and debit cards are issued as smart cards. The microprocessor in the card provides security and stores a list of the most recent transactions.

■   Several countries with national health programs have adopted smart cards for their members.

■   Many countries issue smart cards for the use of pay telephones.

In addition to these, other applications for smart cards include computer/Internet user authentication and nonrepudiation, merchants' gift cards, physical access to secure facilities, hotel cards (that act as both chits and key), mass transit passes, electronic road toll, product tracking, national ID cards, drivers licenses, and passports.

8.3 Passwords

Passwords provide strong, although not absolute, and inexpensive protection in many situations. When someone becomes a legitimate user of a network or a network service, both a login name and a password are issued by the network owner or the service provider (the issuer). A person trying to log into a remote computer or into an account has to type both items for complete identification. Even a simple transaction, such as purchasing an item online, often requires opening an account and obtaining a password. Once a password is issued, the user can change it. In fact, it is good practice to change passwords on a regular basis.

Passwords are currently the only inexpensive, popular, and practical way for a person to identify himself remotely (there have recently been experiments in remote identification and authentication using an array of personal questions, but the reliability of this technique is still unknown). Smartcards and biometric authentication (Section 8.2) are becoming more common, but are still too expensive or unreliable for general use. A password sent on a communications line should, of course, be encrypted, and this issue is discussed in Section 12.10. Password identification is a simple technique, but it involves two types of risk.

One risk is that the password is kept somewhere in the issuer's computer and may be located and stolen. The solution is to encrypt all passwords and keep only the encrypted results. The issuer deletes the original password and keeps a file with the login names and encrypted passwords of all the users. Encryption involves a key and all the passwords are encrypted with the same key. Normally, encryption methods are symmetric; the same key used to encrypt data is also used to decrypt it. In order to keep the passwords secure, even the person who has the encryption key and who encrypts the passwords should not be able to decrypt them. Thus, for better security, password encryption should be done with a one-way encryption algorithm, where no decryption is possible.

This insert discusses the concept of one-way encryption and how UNIX handles passwords. Despite the "UNI" in its name, UNIX (in its current flavors) is a multiuser operating system. A computer running UNIX has a special password file, where the names and passwords of all the users are stored. Not surprisingly, this file was the main target of hackers, because the list of all user names and their passwords made the hacker as powerful as the administrator. At a certain point, UNIX started using encrypted passwords. This change in UNIX reflects the difference between keeping information secret and opening it up. When the passwords are not encrypted, they have to be kept secret and can therefore be stolen or compromised by insiders as well as by outsiders. When they are encrypted, they can be open to anyone. The password file can be readable by anyone and no one can go back from an encrypted password to the original password. Bitter experience, however, has taught UNIX administrators and implementors that it is best to keep the passwords encrypted and the password file as inaccessible as possible. (In other words, combine the benefits of secret policy and open policy.) Current UNIX versions have a password file where the passwords are encrypted with a special, one-way encryption method. An entry in this file has the following fields:

■   Login name. This is a short name, such as johndoe, assigned by the UNIX administrator when a new account is opened. It cannot be changed by the user.

■   Encrypted password. This is a string of bits, the result of encrypting the password. When a new user account is opened, a standard password, such as user, is assigned, and the user is supposed to change it as soon as possible to a secure password.

■   A short string of bits that's referred to as salt. This is appended to the password before it is encrypted, to make a dictionary search of passwords more difficult. The salt is discussed below.

■   A user identification number. This is the number used by UNIX to identify the user. It is easier to use this number, which is an integer, than to use the login name, which is a string of characters. (Each character has a character code, so a string of characters can be considered a number, but this number is normally too long and therefore inconvenient for the operating system.)

■   The group identification number. This identifies the user as a member of a group of users for file access purposes. Each file has a 9-bit access permission code that specifies what kind of access (read, write, and execute, see page 69) the file's owner, the group members, and the rest of the users have.

■   The real name of the user. This is a long string that identifies the real user, in case users have to be contacted personally.

■   The name of the user's directory. This is used by UNIX to locate the user's files.

Next, we discuss ways to implement one-way encryption and we start with a simple permutation. Assume that a password is a string of exactly eight characters. In ASCII, each character has an 8-bit code, so the password becomes a string of 64 bits. Such a string can be securely encrypted by permuting it, because there are 64! permutations of 64 bits. Such encryption is not one-way because every permutation has an inverse, but this idea can be refined and extended in various ways. One extension is to apply the same permutation n times, and compute n from the original password. A hacker trying to reconstruct the original password cannot compute n and therefore cannot perform the reverse permutations. A simple way of computing n is to start with the numeric codes of the individual characters, add the codes, and retain some of the bits of the sum.

Here is an example using 4-character (equivalent to 32 bits) passwords. As our permutation we select a 1-bit rotation to the left. We start with the string qP3$ as our password. The four ASCII codes are $71_{16} = 01110001$, $50_{16} = 01010000$, $33_{16} = 00110011$, and $24_{16} = 00100100$ and their sum is 100011000. The rightmost four bits of the sum are $1000 = 8$, so we apply our permutation eight times. Rotating the original 32-bit string 01110001|01010000|00110011|00100100 eight times to the left produces 01010000|00110011|00100100|01110001. (Rotation is not a secure permutation, but it makes for a simple example)

This example isn't secure, because the hacker can try all the possible values of n. starting from $n = 0$, the hacker has to perform the four simple steps: (1) Perform the inverse permutation on the encrypted password, obtaining a character string S. (2) Add the ASCII codes of the characters of S. (3) Retain the four rightmost bits of the sum. (4) Compare it to n. If the two don't agree, increment n by 1 and repeat the steps.

We clearly need a more complex encryption method. We can start with the original password, compute another number m (perhaps by performing the exclusive-or of the ASCII codes, instead of adding them arithmetically), then execute the original encryption method m times, using a different permutation. We can then compute another number p and execute the original encryption method p times, using a third permutation. This can be repeated x times, where x is also computed from the original password.

◇ **Exercise 8.3:** Suggest another variation of the permutation approach to a one-way encryption algorithm.

More sophisticated approaches to one-way encryption use hash methods. Several secure hash algorithms are currently known and some are designated SHA (secure hash algorithm). The terms "digest" and "digital signature" are also commonly used because these algorithms are employed to generate digital signatures. Popular hash methods are SHA-256 [csrc 04] and MD5 [MD5 04].

Like any encryption algorithm, any method we choose has to go through public scrutiny for a certain length of time before we can be reasonably certain that it is secure and cannot be broken by computer analysis. Even after years of use, someone may find a way to break a one-way encryption, which is why it is wise to combine one-way encryption with an inaccessible password file.

UNIX uses a one-way encryption method based on the data encryption standard (DES), because there is no known way to invert this encryption method in a reasonable time. Because of the popularity of DES, there are hardware circuits that perform fast DES encryption and decryption, which is why UNIX uses a variant of DES. Computers, however, are becoming faster all the time, so at a certain point it will be possible to break UNIX encryption by brute force in a short period of time. This is why UNIX administrators and developers have been trying for the last two decades to defend against fast implementations of their encryption method.

One idea to protect UNIX password encryption is to have a shadow password file. The visible password file will be just a fake, placed in the computer to bait any would-be attackers, while the real password file will be hidden. In addition, any repeated login attempts will be logged and scrutinized by human operators as soon as possible. Unfortunately, past experience has shown that the bad guys will catch on to any such scheme very quickly.

Another proposal is to modify the existing DES version used by UNIX and simply add rounds to it, to make it much slower to crack by brute force. The original DES algorithm computes 16 rounds, but increasing this to 1000 rounds may make it secure for current computers. If this approach proves useful, the number of rounds may simply be increased periodically as computers get faster.

The concept of salt has already been mentioned. Salt is a short, random string of characters appended to a UNIX password to make it more difficult to find valid passwords. When a user enters a password during a login procedure, the salt is appended to the password and the resulting string is encrypted and is compared to the encrypted password in the password file. This makes it more difficult for a hacker to crack passwords with the dictionary method, because if two users select the same password, say `sesame`, their passwords will have different salts appended and may become, for example, `sesameU0` and `sesameF2`. If a word in a dictionary encrypts to `sesameU0`, then only one of the two `sesame` passwords has been compromised (the dictionary attack is discussed below).

Another password risk is that a user may forget a password. This is common because a computer user normally has several (sometimes many) passwords. If the password protects a resource that's important to the user, the user simply loses access to the resource. An example is disk space allocated by a company to users (free or paid for). If a user loses his password, he loses all his data files. His account is erased, and a new password is issued. The company does not keep the original passwords, only the encrypted ones, and they cannot be decrypted.

A solution recommended by some security experts is to list all a user's passwords in a file and encrypt that file by a strong encryption utility. The encryption code is another password that the user has to memorize, but this single password provides insurance against losing any other password. There is, unfortunately, a human factor that comes into play in such a situation. The user may change passwords, delete old ones, and add new ones, and "forget" to update the encrypted file because of laziness.

(The Macintosh operating system has a built-in utility called `Keychain` where passwords and other sensitive information can be stored and encrypted. Of the many password encryption utilities available for the Windows operating system, only the shareware *Password Keeper 2000* is mentioned here. We quote [gregorybraun 05]: "This utility lets you store your frequently-used passwords as well as edit and print them. Each password file that you create can contain up to 1,000 account entries. Password Keeper data files are stored in an encrypted format to prevent unauthorized users from accessing and viewing them.")

However, if the passwords are important to the issuer, they may be kept by the issuer (at the risk of being compromised by an employee or an outsider) and a forgotten password may be sent to the user upon verification. An example is an online business with a large customer base that wants to make it both safe and convenient for online customers to order merchandise. When a new user opens an account, the merchant's computer issues a user (login) name and a password and also asks for other identification, such as an email address, a birthdate, and a personal question and its answer. When the user declares a lost password, the merchant's computer asks the personal question. On receiving the correct answer, the computer sends the password to the email address originally given by the customer. This method provides reasonable security, but requires the user to remember that the email address is kept by the merchant. If the user changes his email address, he has to log in with his password, then notify the merchant's computer of the new address.

It's no wonder that hackers try to crack passwords. With a password at hand, a hacker can easily log into an account and cause much damage. The account owner may later have a hard time recovering from the damage and convincing other victims that he is not responsible for the misuse of his account. One way to crack a password is to guess it. Statistics (more precisely, unfortunate statistics) tells us that many users select easy-to-remember passwords that are also easy to guess. The most common bad passwords are listed here and should be avoided.

■   A valid word in your language. Something that appears in a dictionary.

■   A word spelled backwards.

■   Any names, whether first, last, street names, or place names.

■   Any names with the first letter in uppercase.

■   A car license plate number (even if it is not your car).

■   A number. Avoid using telephone numbers, government identification numbers, such as the social security number in the United States, dates such as someone's birth-date, house numbers, or room numbers.

■   Any string similar to your login name.

> For example, if the login name is "abc," then "abc," "cba," and "abcabc" are excellent candidates for [guessing] passwords.
> —F. T. Grampp and R. H. Morris [Grampp and Morris 84]

[Grampp and Morris 84] looked at more than 100 password files in various UNIX-based computers and discovered that 8–30% of all the passwords in those files were either identical to the account (login) name or could be guessed by using simple variations of it. Section 3.4 lists the tests performed by the Internet worm to crack passwords in computers it invaded.

◇ **Exercise 8.4:** Search the Internet, the computer security literature, and your operating system for default passwords (passwords that come with an operating system or with other software and should be replaced immediately).

The dictionary attack. An alternative method of password cracking is the dictionary attack. Imagine a hacker breaking into the main computer of a large company and copying its password file. The file contains many login names and encrypted passwords. The hacker cannot decrypt the passwords, but he can use a dictionary of words (without their definitions) and with the help of a fast computer encrypt every word in the dictionary and compare the encrypted result to all the encrypted passwords in the stolen password file (Figure 8.4). If a user has selected a password that appears in the dictionary, this method will identify it. This method was actually used by the German hacker caught by Clifford Stoll [Stoll 88, 90, 04]. An obvious defense is to make the password file readable only by the administrator (or super user) of the network or organization, but a hacker may sometimes crack an administrator's password or find a way to gain super user status.

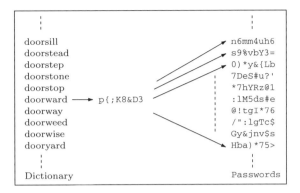

Figure 8.4: A Dictionary Attack.

A more general password cracking method is a hybrid dictionary attack. It goes over all the words of a dictionary, encrypts every word, and then encrypts the word after appending a number to it. Thus, if the word **attack** has been encrypted and tried, the method tries **attack1**, **attack2**, and so on. This is based on human nature. When a user is told to change a password periodically, many tend to simply append a digit to their existing password.

An even more general dictionary attack is to try a brute force approach where every combination of letters and digits (up to a certain length) is tried, encrypted, and compared to all the encrypted passwords in the password file. There are 26 letters and 10 digits, so there are 36 passwords of length 1, 36^2 passwords of length 2, and so on. These numbers grow very rapidly, so even the fastest computer may not be able to try all the passwords of up to, say 12 characters, but many users tend to use short, easy to remember passwords, and these may be cracked in this type of attack. Along the same lines, don't use the reverse of a word found in a dictionary, or the word preceded or followed by one digit.

As a result, the following guidelines should be kept in mind, when selecting a secure password:

■ Select a reasonable length, at least 6 to 8 characters.

■ Have several unique characters. Something like mmmmm is easy for someone looking over your shoulder to memorize.

■ Make sure you have at least one digit and at least one uppercase and one lowercase letter. Punctuation marks should be included whenever possible, but many operating systems restrict the choice of those characters.

■ The password should not be a recognizable word (even in a foreign language). Remember, there are password cracking programs that can go through millions of words in seconds.

■ It should not be a name, address (even old), telephone number, social security number, passport number, car license plate number, or abbreviations of the above.

■ Don't select mathematical or physical constants such as the digits of π or e, even in reverse.

- Don't select letters or digits that are consecutive on the keyboard, such as `qwerty`.

- The name of the current month is similarly an especially bad choice for a password.

> Then I decided to try everything from around 1900 until now. That sounds like a lot, but it's not: the first number is a month, one through twelve, and I can try that using only three numbers: ten, five, and zero. The second number is a day, from one to thirty-one, which I can try with six numbers. The third number is the year, which was only forty-seven numbers at that time, which I could try with nine numbers. So the 8000 combinations had been reduced to 162, something I could try in fifteen or twenty minutes.
>
> Unfortunately I started with the high end of the numbers for the months, because when I finally opened it [Kerst's safe], the combination was 0–5–35.
>
> I turned to de Hoffman. "What happened to Kerst [Donald] around January 5, 1935?"
>
> "His daughter was born in 1936," de Hoffman said. "It must be her birthday."
>
> —Richard P. Feynman, *Surely You Are Joking, Mr. Feynman.*

◇ **Exercise 8.5:** A possible password may be a permutation of a familiar word or phrase. Thus, a password may be the permutation `scrumrewpdaoyses` of the 16-letter phrase `my secure password` (without the spaces). Is such a method secure?

A simple method to select a secure password that's also easy to memorize is to select a familiar phrase or quotation and pick up the first letters of its words, replacing occurrences of to, `too`, and `two` with 2 and occurrences of `for` and `four` with 4. As an example, the phrase "In 96 I got married to YOU! for life" results in the secure password `I96Igm2Y!4l`. A mixture of initials and dates may also be secure. Someone named Arthur C. Lark who owns a Dodge car and whose birthday is 12 November, 2004 may select the semirandom password ACL111204DOD and pray that he'll remember it. The first line (or any memorable line) of a poem or a book may also serve as a secure and easy-to-remember password, but all the spaces should be squeezed out. Examples are *LetMeNotToTheMarriage*, *ItWasTheBestOfTimes*, and *ForAlongTimeIusedToGoToBedEarly*.

A more complex, two-step method that's the favorite of many puzzle and crossword enthusiasts is to start with a short, familiar phrase, perhaps just 2–3 words. Step 1 replaces the first character of the first word by "!" (the keyboard key that corresponds to uppercase 1), then replaces the second character of the second word by "@", and so on. Step 2 eliminates all spaces and changes every other character (except punctuation marks) to uppercase. As an example, start with the phrase `let's be ready` and apply step 1. The result is `!et's b@ re#dy` which step 2 turns into `!eT'sB@rE#dY`, a secure password that's hard to memorize but easy to recreate.

In addition to the above suggestions, this author would like to offer the following ideas. Don't share a password with friends or relatives. Change passwords periodically, but don't go back to old ones; they may already have been cracked by a hacker. Don't write your password anywhere, especially on a paste-it note stuck on your monitor (or even thinly disguised in your address book), and use different passwords for different accounts. Many users apply 2–3 letters taken from the account name as part of the password. Thus, a password for Yahoo may start with `ya` and one for Amazon may start with `am`. This may be secure enough if the passwords are as long as possible.

A security-conscious organization should have a password filter that checks every password selected (and typed) by a user for strength, and issues a mild warning to the user when it discovers a weak password. The warning should be mild, because a strong warning or an ultimatum (either replace your password or your account is closed) may infuriate the user, who may then use his far more superior intelligence to thwart the stupid computer that's trying to tell him, a human, what to do. Also, all schemes requiring a user to replace passwords periodically should use tact to convince the user that the request makes sense and is important. Here is a short list of what users can do (and actually do) to defeat a computer telling them to change a password.

- Submit the existing password as a new one.

- If the computer has been programmed to reject the current password as a new one, a user may have two passwords and simply swap them all the time.

- A similar, bad scheme is to change the current password for a new one, then immediately change it back to the original password.

- If the computer is reprogrammed to remember a user's n previous passwords and it insists on a new password every month, an irate user may decide to use the name of the month as a password. Not only is the name of the current month a terrible choice for a password, but the previous passwords stored in the computer may fall into the hands of a hacker and provide him with a clue to guess the next password with.

⋄ **Exercise 8.6:** Given that the three previous passwords of a user were `qwerty`, `poiuyt`, and `asdfgh`, what's a good guess for the next password?

Some passwords are used locally. A user may type a password to let his computer identify him as the owner. Other passwords are remote. A user may type a password which is then transmitted through the Internet to identify the user to a remote location. A hacker desperate to find someone's password may intercept all the data packets sent from the computer and search for passwords or credit card numbers. A solution is to encrypt a password sent through the Internet, but consider the following. A hacker may intercept the encrypted password and simply send this encryption in the future. One solution is to change the password encryption method all the time, but a better approach is the secure socket layer protocol (SSL, Section 12.10) that's based on certificates issued by trusted sources. Exercise 10.2 proposes another approach to a solution.

In the 1970s and 1980s, fewer users had personal computers, and many had only terminals. A terminal would connect to a central remote computer to enable the user to run programs. In those days, a hacker could often tap the line connecting the terminal to the computer and intercept passwords. Terminals became smart over time and could be programmed. A typical program for a smart terminal was a script (also called a macro). It started with the escape character, followed by a name, followed by a string of characters. This associated the name with the string, so typing the name would be identical to typing the string. For early hackers, such a facility was a Godsend. The hacker with access to the terminal could, for example, reprogram the `return` key to execute a normal return, followed by his malicious program. Often, it was possible to send a terminal a character string starting with an escape and there was no need to have physical access to the terminal. Each technological era has its own security problems.

> Treat your password like your toothbrush. Don't let anybody else use it, and get a new one every six months.
>
> —Clifford Stoll.

◇ **Exercise 8.7:** Search the Internet for commercial devices for local identification (fingerprints, voice prints, and facial identification).

Social engineering. When sophisticated technical methods fail to disclose a password or other desired information, a clever, determined hacker may resort to social engineering. This term refers to ways of exploiting human vulnerabilities and weaknesses. A hacker who badly wants to penetrate the network of an organization, may start by obtaining some telephone numbers of employees. The hacker may then call an employee, pretending to be a security officer from the computer security department or an outside consultant hired to increase security, and ask the employee to cooperate in a test procedure. The hacker may ask the employee to enter a long sequence of complex commands, then claim that there is a problem or that something didn't work. The hacker then asks the employee to try again. After a long sequence of mysterious commands, the hacker again seems disappointed. After a few tries, the hacker starts showing signs of impatience and the employee may feel embarrassed at his inefficiency. At a certain points the hacker says: "This doesn't seem to work. Why don't you just give me your password and I'll try it from here." Someone reading this description might claim that such an approach is stupid because no one would be that naive, yet experience shows that such attempts sometimes succeed.

The following telephone call, from a hacker to a vulnerable employee, perhaps a receptionist, is similar. It exploits the uncertainty and hesitation many employees exhibit when they have to make a quick technical decision.

"Quick! This is John from the security department! I need the password for the xyz account! Quick! We've just discovered a virus and I have to eradicate it immediately. You don't know where it is!? Well, I'll show you how to get it from your computer and if you do that for me, but quick, I won't tell anyone how slow you are."

In the same category belong attempts such as email purportedly coming from the boss, asking to open an attachment, or claiming to be from Microsoft, urging the receiver to open an attachment that will patch a security weakness.

Viruses and worms also use social engineering techniques to lure uninformed email users to click on infected attachments. A common approach is to send messages promising pictures of celebrities. Year 2002 in Appendix B lists three examples.

Good defense against social engineering is for an organization to have a clear policy for the disclosure of passwords. It should spell out who is and who is not entitled to an employee's password.

[Mitnick and Simon 02] is a detailed description of the exploits of a real hacker in the field of social engineering.

◇ **Exercise 8.8:** Use your knowledge of human frailties to come up with more approaches to social engineering.

Social Engineering: Definitions.

Feeding misinformation to people to obtain real information.

Manipulating people psychologically to get useful data.

Using certain keywords in conversation to dupe listeners into giving away personal details.

Obtaining sensitive information by relying on weaknesses and vulnerabilities of people rather than on technical means.

A new form of the old confidence game.

A hacking technique related to social engineering is dumpster diving. A hacker may search through the garbage of a company, looking for computer printouts with passwords, login names, source codes, and customer account numbers. This is why it is important to shred paper documents, even those that seem innocuous (Section 10.2).

Sniffing. Sniffing (more precisely, network sniffing or packet sniffing) is the case where a hacker monitors the traffic to and from a certain site, attempting to identify information (such as passwords, account names, and IP numbers) that may be used later for an attack. The sniffer is a wiretap device, similar to the ones used to tap telephone lines, that works in connection with software. The sniffer collects the bits sent on the network line to a certain network node, while the accompanying software tries to make sense of the bits by identifying the elements of network protocol (IP and TCP headers, passwords, and IP numbers) or at least converting the bits into human-readable format.

There are even (legal) hardware devices and software programs developed for legitimate uses that can be abused by hackers for sniffing. Recall that logging into a remote network node requires sending a password to the node. A hacker monitoring traffic to the node can easily recognize the password.

Fortunately, the Internet is distributed and has no central location. This means that no sniffer can listen to all the traffic on the Internet (an impossible task anyway, considering the amount of data sent all the time). Any local-area network, however, connects its member nodes with a single line, which is why a tap on this line may reveal all the network traffic.

An obvious solution is to encrypt all network traffic, including passwords and login attempts. This prevents direct reading of sensitive data, but a sophisticated hacker can gain some information (such as the types of modems and routers used in the network) even from encrypted data.

[packet-sniffing 04] sells several software tools for detecting packet sniffing on a network. [Orebaugh and Ramirez 04] is a new book that attempts to cover the entire area of packet sniffing.

Case study. Larry, a pharmacist (not his real name), decided to subscribe to ICQ, a popular instant messaging service. One morning he realized he could no longer log into his account. The service kept rejecting his password. After consulting with friends and with experts on the Internet, he realized that someone got hold of his password, logged into his account, and changed the password. Because of its popularity, ICQ has continually been the target of hackers.

The real problem started when the hacker, posing as Larry, started sending Trojan horses as email attachments to everyone on Larry's address book. The recipients, believing the messages came from Larry, clicked on the attachments and infected their computers, which gave the hacker control over those computers as well.

Internet security volunteers from [spywareguide 04] became involved. They messaged the hacker, who demanded money for releasing the account. He was tracked to a university in Holland, which made it slow and legally difficult to identify and apprehend him. The spywareguide workers made sure the victims understood what had happened and showed them how to delete the Trojan horse. The management of ICQ was approached and took several days to close Larry's account.

Once the worst was over, the security people set up to find out how the hackers managed to hijack Larry's account. What they found may astound the reader, but was a familiar story to them. Larry used his name "Larry" as both his login name and his password, which made it trivial for the hacker to guess both. In addition, Larry's ICQ unique identification number was only six digits long, identifying him as a long-time ICQ user, someone who may have a large address book and may be worth attacking.

The conclusion is obvious; your password is the only protection you have from criminals on the Internet. Selecting a weak password is like leaving your doors and windows open or leaving your car key in the ignition.

⋄ **Exercise 8.9:** What is the most common bad password inexperienced people tend to select?

Table 8.5 lists the results of a quick survey made by this author in early 2005. A total of 6828 passwords used on a large university campus were examined and 5667 of them, a full 83%, were found to be in one of seven categories of weak passwords as listed in the table. Generally, password information is sensitive and is not available even to those working closely with the operating system. However, the administrators in charge of campus communications have come up with a new, secure password check and replacement policy, and users were forced to change their passwords within a period of a few days. When a user changed a password, the old password became available for this survey. The results are discouraging.

Defacing Web sites. You sit at your computer, browsing the Internet, admiring your new high-speed Internet connection, clicking here, clicking there, surfing from site to site, having a good time (instead of exercising or spending time outdoors). Today, however, is different. Today you are going to start writing a book on computer security, using Internet resources. You use a search engine to find a Web site on Internet security, you go there and to your surprise you find a single cryptic message scrawled out, announcing something negative and unclear and full of mistypes. You have just seen an example of a network attack. The Web site, like many others, has been defaced.

Defacing a Web site is a common Internet attack. It has already been mentioned in Section 7.3 in connection with DNS poisoning. Defacing occurs when a hacker modifies

Number	Percent	Type of password
33	0.48	A single character
151	2.21	Two characters
911	13.3	Three characters
946	13.9	Four letters
1353	19.8	Five letters of the same case
1280	18.8	Six letters of the same case
993	14.5	Words in dictionaries
5667	83.0	Total weak passwords

Table 8.5: Typical(?) Distribution of Weak Passwords.

the content of a site to display offending or provocative data. This attack is normally perpetrated as a way for the hacker to object to a specific site, to an organization, or to an action or policy carried out by someone perceived by the hacker to be associated with the site. The hacker uses the medium of the Web site to advertise his message. Sometimes, a hacker defaces a site just to prove (to himself) that he controls the Internet. Defacing, also known as the graffiti of the Internet, is surprisingly common. In a survey conducted by the FBI in 2000, 19% of the responders reported some kind of defacement. Web site defacing is done by exploiting a vulnerability in the software run by the site server or a bug in the server's routine that executes the communications protocols. However, password cracking and social engineering are also sources of information to a would-be defacer.

> The medium is the message.
> —Marshall McLuhan

Like many other attacks, the best defense against Web site defacing is to check for software updates and install the latest version of the operating system and server being used by a site. Another solution is to keep a copy (a mirror) of the Web site on a separate disk, and use it periodically to refresh the original data. This way, if the original Web site data becomes corrupted, the damage would automatically be corrected from the mirror after a while. The mirror should be kept on a separate disk to minimize the chance that a hacker would corrupt it at the same time that the original is defaced.

The site [attrition-mirror 05] used to track this type of attack and keep (until 2001) copies of defaced Web sites. It reports an average of 10 defaced sites daily, with up to 100+ sites defaced on certain bad days.

Back in July 2003, the following story appeared in many publications concerned with various aspects of the Internet:

"A hacking contest slated for this weekend could produce a rash of Web-site defacements worldwide, according to a warning issued Wednesday by security companies and government Internet security groups.

The hacker defacement contest is expected to kick off on Sunday. The contest supposedly will award free hosting services, Web mail, unlimited E-mail forwarding, and a domain name of choice for the triumphant hackers, according to a Web site promoting the contest."

In may 2001 the Microsoft site `streamer.microsoft.com` was defaced by a group calling itself Prime Suspectz. The original site was replaced with the message, "Microsoft Owned. Where is the security?" The point was that the attack exploited a vulnerability in version 5 of Internet Information Server (IIS), a product of Microsoft.

In the United States, telephone numbers are 10 digits long. The leftmost three digits are the area code and the next three digits are the prefix. Thus (123) 456-7890 has area code 123 and prefix 456. A large organization may have thousands of telephone numbers, but they often constitute a contiguous range of 4-digit numbers within the same prefix, such as 456-1000 through 456-3200. A hacker who knows some telephone numbers of an organization, such as 456-1544 and 456-2730 can dial the 1000 numbers preceding 456-1544, all the numbers from 456-1544 to 456-2730, and the 1000 numbers following 456-2730, looking for a number that responds with a modem tone. This is a brute force approach for locating a backdoor into the organization.

A war dialer is software (often obtained for free from hackers' Web sites) that can identify telephone numbers that are hooked up to a computer modem. Examples are `BlueDial`, `ToneLoc`, and `PhoneTap`. It is used by hackers to identify potential targets. The program dials all the telephone numbers in a specified range and identifies those numbers that successfully connect to a modem. An advanced war dialer can sometimes also identify the particular operating system running in the computer and detect modem, fax, or PBX tones. A more aggressive version may also try to break into the computer by trying all the login names and passwords in a predetermined list. Commercial war dialers, also known as modem scanners, are also used by network administrators to identify unauthorized modems in their network. Such modems can provide easy access to an organization's network.

Imagine a large university campus, with 10,000+ computers and thousands of users, many of them professors who may not know much about computers and computer security, but have private offices and feel that they are privileged on the campus. A professor decides to hook up a modem to his office computer in order to receive special data, not generally available on the Internet, from a research institute through his office telephone and modem. This innocuous action opens up a backdoor in a campus that may otherwise be very secure, and may allow a hacker to introduce malicious software into campus computers. The point is that it's difficult for campus administrators to identify this security weakness. They have to war dial all the campus telephone numbers periodically, and hope that any unauthorized modems will be up and running while this test is in effect.

◇ **Exercise 8.10:** Once a hacker breaks into one computer on a campus, how can he penetrate to other computers?

In the movie *War Games* (1983) a young hacker uses a primitive version of a war dialer, which gave this type of software first the name "wargames dialer" and later "war dialer."

A phreaker is a hacker "specializing" in telephone-related hacks and the war dialer is one of the most important tools in the phreaker's kit.

Today, with more and more users connected to the Internet through cable or DSL which are open all the time and require no telephone numbers and no dial up, fewer people use modems, resulting in a smaller chance of identifying modem telephone numbers.

Perhaps the best defense against a war dialer is the call back technique, where the operating system has a telephone number associated with each username. When a user dials up the modem and logs in, the telephone hangs up, then calls back the telephone number associated with the user. This makes sense for an organization whose users work off site at fixed locations, but it cannot be used in general.

A security-conscious administrator should personally determine those users who really need dial-in access and deny such access to others. The privileged users should be made to select strong passwords and change them regularly. A stronger defense is to ask for a second password whenever a user logs-in from the outside. This makes it considerably harder for a hacker to crack passwords. Another good habit is to log all dial-in attempts (especially failed attempts) and personally verify each week a sample of them with the relevant users.

> If kings and great men had occasion to authenticate any
> document, they subscribed the "sign" of the cross
> opposite to the place where the "clerk" had written
> their name. Hence we say, to sign a deed or a letter.
>
> —David N. Carvalho, *Forty Centuries of Ink*

9
Spyware

Spyware is the general name of an entire range of nasty software that runs on a computer, monitors the users' activities, collects information such as keystrokes, screen images, and file directories, and either saves this information or sends it to a remote location without the knowledge or consent of the computer owner.

Spyware has recently become one of the biggest topics in computer security. Users who are wizards at avoiding virus-riddled email and always install the latest updates of the operating system are finding to their surprise that in spite of all their efforts their computers are loaded with spyware. And what makes this problem worse is that most spyware is particularly tricky to get rid of.

The various flavors of spyware, such as adware (Section 9.7) and researchware (Section 9.8.1) have become so prevalent and wide reaching that in April 2004 the Federal Trade Commission, a United States Government consumer protection agency, conducted a one-day workshop to explore the issues associated with the effects of information-gathering software [FTC-work 05]. The FTC also accepts complaints about spyware, issues publications to educate the public about this menace, and maintains Web sites on privacy [FTC-privacy 05] and information security [FTC-infosecurity 05].

In addition to the FTC, legislators have become aware of spyware and have been trying to do something about it. In 2004, the United States Congress introduced legislation to fight spyware and its varieties. This act, dubbed SPYBLOCK (for software principles yielding better levels of consumer knowledge) makes it illegal to install software on someone's computer without the owner's consent and also requires reasonable uninstall procedures for all downloadable software (spyware is often meant to be virtually impossible to remove).

Generally, SPYBLOCK requires a dialog box that informs the user that clicking a button will download a certain program and clicking another button will uninstall it. However, if the software has some of the features listed below, more specific disclosure about the operations of the software is required.

- Features of spyware. The software collects information about the user and transmits it to a third party.

- Features of adware. The software causes pop-ups or other advertisements to appear on the user's screen.

- Features of zombie generator. The software sends data to third parties for purposes unrelated to what the user is doing. Typically, these messages help to hijack the computer and eventually use it to send spam or DoS messages.

- Features that modify user settings without the user's consent. The most common such feature is to change the home page of the Web browser.

In addition to this, SPYBLOCK absolutely prohibits programs designed to trick users about who is responsible for content a user sees. A typical example is spyware that causes a counterfeit replica of a Web site to appear whenever the user tries to surf to the legitimate site. Such spyware has been used to fraudulently obtain personal financial information from users confused by dummy Web sites.

9.1 Introduction and Definition

Unfortunately for the lawmakers, it is impossible to even define spyware rigorously. A recent attempt in California (SB 1436) to prevent the installation of spyware on an unsuspecting computer, defines spyware as follows:

Spyware is an executable computer software program that is installed on a user's computer without the knowledge of a computer user by a computer software manufacturer, computer software controller, or Web site operator, and that does either of the following:

(1) Gathers and transmits to the provider of the computer software, to a third party, or to a remote computer or server any of the following types of information:

(A) The personal information of a user (e.g., name, address, etc.).

(B) Data regarding computer usage, including, but not limited to, which Internet sites are or have been visited by a user.

(2) Operates in a manner that is intended to confuse or mislead the user concerning the identity of the person or entity responsible for the performed functions or content displayed by the computer software.

This is a good definition, but readers of this chapter will see that there are already programs such as adware and researchware, that satisfy this definition and yet are considered by many to be different from spyware. The field of computing is related to mathematics, but is not as rigorous and does not always allow for precise definitions and statements.

Since it is virtually impossible to define spyware, any given computer program should be declared spyware if it passes certain tests. The following list proposes such tests and experts can add many more. When presented with a program whose behavior is known and we want to find out whether it is spyware, we ask the following questions and consider the program spyware if the answers to n of them are positive (where n is determined by the leniency of the individual evaluating the software).

■   Is the application file name similar to an important operating system name?

■   Is the program similar to a known Trojan horse?

■   Does the user have to pay a fee to remove the program?

■   Does the program exploit any (even as yet unknown) security holes to propagate and install itself on computers?

■   Does the program log various activities in the computer stealthily?

■   Does the program have a long and confusing software license that uses legalese or unfamiliar technical terms?

■   Is the program useful, popular, and also free or almost free? (if yes, there may be a spyware Trojan horse lurking within).

■   Does the program modify the browser's home page or redirect Internet searches without the user's knowledge?

■   Does the program look for anti-spyware applications in the computer?

■   Does the program try to reinstall itself after it has been deleted (by keeping invisible copies on the disk).

⋄ **Exercise 9.1:** Add another question based on the fact that it is easy to locate complaints on the Internet.

We first consider the question of who installs such software; who are the spies? It turns out that there are many types of spies and they have different reasons to spy. Following are the main categories.

■   Spouses. When relations between a married (or even a live-in) couple start deteriorating, one of them may install spyware on the other's computer, or even on their shared computer. Some experts even claim that this is the primary use of keystroke loggers. In fact, there are known cases where *both* spouses install spyware on the same computer. In such a case, the advantage is normally on the side who installed it first, because they can tell, from the spyware they installed, that the other side has installed similar programs later. This not-so-funny situation may be called a spy versus spy arms race or duel.

■   Parents. More and more parents discover that the best way to restrict the use of the family computer by children is to spy on them. This is arguably one of the few legitimate uses of spyware. (There is software for parental supervision, especially designed to restrict the privileges of certain users on a computer, but this software is far from satisfactory.) We often hear about children abducted by adults they met on the Internet, which suggests that turning children loose in the Internet is like letting them roam city streets known to be dangerous.

A case in point is a free program titled "Spy on your kids" that's freely available for the Macintosh (OS X). The program hides itself from the user, records keystrokes, and can regularly capture the screen. It is available from [Jack Moratis 04] who justifies it by saying "Unsupervised use of the internet can lead children to sneak around behind your back or it could lead to them isolating themselves in their room as they lose touch with the real world. Monitoring your child's computer use is a key way to diagnose problems and it may even save your child from impending danger."

One response to this program found on the Internet claims "Any parent who needs to spy on their kids has some more serious problems to address than how to spy on their kids. Why not use your coding talent to produce some software that promotes trust between parents and kids, or anybody else for that matter. Feh!"

- Bosses. This may be another (sometimes) legitimate use of spyware. An organization expects its employees to use their work computers only for work, not for private uses and certainly not for questionable uses, such as shopping or surfing pornographic sites. The organization must have a clear privacy policy, and should have some way of checking and identifying malingerers.

- Children. In many households, the children are more technologically advanced than their parents, and a child may decide to spy on his parents for fun or to obtain the password they use to limit his access to the computer. This application of spyware is very common and is especially easy since the necessary software can often be freely obtained from hackers' underground Web sites.

- Corporations. They spy on each other to obtain commercial secrets. Almost any commercial organization has sensitive data (such as new product information, pending patents, and planned mergers) on its computers, and many do not realize how easy it is for a competitor to steal this data by installing spyware on a key computer. Even small and very small businesses suffer from this problem and may have to install and run special software that identifies spyware. (See page 68 for a similar example of a print shop attacked by a virus sent by a competitor.)

- Identity thieves. Often an identity thief can easily install spyware on a public computer located in a public library, Internet cafe, or university lab. Such spyware can then transmit information on computer users to the thief and some personal information left on a public computer by a careless user may be enough to start the thief on stealing the user's identity (Chapter 10). Obviously, no one should enter personal data into a public computer.

- Hackers and criminals. A hacker may install spyware on a computer in an attempt to collect passwords. A criminal may do the same in order to collect financial and personal information. In extreme cases, a criminal may install spyware that identifies important and sensitive files and encrypts them, thereby holding them hostage. A message left by the spyware explains what happened and tries to extort money from the user/owner by offering to sell them the encryption key. Reports of such nasty attempts actually appeared in May 2005, but security experts point out that such an extortionist has to expose himself in order to collect the ransom, which makes this type of crime unattractive.

■   Law enforcement. The law, as usual, always lags one step behind the criminals, but law enforcement agencies have finally discovered how to legally use spyware to collect information from computers owned or used by crime suspects. A case in point is a keystroke logging program installed by the American government to capture a password that was later used to access files on a computer owned by jailed mob boss Nicodemo (Little Nicky) Scarfo and his son.

■   Commercial adware, also known as pestware, and parasitic software. Such software (sometimes only cookies) displays unwanted advertisements by taking the user to certain Web sites. Adware may also open new Web pages (popup windows) for these commercials. Adware generally doesn't send data from the computer, so it cannot be called "pure" spyware. Still, adware is steadily becoming more sophisticated. New versions log the user's Internet shopping history and surfing habits (such as news sites, music sites, or sites for movies) and focus the advertisement based on this information. In order to sweeten the bitter taste of adware, Performics, a company specializing in services and technologies for leading multi-channel marketers, has prepared a code of conduct for adware. It recommends habits such as "all clickable events should be initiated by the user" and "an ad publisher should not use ISPs services to interfere with the ads of another ad publisher." The code of conduct is available at [performics 05].

■   Commercial (again) trying to obtain usage data from their customers. A company that makes scanners, for example, also provides a special utility to use their hardware. The company may include a spy routine in this utility, to collect usage data from the user and transmit it periodically and silently to a Web site owned by the company. The data collected may include the number of pages scanned since the last transmission, how many were scanned in color, and how many pages were saved in JPEG, GIF, and other image formats. Such data is anonymous and is used for statistical purposes only, but even this is considered by many an intrusion of privacy and is included in the spyware category. Section 9.6 discusses this practice of remote reporting. The special case of researchware is discussed in Section 9.8.1.

(See discussion on page 30 on how to perturb data for such a purpose. Also, it's hard to imagine a scanner maker having enough time and money to hire personnel to read every report sent from a user site; such data collection can only be for statistical purposes.)

The next three sections discuss other examples of spyware users.

9.2 RIAA and Spyware

The Recording Industry Association of America (RIAA) is the trade group that represents the United States recording industry. Its mission is (quoted) "to foster a business and legal climate that supports and promotes our members' creative and financial vitality." The RIAA members constitute about 90% of the companies that make up the music industry in the United States.

The music industry has known for a while that people illegally download and swap music through file-swapping computer programs such as Napster (now deceased), Kazaa,

Morpheus, and Grokster. In the last few years, the RIAA has become more and more active in pursuing, locating, and prosecuting individuals in well-publicized attempts to scare and stop those who swap music. These facts are well known and will not be discussed here. The topic of this section is to show how the RIAA finds its "persons," because this involves privacy issues and can also teach the reader something about both spyware and anti-spyware.

The key to locating an illegally swapped file is the shared folders that are used by the file-swapping services. When a computer has a shared folder, any file sharing activity in the computer can be monitored from the outside. The RIAA joins a file-swapping service, and then uses special programs (bots) that search for specific files. Once such a file is found in a shared folder, the RIAA bot downloads it and checks to verify its content. If the file turns out to be a copyrighted song or other piece of music, it may end up as evidence in court.

Once an illegal file has been located in a computer, the RIAA still needs to identify the owner of the computer. The first step is to identify the IP address of the computer (although this can be made difficult if the data is routed through an anonymous proxy server). The second step is to find out which ISP was assigned that IP number, and the last step is to convince the ISP to locate and disclose the user's name and address.

We intuitively feel that locating the creator of a dangerous computer virus through his IP address is a good thing, but identifying file-swappers in this way makes some people wonder about privacy on the Internet.

Once a pirated file is located, the RIAA uses software to examine metadata often found in mp3, jpeg, and other types of files such as Microsoft Word. Metadata in an audio file may include the artist's name, song title, recording company, and date of recording. Many mp3 players even display this data when the music is played. However, when a file is copied or ripped, new metadata may be added showing what software did the ripping or the name (pseudonym) of the original hacker who prepared the file. This information is important to the RIAA, but the point is that obtaining it is done by software that some would consider spyware.

> Microsoft will provide the resources for ripping MP3 files in Windows XP after all. But there is a catch: Consumers will pay extra for it.
> —From `news.com.com`, 14 July 2001.

When the RIAA has a file, its incriminating metadata, an IP address, and a name and a physical address, its lawyers may decide they are ready to prosecute.

The solution, for those who want to continue to swap files (a practice not recommended by this author), is to disable the sharing (sometimes called "uploading") feature of the program used for file swapping. If the program has a "supernode" feature, it is better to turn it off too. Reference [Duke 05] shows how to do this for many file sharing services, but don't complain to this author if you get in trouble with the RIAA before or after following these ideas. Another remedy is to avoid music files by artists who are RIAA members (see [RIAA 05] for a list of members).

The zealousness of the RIAA in pursuing song swappers has resulted in claims that they sue people who don't own or use computers and may even sue the dead (see box below).

Gertrude Walton was recently targeted by the recording industry in a lawsuit that accused her of illegally trading music over the Internet. But Walton died in December 2004 after a long illness, and according to her daughter, the 83-year-old hated computers.

More than a month after Walton was buried in Beckley, West Virginia, a group of record companies named her as the sole defendant in a federal lawsuit, claiming she made more than 700 pop, rock, and rap songs available for free on the Internet under the screen name "smittenedkitten."

Walton's daughter, Robin Chianumba, lived with her mother for the last 17 years and said her mother objected to having a computer in the house.

—A news item on Friday, 4 February 2005.

9.3 Terrorism and Spyware

Spyware can be used to launch a DDoS attack. Such attacks have already occurred and were often aimed at anti-spyware Web sites. If a spyware perpetrator can find the time and is willing to spend the effort it takes to attack an anti-spyware site, imagine the effect that a concerted, well-organized attack by terrorists using both spyware and bombs can have on a country, its citizens, and its economy.

It is a little-known fact that the most popular type of computer software is a screen saver. People love those active, colorful patterns that adorn the computer screen when it is not in use (and a personal computer tends to be unused most of the time). With this in mind, imagine a new company, *ScreenSavers R Us*, coming up with a revolutionary screen saver with a patriotic theme. The program costs very little, and it is fully functional even if it's unpaid for. Obviously, there are going to be many copies of this program, used all over the globe, in a very short time. (An alternative is to release a patriotic computer game, full of anti-terrorist action, because computer games are also popular.) Unbeknownst to the users, however, this program is also a Trojan horse set to activate on 11 September of next year and unleash a coordinated DDoS attack that will also result in cutting off the income sources of many companies and will have an adverse effect on the economy.

Even though ScreenSavers R Us practically gives the software away, it still makes money by being an affiliate network. The company's Web site carries ads by well-known brands such as Amazon, Dell, and Target. These ads are seen by anyone surfing to the site in order to download the screen saver, and if the visitor buys anything from any of those sponsors, ScreenSavers R Us gets a small commission. Notice that the sponsors do not check the background, performance, or reputation of ScreenSavers R Us; they are only interested in the size of the commission they fork out. In fact, ScreenSavers R Us doesn't even have to write to any of the sponsors, fill out an application to become an affiliate network, or fulfill any requirements. All it has to do is read an agreement and perform the "click of allegiance" to accept its terms.

Think about it! ScreenSavers R Us is distributing to unsuspecting consumers a screen saver that's actually a ticking time bomb, and while doing this it also makes money each time a consumer buys something from a sponsor.

On the appointed date, the Trojan horses buried in the screen savers spring into action. They instruct their host (zombie) computers to launch a DDoS attack against very specific targets that include medical facilities, critical government Web sites and media information outlets. Now imagine that ScreenSavers R Us was originally founded by a terrorist organization, and they complement the cyber attack with a physical 9/11-style attack on civilians. The result is an unusually large number of casualties, because the medical and government computer networks designed to help in such a case have been incapacitated by the DDoS attack.

As if all this is not enough, the DDoS attack is followed by a flood of emails loaded with propaganda and viruses and sent by the screen saver zombies to hundreds of thousands of computer users, to create further panic and chaos.

Such a combined attack, involving physical violence and cyber crime, could be devastating to any country.

◇ **Exercise 9.2:** Does this sound far-fetched (See also exercise 2.17)?

9.3.1 ParasiteWare

There is an interesting twist to the concept of affiliate networks and it involves a new type of software, the parasiteware. Parasiteware is any adware that overwrites certain affiliate tracking links. Here is a typical scenario. John joins eBates. He is given a computer program, a parasiteware, and is presented with a list of stores to shop at. Those stores pay a commission to eBates (located at [eBates 05]) on John's purchases and eBates pays that commission (or part of it) to john. If this is all the parasiteware does, it does not pose any security threat.

9.4 Political Contributions

In the United States, contributions to political parties and political campaigns cannot be anonymous and must be made public by law. The name, address, and occupation of every contributor become public knowledge, as well as the amounts of individual contributions. This law is the result of unfair political influence gained in the past by anonymous contributors. (The law regulates only "hard money" contributions, but it is also possible to contribute "soft money" which is not regulated by this law.)

This law makes sense, but also serves as an example of government-imposed invasion of privacy, which is why many may consider it a sort of spyware. Contributors know that any donation they make will become public knowledge. The following organizations make it easy to search for political contributions.

■   OpenSecrets (the center for responsive politics, located at [opensecrets 05]) is a non-partisan, non-profit research group based in Washington, D.C. This organization conducts research on campaign finance issues, including names, addresses, and amounts of contributions made by individuals. Currently (late 2004), OpenSecrets maintains data about contributions to the 2004 elections in the United States as well as on contributions going back to 1990. This data includes hard money and soft money contributions. This data can be sorted by zip code, year, and donation amount, thereby making it a very valuable resource to those looking for personal information.

■ The FundRace: This is a useful Web site created and maintained by the Eyebeam research group [fundrace 05] which is trying to illustrate how contributions shape elections. The site maintains a city mapping tool that shows the ratios of Democrats and Republicans in individual states and cities in the United States. The data is based on records filed with the American government of contributions by individuals to a single Republican or Democratic presidential campaign or national committee during 2003 and 2004.

■ The Voters' Self Defense Manual [vote-smart 05] is a 53-page publication from *Vote Smart*, a citizen's organization. It describes project Vote Smart, an online database with information on members of Congress in five basic categories: biographical information, issue positions, voting records, campaign finances, and interest group ratings. This is a useful resource for anyone interested in the members of Congress and their activities, but some may view it as an intrusion on privacy.

The political contributions law and the resources above make it easy to obtain certain items of personal information on many individuals.

⬦ **Exercise 9.3:** Search [opensecrets 05] for political contributions made by a person of your choice.

> There's a lot of money in the Internet. On the last count of malware I did, only 10 percent was written by teenagers. Ninety percent is developed by criminals. This malware is designed for criminal needs such as stealing money, distributing spam, and Internet rackets.
> —Eugene Kaspersky, Kaspersky Labs, `http://www.kaspersky.com`.

9.5 Distribution of Spyware

How can you have your computer riddled with spyware? Simple, just use it. It is well known that certain Web sites such as [HastaLaVista 04] that provide serial numbers for pirated software, also download spyware in the process. Unfortunately, even something as innocent as downloading a movie trailer and watching it can result in more than one spyware program being loaded and installed in the process. A frightening prospect!

An especially disturbing example of spyware with a twist was a program called *LoverSpy* that was advertised for a while by sending large quantities of email (spam) to people with email addresses. LoverSpy was touted as easy-to-use, inexpensive spyware that can spy on spouses, children and so on, but the frightening aspect of LoverSpy was that it could be installed on any computer by sending an electronic greeting card. The card carried a Trojan horse that installed an activity monitor and emailed the result to the card sender periodically. (This type of stealth installation is sometimes referred to as a drive-by download.) LoverSpy monitored and recorded activities such as email, Web sites visited, instant messaging communication, passwords, files, and keystrokes.

Imagine someone using a work computer, checking their email, finding a greeting card, and opening it, only to have spyware surreptitiously installed on their computer. When such spyware is later discovered by the boss, the hapless worker gets in trouble and may loss credibility, a promotion, or even the job itself.

Theoretically, the best defense against spyware is to (1) install anti-spyware software and run it often to detect and remove suspicious programs, (2) install a firewall that monitors transmission of data outside the computer (Section 7.6), and (3) encrypt all sensitive data stored in the computer (all the files with personal or commercial data). Even this is not completely secure. Anti-spyware software (especially the free varieties) may install its own adware (Section 9.7). Spyware that logs keystrokes may save them in the computer, perhaps as an invisible file. The spy (spouse, child, boss, employee) may personally access the computer and copy this file to a removable disk or print it. The spy may log into the computer remotely and retrieve the file periodically, or may even use software that has a backdoor, that allows the spy, but no one else, to remotely access the computer and retrieve the file. The Bugbear worm (year 2002 in Appendix B) installs a backdoor that opens port 36794 and waits for commands from its author. The commands order the worm to perform actions such as copy files, list files and deliver the list to the hacker, delete files, start processes, terminate processes, list processes and deliver the list to the author, deliver saved keystrokes in encrypted form, and deliver various items of information about the infected computer to the hacker.

Backdoors have already found their way into main stream literature. The character Nedry in the novel *Jurassic Park* builds a backdoor in his software and uses it later to turn off the electronic alarm system in the park so he could sneak into a storage room, steal dinosaur DNA, and sell it to a park competitor.

And partly it was insurance for the future. Nedry was annoyed with the Jurassic Park project; late in the schedule, InGen had demanded extensive modifications to the system but hadn't been willing to pay for them, arguing they should be included under the original contract. Lawsuits were threatened; letters were written to Nedry's other clients, implying that Nedry was unreliable. It was blackmail, and in the end Nedry had been forced to eat his overages on Jurassic Park and to make the changes that Hammond wanted.

But later, when he was approached by Lewis Dodgson at Biosyn, Nedry was ready to listen. And able to say that he could indeed get past Jurassic Park security. He could get into any room, any system, anywhere in the park. Because he had programmed it that way. Just in case.

—Michael Crichton, *Jurassic Park*, 1991

In response to spyware, software makers started developing anti-spyware software tools. Such a program searches the disk for executable files with known signatures and alerts the user to them. New spyware is introduced all the time and its signatures change, so anti-spyware software must be updated regularly, like anti-virus software.

The freeware *Spybot* [Spybot 04] is a good example of such a tool. It searches the files for particular signatures that it associates with spyware and alerts the user to decide whether to remove them. The commercial anti-spyware software *Spy Sweeper* from [Spy Sweeper 05] is another example. In January 2005, this program had a data base with tests for 46,536 spyware threats (many of them cookies). *Ad-Aware*, from Lavasoft [Lavasoft 04] is another commercial utility. It works similarly, but finds a different set of nasties. Any personal computer should have several such tools and the owner should update and run them regularly. There are other titles of similar software tools, but the above can normally rid a PC of virtually all the spyware "on the market."

Ad-Aware is designed to provide advanced protection from known Data-mining, aggressive advertising, Parasites, Scumware, selected traditional Trojans, Dialers, Malware, Browser hijackers, and tracking components. With the release of Ad-Aware SE Personal edition, Lavasoft takes the fight against Spyware to the next level.

—From [Lavasoft 04].

Examples of commercially available keystroke loggers are Spector Pro and eBlaster (both by [SpectorSoft 04], both currently in version 5.0). The latter even sends reports back to the spy over email. Both programs offer stealth mode, in which they reveal no trace of their existence. Several recent spy programs even have remote-installation capabilities. They can be sent as email attachments to the potential victim, and will install themselves when clicked on by the (normally trusting) victim. This is an example of a drive-by download. In their advertising, the makers of such software claim that the programs are useful for parents who want to keep an eye on kids' computer-use habits, but they also tend to have testimonials from customers who use the software to spy on spouses and competitors.

Spector Pro contains seven integrated tools that record: chats, instant messages, emails sent and received, web sites visited, keystrokes typed, programs launched, peer to peer file searching and swapping—plus, Spector Pro provides the equivalent of a digital surveillance tape so that you can see the EXACT sequence of EVERYTHING your family members or employees are doing on the computer. All seven tools work together at the same time, secretly saving all the recordings in a hidden location only you know about.

... Spector Pro has been awarded PC Magazine Editors Choice as the best Internet monitoring software for recording computer activity.

—From `www.SpectorSoft.com`.

Encrypting a file implies that the file has to be decrypted every time it is used, then encrypted again. Such a tedious process is an ideal candidate for automation, which is precisely what the well-known PGP software does. PGP has a virtual disk option, where all the sensitive files are moved to a section of the hard disk that's declared a virtual disk. This section is mounted separately, it looks like a separate drive and can be activated by a password. All files written in this section are automatically encrypted each time they are saved and are also automatically decrypted whenever they are opened. The sensitive data is always encrypted (except when it is processed) and the encryption and decryption steps are transparent to the user, except for small but sometimes noticeable delays when files are opened and saved. This is another example of a sophisticated use of cryptography for computer security.

A case study. In late 2004, the United States Federal Trade Commission (FTC) filed the first spyware case against Seismic Entertainment Productions Inc., Smartbot.Net, Inc., and Sanford Wallace, a (supposedly former) spammer. The three have been charged of infecting many computers with spyware, and then offering the computer owners special spy-deleter software for $30 to correct the problem. The spyware in question had modified the Web browsers on the affected computers, and added software to download advertisements in the form of pop-up ads. Surprisingly, the FTC did not ask the court to punish the defendants, only to compel them to remove the offending spyware, to cease their spyware operations, and to produce documents related to their internal marketing. Whether this will serve as a deterrent to future spyware makers and dealers remains to be seen.

Spyware has become such a plague that the United States Congress opened hearings, on 29 April 2004, on the subject, in order to prepare legislation to fight it. The proceedings of these hearing are available at [house 04].

Another evidence for the prevalence of spyware is provided by the following numbers. They were compiled in late 2004 by Webroot, an anti-spyware firm, located at [webroot 04] that makes the SpyAudit anti-spyware program and other tools. Webroot scanned more than 10,000 computers installed in about 4,100 companies and found them riddled with spyware. The large majority of spyware found was cookies, which may be annoying but are harmless. In addition, 5% of the computers had spyware and 5.5% had Trojan horses, which are similar to spyware. Another survey, this time of personal home computers, found an even worse situation. An average of 26 nasty software items (consisting mostly of cookies, spyware, adware, Trojans) was found on these private computers.

⋄ **Exercise 9.4:** Search the Internet for this and other spyware audits.

9.6 Remote Reporting

Remote reporting is an old concept, used in computers since the 1970s. This term refers to data transmitted automatically by a piece of hardware when it detects urgent or unusual conditions in a computer. The following examples are typical:

■ In a multiuser computer, certain powerful instructions are privileged and can only be used by the operating system. When a user program tries to use a privileged instruction, the computer hardware generates an interrupt that invokes an operating system routine. The routine may simply display an error message on the user's screen and terminate the user's program, but it may also send a report to the computer administrators for further investigation.

■ When a printer runs out of paper or becomes jammed, sensors in the printer may send a report to the computer operators, so that the problem can be corrected quickly.

Nowadays, in the age of personal computers and spyware, remote reporting has taken on a new, more sinister face. Commercial entities, even reputable ones, sometimes decide to use a mild version of spyware to gain a competitive edge. The chance of knowing more about their customers and how their products are used is simply too tempting to pass up. A typical example is a printer maker. Every printer is different, so a printer maker always provides software to drive their printers on various platforms. The software may contain a remote reporting feature that collects data about the use of the printer and periodically sends it to the printer maker for statistical use. The data may include items such as the number of pages printed, how many were in color, and the page coverage (how much of each page was covered by ink).

A case in point is the Lexmark Corp., a maker of laser and inkjet printers. In November 2004, several reports appeared in the `comp.periphs.printers` Usenet news-group claiming that Lexmark printer drivers contain spyware that monitors the use of the printer and reports back to `www.lxkcc1.com`, a Web site owned by Lexmark. This practice was discovered by users who installed special firewalls that monitor data sent outside the computer by various programs.

Lexmark initially denied the rumors, then admitted the existence of the tracking software, but claimed that (1) its software license includes a statement about the silent monitoring, (2) no personal data is collected by its software, and (3) it is impossible to identify any individual user. The company even claimed that the software has a name, *Lexmark Connect*. Such data is obviously useful to Lexmark and can be used to help plan the next generation of printers.

In response, users point out that (1) very few people read long, complex software licenses, warnings, and copyright statements, (2) once someone has purchased a printer, the only way to use it is to agree to the software license, and (3) after the software is installed, it prompts the user to fill out a registration form with the user's name, address, and the printer's serial number, thereby making it possible for Lexmark to track the printing habits of individual users.

Other points to consider are (1) many users have software installed for them by an expert, who becomes the one to agree to the software license, (2) sometimes a computer is purchased with a printer as a package deal and the software is preinstalled in a store, (3) a user who has read the license and noticed all its points is only human and may forget some of the conditions, especially after reading many such licenses, and (4) many have come to consider software licenses and the need to click to accept them (the click of allegiance) an unnecessary nuisance.

It is clear that many users object to data being sent back to a manufacturer silently, surreptitiously, and involuntarily. Even a user who has carefully read the license and knows about the remote reporting feature may become suspicious when they actually notice a printer "calling home." Such behavior resembles spyware too much for users to feel comfortable with. The result may be a growing suspicion of customers toward Lexmark that may translate into declining sales.

Proponents of the "calling home" approach claim that programs that send data back to the manufacturer offer important advantages for the consumer. A printer maker may establish a subscriber service where a printer notifies the company when toner or ink runs low, and the company responds by automatically delivering a fresh supply and charging the customer. A possible solution may be for a company to start offering such a service, or at least to notify the user each time the program intends to transmit data (and to display the data about to be sent).

Both Microsoft, the makers of the Windows operating system and Apple with the Macintosh OS X have implemented a procedure for error reporting. When the operating system senses that a program has quit abnormally, it (the operating system) gives the user a chance of filling out an error report and sending it to the manufacturer. Such open policy cannot reasonably be considered spyware and can perhaps be adopted by printer makers and others.

Lexmark is also notorious for its strict policy about third-party cartridges. A Lexmark toner cartridge has a special chip and the printer will not accept a cartridge that doesn't have this chip (Lexmark is not the only printer maker that has this policy). Original Lexmark cartridges are therefore expensive, which has prompted other companies to copy the chip and make compatible, but less expensive, cartridges. Lexmark has sued one such competitor, Static Control, that makes imitation chips called Smartek. These chips allow printer owners to use Static's after-market laser toner cartridges for printers made by several manufacturers.

In its law suit, Lexmark claimed that the Smartek chip violates the 1998 DMCA law enacted in the United States to limit Internet piracy. Under this law, it is generally unlawful to circumvent technology that restricts access to a copyrighted work or sell a device that can do so.

Lexmark has claimed that the Smartek chip mimics a technology used by Lexmark chips and thus unlawfully tricks the printer into accepting an after-market cartridge. Fortunately, the United States Congress also included exemptions in the DMCA explicitly permitting activities such as law-enforcement activities, encryption research, security testing, and interoperability.

The last of these, interoperability, permits the mimicking of technology "for the purpose of enabling interoperability of an independently created computer program with other programs." The interoperability exception, combined with a legal claim about the traditional fair use rights enshrined in United States copyright law, has resulted in Static Control winning on appeal (and the rest of us benefitting from competition). Static Control's site [scc-inc 04] has more information on this case.

For more that a century, industrialists and marketers have realized that for many products, the "real" money didn't come from the selling of the big item at a huge, one-time premium, but rather from the periodic sale of inexpensive support items necessary for the operation or maintenance of the big item. Smart business people realized that if you practically give away the big item, the money to be made on the regular sales of the little support items translates to huge profits.

The classical example of this pricing strategy comes from the business of razors. Makers of razors and razor blades sell their razors at or below cost, and make money from the sale of their proprietary, patent-protected razor blades.

Several decades ago, the United States government enacted the Sherman and Clayton Anti-Trust acts to prevent anyone from being subjected to this sort of business practice. These acts dictate that consumers cannot be forced to use a particular supply, nor can a warranty be voided because a consumer did not use the high-priced, name-brand supply. This applies to any product that needs a regular supply of anything.

9.7 Adware

Generally, adware is software that downloads advertisements and displays them on a computer. These advertisements are referred to in the advertising industry as interstitials or pop-ups. Various flavors of adware can do more than that. For example, they can profile your online surfing and spending habits. Some adware comes as a virus or a Trojan horse, and is definitely spyware, while other adware is voluntarily installed by computer owners on their machines. In order to entice users to install adware on their computers, the adware is often promoted as free software that cleans up the computer by finding and identifying spyware and other "objectionable" software. This is an example of a free item that comes with a hidden cost. A case in point is PurityScan [purityscan 05], a company that offers free software to scan a computer and find undesirable content.

> It's a fact—inappropriate files can make their way onto your computer when you surf the Internet. PurityScan is a safe and easy way to discover if undesirable files are on your computer.
>
> —From PurityScan.

The catch (or hidden cost) is that the PurityScan software modifies the Internet browser installed on the computer. Once PurityScan is installed, pop-up ads appear on the screen every time the browser is launched. A user who finds this practice annoying, can get rid of the unwanted ads by uninstalling the PurityScan software, but the point is that the ads appear as long as the software is installed, not just when it is actually used.

This catch is mentioned in PurityScan's user's agreement, but as discussed on page 223, few people read long, complex software licenses. The inescapable conclusion is: read your software license, especially if the software is free.

Someone with experience (especially bitter experience) with computer security issues would tend to recommend against using free software or services that come with hidden costs, especially since they may involve even higher costs in the future. An unscrupulous company may start by selling pop-up ads, but may later be tempted to "extend" its software to look for personal information and browsing patterns in host computers and sell this information to marketing organizations.

The final choice, of course, is in the hands of the user who should, as always, use common sense.

> Any software application in which advertising banners are displayed while the program is running is called Adware. And any software that sends data back to a third party—WITHOUT ASKING the user—is Spyware.
>
> —From `www.adware.info`

Table 9.1 lists the top ten spyware programs of 2004. It is obvious that virtually all are adware.

	Name	Vendor	Type
1	Gain	`www.gainpublishing.com/`	adware
2	Claria (Gator)	`www.gainpublishing.com/`	adware
3	Gamespy arcade	`www.gamespyarcade.com/`	adware hidden in a game
4	Hotbar	`www.hotbar.com/`	monitors browsing activity
5	Ezula	`www.ezula.com/`	adware
6	BonziBuddy	`www.bonzi.com/`	tracks all usage, changes browser homepage
7	Weathercast	`www.WhenU.com/products.html`	ads in weather forecasts
8	LinkGrabber 99	`www.Netjumper.com/`	ads in browser
9	TOpicks	`www.topicks.com/`	adware
10	Cydoor	`www.cydoor.com`	adware

Table 9.1: Top Ten Spyware of 2004.

9.8 Spyware?

The following example illustrates how a useful, well-designed piece of software can be abused. The well-known Internet search engine Google has come up with *Google Desktop Search*, a utility [Google 05] that prepares an index (or cache) of many types of files on a computer. Once the index is ready, the user can easily search the computer for files with certain keywords. In addition to text and other types of document files, this search includes Web sites visited in the past, email messages, and bookmarks. Google Desktop Search is definitely a useful program, but poses a hidden danger. When used on a public computer, it allows a miscreant to locate important personal information left by others.

> Google Desktop Search is how our brains would work if we had photographic memories.
>
> —`http://desktop.google.com/about.html`

Libraries, university labs, and Internet cafes have public computers that are continually used by many people. Careless users may enter passwords or credit card numbers into such a computer, and these may later be discovered by a hacker. All that such a bad guy has to do is install Google Desktop Search, hide its icon, leave it for a few hours to generate its cache, and then use it to locate keywords such as "password," and "master card." When done, the hacker can delete the utility and its cache in order to cover up his tracks. This scenario applies also to a home computer with several users.

Because of this and similar dangers, a careful user should never conduct important business at a public computer. The owner of a public computer should search as often as possible for spyware and utilities such as Google Desktop Search and delete them. Most operating systems have a routine that displays all the active processes on the computer and can reveal the presence of active but hidden spyware and other suspicious software.

9.8.1 Researchware

It is clear that keystroke loggers and screen capturers are spyware, as are many other types of rogue software. There are, however, invasive and secretive programs that are touted by their developers as adware or researchware, while others consider them as bad as spyware.

Consider the case of comScore Networks [comscore 04], a company that helps other companies improve their marketing, sales, and trading strategies by providing them with insight on consumer behavior. The following quote, from comScore's site, shows how it gains this insight: "...based on a continuously captured view of a representative cross-section of more than 2 million global Internet users—the largest consumer panel."

In order to accomplish its task and continuously capture the views of millions of online users, comScore has developed software titled *marketscore*. This application is voluntarily installed in the computers of many Internet users (whom comScore calls *panelists*) who participate in comScore's market research and who in return receive from comScore benefits such as server-based virus protection, improved Internet performance, sweepstakes prizes, and the opportunity to help shape the future of the Internet.

Once marketscore is installed on a computer, it routes all the Internet traffic of the computer through comScore's computers. Every data packet sent from a panelist's computer arrives first at comScore's server where it is examined and then forwarded to its destination. Every packet destined for the panelist is similarly routed through comScore's server, where it is also examined and forwarded to the panelist's computer. Even secure data transfers, which employ the secure socket layer (SSL, Section 12.10) protocol, are examined. An encrypted data packet arriving at the comScore server is decrypted, examined, and then re-encrypted and sent on its way.

This process, which is completely transparent to the computer user, allows comScore to capture a complete picture of the panelist's online activities. Every Web site visited, every page viewed, every ad seen, every promotion used, every product or service purchased by the panelist (including the prices paid) are recorded and used by comScore to provide its client companies with insight on consumer behavior.

In addition, comScore sends its panelists surveys asking about their offline commercial activities, such as supermarket purchasing, their use of manufacturers' coupons, or automotive registrations, and this information is also included in the company's statistical reports and improves its insight on consumer behavior.

ComScore claims that its panelists are fully aware of its practices, but are safe because the company removes any personal information it receives from the participants and sends its clients only statistical data on E-commerce sales trends, Web site traffic, and online advertising campaigns.

The claim is that spyware is software that's planted in a computer without the computer owner's knowledge, whereas researchware is downloaded into a computer with the owner's permission. Also, spyware is hidden in the computer, while researchware can be located and deleted by the owner/user at will.

These activities have turned comScore in just a few years into an important Internet research provider (IRP, not to be confused with ISP). Its research service is regarded as one of the best and its clients include large companies, universities and media outlets.

With such success, trouble was bound to ensue. Privacy advocates got wind of comScore's activities (and similar operations by other organizations) and are warning consumers against them, claiming that software like marketscore is nothing more than spyware. After all, it sniffs and tracks every step a user takes on the Internet, and the user has to trust comScore to ignore and delete any personal data. Also, marketscore is software and is therefore vulnerable to viruses. If a virus invades marketscore, all the information available to comScore may become available to the virus' owner.

In its defense, comScore calls its software "researchware" and tries to convince security experts, ISPs, and the general public that researchware (and similar programs that collect data) is not spyware. The point is that the voluntary nature of marketscore participation makes it a legitimate application of computers and networks for research purposes. Spyware, in contrast, is *unknowingly* planted in victims' computers.

In response, consumer and security experts point out that legitimizing labels such as adware and researchware may lead to many new software applications that "live" in the wide gray area between (definitely bad) spyware and (useful and legitimate) researchware. A possible result of this battle may be government intervention in the form of a law or an agency that will try to precisely classify each software product as spyware, adware, researchware, system monitor, data miner, or something else. Another, unavoidable result will be additional confusion for computer users. The vast majority of computer users know very little about their computers and how data is moved into and out of the computer. Such users may be lured by promises of gifts and may never realize the kind of information that's collected about them.

The success of comScore has prompted other companies to release software that detects the presence of marketscore and can delete it. One of the major players in this field is Webroot, an Internet security company (see [webroot 04]) that developed *Spy Sweeper*, a utility that promises to locate and uproot not just spyware and adware, but other types of software such as system monitor, researchware, and other "pests" that transmit personal data and may potentially be as damaging as viruses and worms.

◇ **Exercise 9.5:** search the Internet for other companies that develop and promote anti-spyware programs.

Ten Basic Facts About Spyware

The following ten paragraphs are not exactly the ten commandments of spyware, but they summarize its important attributes and the features that distinguish it from other types of rogue software.

■ Spyware started as software that records keystrokes and captures the monitor screen periodically, but has since "matured" in unforeseen ways. The newest breed of spyware can open a port in a computer and protect it with an easy-to-guess password. Any hacker scanning the Internet can find these vulnerable computers, guess the password, and transmit dangerous software. Thus, new spyware can create security weaknesses.

■ The use of spyware is restricted by law in the United States and in other countries. Thus, before trying to install spyware on someone else's computer, a potential spy should consider the legal ramifications of this act and its possible consequences. More federal and local laws governing spyware can be expected in the future.

- Spyware is constantly becoming more sophisticated and less expensive, which makes it more and more popular.

- Spyware is made easy to install, easy to use, but hard to remove, and these features also increase its popularity.

- Adware and researchware are not the same as spyware. Spyware is not generally written and distributed by commercial entities or market researchers. These bodies write and attempt to distribute software that can be classified as rogue or at least as invading privacy, but spyware is much more invasive and constitutes a threat, not just a nuisance.

- Spyware is often hawked as monitoring software, which disguises its real applications. However, its makers and sellers are aware of the potential spying power of their software and should warn potential buyers of any possible abuses of their monitoring software. Instead of warning buyers, the makers of spyware often make buyers agree (with the instantaneous click of allegiance) to release them from any liability in the use or abuse of the software.

- Spyware is made difficult to remove and to detect, but it is not absolutely invisible; it can be detected, yet spyware makers often try to convince potential purchasers that the software is untraceable.

- Spyware can be planted in a victim's computer from the outside, as a Trojan horse, exploiting any vulnerabilities or security weaknesses as any other rogue software.

- Most spyware transmits the data it collects. Therefore, deleting sensitive data, such as log files, browser caches, and cookies, may not protect a computer user from loss of data by spyware.

- The best way to detect and delete spyware is by using anti-spyware on a regular basis. However, even this cannot guarantee a clean computer, which is why a careful computer user should use common sense and should (1) read reports on the Internet about new types of spyware, (2) avoid software from unknown or untrusted sources, and (3) avoid surfing to Web sites where a careless click may download spyware to the computer.

[spywareguide 04] is a Web site with much information about spyware, anti-spyware, and related topics. [Wyatt 04] is a book helping users of Windows XP to fight spyware as well as other problems specific to that operating system.

> I'm not a spy or anything. I did all the work sitting at a little desk in a little room on the third floor. I wrote a report, and that was that.
>
> —Tom Clancy, *Patriot Games*

10
Identity Theft

Identity theft is the crime of pretending to be someone else. The thief goes to the trouble of obtaining someone's identity in order to gain financially from fraud, leaving the victim to sort out the resulting mess as best they can. Identity thieves use three main methods to obtain personal information:

■ Installing spyware on personal computers, computers at public places, and computers in offices and other places of work. Such spyware acts as *snoopware*, and provides the thief with sufficient personal information to steal someone's identity.

■ Stealing data files from E-commerce sites, government agencies, and other entities that maintain large consumer and citizen data bases.

■ Phishing. This is the topic of Section 10.4.

There are also secondary sources for personal information such as stealing letters from mailboxes, searching trash cans for useful garbage, mostly computer printouts, and sending baited mail or email to unsuspecting or vulnerable persons, promising free gifts or cruises and asking for personal data. Spyware is the topic of Chapter 9. This chapter discusses the latter two methods.

The Federal Trade Commission made public some startling statistics on identity theft this week. According to their own survey data, 27.3 million Americans have been victims of identity theft in the last five years, and a whopping 9.9 million people joined this unfortunate list in just the last 12 months. The crime, the FTC found, costs consumers $5 billion, but the damage is not, according to the FTC, limited to individuals; the commission's survey also found that businesses lost nearly $48 billion last year in cases of identity theft.

—From [ftc 04].

10.1 Introduction

A rare crime in the past, identity theft has become prevalent in the age of the Internet because of the greater availability of personal information in various computerized data bases. More and more files and data bases contain personal information such as names, physical addresses, email addresses, telephone numbers, and government identification numbers (in the United States, the social security numbers). A news item noticed by this author in late October 2004 tells about a hacker breaking into a computer at the University of California, Berkeley, stealing files with personal information of 1.4 million Californians. The information was gathered by a researcher, a social scientist, from government sources without the knowlege or consent of the individuals involved. Such cases are becoming common. Not every identity thief is a hacker or a professional criminal. A news item broadcast on CNN in early November 2004 tells about a cancer patient whose identity had been stolen while he lay in hospital. After weeks of double agony for the victim, the thief was caught and turned out to be a technician at the hospital, who happened to have access to the patient's information.

In the United States, the key step to stealing someone's identity is to obtain that person's social security number. Based on this number, the thief can obtain bona fide identification documents, such as a driver's license and credit cards. With those, the thief may purchase merchandise and draw cash. The thief may also use the credit background of the victim to apply for loans, and may even obtain a job, not pay any taxes, and wait for the tax authorities to demand the money from the victim. There are known cases of victims of identity theft getting arrested for crimes committed by the thieves.

Even governments have finally become aware the role played by the social security number (SSN) in identity theft. A law (that started its life as SB168) enacted in California in early 2005 is designed to thwart identity theft by restricting the use of social security numbers by bodies other than government agencies. Among other clauses, this law says that companies cannot post or display social security numbers, print them on identification cards or badges, print an SSN on anything mailed to a customer, require people to transmit an SSN over the Internet (through e-mail, for example) unless the connection is secure, or require people to log on to a Web site using an SSN without a password. One publication of the state of California that discusses the relation between the SSN and identity theft is [Calif-gov 05].

Experts who talked to many victims of this crime paint the following picture of a typical identity theft. Mr and Mrs Smith apply for a new, low-interest mortgage on their home. To the best of their knowlege they have excellent credit and don't owe money to anyone. When their loan application is processed, the bank obtains their credit report, which shows many open, outstanding accounts to stores, credit card companies, and E-commerce sites. In the language of loan officers, these are negative accounts, so their loan application is refused. The Smiths are first surprised, then puzzled, and finally devastated. Their case is complicated by the additional fact that the thief actually

made the minimum payments of the credit cards balances, which allowed him more
time for his activities and made the police investigators suspicious of the Smiths.

The victims normally take months to discover the identity theft and on average
they have to pay about $1000 in legal fees and damage repair of their credit. The thief
is many times apprehended, but is normally sentenced to only probation or a short
prison term, punishment that many thieves feel makes this type of crime pay very well.
In addition, light sentences also discourage law enforcement agencies from prosecuting
identity theft crimes. In a democracy, prosecution is a slow, expensive process, and a
prosecutor or a district attorney may decide that releasing an identity thief would free
scarce resources that could then be used to prosecute more serious crimes.

In response to the growing threat of identity theft, the Unites States Congress
passed a tough new identity theft bill, signed into a law by the President in July 2004,
that adds two years to prison sentences for criminals convicted of using stolen credit
card numbers and other personal data to commit crimes. Violators who use such data
to commit "terrorist offenses" would get five extra years. In the signing ceremony the
President said "Like other forms of stealing, identity theft leaves the victim poorer and
feeling terribly violated. The criminal can quickly damage a person's lifelong effort to
build a good credit rating."

Spyware for identity theft. The discussion of spyware in Chapter 9 makes it
obvious that spyware, even the less-sophisticated programs designed for use by parents
and bosses, can become a dangerous tool in the hands of an identity thief (who in
turn considers it a treasure trove). The thief installs spyware remotely, as a Trojan
horse, normally by sending the spyware application as email attachment and duping
the recipient to click on it (an example of a drive-by download).

◇ **Exercise 10.1:** Can you think of any legitimate scenario where a parent or employer
would need to use remote installation to install a monitoring program?

A case study. The case of identity thief Juju Jiang has been well publicized. He
had covertly installed keylogging spyware on computers in about 14 New York branches
of the Kinko company. Kinko's has grown from a supplier of stationery, copy services,
and college textbooks to a full-fledged Internet cafe where customers rent time on personal computers and use Internet services. For over a year Juju captured more than
450 names and passwords that he used to access bank accounts and open new accounts
online. Jiang was finally caught and pleaded guilty in July 2003, but this case implies
that there must be many similar, undiscovered cases of identity thieves exploiting the
easy access to public computers.

(Jiang was caught when he used one of the stolen passwords to access a computer
by means of `GoToMyPC`, software that makes it easy to access a computer remotely. The
computer owner was home at the time and suddenly saw the cursor on his screen move
about and files open as if by themselves. He then saw an account being opened in his
name at an online payment transfer service.)

◇ **Exercise 10.2:** Obviously, it is risky to type a password outright in a public computer
even if no one is looking. Suggest ways to type a password (or any other text) indirectly,
to confuse any spyware.

Because of the prevalence of identity thefts, there are several precautions that everyone must take. The most important ones are the following:

■   Monitor your credit on a regular basis. This is the best way to discover identity theft. Any suspicious or unrecognizable items such as a wrong change of address, unknown open financial accounts, or negative statements by anyone should be cause for concern. Similarly, we all receive monthly billing statements from banks, credit cards, and utility companies and those should also be checked for errors, unusual activity, and unknown, unrecognizable items. In the United States, an individual is periodically entitled to a free credit report which can be applied for from the large credit reporting companies such as EquiFax, Experian, ConsumerInfo, and CreditReporting.Com.

■   When applying for a loan, a credit card, or rental housing, always request that your identification number (in the United States, the social security number) be erased once the application is processed. If the application requires a credit report, ask for the report to be shredded once the application is processed.

■   Persons in the United States should request their social security earnings and benefit statement at least once a year and check for signs of fraud. This statement can be applied for online at [ssa-gov 04] or by filling out form SSA-7004 obtainable at [ssa-form 04]. The statement is mailed to the consumer by the government.

■   Shred old and unneeded documents (Section 10.2). This author's experience suggests using a cross-cut shredder for best results and to avoid the huge piles of narrow slips of paper left by a straight-cut shredder.

■   Replace your mailbox with a lockable one. One way identity thieves obtain personal information is by stealing it from mailboxes. Security-conscious persons should consider renting a mailbox in a post office (another example of a trade-off between security and convenience). Anyone going on vacation or planning to stay away from home should arrange for their mail to be picked up by a trusted person or be kept in the post office.

◇ **Exercise 10.3:** What personal information useful to an identity thief can be found regularly in a mailbox?

■   An identity thief may call you, claiming to be from a loan company that gives out loans at a low interest rate. It is important not to give out personal information over the telephone, unless you personally know the person on the other side. Along the same lines, don't print your social security number on personal checks and don't let merchants write it on your checks as an identification.

■   Check your wallet and remove anything you don't use on a regular basis. There is no need to have in your wallet or carry on your person bank account numbers, passwords, a birth certificate, or your social security card. Unfortunately, in the United States certain people must carry their medicare or another health insurance card that uses the social security number as identification.

■   Passwords are now routinely used by financial institutions to verify transactions. If a password is optional, get one (and follow the guidelines for secure passwords listed in Section 8.3).

■   Be paranoid rather than vulnerable. Check your mail and email with suspicion. Don't just assume that a letter you received was really sent by a person known to you or that an email received really came from the source address on the email and is going to the destination address you specify. Remember how spoofing (Section 7.3) works and how spammers use it. Identity thieves use it in much the same way to obtain your personal data. You may receive email that seems to have come from a familiar store or online merchant and asks you to click on a link to update your personal information. You click and are directed to a Web site that looks identical to the store's or merchant's site, where you are asked to enter your password. Be suspicious. It is best to type the store's URL manually rather than use the convenience of a click.

■   Page spoofing is a technique hackers and thieves use to route your email or Web site request to a different address. If a Web form has a return address such as `http://www.BofA.com@thief.biz/index.html`, your reply will go the address following the "@" sign instead of to the Bank of America.

■   The use of security software is recommended. At a minimum you should have on your personal computer a firewall, antivirus, and anti-spyware software. The latter two should be updated regularly with the latest definitions and security patches.

■   Bypass registration. Many magazines and newspapers keep their content on the Internet and will let anyone read it for free. Some, such as the *New York Times*, require (free) registration. Beside being tedious, typing your name, address, email and other personal information may help identity thieves and should be avoided as much as possible. An attractive solution is to use the free service offered by `www.bugmenot.com`. You type in the site you're trying to access and you immediately receive a username and password that will let you in. No personal information needs be typed or sent over the Internet.

■   Fake an email address. Often, a Web site asks for an email address to send a confirmation to. Similarly, someone at a party may ask for your email for a flimsy reason. Anyone who needs a temporary email address can use the free service offered by [mailinator 04]. You simply select an email address of the form `xxx@mailinator.com`, where `xxx` is any string and give it to someone you'd like to hear from once, but not more than once. When a message is sent to that address, it is deleted after a few hours, giving you a chance to read it. This foils any would-be identity thief or spammer who collect email addresses. Similar services are offered by [dodgeit 04], [spamgourmet 04], and [spambob 04].

■   A disposable credit card number? Yes, such things are offered by Citibank. Such a number can be used just once for online shopping (not for purchases where the actual card has to be swiped). It takes time to apply for such numbers, but they increase security.

■   Rotate your IP. A hacker planning to break into your computer starts by finding your IP address. For a subscription fee of $30 a year, `anonymizer.com` will change your IP at random very often while you surf, thus strengthening your Internet security.

⋄ **Exercise 10.4:** What's wrong with people knowing your IP number?

■   Turn off html. Email messages are sent in either plain text or html formats. It turns out that a spammer can embed special html commands in an otherwise innocuous-looking email message. Such code tells the spammer whether the message has been read and for how long. Many email programs make it possible to turn off "display html" in the preferences.

This long list looks intimidating, but there is some help. The identity theft resource center [idtheftcenter 04] offers information, resources, and help to victims of identity theft.

One way to gain extra protection when surfing the Internet is to use a proxy server. A proxy server is a service that "sits" between your computer and the Internet. It serves many Internet users by saving the most-popular Web sites in its buffer (or cache). When a user requests a cached page, the proxy server can serve it immediately. A special type of a proxy server is an anonymous server. It hides the IP addresses of its users, thereby allowing them to surf anonymously. A Web site that's being visited from an anonymous server cannot locate the IP address of the visitor, which gives the visitor some protection. The point is that a Web site may collect the IP addresses of its visitors and use this information to limit what certain visitors can see and to monitor visitors' surfing patterns. However, the anonymous proxy server itself may collect the IP numbers of its visitors and abuse this information, which is why it is recommended to choose a reputable anonymous proxy server (which rules out most of the free ones).

10.2 Shredding

Old magnetic and optical storage media should be thoroughly destroyed, not just thrown away, when it is no longer needed, because people tend to forget what they put on old disks and CDs. A single CD may have old bank and tax records and personal correspondence that may prove a treasure trove for a wrongdoer looking to steal identities. Banks, mortgage companies, and medical and dental offices should especially pay attention to the problem of getting rid of old, personal information. The following paragraphs offer some ideas on how to handle old storage media in order to protect personal information and privacy.

■   Encrypt personal files. Many strong-encryption programs, commercial, shareware, and free, are available for all computer platforms. The well-known PGP software is the first example that comes to mind, and there are many others. Remember that the protection is provided by the encryption key, not the encryption algorithm, so be sure to choose strong keys as discussed in Section 8.3.

■   On a magnetic disk, it is not enough to simply delete old files. Deleting a file only removes it from the disk directory and marks the space occupied by the file as available, so that other data can be written in it. However, as long as no data has been written in this space, an expert may recover the original, deleted data, or at least parts of it.

Apparently there are many security-conscious people who own paper shredders who don't know or don't care about residual information from their deleted computer files. But there have been many people in recent history who have learned about this issue the hard way. That's how U.S. Senate investigators got evidence on Col. Oliver North. Email messages that North believed to be deleted were found and used against him in litigation. A total of 758 email messages were sent, involving him in the Iran-Contra affair, and every one of them was recovered. Ironically, this problem becomes more difficult if you make backup copies of everything on your computer, as you should.

—From `http://www.akdart.com/priv9.html`

- A magnetic disk can be erased by reformatting it, but not all reformatting utilities do a good job. It is safer to erase a disk by degaussing it first, and then formatting it. Degaussing is the process of passing the disk through a strong magnetic field that erases the data bits recorded on the disk. (The unit of measure of magnetic inductive force is the gauss, named for mathematician Karl Friedrich Gauss.)

- When new data is recorded "on top" of old one, it erases the old data. This is referred to as data wiping. Thus, a disk can be erased by filling it up with (perhaps random) data, but the entire disk must be filled up, to ensure that no old data remains.

- A disk can be physically destroyed by exposing the platters and cutting or physically damaging each. This is easy to do with a floppy disk, but a hard disk has to be disassembled first.

- Old CDs and DVDs can be shredded. Many high-quality shredders are powerful enough to shred the heavy plastic of these media. However, it is the opinion of this author that it is enough to bend and fold a CD several times and make sure the metallic layer (that looks like very thin aluminum foil) has cracked. A few more foldings will actually break the CD, and the really paranoid will throw each piece in a different trash container.

- A commercial service that shreds documents may want to retain the inner hub of all CDs shredded (this is where the serial number of the CD is written, Figure 10.1) to prove that they were in fact destroyed, and not just thrown in the trash.

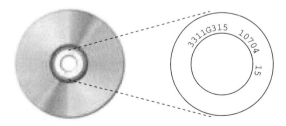

Figure 10.1: The Inner Hub of a CD.

■   Old, unneeded paper documents should be shredded. A cross-cut shredder is recommended for best results and to avoid the huge piles of narrow slips of paper left by a straight-cut shredder.

■   When applying for a loan, a credit card, or rental housing, always request that your identification number (in the United States, the social security number) be erased once the application is processed. If the application requires a credit report, ask for the report to be shredded once the application is processed.

(The following news item appeared on local television in San Diego, California in early November 2004. Someone had found in a dump a large quantity of documents with sensitive personal information of people who applied for mortgages. The mortgage company in question was contacted and its president explained that the company went out of business sometime earlier and hired a disposal professional to shred its documents. Instead of shredding the documents, the professional simply dumped them in the trash.)

> It never ceases to astonish me what organisations leave in refuse piles without first giving them a session with the paper shredder.
>
> —Hugo Cornwall, *The Hacker's Handbook* (1985).

10.3 Internet Cookies

Online shopping is so common nowadays that we take it for granted. It's easy to surf to an online store, select an item, place it on a "shopping cart" and either order it or ignore it and forget about it. When the item is ordered, the customer provides a name, address, and credit card information, but before the item is ordered the shopping cart is simply a record in the online store's computer with the item's information and whatever is known about the customer (often just an IP address). Now consider the following typical situation. The customer places an item in the shopping cart, then surfs to another store to compare items and prices. If the customer returns to the original store within a reasonable period of time, ready to order the item, the store's computer should be able to identify the customer and associate him with a waiting shopping cart.

This problem was recognized in the early days of E-commerce and is handled by adding a simple feature, cookies, to Internet browsers. A cookie is a small text file, with an expiration date, sent by the store (or by any site the user visits) and kept by the browser until it expires or until the user explicitly deletes it. When a potential customer visits an online store, the store's computer looks for any cookies in the customer's browser area. If it finds a cookie with the store's URL, the cookie's content identifies the customer to the store, which can then reconstitute any past shopping cart, shopping habits, and browsing habits of the customer.

A simple application for cookies is to identify an online visitor to a Web site (such a visitor may also be a customer). Imagine the Web site of URL `www.rollers.info`. Once someone connects to this site, the site search for cookies that start with the string `UserID` and end with `www.goto.com/`. If no such cookie is found, the site sends a cookie with the following format:

```
UserID    F9D3AEC40583962D    www.rollers.info/
```
The site then creates a record on its computer that associates the visitor with the identification string `F9D3AEC40583962D`. On subsequent visits, the site will find this cookie in the visitor's computer and will use it to identify the visitor.

⋄ **Exercise 10.5:** Suggest other applications for cookies.

The mechanism of cookies is certainly handy and contributes to the usefulness of the Internet and its resources. However, it allows Web sites to store something in a user's computer and therefore has a potential for abuse. One example of such abuse is an employee of company `A` who knows the meaning of cookies installed by `A` on computers. The employee then quits `A`, is hired by `B`, a competitor of `A`, and uses his knowledge to read cookies installed by `A` to benefit `B`. Another example is a boss going through the cookies stored in an employee's work computer to discover the Internet surfing habits of the employee. The boss cannot tell what each cookie means, but cookies from online merchants imply shopping on company time, and cookies from adult sites may imply objectionable use of company time and resources. The boss, of course, may do more than cookie checking. He may actually install spyware on all employee computers and log keystrokes, email sent, and other information on the employee's use of the computer.

The good news about cookie security is that no one has yet found a way to employ cookies to install a virus or to execute any other type of remote attack.

Every browser has user-controlled settings that limit the cookies that a site can store in the browser. Typically, a user can set the browser to (1) always accept cookies, (2) ask the user for each cookie sent, (3) ask the user for each site visited, and (4) reject all cookies.

Rejecting cookies may be a safe approach for careful users, but some sites don't work without them. For example, Wells Fargo bank provides several useful online services to its customers, but those services are controlled by cookies. A computer owner may always check all the existing cookies and manually delete all cookies from unknown sources. There are also utilities that allow the user to edit cookies, delete them, add new cookies, and move cookies from browser to browser.

10.4 Phishing

When identity thieves fail to locate victims with the help of data stolen on the Internet, they frequently resort to what has become known as phishing. In this type of scheme, the criminal sets up a Web site that resembles a familiar E-commerce or bank site. The idea is to dupe innocent consumers into entering personal information while trying to open an account or apply for a loan at the fake site. A common variation on this technique is to send an email message to someone, informing them that their personal information (bank account details, credit card numbers, dates of birth and so on) has been lost or is being audited, and asking to re-enter the information. Many vulnerable people fall for such schemes, especially if the message appears to have come from a legitimate site, such as a bank or a large online merchant. Security workers in this area believe that phishers are able to convince up to 5% of recipients to respond to them.

The following is a typical example of phishing, one among many sent to this author. This one relies on social engineering, trying to confuse the reader and elicit a quick response.

```
Date: Sun, 28 Nov 2004 11:18:46 -0500
From: eBay <eBay@eBay.com> Add To Address Book
Subject: Account Violate The User Policy Second Notice
To: david.salomon@csun.edu

Dear valued customer

We regret to inform you that your eBay account could be suspended if you don't
re-update your account information. To resolve this problems please click here
and re-enter your account information. If your problems could not be resolved
your account will be suspended for a period of 24 hours, after this period your
account will be terminated.

For the User Agreement, Section 9, we may immediately issue a warning,
temporarily suspend, indefinitely suspend or terminate your membership and
refuse to provide our services to you if we believe that your actions may cause
financial loss or legal liability for you, our users or us. We may also take
these actions if we are unable to verify or authenticate any information you
provide to us.

Due to the suspension of this account, please be advised you are prohibited from
using eBay in any way. This includes the registering of a new account. Please
note that this suspension does not relieve you of your agreed-upon obligation to
pay any fees you may owe to eBay.

Regards, Safeharbor Department eBay, Inc
The eBay team.

This is an automatic message. Please do not reply.
```

Naturally, as phishing and its dangers become familiar to the public, consumers become aware of the danger and look and think twice before entering any sensitive information. In response, the phishers have also become more sophisticated. They find ways to send messages that look legitimate and even have the correct sender's address. It is common to receive messages from a bank or other online site that say: "We will never ask you for your password. If you receive such a request from us, let us know."

Experts suggest a simple and useful way to handle phishing. If you receive a request for personal information or for a donation that seems to come from a bona fide, familiar source, don't answer it and don't follow any instructions to go to a Website. Instead, get in touch with the source (using the email address, physical address, or telephone number you always use) and ask them to confirm the request. If you decide to use the email address, wait! The phisher may have modified it in your address book. Better use the telephone.

Some phishing attempts arrive as an html form where the recipient can input the information directly into the form. This is convenient but risky. Responding to email forms should be avoided as much as possible.

Check your bank balance regularly and compare it to the bank statement to ensure that all the transactions are legitimate. It is even more important to do this with credit and debit cards. Today, aware of phishing and other identity theft "techniques," banks and credit card companies call the consumer for any unusually large or suspicious transactions, but the consumer should have the ultimate responsibility for his financial situation. There are credit and bank monitoring services that will watch your accounts for you (or rather, for a fee), but it is this author's opinion that this type of work should best be done by the individual, except in rare cases.

Credit and Bank Monitoring Services

- 3-1 Bureau Credit Reports—Instant Online Delivery.

  This service provides fast online access to all credit reports, including Experian, Equifax, and Trans Union. It also has information on who has been checking your credit reports and on creditors' addresses. There is free customer service to help in resolving inaccuracies.

- ConsumerInfo Credit Monitoring E-mail Reporting.

  This is a service that offers unlimited Experian credit reports. Once you enroll, you can see your updated credit report at anytime. This service also emails its members alerts of changes to their credit reports. It also monitors members' credit reports on a daily basis to discover any fraudulent activity, new inquiries, new accounts, and late payments—all within 24-hours. The service features credit dispute forms and tips. This gives members the ability to easily correct mistakes in credit reports.

- Equifax Credit Reporting.

  Equifax protects its members against identity theft and minimizes its impact on victims. Membership includes weekly email alerts of credit changes and identity theft insurance (with a deductible and other limits). Members have access to one initial Equifax credit report and there is a charge for any additional reports.

- Experian Credit Reporting Services.

  CreditExpert provides its members with powerful tools to help them manage and protect personal credit information in real time. Members get unlimited access to credit reports, scoring tools, and credit advice. An added benefit is early warning of fraudulent activity or identity theft.

- Know Your Loan Rate.

  Know Your Own Loan Rate advertises itself as a unique and really useful service. It surveys lenders and uses the information thus obtained to provide potential borrowers with an estimate of what they can expect to pay based on their credit scores and other factors. Such a service may prove useful to those planning to buy a house.

- Social Security Statement (in the United States). The Social Security Statement estimates the future Social Security benefits that an individual can expect and explains how to qualify for those benefits. This statement is free. It is possible to request a

Social Security Statement online. At present, however, the statement itself is provided by mail only, not online, and takes 2–4 weeks.

■   TransUnion Credit Report Service.

Offers its members a free credit report, credit score and analysis, and borrowing power analysis. This service has the following features (quoted directly):

1. Weekly Fraud-Watch Emails. Receive weekly email alerts to changes in your report. Immediately find out about credit report changes including fraudulent activity, new inquiries, new accounts, late payments, and more.

2. Quarterly Access to Your Credit Report. Receive a brand new credit report four times per year. Reports are easy-to-read with color graphics and free interactive guide.

3. Credit Score Monitoring. Receive updated credit scores four times per year Includes personalized analysis with tips for improving your score.

4. Borrowing Power Monitoring. Receive updated analysis of your debt/income relationship four times per year. Includes custom hints for improving debt management.

5. Powerful Tools and Analysis. Graphical trending helps you manage your progress. View colorful charts and graphs on changes in your debt, income, credit score, and more.

For actual addresses of these and similar services, see [creditexpert 05], [creditreporting 05], [equifax 05], [knowyourloanrate 05], [qspace 05], [ssa-stat 05], and [TransUnion 05].

Around 2003, phishing and other aspects of identity theft had become so prevalent that most experts have decided to upgrade identity theft from "just" e-crime to an endemic online threat. One result of this realization is that financial institutions, online retailers, and others who have a wide online customer base are trying harder than ever to secure their data and protect their customers. Another aspect of increased identity theft is that technology companies are developing new products and are offering new services to counteract and curb, or at least greatly reduce, online identity theft. Here is a list of current products available at the time of writing (late 2004).

■   The Anti-Phishing Working Group (APWG). This is an industry association focused on eliminating the identity theft and fraud that result from the growing problem of phishing and email spoofing. APWG is located at [APWG 04].

■   Antiphishing toolbars. One phishing technique uses spam to lure vulnerable individuals to a certain URL designed to look like a legitimate online store or an e-commerce site. Once there, the potential victim is lured into entering personal information. An antiphishing toolbar is a small, free applet offered by several ISPs, such as AOL and EarthLink and by legitimate online e-commerce sites such as eBay. The program adds to the user's Web browser a new toolbar that warns the user about Web sites that try to hide their true identities.

■   Antiphishing services. A typical antiphishing service employs a distributed network of sensors to monitor email traffic, news groups, and Web domain registrations in an attempt to spot new scams, such as phishing attacks. When a sensor locates a fraudulent Web site, it alerts its subscribers (both individuals and companies) by email. Such services are currently offered by MarkMonitor Inc. (FraudProtect), Symantec Corp. (Online Fraud Management Solution), VeriSign Inc. (AntiPhishing Solution), and NameProtect Inc.

■ Smart cards (Section 8.2). Traditional credit cards have a magnetic stripe with some information about the card holder, but the new smart cards, such the one shown in Figure 10.2, have a small computer (a microprocessor with memory) embedded in them, so they can hold much more information and can update it. As an example, a smart card can store biometric information to authenticate its owner, as well as long, multidigit PINs. Smart cards are already used extensively in certain European countries to verify the identity of purchasers. The hope is that just stealing someone else's account number will not be enough for the thief to use the account. Also, a thief stealing someone's smart card will not be able (and may not even try) to use it because of the biometric information in the card.

Figure 10.2: A Smart Card.

■ Fraud screening and prevention. When a thief gets hold of someone's credit card number, they try to use it immediately, and spend as much as possible, often on extravagant or useless items. Such an unusual activity can be used as an indication of a problem if immediately detected by the credit card company. In addition, the geographic location of the thief and the victim may be different, providing another clue to a potential identity theft. Such indicators are commonly used by credit card companies to detect fraud while it is happening. There are even companies, such as VeriSign, ClearCommerce Corp., and CyberSource Corp., that offer services in this area. They follow the purchasing habits of an individual with a credit card, flag any suspicious pattern, and notify the card issuing company.

■ Consumer authentication services (see also Chapter 8 for this topic). It is well known that a simple password isn't very secure, because many users select easy-to-guess passwords and many hackers know how to guess and steal passwords. As a result, security experts have been working on stronger authentication procedures. Typical examples of such procedures are RSA SecurID and the unified authentication program of VeriSign [Verisign 04].

RSA security, a leading developer of encryption techniques and devices, has developed a two-step authentication process known as RSA SecurID [RSASecurID 04]. Network and desktop users identify themselves with two unique factors—something they know (a password or a PIN), and something they have (an authenticator)—before they are granted access to a secured network, computer, site, or service. A SecurID authenticator can be hardware or software. A hardware authenticator comes as a key fob, a card, or a PINpad (the latter is a small, credit-card-shaped device with a 10-key keypad on the card). These authenticators are manufactured and sealed with an integral lifetime battery. No user maintenance or battery replacement is required. A software authenticator (available for Windows, Palm, Blackberry, and various mobile telephones) is a PINpad displayed on the screen.

To log into a site with SecurID, the owner enters a password and uses the authenticator to send an additional code to the site. The additional code is unique and is always different. A new code is generated by the authenticator every 60 seconds. At the site, the RSA authentication manager knows which code is valid at that moment in time for that user/authenticator combination. This type of authentication is much safer than just a password, but is more expensive.

The VeriSign unified authentication scheme is based on a portable hardware device called a USB hybrid token that generates one-time passwords (OTPs). The user presses a button on the device, and an OTP is displayed, ready for immediate use. The user then enters their static password and the OTP for secure authentication. If authentication is done from a computer that has USB connectivity, the hybrid token can be plugged into the computer and it sends the OTP automatically. The user still needs to enter their static password.

A Case study. A suspected Russian mobster was charged on 10 November 2004 with identity theft in a phishing-style scam.

Andrew Schwarmkoff, 28, was arraigned in a Boston-area district court on multiple counts of fraud, identity theft, larceny, and receiving stolen goods, the *Boston Herald* reported Wednesday. He used phishing attacks—phony e-mails that demand recipients provide their credit card and bank account numbers or risk losing access to the cards or accounts—to collect the confidential information.

When police arrested Schwarmkoff Friday, they reportedly found credit card scanning devices, over 100 identity cards with bogus information, $200,000 worth of stolen merchandise, and nearly $15,000 in cash.

Schwarmkoff was ordered held on $100,000 cash bail.

According to the Herald, sources close to the case said investigators believe Schwarmkoff is a member of the Russian mob, but has not cooperated with the authorities.

"Would you?" the Herald quoted the source as asking. "Schwarmkoff is more content to sit in jail than risk the consequences of ratting out the Russian mob," the Herald quoted him as saying.

(From `http://www.techweb.com/wire/security/52600627`, November 10, 2004.)

10.5 The Homograph Threat

The resemblance of the Latin letter "O" to the digit "0" has long been a source of confusion to programmers. In the old days of computing, printers produced the same glyph for both characters. Later, a zero got a slash added and became ∅. Currently, editors, word processors, and high-resolution printers easily distinguish between the two characters in print and on a display, but the problem of similar glyphs has returned in early 2005 to haunt computer users again, this time in the form of a security hole dubbed the *homograph threat*.

> Homograph (noun). One of two or more words that have the same spelling but differ in origin, meaning, and sometimes pronunciation, such as fair (pleasing in appearance) and fair (market), wind (blowing) and wind (your watch), or bow (and arrow) and bow (to my superior wisdom).
>
> —From `http://www.yourdictionary.com/`.

In its crudest form, this threat may be realized by a phisher who exploits the similarity of the two Os to register a domain name such as `www.micr∅s∅ft.com` and then try to lure unsuspecting visitors to this site in an attempt to obtain personal information. This doesn't seem a serious threat because current Web browsers display different glyphs for "O" and "0", thereby making it easy to distinguish between them, but the next step in this threat is to use foreign language glyphs in domain names.

⋄ **Exercise 10.6:** How can a phisher lure visitors to a site like `www.micr∅s∅ft.com`?

The new homograph threat, discovered by Evgeniy Gabrilovich and Alex Gontmakherm is described in [homograph 05]. It stems from the new Web initiative that makes it possible to register domain names in character sets other than Latin. This is a worthwhile development that will allow more people to benefit from the Web and the Internet, but it has its downside. Often, the glyph of a character in a foreign script resembles (or is even identical to) that of a Latin character, and this is what creates the homograph threat.

⋄ **Exercise 10.7:** Try to register domain `www.micr∅s∅ft.com`.

The problem is easy to understand (and unfortunately, also easy to exploit). Certain Cyrillic characters (Figure 10.3) have glyphs identical to the Latin letters a, e, p, and y (although the Cyrillic p is pronounced like the English r). A trouble maker can register the domain `yahoo.com` where the y comes from the Cyrillic alphabet, and then lure unsuspecting visitors to this site. The point is that certain browsers, most notably Firefox, Safari, and Opera make it impossible to distinguish between such a domain and the authentic yahoo site. Both are displayed with the same graphics. The older Internet Explorer, on the other hand, does distinguish between different character sets, thereby making it easy for the user to detect such "forgery."

As an example, try to create a local html file on your computer with the link `http://www.p&#1072;ypal.com/`. When Safari opens this file, the link displays as `http://www.paypal.com/`, is misleading and points to a site different from `paypal.com`. When the same file is opened in Internet Explorer and the user clicks on the link, the URL is displayed as `http://www.pɨypal.com/`, indicating a problem.

АБВГДЕЁЖЭИ
КЛМНОПРСТ
УФХЦЧШЩЪ
ЫЬЭЮЯ

Figure 10.3: The Cyrillic Character Set.

Readers of this book may already know enough about the way hackers operate and may know how easy it is to extend this threat to something really serious. A miscreant may register a domain similar to that of a bank but using characters from a different script, lure visitors to his site, and get their passwords by a trick similar to the Trojan horse that replaces the login procedure (Chapter 4). The forged site asks the user for an account number and a password, then displays the message "wrong password, please try again" and immediately forwards the user to the legitimate site. When the user tries again, the password is accepted by the real site, the user has no reason to suspect anything, and the fraudster has harvested another account number and password. Such an operation may go undetected for a long time (especially as more and more bank customers bookmark the forged domain for convenience) and be extremely profitable to the perpetrator while becoming a new headache for security experts and for the rest of us Internet users.

A possible solution is to modify all the Web browsers to display characters from different scripts in different colors, but this will most likely be frowned upon by activists from the international association of the color blind, thereby giving new meaning to the phrase "you cannot satisfy everyone" (just a joke).

A better solution (only for the Safari browser on the Macintosh, but very useful until Safari is patched) is a free program called *Saft Lite* by Hao Li [SaftLite 05]. It intercepts URLs that contain any non-Roman alphabet characters and displays an alert giving the user the option of not surfing to that URL. For the paypal example above, the message says:

"The URL on your location field is shown as `http://www.paypal.com/` though the real (spoofing) URL (may look like the same) is `http://www.xn--pypal-7ve.com/`." (Grammar due to Hao Li.)

A sibling may be the keeper of one's identity, the only person with the keys to one's unfettered, more fundamental self.

—Marian Sandmaier

11
Privacy and Trust

In this age of computers, the Internet, and massive data bases that never lose or forget anything, it is no wonder that we feel we are losing our privacy and we get very concerned about it. The reason for this loss can be found in the phrase "once something is released into the Internet, it can never be completely deleted." We give away bits and pieces of personal information all the time, but we give them to different entities, at different times, and through different media such as paper or verbally. We therefore expect these pieces of information to disappear or at least to stay separate. The nature of the online world, however, is such that individual pieces of information tend to gravitate toward one another and coalesce into solid objects called personal records.

A personal record is an important tool in the hands of marketers, public opinion researchers, social scientists, physicians, statisticians, and also (as readers of this book can easily guess) criminals. More and more countries are coming to grips with this problem and are adopting privacy laws that make it difficult to collect unauthorized information and that specify when and where such information has to expire or be explicitly deleted or erased.

An important organization devoted to protecting our online privacy is the Online Privacy Alliance [privacyalliance 05] whose mission statement reads "We will lead and support self-regulatory initiatives that create an environment of trust and that foster the protection of individuals' privacy online and in electronic commerce."

This chapter starts with a short survey of privacy issues and general tools and techniques for maintaining online privacy. It continues with a detailed discussion of the important topic of children's online privacy, and it concludes with a section on trust and how to create it in online visitors, shoppers, and potential customers.

11.1 Privacy Issues

Privacy has two faces. The first, traditional face has to do with seclusion from intrusion or the right to be let alone. The second face, formulated in the 1960s in response to the rapid development of computers and data bases, deals with informational self-determination, the right to control the collection, disclosure and use of information about oneself. Nowadays, privacy is closely connected to computer security, and many feel that our privacy is rapidly dwindling because of actions of hackers, spammers, and online merchants, and of mistakes made by government agencies and other organizations that have large collections of private data.

> I want to be let alone.
> —Greta Garbo in *Grand Hotel*, 1932.

The issue of privacy is further complicated because privacy, even though a fundamental human right, is not absolute. It has to be balanced with accountability. Privacy should be respected, but should not provide impervious and permanent cover for criminal activity. (The Introduction mentions a few people who kept to themselves.) This section discusses various aspects of privacy as affected by the Internet.

Geolocation is the name of a new, disturbing trend on the World Wide Web. Web sites examine the IP address of a visitor and use it to try to determine the visitor's physical location (at least country, preferably state or province, and ideally down to individual zip codes or organizations). Once known, the geographic location of the viewer determines what the Web site will display and what the visitor will be allowed to do. The following examples illustrate the applications of geolocation.

■   A person in a large city is looking for a Chinese restaurant. Typing this phrase into certain Internet search engines may result in Chinese restaurants in just that city.

■   A sport team may sign a contract with a local television station to broadcast their games in city A. The team may then elect to have some games shown for free on their Web site, except to visitors from A, who find these games blocked because of the contract. Similarly, certain movies may be shown only to visitors from certain countries.

■   A gambling casino in country X may have to block bets coming from country Y because of legal reasons.

■   A company may display certain prices for its products to the general public, but changes to lower prices when someone from a competing company visits their site.

■   A candidate for a public office may display material on job creation to visitors from one county and information on crime fighting to visitors from another county.

■   A company that caters to customers from many countries may display prices in different currencies depending on the geographic location of a visitor.

■   The well-known Google search engine allows its advertisers to target ads to visitors according to their city or distance from a given location.

■   Yahoo has a Web auction site that auctions Nazi paraphernalia. It had to block these auction items to French visitors because of a French court order.

◇ **Exercise 11.1:** Think of a geolocation application for a news agency.

People's opinions on these geolocation schemes and restrictions vary. Most agree that not all of them are bad, and that geolocation cannot identify individual users. Proponents of geolocation claim that it helps Web content providers to cater to different tastes of viewers and to comply with laws in different countries, but privacy advocates consider geolocation techniques unethical and worry that further expansion of this trend would lead to misleading information and reduced privacy. The following quotation, from privacy advocate Jason Catlett, summarizes this worry.

> The technical possibilities do allow a company to be two-faced or even 20-faced based on who they think is visiting.
> —Jason Catlett, `http://www.junkbusters.com/aboutus.html`

Geolocation works by examining the IP number of the visitor. The allocation of IP numbers by ICANN is public information, so anyone can collect the entire Whois data base (located at [arin 04]) and find out who is assigned a given IP number. The identification is complicated by the fact that certain entities (large ISPs, companies, universities, and government agencies) have been assigned a block (or several blocks) of IP numbers and have privately assigned these to their members/customers, sometimes dynamically. For example, a search for IP `130.166.2.76` results in the following information

```
OrgName:    California State University, Northridge
OrgID:      CSUN
Address:    18111 Nordhoff St
City:       Northridge
StateProv:  CA
PostalCode: 91330
Country:    US
NetRange:   130.166.0.0 - 130.166.255.255
```

(followed by many more lines). We see that this university has been assigned the entire block of $2^{16} = 65,536$ numbers `130.166.x.x`, and only their network administrators can tell who is located at `130.166.2.76`.

However, because of the growing importance of geolocation, several companies, among them Digital Envoy Inc. [digitalenvoy 04], Quova Inc. [Quova 04], and Akamai Technologies [Akamai 04], have been trying to narrow the actual locations of IP numbers by tracing data packets as they are forwarded between Internet routers. The result is data bases where IP numbers are identified by country, province, postal code, time zone, and even organization. Currently, such data bases claim better than 80% accuracy, and sometimes up to 99%.

Web crawling. We are all familiar with Internet search engines. In fact, life on the Internet without them would be difficult, dull, and unproductive to most users. A search engine has two parts, a crawler and a ranking algorithm. The crawler is a program that collects Web sites and stores them in a data base. The ranking algorithm searches that data base for a work or a phrase, finds all the pages that contain that word, and ranks them.

A Web crawler is given an initial URL or a set of initial URLs. It visits one of them and analyses its content, looking for hypertext links that point to other Web pages. The crawler then visits those pages and examines each for new links. The process continues recursively until no more unvisited links are found. The crawler then starts with the next URL on the list of initial URLs. Figure 11.1 shows a small fragment of typical html text with links.

A `spider` starts with an initial list of URLs that have many links. Examples of such URLs are `yahoo.com` for general reference, the Internet movie database (`www.imdb.com`) for movie information, `hometown.aol.com/TeacherNet` for educational resources, and `vlib.org` for literary resources. Such a list can be started by using another `search engine` to search for Web pages containing phrases such as "many links," "the most links," "art resources," or "all about music." Once an initial list of URLs has been established, the `spider` can follow every link from each of the URLs on the list. When those Web pages are input into the data base, the number of links in each is counted, and those pages with the most links are added to the initial list.

Figure 11.1: A Sample HTML Text With Links.

Notice that a Web crawler doesn't actually propagate itself to different computers on the Internet, as viruses do. The crawler resides on a single machine and only sends HTTP requests to other computers on the Internet for documents, just as a Web browser does. The crawler is a recursive program that looks for links.

As long as a crawler is limited to a search engine, no one would object to it, but any Internet user can implement (or buy) and use a crawler. Here is one questionable commercial application of such a private crawler. Back in 1997, an article in the *San Francisco Chronicle* reported that Barnes and Noble, a major online and offline American bookseller, had implemented a crawler to examine Web pages of private individuals for their reading habits and preferences. The information collected in this way was then used to email those individuals book offers based on their perceived reading habits (dear John, as a murder enthusiast we have an offer, a free gift, and a surprise for you...). Once this practice was unveiled by the newspaper, Barnes and Noble discontinued it, but a precedent had been set. Once again the Internet is being used to pry information that most people would rather keep private.

⋄ **Exercise 11.2:** (Tricky.) What's a free gift?

11.2 Online Privacy

One (although not the only) outlet through which our personal information is leaked out are the many online commercial entities. When we make an online purchase, we are asked to provide our name, address, and other information, followed by our credit card data. Often, a purchaser is asked to open an account and select a password. Thus, the various online merchants have much information on consumers and have a responsibility to ensure its privacy. Nevertheless, this information tends to leak outside and spread either because the merchant decides to sell it or because it is stolen by an insider or by a hacker breaking into a computer.

As these problems become prevalent, more online commercial sites advertise privacy policies that promise either "we will never sell your personal data" or "we don't keep your credit card number." Such promises are encouraging but consumers should not absolutely rely on them. There are certain steps consumers can take (and certain rules to keep in mind) to protect themselves. The most important ones are listed here.

■   When a Web site asks you to register or to provide information, look for its privacy policy and read it. If this policy is easy to find and easy to understand, chances are it is credible. The link to a site's privacy policy should be right on the home page and should be clearly visible. The policy itself should say exactly what information the site collects, what it is used for, and whether it is shared with anyone else. The policy should have an option for the user to restrict sharing or selling of information. If a Web site, especially a commercial one, doesn't have a privacy policy or if the policy is hard to find or difficult to understand, consider the site suspicious.

■   Look for a privacy seal in Web sites that ask for personal information. These seals, a recent innovation, should make the user fairly confident that a Web site is abiding by its posted privacy policy. Two organizations that issue such seals are [truste 05] and [bbbseal 05]. Finding a seal of approval in a Web site should give a consumer confidence that the site is legitimate and can be trusted. It also provides a mechanism for handling complaints by consumers who feel that their privacy has been violated. The seals also mean a company has instituted procedures for practicing what it preaches about privacy protection. If you don't find a seal at a Web site, better have second thoughts.

■   Keep your password secure and secret. Remember the various methods of social engineering used by the many scammers, spammers, and phishers (or review Section 8.3 if you forgot).

■   Web browsers have become important. We use them in our daily lives to communicate, to obtain information, and to do business. It is therefore crucial to use a secure browser that complies with an industry security standard, such as Secure Sockets Layer (SSL, Section 12.10) that encrypts or scrambles sensitive transaction information.

■   Lastly, when shopping online, print and save a copy of any purchase order. This document has the all-important confirmation number that will be needed in any future communications with the seller.

These are the basic rules. Others can be found at [truste 05] and [bbbseal 05].

When ordering merchandise online, the seller has to have the real name and address of the purchaser, but in other online situations privacy can be protected by remaining anonymous and by using an intermediary.

Anonymizers work by giving a person an untraceable alias. This is a useful tool for certain applications, but it works both ways because anonymizers can protect law-breakers. Intermediaries (or infomediaries) negotiate on behalf of a user or a consumer the amount of personal data released to any given Web site. Software tools for either approach exist and some are described here.

■   *Anonymizer* from [anonymizer 05] redirects all communications to and from a computer through the servers of `anonymizer.com`. The program also uses SSL (Section 12.10) to encrypt all communications to and from the computer it is installed on. When the owner of a computer sends a message to a site `xyz.com`, *Anonymizer* encrypts the message and routes it to `anonymizer`'s server, where it is decrypted and sent to `xyz.com` with `anonymizer.com` as the sender's address. Thus, any responses from `xyz.com` are sent to `anonymizer.com`, where they are encrypted and sent to the originating computer. The result is that `xyz.com` doesn't know who the real sender is, anyone listening on the connection between `anonymizer.com` and `xyz.com` has no idea who the real sender is, and anyone eavesdropping on the communications between the computer and `anonymizer.com` has to defeat the encryption, a nontrivial task.

■   *WebSecure*, from [freedom 05] works similarly, but uses stronger encryption. United States law limits the strength of encryption used by individuals, but `freedom.net` is located in Canada. WebSecure also allows the user to specify up to five online aliases and anonymous profiles.

■   *Crowds* is a research project [Reiter and Rubin 98] conducted at Bell Labs. It protects the anonymity of a user by blending the user in a crowd. A large group of geographically diverse users becomes a crowd. When a crowd member issues a request for data, the request is routed through another member, making it impossible to track a group member individually.

■   The *Onion routing* project [onion-router 05] is a research project of the United States Naval Research Lab (NRL). The assumption is that two parties want to communicate and may even agree to authenticate themselves to each other, but want to keep their communication private. The project employs a technique where each message is forwarded several times through a series of routers before it reaches its destination.

■   *DigitalMe* is a discontinued infomediary service from Novell. The idea was to have a member submit personal information, including names and passwords (as real or as fake as the member decides) and have the service use it to automatically fill out forms at Web sites. The member gets a chance to review each form before it is sent by the service.

■   *Jotter* (also discontinued) is a similar tool. The user enters personal information (normally only partly real) for various sites, and the program later produces the right user profile for each site visited.

- *Lumeria* is an infomediary service based on the belief that if personal information of users is valuable to companies, they should be willing to pay for it. A consumer can get in touch with Lumeria and submit a personal profile including areas of interest. Marketers send advertisements to Lumeria. If a consumer indicates interest in, for example, cosmetics, Lumeria will forward the consumer ads in this area. This way, the consumer remains anonymous to the marketers. The company also has an anonymizer service where it provides wrong cookie information to commercial Web sites.

In addition to anonymizers and infomediaries, there exist other services and techniques that aim to increase privacy. One example is [junkbusters declare 05], free software that has the addresses of all major vendors of personal information. You can use this program to draft letters to these vendors, asking to remove your name from the lists they sell.

11.3 Children's Privacy

In many households, the children are more comfortable with computers, computer communications, and the Internet than their parents. The Internet, and especially the World Wide Web, is a tremendous resource for children. It gives young people a chance (in fact, many chances) to receive new ideas, explore the world, learn many topics, and chat with their peers. However, the Internet has its own dangers, some as serious as those found in the real world. Web sites with harmful and objectionable material can confuse a child. Predators who offer to secretly meet with the child can change overnight from a virtual threat to a real danger. Miscreants may convince a child to click on an email attachment that will place spyware in the computer, thereby creating a risk for the entire family.

The terms "harmful" and "objectionable" normally refer to pornography, profanity, and hate material, but readers of this book already know that these terms also include spam and misleading advertising specifically directed toward children.

There are several public interest organizations dedicated to protecting the privacy and safety of anyone, but especially of children, on the Internet. One such organization is GetNetWise. Located at [getnetwise 05], this organization is funded by a wide range of Internet industry corporations and public interest organizations. The GetNetWise coalition wants Internet users to be only "one click away" from the resources they need to make informed decisions about their and their family's use of the Internet.

The national center for missing children, located at [missingkids 05], has a cyber tipline where anyone can report cases of sexual exploitation (especially resulting from online communications) of children.

A similar organization is the privacy rights clearinghouse, a public interest body located in San Diego, California. It has researched the topic of children's privacy and safety on the Internet, and has come up with a list (see [privacyrights 05]) of threats that exist especially for children and ways for parents and educators to combat them.

The main protection children have on the Internet is parental guidance and supervision. Parents should take the time to involve themselves in their children's activities and apply their life experience to advise the child on what is bad, misleading, and dangerous. This is true even if the parents know nothing about computers and the Internet. When the parents cannot or will not spend the time and the effort, the child suffers, period! Following is a list of tips for parents on how best to protect a child's privacy and safety on the Internet.

■   Privacy policy. Parents should read the privacy policies of Web sites frequented by a child. If anything looks unusual, suspicious, or unclear, advise the child to forgo the site. Older children should be taught to do the same themselves.

■   Consent. In the United States, federal law requires a parent to decide whether or not they consent to their child giving information to a Web site. Children should be taught (repeatedly, if necessary) not to give any information without parental consent.

■   Web seal. Many Web sites have "seals of approval" to build trust in visitors. One organization that issues such seals is [truste 05]. The following short quote explains what this seal does for an online business.

"Build trust and drive revenue with the TRUSTe privacy seal. Displaying the TRUSTe seal demonstrates that your site complies with our best practices. Call TRUSTe to sign up, and let consumers know they can trust you more than other businesses when it comes to online privacy."

The truste organization checks sites and audits their privacy practices. It also helps in resolving disputes. The Council of Better Business Bureaus has a similar Web seal program, see [bbbseal 05]. Finding such a seal of approval in a Web site should give a parent confidence that the site owner is not out to cheat vulnerable people, especially children.

■   Contracts. Often, children, especially teenagers, can be made more responsible for their online actions and behavior by signing a contract with their parents. Such a contract increases the self-importance of the child and should therefore be written in a simple language employing basic, nonlegal terms.

The Federal Trade Commission of the United States has an example of such a contract at [FTC-CONT 05]. Figure 11.2 shows this agreement (but see [getnetwise-ctrct 05] for another example).

■   Family rules. A list of rules that have to be obeyed by anyone in the family may go a long way. Such rules may include the following:
1. Never give out identifying information such as family information, home address, school name, or phone number in chat room discussions and when visiting Web sites. Even email addresses should be handled carefully and not given to strangers met online. The same is true for family pictures.
2. Passwords should be kept private and secret. When someone pretending to be authorized or important asks you in a chat for a password, refuse to give it and leave the chat immediately.
3. Similarly, when you receive a threatening, suggestive, or just plain uncomfortable message, quit without an argument.

Cyberspace Passport

These rules are for my safety. I will honor them when I go online.

- I can go online _____ (Time of day) for _____ (How long)
- It's ____ OK ____ not OK for me to go online without a parent.
- I understand which sites I can visit and which ones are off limits.
- I won't give out information about myself or my family without permission from my parents.
- My password is my secret. I won't give it to anyone.
- I will never agree to meet an online pal, or send my picture, without permission from my parents.
- I know an advertisement when I see one. I also know that animated or cartoon characters aren't real and may be trying to sell me something or to get information from me.
- I will follow these same rules when I am at home, in school, or at the library or a friend's.

Figure 11.2: A Sample Child's Online Contract.

4. Computer use, like television watching, should be limited. Everyone should understand the meaning of the word "addiction" and should set a daily maximum amount of time of Internet surfing.

5. If at all possible, the family computer should be kept in a family room rather than in a child's room. This rule is especially difficult to keep when children become teens and insist they know better.

6. A cooperative child should be encouraged to disclose the names and addresses of any online friends and buddies. Everyone should be taught that face-to-face meetings with online friends can be dangerous. An Internet search provides a list of children that went missing as a result of such a meeting.

7. Similarly, a child should be encouraged to disclose what Internet services they use. A parent may pretend to be computer illiterate asking for help and information from the child.

8. It's a useful rule to assume that strangers on the Internet are never who they claim to be. A chat partner claiming to be a teen ager often turns out to be an adult (and possibly dangerous).

9. A similar rule should explain that not everything we read online is true, especially offers, and most especially offers that look too good to be true.

(End of list.)

Someone who is not in the "business" (of marketing) may not realize that children constitute a large segment of the consumer population. Market researchers may try to use the Internet to learn about the preferences of children. Advertisers see the Internet as a natural ground for advertising, and they generate special Web sites that lure young visitors. Such a site may advertise merchandise for children and promise gifts for filling out surveys, disclosing personal information, and joining clubs.

A toy maker, for example, is naturally interested in selling to children. An agent for such a company may visit chat rooms pretending to be an action figure or a comics hero and chat with children. Once a child discloses an email or a physical address, the company sends a message or a letter purportedly coming from the hero and offering merchandise. A child being tempted in this way may not realize the difference between the world of comics and the real world, and may give his parents a hard time asking for (perhaps unsuitable or expensive) toys.

Even more serious are attempts to have a child click on various links that send cookies and adware to his computer. The result may be a large number of advertisements especially targeted for the child, sent to the computer in a seemingly unending stream. Parents should turn off cookies if possible and run anti-spyware software regularly to discover unwanted software.

⋄ **Exercise 11.3:** Are children especially vulnerable to rogue software?

So far we have concentrated on commercial Web sites catering to children, but there is still the bigger problem of sites with objectionable material or content unsuitable for children, such as pornography, obscenity, violence, and hatred. The best approach so far to block kids' access to such sites are various software filters. A filter obeys the commands of its owner, who is identified by a password. Its main task is to block access to certain sites, but it may provide other useful services such as (1) It can prevent users from surfing the Internet during certain times. (2) It maintains an activity log of Web sites visited, pages received, and cookies saved. (3) It regularly and automatically connects to its maker to receive fresh lists of new Web sites that the owner may want to block. (4) It has search features that return porn-free results or can be filtered in any desired way.

This type of software is easy to locate by searching the Internet under "parental control software," but here are three examples.

■ NetNanny, from [netnanny 05] is touted as the only family control software that includes family-safe filtered search, an Internet monitor, Web site filtering, time limits, chat recording, newsgroup blocking, and privacy controls.

■ CyberSitter, published by [CyberSitter 05], is advertised as software designed primarily for home, educational and small business use. It records all Instant Messenger chat conversations for AOL (AIM), and Yahoo Messengers. It provides over 30 categories of filtering, making it the most complete Internet filter available. Filters are updated automatically. It allows parents to override blocked sites, add their own sites to block, and specify allowable times to access the Internet. It maintains a detailed log of all Internet activity and violations. It will even send a daily report to parents by email.

■ CyberPatrol, made by [cyberpatrol 05], features the following: Block harmful websites and newsgroups. Restrict chat and instant messaging. Filter Web based email. Manage time online and access to programs. Control program downloads. Protect personal identity.

In general, parents looking for software that allows filtering and control should look for the following features:

- The first user to launch the software becomes its owner and can select a password that will authorize him to turn the software on and off, set parameters, and select options.

- The software should block outgoing messages with personal information. This is an ideal feature that state of the art of artificial intelligence cannot achieve. The best that can be done at present is to block any strings that resemble an email address, a telephone number, or any names of family members.

- Similarly, the software should block incoming text that has offensive language, but this is also an as-yet unachieved goal of artificial intelligence. The best the owner can do is enter a list of words and ask the software to block any message that contains any of them.

- It should limit the total amount of connect time and also limit Internet access to certain hours.

- It should allow its owner (typically a parent) to view and edit the list of blocked Web sites, including Internet relay chats (IRCs) and usenet newsgroups.

- It should offer criteria for blocking certain sites automatically. The html standard supports a `meta` tag which is used to describe a site. A parent should be able to instruct the filtering software to block any site that features a `meta` tag such as `<META NAME="keywords" CONTENT="sex, breast, poison">`.

- Filtering software should be updated often to reflect newly-discovered threats and new features of the operating system.

- Many ISPs are continually developing tools and features to control spam and objectionable material. An ideal filtering program should know about such tools and features and use them.

Current filtering software is never ideal, but is being developed and is getting better all the time. Here is a simple example that illustrates the difficulty of filtering. If the software is instructed to block Web sites that have the word "breast" in them, it may block sex sites, but also medical sites and sites that offer chicken recipes. The significance of a keyword has to be judged by its context. The conclusion? Software for filtering and control is useful but cannot replace parental supervision and judgement.

Chat rooms and instant messages are two services offered by commercial online organizations such as AOL, Yahoo, and MSN and by Internet relay chat (IRC). Both services are very popular with children because they allow a child to appear older and because children tend to have free time. Unfortunately, these facts are also known to the bad guys, and they often participate in chats, pretending to be children and phishing for addresses, passwords, and other personal information. Even worse, sexual predators have been known to try to lure children to meet them physically, sometimes with disastrous results.

Here is what may happen in a sexual abuse case (see also [chatdanger 05]). The perpetrator lurks in a public chat room looking for a vulnerable child. When he (most sexual predators are male) finds someone who seems both a child and vulnerable, he invites the child into a private area of the chat room to get better acquainted. His first tactic is to create a comfort level, typically by posing as a young person about the same age as the intended victim. Next comes private chat via an instant message service followed by email, telephone conversations, and finally, a face-to-face meeting.

Because of the importance of this topic, there are several sites that deal with protecting kids and families from the dangers of online communications and making the Internet and technology fun, safe, and productive for the entire family. See, for example, [chatdanger 05], [safekids 05], and [protectkids 05].

11.4 Trust

The dictionary defines trust as "firm reliance on the integrity, ability, or character of a person or thing," but in the online world trust is defined as the expectation that one's vulnerabilities will not be exploited. Trust, specifically online trust, is perhaps the most important reason why users surf to certain Web sites while ignoring other sites.

In real life (the offline world) we try unconsciously to build trust by adopting certain facial expressions, looking the right way, saying the right things in the right tone, and using body language that our fellow humans understand. None of these methods work online, so substitutions must be found. A well-designed, smart, and straightforward Web site is the first step toward establishing online trust.

If many people visit the Web site of a company each day, but very little new business is generated, the reason could be lack of trust. Bear in mind that each visitor has located the site and took the time to visit it, implying that they had expectations from it, but most went away immediately, which means they were somehow disappointed.

Even beginners have heard of viruses, spam, and spyware, and therefore know that online interaction involves risk and that computers are vulnerable. Thus, users, online shoppers, and Web surfers look for sites they can trust. The degree of trust they expect is inversely proportional to the risk involved in the interaction. A sick person following medical advice offered on the Internet faces more risk than someone purchasing a low cost item, and therefore looks harder for a site that can be trusted.

How can a Web site, whether informational or commercial, be designed to convey trust? Perhaps the two main features that help are usability and credibility. The simple fact that a Web site is easy to use contributes to increased trust on the part of a user. Similarly, a credible site, a site that conveys honesty, professionalism, and expertise, will reduce a visitor's feeling of risk and will therefore be considered trustful even by first-time visitors.

Secondary factors in creating trust are style, color, and layout of text, amount of information on the screen, and speed of download (a site with many small images takes the browser longer to download, construct, and display). It has been shown that lines of centered text which have a ragged left margin are harder to read than left-justified text. Text in italics or in boldface is similarly more demanding and results in slow reading. Readers also prefer warm colors (red, orange and yellow) to cool colors (violet, blue, and green). As a result, it is easy to design a Web site that will be demanding on the user and will therefore convey low trust.

After reading so much about miscreants, fraudsters and wrongdoers in this book, readers can easily draw the obvious conclusion from the preceding paragraphs. A hacker can also employ the tips given here in order to set up an attractive Web site, a trap. This is why reputation also enters the picture. An unscrupulous operator can easily design an attractive site, but can hardly develop a reputation, much less a solid one. Recommendations are also a big contributor to trust. A Web site that can boast references and support from recognized and respected entities and individuals generates more trust.

Another factor that tends to be ignored is the loss of trust. Once users lose trust in a site, it is slow and difficult to recreate this trust (see the answer to exercise 2.15).

Online commerce (or E-commerce) is very different from traditional business. Many cues are available to a customer in a traditional store. The neighborhood, the age of the store, its decoration, the selection of products, and the personnel are a few examples. An online business, on the other hand, has only its Web site to confront a new customer. If the site isn't attractive, clear, and easy to use, the customer loses trust and may "walk" away.

> Trust me, I know what I'm doing.
> —A common phrase.

The following list applies to commercial Web sites and offers the site's owner tips for increased trust.

■ Pay special attention to how customers' billings and payments are handled. A mistake in this area, even in favor of the customer, diminishes trust considerably.

■ Use the SSL protocol (Section 12.10) to encrypt all sensitive transactions. This is obvious and has become prevalent. It is rare to find a commercial site that doesn't use encryption.

■ Customers tend to complain when something goes wrong, but a few also send praise when they are satisfied. Collect those positive responses and make it easy for prospective customers to find them (but they have to be real).

■ Pretend to be a customer and use your own site to make purchases. This is the best way to learn about any downside in your Web interface and to come up with ideas that will make shopping experience at your site simple, pleasant, and reassuring.

■ One way for merchants to compete by reducing prices is to raise the rates they charge for shipping and handling (S&H). As a result, the total cost of a small, inexpensive item may almost double once the S&H is included, which may irritate many customers and lead to cancellation of orders and loss of trust. Marketing researchers often recommend to tie the S&H to the cost of an item (so an inexpensive item will also be inexpensive to ship) instead of to its weight. A large inexpensive item, such as a garden rake, is expensive to ship, and therefore shouldn't be sold online. On the other hand, a heavy, expensive item, such as a table saw, is normally shipped (and not carried by the purchaser) even if bought in a store, so an online merchant can charge more in S&H for it.

- An important reason to have an online business is the smaller number of employees required. Salaries are normally a large item of expense in a business, so the number of employees is important. Still, even an online business should make it easy for customers to talk to a person, which is why a toll-free telephone number and a 24-hour online chat are important tools that increase customers' trust. Remember, computers are notoriously weak in intelligence and can't hold an intelligent conversation, which is why people hate to talk to computers. Browsing [versiontracker 05], an Internet site that lists new software daily, this author often notices users' evaluations of software that claim "to me, the single most-important feature of a software developer is its responsiveness to users' questions and complaints."

- A publicly-held company must report its finances to the government. If the company is doing well, it's a good idea to display important positive financial data prominently in the Web site. (However, if the company is doing badly, there is no need to worry about displaying data since the company may soon be out of business anyway.)

- Customers hate long-term contracts. Companies (such as weight-loss providers and fitness centers) that traditionally lose customers after a short period insist on long-term contracts. If your business isn't like that, try to offer short-term contracts or no contracts at all.

- Similarly, if at all possible, avoid asking for any money up front, it diminishes trust.

- Register with the local better business bureau or any similar consumer organizations in your area and advertise this fact in your site.

- Pretend to be honest (just joking; be honest) and post as many prices, contracts and agreements as possible prominently on your site.

- Make sure it's easy to see on your site how long you've been in business and the size of the business (number of customers, employees, products, warehouses, etc.)

- Try to innovate. Look at other Web sites and try to improve on them. It is generally believed that sites dealing with entertainment, youth, and media are innovative, whereas financial and legal sites are more traditional and rigid.

- It's better to offer choices to customers instead of trying to sell them what you prefer to sell.

- Display your telephone number on every Web page. It's also better to have a street address instead of a P.O. Box and display it too. Remember that a person would like to see real-world contact points. Any information on insurance and dispute resolution also adds to consumer trust.

- Along the same lines, pictures of your employees (the team) and premises may create trust. A simple, modern logo also helps.

- Experience with the psychology of shoppers teaches us that the quality of a Web site and the degree of satisfaction derived from its use transfers to a perceived quality of the product or service offered. In other words, if the customer is satisfied with the site and the process of purchasing, they will tend to be satisfied with what they bought.

> In God we trust, all others we monitor.
> —*Deadly Transmissions*, NSA study, Dec. 1970.

In general, online commercial sites should educate the public, make the online environment more "human," and thereby demonstrate that the Internet can be a safe place to shop regardless of malware, spyware, spam, and other threats. Education is needed because ours is the first generation of online shoppers and customers. Most of us have long been familiar with credit cards and use them routinely in offline situations, in a store or an office, yet many are scared of using a credit card in an online transaction. "I mistrust computers" is a phrase commonly heard. Such a person can be educated by pointing out the following. When you hand over your credit card in a store, the store clerk or employee swipes it and its details are sent, encrypted, to the credit card company through the Internet. In principle, this is no different from using a credit card in an online transaction. The sensitive information is still sent through the Internet and is still encrypted. The main difference is that there is no clerk or employee involved in the process.

The slogan of the American National Rifle Association (NRA) "guns don't kill people, people do," can with justification be modified to "computers do not create fraud, people do" (see also exercise Intro.2). All the security problems, fraud, and computer crime are created by people, but other people fight back by developing technologies such as encryption and digital signatures that create a safer online environment.

Interactive Media in Retail is a British group that promotes safe Internet shopping, trade, and interaction. Their main project is titled *Internet Shopping is Safe* [ISIS 05], and is where the following quotation comes from

ISIS: a keystone in the bridge of trust between shops and shoppers.

ISIS-accredited merchants now account for approximately two thirds of all UK online shopping.

Consumers can shop online with confidence wherever they see the ISIS logo because it certifies that the merchant has:

● registered with the ISIS programme and undertaken to trade in a manner that is LEGAL, DECENT, HONEST, TRUTHFUL AND FAIR.

● had its web site and service reviewed and monitored by IMRG.

● had its Business, VAT and Data Protection registrations checked by IMRG.

To verify the merchant's ISIS certification, simply click on the ISIS logo—a new "ISIS verification" page will open up confirming that specific merchant's certification. If you see an ISIS logo that doesn't correctly link through to the verification page, please report it to IMRG immediately by emailing `ISIS@imrg.org`.

> Wolf: I get the feeling you still don't completely trust me.
> Virginia: I don't trust you at all! You tried to eat my Grandmother.
> Wolf: You don't trust no one.
> Virginia: I don't trust you, no.
>
> —From *The 10th Kingdom*, 2000.

In conclusion, a new online consumer may be hesitant, uncertain, and reluctant to trust an online commercial site and to pay even a discount price for a product or service sold online. The best solution for both sellers and buyers is to create trust using the methods described here and to keep that trust.

◇ **Exercise 11.4:** Now that you have read the first part of this book, develop your own set of the 10 most important security laws.

> Every man should know that his conversations, his correspondence, and his personal life are private.
>
> —Lyndon B. Johnson

> Well, just one more piece, then I'm done. Trust no one, my friend, no one. Not your most grateful freedman. Not your most intimate friend. Not your dearest child. Not the wife of your bosom. Trust no one.
>
> Herod, *I, Claudius,* (1976)

12
Elements Of Cryptography

The discussion of computer security issues and threats in the previous chapters makes it clear that cryptography provides a solution to many security problems. Without cryptography, the main task of a hacker would be to break into a computer, locate sensitive data, and copy it. Alternatively, the hacker may intercept data sent between computers, analyze it, and help himself to any important or useful "nuggets." Encrypting sensitive data complicates these tasks, because in addition to obtaining the data, the wrongdoer also has to decrypt it. Cryptography is therefore a very useful tool in the hands of security workers, but is not a panacea. Even the strongest cryptographic methods cannot prevent a virus from damaging data or deleting files. Similarly, DoS attacks are possible even in environments where all data is encrypted.

Because of the importance of cryptography, this chapter provides an introduction to the principles and concepts behind the many encryption algorithms used by modern cryptography. More historical and background material, descriptions of algorithms, and examples, can be found in [Salomon 03] and in the many other texts on cryptography, code breaking, and data hiding that are currently available in libraries, bookstores, and the Internet.

Cryptography is the art and science of making data impossible to read. The task of the various encryption methods is to start with plain, readable data (the *plaintext*) and scramble it so it becomes an unreadable *ciphertext*. Each encryption method must also specify how the ciphertext can be decrypted back into the plaintext it came from, and Figure 12.1 illustrates the relation between plaintext, ciphertext, encryption, and decryption.

Thus, cryptography hides or obscures the meaning of data, but does not hide the data itself. Hiding data is also a useful computer security technique. A small data file

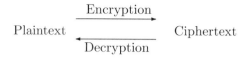

Figure 12.1: Encryption and Decryption.

(the payload) can be hidden inside a larger file (the cover), such that an examination of the cover will not uncover the data and will not raise any suspicion.

12.1 Principles of Cryptography

First, a simple classification. The field of cryptography is huge and covers many methods and approaches. At the most basic level, these methods can be classified into codes and ciphers.

A code is a short symbol or word that replaces an entire message. Codes are secure but are not general purpose. Before a spy is sent to a foreign country he and his runner may agree on a set of codes. The words *happy* and *sad* used by the spy in otherwise-innocuous sentences may indicate good and bad economies in the foreign country, whereas *deep* and *shallow* may be codes for success and failure of the spy's mission. It is easy to see why the use of codes is limited, but it is also true that codes can be broken. If the same spy sends many messages that use the same codes, then clever codebreakers who intercept the messages may eventually guess the meaning of certain codes, and then test their guesses by applying them to future messages to see if the guesses make sense.

A cipher is a rule that tells how to scramble (encrypt) data in a nonrandom way, so it can later be unscrambled (decrypted). Perhaps the simplest example of a cipher is to replace each letter with the one following it (cyclically) n positions in the alphabet. This is the well-known *Caesar cipher*. Here is an example for $n = 3$ (note how X is replaced by A).

```
ABCDEFGHIJKLMNOPQRSTUVWXYZ
DEFGHIJKLMNOPQRSTUVWXYZABC
```

The top line is the *plain alphabet* and the bottom line is the *cipher alphabet*. The plaintext COME BACK is encrypted by this method to the unreadable ciphertext FRPH EDFN. This simple cipher illustrates several important facts about ciphers as follows:

■   Decrypting this cipher requires knowledge of n (3 in our example). Thus, the number n is the *key* of this cipher. Long experience with ciphers has convinced cryptographers that the security provided by a cipher depends on the key, and not on the encryption method. The reason for this is easy to understand. When two persons want to communicate privately, they can develop an encryption method without a key and hope that no one will break it, but when a bank needs encryption for its sensitive operations, it cannot keep its encryption algorithm secret. Many people work for a bank, they come and go and it is inevitable that the details of such a secret algorithm will leak out. It makes more sense for a bank (and for other entities such as government agencies, army units, and spies) to use a well-tested, key-based commercial encryption program and base their security on the key.

■   There are 26 letters in the English alphabet, so n can take the values 1 through 25 (the keys 0 and 26 produce ciphertext that's identical to the plaintext). Thus, the *keyspace* of the Caesar cipher is very small, which makes it easy to break this cipher by trying all 25 keys. A practical, useful cipher must have a very large keyspace. Current cryptographic algorithms are executed on computers and are therefore based on binary numbers. Keys typically vary in size from 64 to 256 bits (see exercise 12.1).

■   In the Caesar cipher, a plainletter is always encrypted to the same cipherletter. Such a cipher is called *monoalphabetic* and it is easy to break because the ciphertext reflects the statistical properties of the plaintext. In English, for example, the most common letter is E. A plaintext encrypted with a monoalphabetic cipher that replaces E with K, will produce ciphertext with K as its most common letter. Section 12.3 describes a simple monoalphabetic cipher designed in antiquity by Polybius. A better approach is offered by a *polyalphabetic* encryption method, where the same plainletter is encrypted to different cipherletters. However, modern ciphers are based on binary numbers, not on letters, so they use different approaches.

12.2 Kerckhoffs's Principle

The entire field of cryptography is based on an important assumption, namely, that some information can be kept and disseminated securely, accessible only by authorized persons. This information is the *key* used by an encryption algorithm.

An important principle in cryptography, due to the Dutch linguist Auguste Kerckhoffs von Nieuwenhoff [Kerckhoffs 83], states that the security of an encrypted message must depend on keeping the key secret. It should not depend on keeping the encryption algorithm secret. This principle is widely accepted and implies that there must be many possible keys to an algorithm; the *keyspace* must be very large. The Caesar algorithm, for example, is very weak because its keyspace is so small. Notice that a large keyspace is a necessary but not a sufficient condition of security. An encryption algorithm may have an immense keyspace but may nevertheless be weak.

Kerckhoffs's Principle

One should assume that the method used to encipher data is known to the opponent, and that security must lie in the choice of key. This does not necessarily imply that the method should be public, just that it is considered public during its creation.

—Auguste Kerckhoffs

It is possible to use a brute force approach to break a cipher. A would-be code-breaker can simply search the entire keyspace—every possible key! There are, however, two good reasons why this approach is impractical and has at best a limited value. One reason is the large number of keys, and the other is the problem of recognizing the correct plaintext once it has been obtained when the right key is tried. Table 12.2 lists the times it takes to check all the keys, for several key sizes n. The table lists the times for the cases where one mega and one giga keys are checked each second (a mega is 2^{20}, about a million, and a giga is 2^{30}, about a billion). It is clear that doubling the key size more than doubles the total number of keys. In fact, for an n-bit key, the number of keys is 2^n, so it grows exponentially with n. Recognizing the plaintext is not easier. If the plaintext is text, it may be recognized by a computer program by looking up words in a dictionary. Even this can be defeated by artificially inserting many nonsense "words" in the text, but the plaintext may be compressed data, or executable machine code. These types of data are random or close to random and may be virtually impossible to recognize. The plaintext may also be image, video, or audio data, and these types, although nonrandom, may not always be easy to recognize.

n	2^n (approx)	Time			
		1M tests/s		1G tests/s	
32	4.3×10^9	4096	sec	4	sec
40	1.1×10^{12}	291	hrs	1024	sec
56	72×10^{15}	2179	yrs	777	days
64	1.84×10^{19}	557845	yrs	545	yrs
128	3.4×10^{38}	10^{25}	yrs	10^{22}	yrs

Table 12.2: The Security Provided by Certain Key Sizes.

⋄ **Exercise 12.1:** Cryptographers often have to refute the following statement: "I can always crack an encrypted message by trying the entire key space. With a really fast computer, I can easily try all the possible 64-bit keys. Besides, I may succeed on the first try." Use real-life examples to illustrate the fallacy of this boast.

12.3 Polybius's Monoalphabetic Cipher

Before we get to the details of modern, computer-based encryption algorithms, we present two examples of old, letter-based ciphers. This section and the next one describe a monoalphabetic and polyalphabetic ciphers developed in antiquity by the same person.

The second century B.C. Greek author and historian Polybius (or Polybios) had an interest in cryptography and developed the simple monoalphabetic cipher that today bears his name. The cipher is based on a small square of letters, so when applied to English text, the number of letters is artificially reduced from 26 to 25 by considering I and J identical. The resulting 25 letters are arranged in a 5×5 square (Figure 12.3a) where each letter is identified by its row and column (integers in the interval $[1,5]$). Encrypting is done by replacing each plainletter with its coordinates in the Polybius square. Thus, the plaintext POLYBIUS␣CIPHER is encrypted into the numeric sequence 35, 34, 31, 54, 12, 24, 45, 43, 13, 24, 35, 23, 15, and 42.

Even though the ciphertext consists of numbers, this cipher is still monoalphabetic and can easily be broken. An experienced cryptanalyst will quickly discover that the ciphertext consists of 2-digit integers where each digit is in the interval $[1, 5]$, and that the integer 15 appears about 12% of the time. The ciphertext may be written as a sequence of digits, such as 3 5 3 4 3 1 5 4 1 2 2 4 4 5 4 3 1 3 2 4 3 5 2 3 1 5 4 2, but this does not significantly strengthen the method. A key may be added to the basic cipher, in accordance with Kerckhoffs's principle (Section 12.2). The key `polybius cipher` becomes, after the removal of spaces and duplicate letters, the string `polybiuscher`. The rest of the alphabet is appended to this string, and the result is the Polybius square of Figure 12.3b.

◇ **Exercise 12.2:** Suggest another way to extend the short key `polybius⎵cipher` to the complete set of 25 letters.

	1	2	3	4	5
1	a	b	c	d	e
2	f	g	h	i/j	k
3	l	m	n	o	p
4	q	r	s	t	u
5	v	w	x	y	z

(a)

	1	2	3	4	5
1	p	o	l	y	b
2	i/j	u	s	c	h
3	e	r	a	d	f
4	g	k	m	n	q
5	t	v	w	x	z

(b)

Figure 12.3: The Polybius Monoalphabetic Cipher.

The monoalphabetic Polybius cipher is sometimes called the *nihilistic cipher* or a *knock cipher* because it was used by the Russian Nihilists, the opponents of the Czar, to communicate in prison by knocking the numbers on the walls between cells. They naturally used the old 35-letter Cyrillic alphabet, and so had a 6×6 Polybius square. Each letter was transmitted by tapping its two coordinates (each an integer in the interval $[1, 6]$) on the wall.

Another variant embeds the digits 6–9 in the ciphertext randomly, to act as nulls or placebos, to confuse any would-be codebreakers or listening jailers.

The monoalphabetic Polybius cipher rearranges the one-dimensional string of letters in a two-dimensional square. The method can therefore be extended by increasing the number of dimensions. Since $3^3 = 27$, it makes sense to have a three-dimensional box of size $3 \times 3 \times 3$ and to store 27 symbols in it. Each symbol can be encrypted to a triplet of digits, each in the interval $[0, 2]$ (these are ternary digits, or trits). If the original Polybius method, using a square, can be called *bipartite*, its three-dimensional extension may be called *tripartite*. Similarly, since $2^8 = 256$, it is possible to construct an eight-dimensional structure with 256 symbols, where each symbol can be coded with eight bits. This may be termed *octopartite* encryption and it is the basis of the EBCDIC (extended BCD Interchange code) used in IBM mainframe computers.

Today, the monoalphabetic Polybius cipher is used mostly to convert letter sequences to numeric sequences. Section 12.4 discusses a polyalphabetic version of this ancient cipher.

12.4 Polybius's Polyalphabetic Cipher

The simple Polybius monoalphabetic cipher of Section 12.3 can be extended to a polyalphabetic cipher. A long key is chosen (normally text from a book) and is encrypted by the Polybius square of Figure 12.3a. The result is a sequence of two-digit numbers.

The plaintext is also encrypted by the same square, resulting in another sequence of 2-digit numbers. The two sequences are combined by adding corresponding numbers, but the addition is done without propagating any carries. Assuming that the plaintext is POLYBIUS␣CIPHER, and the key is the text happy families are all alike..., the two sequences and their (carryless) sum are

Plaintext	35	34	31	54	12	24	45	43	13	24	35	23	15	42
Key	23	11	35	35	54	21	11	32	24	31	24	15	43	11
Ciphertext	**58**	**45**	**66**	**89**	**66**	**45**	**56**	**75**	**37**	**55**	**59**	**38**	**58**	**53**

The digits of the two numbers added are in the interval $[1, 5]$, so each digit of the sum is in the interval $[2, 10]$, where 10 is written as a single 0.

Decrypting is done by subtracting the key from the ciphertext. In our example, this operation is summarized by the three lines

Ciphertext	58	45	66	89	66	45	56	75	37	55	59	38	58	53
Key	23	11	35	35	54	21	11	32	24	31	24	15	43	11
Plaintext	35	34	31	54	12	24	45	43	13	24	35	23	15	42

The carryless addition simplifies the subtraction. Each digit of the ciphertext is greater than the corresponding digit of the key, except for cipherdigits that are zero. If a cipherdigit is zero, it should be replaced by the number 10 before subtraction.

⋄ **Exercise 12.3:** In a 6×6 Polybius square, each digit is in the interval $[1, 6]$. When two digits are added, the sum is in the interval $[2, 12]$, where 10, 11, and 12 are considered 0, 1, and 2, respectively. Is it still possible to add two numbers without propagating carries?

Even though this cipher employs numbers, it is similar to other polyalphabetic cipher because the numbers are related to letters and the letter frequencies are reflected in the numbers. The resulting ciphertext can be broken with methods similar to those used to break other polyalphabetic ciphers. The polyalphabetic Polybius cipher is similar to the one-time pad of Section 12.5 and can provide absolute security if the key is as long as the plaintext, is random, and is used only once.

> Polybius had fared better than most of the leaders and intellectuals that Rome had taken from Achaea. While a prisoner, he met the head of one of Rome's great families, Scipio Aemilianus. Scipio found Polybius good company and exchanged books with him. He took Polybius with him on military campaigns, and he introduced Polybius to Rome's high society.
>
> —From *http://www.barca.fsnet.co.uk.*

12.5 The One-Time Pad

The encryption methods discussed so far start with a plaintext that's a string of characters (letters, digits, and punctuation marks) from a certain alphabet and produce ciphertext whose symbols are drawn from the same alphabet. Modern cryptography is based on computers which use binary numbers, so current encryption techniques assume the binary alphabet whose symbols are 0 and 1. We start with the one-time pad (also called the *Vernam cipher*), a simple, secure, but not always practical algorithm for encrypting binary data. The encryption key of the one-time pad is a long, random binary string that's used just once. The key is distributed to all the parties authorized to use the cipher, and it employs the exclusive-OR (XOR) logical operation to encrypt and decrypt binary data.

The rule of encryption is to perform the XOR of the next bit of the plaintext and the next bit of the key. The result is the next bit of the ciphertext. Similarly, decrypting the next bit of ciphertext is done by XORing it with the next bit of the key. The result is the next bit of the plaintext.

This interesting and important cipher was developed by Gilbert S. Vernam in 1917, and United States patent #1310719 was issued to him in 1918.

The vernam cipher is secure because the resulting ciphertext is a random string of bits. It does not contain any patterns from the plaintext and does not provide the codebreaker with any clues to the plaintext. However, the key has to be long (at least as long as the plaintext) and it should be used just once (the reason for that is explained below). Thus, the one-time pad can be used only in applications where long keys can be distributed securely and often.

It is easy to show that if the keystream of a Vernam cipher is a random sequence of bits, then the ciphertext is random even if the plaintext isn't random. We denote the ith bits of the plaintext, the keystream, and the ciphertext by d_i, k_i, and $c_i = d_i \oplus k_i$, respectively. We assume that the keystream is random, i.e., $P(k_i = 0) = 0.5$ and $P(k_i = 1) = 0.5$. The plaintext isn't random, so we assume that $P(d_i = 0) = p$, which implies $P(d_i = 1) = 1 - p$. Table 12.4 summarizes the four possible cases of d_i and k_i and their probabilities. The values of c_i and their probabilities for those cases are also listed. It is easy to see from the table that the probability of c_i being 0 is $P(c_i = 0) = p/2 + (1 - p)/2 = 1/2$, and similarly $P(c_i = 1) = 1/2$. The ciphertext of the Vernam cipher is therefore random, which makes this simple method unbreakable.

d_i	$P(d_i)$	k_i	$P(k_i)$	c_i	$P(c_i)$
0	p	0	$1/2$	0	$p/2$
0	p	1	$1/2$	1	$p/2$
1	$1-p$	0	$1/2$	1	$(1-p)/2$
1	$1-p$	1	$1/2$	0	$(1-p)/2$

Table 12.4: Truth Table of a Vernam Cipher.

◇ **Exercise 12.4:** In principle, the Vernam cipher can be broken by a brute force approach where every key is tried. This approach is impractical because the key tends to be long, resulting in an immense keyspace. Also, each plaintext produced by such a search will have to be checked. Most such plaintexts would look random and would be immediately ignored, but some may appear meaningful and may have to be carefully examined. However, the chance that a wrong key would produce meaningful plaintext is very small. Advance arguments to support this claim.

In order to achieve good security, the one-time pad should be used just once. The Venona project [NSA-venona 04] run by the United States Army's signal intelligence service during 1943–1980 is a good, practical example of a case where this rule was broken, with significant results. Using the one-time pad more than once breaks one of the cherished rules of cryptography, namely, to avoid repetitions, and may provide enough clues to a would-be codebreaker to reconstruct the random key and use it to decipher messages. Here is how such deciphering can be done.

We assume that two ciphertexts are given and it is known or suspected that they were encrypted with the same random keystream. We select a short, common word, such as the. We can assume that the first message contains some occurrences of this word, so we start by assuming that the *entire* first message consists of copies of this word. We then figure out the random keystream needed to encrypt a series of the into the first ciphertext, and try to decrypt the second ciphertext with this key (a key that we can consider *the first guess*). Any part of this first-guess key that corresponds to an actual the in the first message would decrypt a small part of the second message correctly. Applying the first-guess key to the second ciphertext may therefore result in plaintext with some meaningful words and fragments.

The next step is to guess how to expand those fragments in the second plaintext and use the improved plaintext to produce a second-guess key. This key is then applied to the first ciphertext to produce a first plaintext that has some recognizable words and fragments and is therefore a little better than just a series of the. Using our knowledge of the language, we can expand those fragments and use the improved plaintext to construct a third-guess key.

After a few iterations, both plaintexts may have so much recognizable material that the rest can be guessed with more certainty, thereby leading to complete decipherment.

Even though it offers absolute security, the one-time pad is generally impractical, because the one-time pads have to be generated and distributed safely to every member of an organization that may be very large (such as an army division). This method can be used only in a limited number of applications, such as exchanging top-secret messages between a government and its ambassador abroad or between world leaders.

(In principle, the one-time pad can be used, or rather abused, in cases where the sender wants to remain unaccountable. Once an encrypted message A is decrypted to plaintext B and the one-time pad is destroyed, there is no way to redecrypt A and thus to associate it with B. The sender may deny sending B and may claim that decrypting A had to result in something else.)

In practice, stream ciphers are used instead of the Vernam cipher. Stream ciphers employ keystreams that are *pseudorandom* bit strings. Such a bit string is generated by repeatedly applying a recursive relation, so it is deterministic and therefore not truly random. Still, if a sequence of n pseudorandom bits does not repeat itself, it can be used as the keystream for a stream cipher with relative safety.

12.6 The Key Distribution Problem

The problem of key distribution has already been mentioned. Kerckhoffs' principle (Section 12.2) states that the security of a cryptographic method depends on the encryption key, not the encryption algorithm, being kept secret. In cases where a large group of users is authorized to send and receive encrypted messages, each person in the group has to have the key and is responsible for keeping it secret. The larger the group, the greater the chance that the key will fall into the wrong hands. Also, encryption keys have to be changed from time to time, and distributing the new key securely to a large group of users (especially under difficult conditions, such as a war) is a delicate and complex task.

For many years it was strongly believed that the key distribution problem has no satisfactory solution, but an ideal, simple solution was found in the 1970s and has since become the foundation upon which much of modern cryptography is based.

The following narrative illustrates the nature of the solution. Suppose that Alice wants to send Bob a secure message. She places the message in a strong box, locks it with a padlock, and mails it to Bob. Bob receives the box safely, but then realizes that he does not have the key to the padlock. This is a simplified version of the key distribution problem, and it has a simple, unexpected solution. Bob simply adds another padlock to the box and mails it back to Alice. Alice removes her padlock and mails the box to Bob, who removes his lock, opens the box, and reads the message.

⋄ **Exercise 12.5:** (Easy.) When restricted to physical boxes and keys, this problem has a simpler solution. Once Bob verifies receipt of the box, Alice can mail him the key under a separate envelope. Explain why this solution cannot be applied to the case where the messages and keys are files sent between computers.

The cryptographic equivalent is similar. We start with a similar, albeit unsatisfactory, approach. Imagine a group of users of a particular encryption algorithm, where each user has a private key that is unknown to anyone else. Also imagine a user, Alice, who wants to send an encrypted message to another user, Bob. Alice encrypts the message with her private key (a key unknown to Bob) and sends it. Bob receives the encrypted message, encrypts it again, with his key, and sends the doubly-encrypted message back to Alice. Alice now decrypts the message with her key, but the message is still encrypted with Bob's key. Alice sends the message again to Bob, who decrypts it with his key and can read it.

The trouble with this simple scenario is that most ciphers must obey the LIFO (last in first out) rule. The last cipher used to encrypt a doubly-encrypted message must be the first one used to decipher it. This is easy to see in the case of a monoalphabetic cipher. Suppose that Alice's key replaces D with P and L with X and Bob's key replaces P with L. After encrypting a message twice, first with Alice's key and then with Bob's key, any D in the message becomes an L. However, when Alice's key is used to decipher the L, it replaces it with X. When Bob's key is used to decipher the X, it replaces it with something different from the original D. The same LIFO rule applies to most polyalphabetic cipher.

12.7 Diffie–Hellman–Merkle Keys

However, there is a way out, a discovery made in 1976 by Whitfield Diffie, Martin Hellman, and Ralph Merkle. Their revolutionary Diffie–Hellman–Merkle key exchange method makes it possible to securely exchange a cryptographic key (or any piece of data) over an unsecured channel. It involves the concept of a *one-way function*, a function that either does not have an inverse or whose inverse is not unique. Most functions have simple inverses. The inverse of the exponential function $y = e^x$, for example, is the natural logarithm $x = \log_e y$. However, modular arithmetic provides an example of a simple and useful one-way function. The value of the modulo function $f(x) = x \bmod p$ is the remainder of the integer division $x \div p$ and is an integer in the interval $[0, p-1]$. Table 12.5 illustrates the one-way nature of modular arithmetic by listing values of $3^x \bmod 7$ for 10 values of x. It is easy to see, for example, that the number 3 is the value of $3^x \bmod 7$ for $x = 1$ and $x = 7$. The point is that the same number is the value of this function for infinitely more values of x, effectively making it impossible to reverse this simple function.

x	1	2	3	4	5	6	7	8	9	10
3^x	3	9	27	81	243	729	2187	6561	19683	59049
$3^x \bmod 7$	3	2	6	4	5	1	3	2	6	4

Table 12.5: Ten Values of $3^x \bmod 7$.

⋄ **Exercise 12.6:** Find some real-world processes that are one-way either in principle or in practice.

Based on this interesting property of modular arithmetic, the three researchers came up with an original and unusual scheme for distributing keys. The process is summarized in Figure 12.6. The process requires the modular function $L^x \bmod P$, whose two parameters P (a large prime, about 512 bits) and L should satisfy $L < P$. The two parties have to select values for L and P, but these values don't have to be secret.

Careful study of Figure 12.6 shows that even if the messages exchanged between Alice and Bob are intercepted, and even if the values $L = 5$ and $P = 13$ that they use are known, the key still cannot be derived, since the values of either a or b are also needed, but both are kept secret by the two parties.

This breakthrough has proved that cryptographic keys can be securely exchanged through unsecured channels, and users no longer have to meet personally to agree on keys or to trust couriers to deliver them. However, the Diffie–Hellman–Merkle key exchange method described in Figure 12.6 is inefficient. In the ideal case, where both users are online at the same time, they can go through the process of Figure 12.6 (select the secret numbers a and b, compute and exchange the values of α and β, and calculate the key) in just a few minutes. If they cannot be online at the same time (for example, if they live in very different time zones), then the process of determining the key may take a day or longer.

	Alice	Bob
Step 1	Selects a secret number a, say, 4	Selects a secret number b, say, 7
Step 2	Computes $\alpha = 5^a \bmod 13 = 624 \bmod 13 = 1$ and sends α to Bob	Computes $\beta = 5^b \bmod 13 = 78125 \bmod 13 = 8$ and sends β to Alice
Step 3	Computes the key by $\beta^a \bmod 13 = 4096 \bmod 13 = 1$	Computes the key by $\alpha^b \bmod 13 = 1 \bmod 13 = 1$

Notice that knowledge of α, β, and the function is not enough to compute the key. Either a or b is needed, but these are kept secret.

Figure 12.6: Three Steps to Compute the Same Key.

◇ **Exercise 12.7:** Show why the steps of Figure 12.6 produce the same key for Alice and for Bob.

◇ **Exercise 12.8:** Why should P be large and why should L be less than P?

The following analogy may explain why a one-way function is needed to solve the key distribution problem. Imagine that Bob and Alice want to agree on a certain paint color and keep it secret. Each starts with a container that has one liter of paint of a certain color, say, R. Each adds one liter of paint of a secret color. Bob may add a liter of paint of color G and Alice may add a liter of color B. Neither knows what color was added by the other one. They then exchange the containers (which may be intercepted and examined). When each gets the other's container, each adds another liter of his or her secret paint. A little thinking shows that the two containers end up with paint of the same color. Intercepting and examining the containers on their ways is fruitless, because one cannot unmix paints. Mixing paints is a one-way operation.

12.8 Public-Key Cryptography

In 1975, a little after the Diffie–Hellman–Merkle key exchange was published, Whitfield Diffie came up with the concept of an *asymmetric key*. Traditionally, ciphers use symmetric keys. The same key is used to encrypt and decrypt a message. Decrypting is the exact reverse of encrypting. Cryptography with an asymmetric key requires two keys, one for encrypting and the other for decrypting. This seems a trivial concept but is in fact revolutionary. In an asymmetric cipher, there is no need to distribute keys or to compute them by exchanging data as in the Diffie–Hellman–Merkle key exchange scheme. Alice could decide on two keys for her secret messages, make the encryption key public, and keep the decryption key secret (this is her private key). Bob could then use Alice's public key to encrypt messages and send them to Alice. Anyone intercepting such a message would not be able to decipher it because this requires the secret decryption key that only Alice knows.

> Whitfield Diffie took cryptography out of the hands of the spooks and made privacy possible in the digital age—by inventing the most revolutionary concept in encryption since the Renaissance.
>
> —*Wired*, November 1994

12.9 RSA Cryptography

It was clear to Diffie that a cipher based on an asymmetric key would be the ideal solution to the troublesome problem of key distribution and would completely revolutionize cryptography. Unfortunately, he was unable to actually come up with such a cipher. The first, simple, practical, and secure public-key cipher, known today as RSA cryptography, was finally developed in 1977 by Ronald Rivest, Adi Shamir, and Leonard Adleman. RSA was a triumphal achievement, an achievement based on the properties of prime numbers.

A prime number, as most know, is a number with no divisors. More accurately, it is a positive integer N whose only divisors are 1 and itself. (Nonprime integers are called composites.) For generations, prime numbers and their properties (the mathematical discipline of number theory) were of interest to mathematicians only and had no practical applications whatsoever. RSA cryptography found an interesting, original, and very practical application for these numbers. This application relies on the most important property of prime numbers, the property that justifies the name *prime*. Any positive integer can be represented as the product of prime numbers (its prime factors) *in one way only*. In other words, any integer has a unique prime factorization. For example, the number 65,535 can be represented as the product of integers in many ways, but there is only one set of primes, namely 3, 5, 17, and 257, whose product equals 65,535.

The main idea behind RSA is to choose two large primes p and q that together constitute the private key. The public key N is their product $N = p{\times}q$ (naturally, it is a composite). The important (and surprising) point is that multiplying large integers is a one-way function! It is relatively easy to multiply integers, even very large ones, but it is practically impossible, or at least extremely time consuming, to find the prime factors of a large integer, with hundreds of digits. Today, after millennia of research (primes have been known to the ancients), no efficient method for factoring numbers has been discovered. All existing factoring algorithms are slow and may take years to factor an integer consisting of a few hundred decimal digits. The factoring challenge (with prizes) offered by RSA laboratories [RSA 01] testifies to the accuracy of this statement.

To summarize, we know that the public key N has a unique prime factorization and that its prime factors constitute the private key. However, if N is large enough, we will not be able to factor it, even with the fastest computers, which makes RSA a secure cipher. Having said that, no one has proved that a fast factorization method does not exist. It is not inconceivable that someone will come up with such an algorithm that would render RSA (impregnable for more than two decades) useless and would stimulate researchers to discover a different public-key cipher.

(Recent declassifying of secret British documents suggests that a cipher very similar to RSA had been developed by James Ellis and his colleagues starting in 1969. They worked for the British government communications headquarters, GCHQ, and so had to keep their work secret. See [Singh 99].

> James Ellis, a mathematician and computer scientist, joined GCHQ (then at Eastcote, West London) in 1952, having previously worked for the Admiralty.
> —From `http://www.gchq.gov.uk/`

The following is a comment made by an anonymous reviewer: "Another reason why the GCHQ work was never applied was because no one there believed it to be useful. It took private industry to recognize its worth. In other words, it wasn't just secrecy that prevented its use until it was reinvented in the open literature.")

And now, to the details of RSA. These are deceptively simple, but the use of large numbers requires special arithmetic routines to be implemented and carefully debugged. We assume that Alice has selected two large primes p and q as her private key. She has to compute and publish two more numbers as her public key. They are $N = p \cdot q$ and e. The latter can be any integer, but it should be relatively prime to $(p-1)(q-1)$, a number denoted by ϕ. Notice that N must be unique (if Joe has selected the same N as his public key, then he knows the values of p and q), but e does not have to be. To encrypt a message M (an integer) intended for Alice, Bob gets her public key (N and e), computes $C = M^e \bmod N$, and sends C to Alice through an open communications channel. To decrypt the message, Alice starts by computing the decryption key d from $e \times d = 1 \bmod \phi$, then uses d to compute $M = C^d \bmod N$.

The security of the encrypted message depends on the one-way nature of the modulo function. Since the encrypted message C is $M^e \bmod N$, and since both N and e are public, the message can be decrypted by inverting the modulo function. However, as mentioned earlier, this function is impossible to invert (or, rather has too many inverses) for large values of N. It is important to understand that polyalphabetic ciphers, block ciphers, and stream ciphers can be as secure as RSA, are easier to implement, and are faster to execute, but they are symmetric and therefore suffer from the problem of key distribution.

The use of large numbers requires special routines for the arithmetic operations. Specifically, the operation M^e may be problematic, since M may be a large number. One way to simplify this operation is to break the message M up into small segments. Another option is to break up e into a sum of terms and use each term separately. For example, if $e = 7 = 1 + 2 + 4$, then

$$M^e \bmod N = [(M^1 \bmod N) \times (M^2 \bmod N) \times (M^4 \bmod N)] \bmod N.$$

Here is an example of RSA encryption and decryption using small parameters. We select the two small primes $p = 137$ and $q = 191$ as our private key and compute $N = p \cdot q = 26{,}167$ and $\phi = (p-1)(q-1) = 25{,}840$. We also select $e = 3$ and, using the extended Euclidean algorithm, find a value $d = 17{,}227$ such that $e \cdot d = 1 \bmod \phi$. The public key is the pair $(N, e) = (26167, 3)$, and the decryption key is $d = 17{,}227$. For the plaintext M, we select the 4-character string `abcd` whose ASCII codes are 97, 98, 99, and 100, or in binary 01100001, 01100010, 01100011, and 01100100. These are grouped into the two 16-bit blocks $0110000101100010_2 = 24{,}930$ and $0110001101100100_2 = 25{,}444$. Encrypting the blocks is done by

$$C = M^e \bmod N = 24{,}930^3 \bmod 26{,}167 = 23{,}226,$$
$$C = M^e \bmod N = 25{,}444^3 \bmod 26{,}167 = 23{,}081.$$

Decrypting the two blocks C of ciphertext is done by

$$C^d \bmod N = 23{,}226^{17227} \bmod 26{,}167 = 24{,}930,$$
$$C^d \bmod N = 23{,}081^{17227} \bmod 26{,}167 = 25{,}444.$$

RSA in Two Lines of Perl

Adam Back (`aba@dcs.exeter.ac.uk`) has created an implementation of RSA in just two lines of Perl. It uses `dc`, an arbitrary-precision arithmetic package that ships with most UNIX systems. Here's the Perl code:

```
print pack"C*",split/\D+/,`echo "16iII*o\U@{$/=$z;[(pop,pop,unpack"H*",<>
)]}\EsMsKsN0[lN*11K[d2%Sa2/d0<X+d*lMLa^*lN%0]dsXx++lMlN/dsM0<J]dsJxp"|dc`
```

The security of RSA depends on the infeasibility of factoring large numbers, and this paragraph shows that this problem is equivalent to keeping the private quantity d secret. It turns out that knowledge of d can lead to an efficient factoring of N in the following way. We know that $e \cdot d = 1 \bmod \phi$, which implies that there is an integer k such that $e \cdot d - 1 = k\phi$. From this it follows (by one of the many theorems proved by the great Leonhard Euler) that $a^{ed-1} = 1 \bmod \phi$ for all integers a in the interval $[0, n-1]$. If we now use the notation $ed - 1 = 2^s t$, where t is odd, then it can be shown that there is an integer $b \in [1, s]$ such that $a^{2^{b-1}t} \neq \pm 1 \bmod N$ and $a^{2^b t} = 1 \bmod N$ for at least half of the integers a. We therefore conclude that if such a and b are known, then the greatest common divisor of $a^{2^{b-1}t} - 1$ and N is a factor of N. Factoring N may therefore be done by selecting a random integer a in the proper range and looking for an integer $b \in [1, s]$ that satisfies the property above. With the computing power currently available, this can be achieved quickly and easily.

The value of parameter e is also important. Encryption requires the computation of M^e, so small e implies faster encryption. However, small values of e may also lead to a weaker ciphertext, as the following example illustrates. Suppose that Alice wants to encrypt a message M and send it to three recipients whose public keys are N_1, N_2, and N_3. Suppose also that all three recipients use the same small e, say, $e = 3$ as in our example. Alice can then compute $C_i = M^3 \bmod N_i$ for $i = 1, 2, 3$ and send the three ciphertexts C_i to their recipients. If Eve intercepts the ciphertexts, however, she may have an easy way to decrypt them. She may use Gauss's algorithm to solve the three modular equations $x = C_i \bmod N_i$ for $i = 1, 2, 3$. The solution x will be in the interval $[0, N_1 N_2 N_3)$. We know that $M^3 < N_1 N_2 N_3$, so from the Chinese remainder theorem we conclude that x must equal M^3. Hence, Eve can decrypt the message by computing $\sqrt[3]{x}$. This vulnerability can be avoided by using large values for e or, in cases where the same message is sent to several recipients, by appending a random string to each message in order to make the plaintexts different.

The Chinese remainder theorem states that if the integers n_1 through n_k are pairwise relatively prime, then the system of equations

$$x = a_1 \bmod n_1, \quad x = a_2 \bmod n_2, \ldots, \quad x = a_k \bmod n_k,$$

has a unique solution modulo the quantity $n = n_1 n_2 \ldots n_k$.

Gauss's theorem states that the solution to the system of equations in the Chinese remainder theorem can be expressed as the sum $x = \sum_{i=1}^{k} a_i N_i M_i \bmod n$, where $N_i = n/n_i$ and $M_i = N_i^{-1} \bmod n_i$.

Another potential vulnerability of RSA is its *multiplicative property*. We denote by $\mathcal{Z}_N$ the set of integers modulo N, i.e., $\{0, 1, \ldots, N-1\}$. We similarly denote by $\mathcal{Z}_N^*$ the set of integers $\{a \in \mathcal{Z}_n \,|\, \gcd(a, N) = 1\}$. In the special case where N is prime, $\mathcal{Z}_N^* = \{1, 2, \ldots, N-1\}$. It can be shown that $\mathcal{Z}_N$ is closed under multiplication and constitutes a multiplicative group.

Assume that $C_i = M_i^e \bmod N$ for $i = 1, 2$ (i.e., two messages use the same N). This implies that $(M_1 M_2)^e = C_1 C_1 \bmod N$. The RSA multiplicative property can now be stated as follows. The ciphertext C that corresponds to the plaintext $M = M_1 M_2 \bmod N$ is $C = C_1 C_2 \bmod N$. An attack by Eve on messages decrypted by Alice is possible if Alice has a certain amount of trust in Eve and is willing to encrypt certain messages for her. Suppose that Eve wants to decrypt a message $C = M^e \bmod N$ that she has intercepted on its way to Alice. Eve can select a random integer $x \in \mathcal{Z}_N^*$, compute $C' = C \cdot X^e \bmod N$, and ask Alice to encrypt C'. If Alice complies, she will compute $M' = (C')^d \bmod N$ and send M' to Eve, who can then use the relation

$$M' = (C')^d \bmod N = C^d (X^e)^d = M \cdot X \bmod N$$

to compute $M = M' X^{-1} \bmod N$.

The *cycling attack* poses another threat to RSA security. Given a plaintext M in the interval $[0, N-1]$, it is encrypted to $C = M^e \bmod N$. The ciphertext C is therefore also an integer in the same interval. Thus, M and C are *permutations* of each other. Because of this, there must be a positive integer k such that $C^{e^k} \bmod N = C$ and $C^{e^{k-1}} \bmod N = M$. The cycling attack uses the public key (N, e) and an intercepted ciphertext C to compute the sequence $C^e \bmod N$, $C^{e^2} \bmod n$, $C^{e^3} \bmod N$, and so on, until one of those numbers, $C^{e^k} \bmod n$, equals C. This reveals the value of k and makes it possible to decrypt C by computing $M = C^{e^{k-1}} \bmod N$. Special software has to be used in these calculations, since the quantities C^{e^k} grow very quickly.

Regardless of the key used, some plaintexts are encrypted by RSA to themselves. Thus, $M^e \bmod N$ may sometimes equal M. Such messages are referred to as *unconcealed* and are rare. Nevertheless, RSA encryption software should compare every ciphertext C to its plaintext M and alert the user when an unconcealed message is detected.

The various problems mentioned here are eliminated by the Public-Key Cryptography Standards (PKCS) developed by RSA Security. The interested reader should consult especially PKCS #1 [PKCS 04].

> RSA stands for "resists serious attack."

12.10 SSL: Secure Socket Layer

The following is a dramatization. Alice is hunched over her computer, browsing the Internet. Her wedding to Bob is in a week, and she is still looking for a wedding dress. She has just found a beautiful cream-colored layered chiffon dress that is exactly her size (36–24–36) and is within her price range. It is sold online by `ChiffonDresses.com`. Alice takes out her credit card, ready to send her number and order the dress, but her hand suddenly freezes in midair. She has just remembered that important transactions on the Internet require special security. She checks the bottom-left corner of her screen and yes, there is a small lock, similar to the one shown here, that assures her that the transaction she is about to perform is secure (the URL also changes to `https` instead of `http`). She can order her dress with confidence, being reasonably certain that no one can intercept and steal her credit card number.

This scenario is common. Most of us perform sensitive transactions over the Internet, and we expect them to be private. Online purchasing is one example. Online banking, where a bank account can be reviewed by a customer after a PIN is sent, is another.

This section describes the SSL (secure socket layer) protocol employed by all major Web browsers, as well as by other software, to secure messages sent over the Internet. First, a disclaimer. SSL provides secure communications but cannot guarantee total security. A credit card number or other sensitive information sent over the Internet by the SSL protocol is encrypted and cannot be compromised while in transit. When it arrives at its destination, however, the security provided by SSL ceases and the information may become vulnerable. A dishonest employee may steal it. An insecure data base may be taken over by a hacker and its content copied and misused. The conclusion is simple. Don't trust SSL all the way. Trust it only for communicating your sensitive data. If there is any reason to doubt the integrity of the receiver, don't send the data. The Better Business Bureau [bbbseal 05] is one source that can be employed to evaluate the integrity of a commercial organization.

SSL was developed at Netscape Communications, Inc. in 1994 in response to users' demand for secure Internet communications. It has since evolved and been strengthened considerably by several organizations. Today, the most-common SSL protocol is TLS (transport layer security), and there are other versions of SSL, such as an open version (openssl) and a version for wireless communications (WTLS).

Two recommended references are [Rescorla 00] and [Thomas 00].

As before, we assume two protagonists, Alice and Bob. Alice plays the part of a consumer trying to purchase an item online. Bob is the seller. The SSL protocol proceeds in the following steps:

1. An authentication protocol is executed by Alice to make sure that Bob is really who he claims to be. Bob's public key is sent to Alice as part of this protocol. The protocol is based on the public-key concept and employs RSA encryption and also a trusted third party.

2. Alice selects a random key for encrypting her sensitive information. This key is encrypted with Bob's public key and is sent to Bob.

3. Alice uses this key to encrypt her sensitive data with a fast, strong encryption algorithm such as DES or AES. Bob uses the same key and algorithm to decrypt the data. Several messages can be exchanged this way between the two parties in complete privacy.

It is obvious that step 1 is the most important part of SSL. It provides secure communications over an insecure channel. This step is complex and slow, which is why it is used only for communicating a short (normally 128-bit) key. The sensitive data itself is encrypted with a fast cipher. This step depends on a basic property of the RSA encryption algorithm. Data encrypted with a public key can be decrypted only with the corresponding private key, but data can also be encrypted with the private key and decrypted only with the corresponding public key. With this in mind, we start with a simple authentication protocol. (We use the notation "`<message> key`" to indicate a message encrypted with a certain key.) If Alice wants to authenticate Bob, she can send him a short message and have Bob encrypt it with his private key and return the result.

Alice → Bob: `Authenticate this.`
Bob → Alice: `<Authenticate this> Bob's private key.`

Alice now decrypts this result with Bob's public key. If the result matches her original message, she has authenticated Bob. This simple protocol has two drawbacks, as follows:

1. Alice must know Bob's public key. If Alice and Bob are members of a group— say, both are scientists and have been communicating by email for a while—then their public keys are known to all the group's members because they are included in each email message. However, if Bob is an organization, such as a new online store, Alice may not have its public key. Even if Bob sends his public key to Alice, she cannot be sure that it really came from Bob's store; it could have been sent by Eve pretending to be Bob and trying to steal Alice's card number.

2. Encrypting a message with your private key and sending it to Alice leads to weak security. Remember that Alice has the original message. If she also has its private-key encryption, she may use both to pretend to be Bob.

Our simple protocol needs improvements. The first one eliminates the need to encrypt Alice's message with Bob's private key. Instead, Bob selects a new message, computes its *message digest*, encrypts the digest with his private key, and sends the (plain) message and the encrypted digest to Alice.

Alice → Bob: `Looking for Bob.`
Bob → Alice: `I'm Bob, <Digest[I'm Bob]> Bob's private key.`

The digest of a message is a function of the message with the following useful properties: (1) it is practically infeasible to compute the original message from its digest and (2) the chance of finding another message that will produce the same digest is extremely small. In practice, a digest is a hash function that hashes text of any length to a small (typically 128-bit) number. The SHA-1 hash function is currently popular as a digest generator. It has replaced the (somewhat similar) MD5 function, which is described below.

With this protocol, Bob still has to send a message (I'm Bob) and the encrypted version of its digest (this is known as a digital signature), but now he can select the message, which gives him more protection from an unscrupulous Alice. The protocol constitutes authentication because Alice has a plain message and the private-key encryption of its digest. She can decrypt the digest, digest the message, and compare the two digests. There is still the problem of having Bob's public key and being certain that it is Bob's, and no one else's public key. Here is what may happen if Eve pretends to be Bob.

Alice → Bob: `I'm looking for Bob.`
Eve → Alice: `I'm Bob, Eve's-public-key.`
Alice → Bob: `Are you?`
Eve → Alice: `Of course I am, <Digest[Of course I am]> Eve's private key.`

The solution to this dilemma involves a third, trusted party, an escrow, that issues *certificates*. When Bob opens his store, he applies for a certificate from an escrow. The escrow company sends an inspector to check Bob and his facilities and to look at their operations and verify their identification. If all is satisfactory, a certificate is issued, but it has an expiration date and has to be renewed periodically. Admittedly, this solution is not elegant. In principle, we would like a protocol that involves just the two communicating parties, but in practice a third party is needed. A certificate contains the following fields Figure 12.7:

1. The name of the certificate issuer (the escrow)
2. A digital signature of the certificate issuer
3. The name of the subject, Bob (the entity for which the certificate is issued)
4. The subject's public key
5. The certificate's expiration date

Figure 12.8 is a detailed listing of the fields of a typical certificate. The issuer part and the subject part have the fields C (two-letter international country code), ST (state or province), L (locality), O (organization name), and OU (organizational unit).

Many organizations apply for certificates, so there must be many certificate issuers. Alice doesn't know all of them. She can be expected to know only a few. There is therefore a need for root certificate issuers. Every leading Web browser comes with a list of root certificates preinstalled. A root certificate (also known as a *CA* or *certificate authority*) belongs to a trusted authority that can issue certificates to other, smaller certificate issuers after checking each to make sure it can be trusted. The encryption preferences (or security preferences) menu of the browser can display the list of CA certificates it knows. If the certificate has expired, the browser displays a dialog box

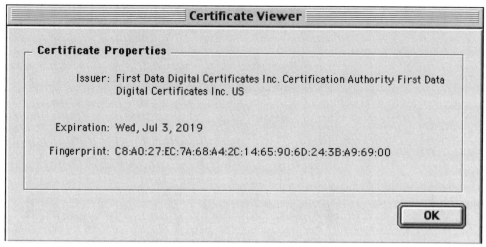

Figure 12.7: A Certificate.

similar to Figure 12.9 that gives the user a choice to continue the sensitive web session or terminate it.

With certificates, the SSL protocol proceeds as follows:

Alice → Bob: `I'm looking for Bob.`
Bob → Alice: `I'm Bob, Bob's certificate.`
Alice → Bob: `Are you really?`
Bob → Alice: `Definitely, <Digest[Definitely]> Bob's private key.`

It is the certificate that provides Alice (or, in practice, her Web browser) with Bob's public key. To verify that this is really Bob's certificate, Alice's browser reads the certificate's issuer name (say, Y) and signature from the certificate. The digital signature contains the issuer's own certificate, which has been issued by one of the root issuers (call it X). The browser has a list of the root certificate issuers, and it communicates with root issuer X to verify the certificate of issuer Y. This is a slow, tedious process, so it is used as little as possible.

Eve may try to impersonate Bob in this protocol, so we have to keep her in mind. She can execute step 2 in the protocol, because she may have Bob's certificate from a past transaction with him, but she cannot execute step 4 because she doesn't have Bob's private key.

The protocol above is the first and most important step in the complete, three-step SSL protocol. Once it has been executed, Alice is confident that she is dealing with Bob and that she has his public key. In the second step, Alice (or rather her browser) selects a random number to serve as a secret key and sends it to Bob, encrypted with his public key, as a short message. Only Bob can decrypt this message, but again we have to place ourselves in Eve's shoes. What can she do? She cannot decrypt this short message, but she can damage it on its way to Bob. This may be useful to Eve, so the SSL protocol must have a way for Bob to identify damaged messages. One way of verifying a message

```
Certificate:
Data:
Version: 1 (0x0)
Serial Number: 0 (0x0)
Signature Algorithm: md5WithRSAEncryption
Issuer:
  C=US,
  ST=NC,
  L=Cary,
  O=My New Outfit, Inc.,
  OU=Sales,
  CN=ntbox.somewhere.com/Email=me@somewhere.com

Validity
  Not Before: Oct 7 04:19:24 1999 GMT
  Not After : Oct 6 04:19:24 2000 GMT

Subject:
  C=US,
  ST=NC,
  L=Cary,
  O=My New Outfit, Inc.,
  OU=Sales,
  CN=ntbox.somewhere.com/Email=me@somewhere.com

Subject Public Key Info:
Public Key Algorithm: rsaEncryption
RSA Public Key: (1024 bit)
Modulus (1024 bit):

00:c9:dd:68:31:ca:1c:ab:74:7c:21:a8:de:71:22:
25:ec:48:dd:54:34:b5:b8:be:ad:96:cf:56:ad:a2:
7d:9f:81:d5:62:3a:f1:c2:03:4d:8d:73:a3:cb:ac:
f8:f4:d7:95:0d:3f:9e:2c:8f:5f:d3:40:91:09:79:
21:c4:8b:f6:0a:3b:2c:c7:42:3d:2c:c3:5b:17:68:
58:2e:47:42:1e:24:41:1d:59:ba:57:0c:26:63:2e:
46:55:72:e5:1e:61:6c:6e:c2:73:ad:e0:68:ed:70:
a9:43:73:69:b5:c3:9f:64:54:d6:12:11:f3:10:38:
42:e8:54:82:23:f7:20:26:03

Exponent: 65537 (0x10001)

Signature Algorithm: md5WithRSAEncryption

4f:27:7b:c5:f1:52:33:bc:f8:50:19:b9:98:e6:3b:08:9b:4b:
7b:24:f8:80:10:18:a4:25:6a:39:b1:75:35:05:64:54:ec:5e:
e4:c1:88:fb:7f:72:d1:32:f4:8c:0d:08:28:7e:7e:a5:5f:61:
9c:cc:b4:5c:13:f0:71:a8:d0:56:58:11:e6:b8:35:0a:01:b7:
72:7f:e8:a7:b6:82:aa:52:5d:05:29:d8:48:ba:26:8e:ed:41:
38:86:b8:62:2e:9a:f1:be:99:3c:20:76:57:0f:70:4b:a6:18:
82:aa:90:0c:1f:18:05:c3:98:b8:20:9e:e5:64:02:0d:01:4e:
c4:4e
```

Figure 12.8: A Detailed Certificate.

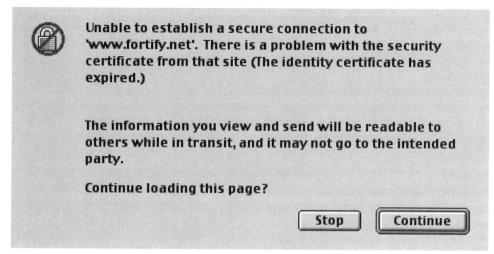

Figure 12.9: An Expired Certificate.

is to append to it a message authentication code (MAC) that consists of a digest of the message and of the secret key. Eve doesn't know the secret key, so she cannot generate the MAC. Here is the revised protocol

Alice → Bob: `Is this Bob?`
Bob → Alice: `I'm Bob, Bob's certificate.`
Alice → Bob: `Are you really?`
Bob → Alice: `Definitely, <Digest[Definitely]> Bob's private key.`
Alice → Bob: `You have been authenticated.`
Alice → Bob: `Here is our new key <secret-key> Bob's public key.`
Alice computes: `MAC=Digest[My CC # is 12345, secret-key].`
Alice → Bob: `<My CC # is 12345, MAC> secret-key.`

Bob knows to expect two-part messages, where the second part consists of the MAC of the first part. Any corrupted message can easily be identified by Bob. Once Bob has received the new secret key (normally, 40, 56, or 128 bits) from Alice, the two can exchange messages with confidence. The messages are encrypted with this key by a secure, fast algorithm, such as DES or RC4.

As noted earlier, SSL was developed at Netscape Communications in 1994. Just a year later, several hackers discovered a weakness in the Netscape implementation of the first SSL version. It turned out that the secret key was selected by a pseudorandom number generator (PRNG) whose seed was a combination of the current time (just the seconds and microseconds) and the process id. Netscape programmers believed that such a combination was sufficiently random and would lead to pseudorandom numbers that could be used as secure keys. However, someone intercepting information packets sent by a browser can have a good idea of the time (in seconds) when the packets were generated. Also, someone with access to any account on the operating system where the Netscape browser is running can find the id of any process. The microseconds part of the seed can then be found by trying the million values between 0 and 999,999. It seems that Netscape has since improved the way the seed of the PRNG is computed.

> To understand the rest, you ought to have a notion
> of two areas in computer science: digital libraries
> (databases) and digital magic (cryptography).
>
> —Dmitri Asonov

A
l33t Speak

The term "l33t Speak" (pronounced "leet") refers to a language or a notational system widely used by hackers. This notation is unique because it cannot be handwritten or spoken. It is an Internet-based notation that relies on the keyboard. It is simple to learn and has room for creativity. Web site [bbc 04] is just one of many online references to this topic.

Many other artificial languages or notational rules have been described or used in literature. The following are a few examples.

Elvish in J. R. R. Tolkien's *The Lord of the Rings*.
Newspeak in George Orwell's *Nineteen Eighty-Four*.
Ptydepe in Václav Havel's *The Memorandum*.
Nadsat in Anthony Burgess' *A Clockwork Orange*.
Marain in Iain M. Banks' *The Player of Games* and his other Culture novels.
Pravic in Ursula K. LeGuin's *The Dispossessed*.

The history of l33t speak is tied up with the Internet. In the early 1980s, as the Internet started to become popular, hackers became aware of themselves as a "species." They wanted a notation that will both identify them as hackers and will make it difficult for others to locate hacker Web sites and newsgroups on the Internet with a simple search. Since a keyboard is one of the chief tools used by a hacker, it is no wonder that the new notation developed from the keyboard. The initial, tentative steps in the development of l33t speak have simply replaced certain letters (mostly vowels) by digits with similar glyphs, so *A* was replaced by 4 and *E* was replaced by 3.

It was the development of sophisticated computer games in the early 1990s that boosted the popularity of l33t speak and prompted hackers to enrich it with features. Gamers started developing their own language, based on phrases heard in games, and hackers who played games (and there are many of them) naturally wrote such phrases in l33t speak. An important example is the phrase "I am elite," whose l33t speak version is "1 4m 3l1t3." Hackers are notoriously bad spellers, so this phrase got first corrupted to "1 4m 3l33t," then mutated to "1 4m l33t," which gave l33t speak its current name. The final boost to the popularity of l33t speak was given by a very popular web comic called Megatokyo.

Like any other language or notational system, l33t speak has its grammar rules, but they are flexible, allowing users to be creative. The basic rules for replacing letters with digits and other keyboard characters are listed here, but new rules appear all the time and either become popular or are forgotten.

$$A \rightarrow 4, \ E \rightarrow 3, \ I \rightarrow 1, \ O \rightarrow \phi, \ O \rightarrow (), \ U \rightarrow |\_|, \ T \rightarrow 7, \ D \rightarrow |), \ W \rightarrow \backslash/\backslash/, \ S \rightarrow \$$$

(Notice the two versions of O.) Connoisseurs of l33t speak talk about classifying versions of this notation into classes or levels such as light l33t, medium 1337, hard |_337, and ultra |_33⁻|⁻.

In l33t, z is used instead of s to construct the plural, f is generally changed to ph, and a short u is often replaced by the pair $\phi\phi$.

The term "digram" is used in English to indicate a pair of characters and l33t speak employs ϕd and ϕr to express the digrams "ed" and "er." For example, "1 4m 4 l33t h4xϕr" can be used instead of "1 4m 4 l33t h4ck3r." (In ultra, this would be spelled "1 $\phi\backslash/\backslash/|\backslash|z\phi r$.")

Punctuation marks are sometimes omitted, and are rare in higher levels of l33t speak. Many chat programs allow the user to type only one sentence at a time, so there is no need for end-of-sentence periods. On the other hand, since l33t speak is commonly used to express surprise or pleasure, exclamation marks are popular and are sometimes repeated several times (a practice strictly prohibited by traditional copy editors). Low levels of l33t speak may use commas, but even those humble punctuation marks are omitted in the higher levels.

The vocabulary of l33t speak is mostly a corrupted form of English, but many phrases and spellings are unique to l33t speak. Here are some examples.

$\phi w|\backslash|$ or $\phi wn3d$. A popular l33t speak word. Its (very loose) meaning is "beaten" but it can also express awe, as in, "I ϕwn3d you" which means "I have beaten you good and proper", or ϕwn4ge!" which means "That was very nifty."

w$\phi\phi$t. This word, derived from "hoot," is interpreted to mean "yay," and is commonly used to express victory.

13wt. A misspelling of "loot" that came to mean a treasure, good merchandise, or possessions. Its most common use it to refer to pirated software, to items in a game, or promotional giveaways.

h4xϕr. The word for hacker or a skillful person. This is the most common occurrence of the ϕr digram.

ph33r. Fear. Most-commonly used in phrases such as "Ph33r m3!" or "Ph33r |\/|y 1337 sk1llz!" It can also be spelled "ph34r."

sk1llz. A word derived from "skill" and referring to skill in some online activity such as programming or hacking. Often used in conjunction with "m4d." As a general rule, if one has sk1llz, one is to be ph33r3d.

m4d. Mad, commonly used as a descriptive term meaning great, for example, "h3s gφt m4d sk1llz."

jφφ. You, often used in phrases like "jφφ d34d fφφ."

fφφ. Fool, someone not bright or skillless.

In any event, it's not a matter of liking or disliking, not a matter of skillful or skillless (how many Ls does that have?). No. When it comes to penguin shuffling, it's your patriotic duty.

—Anonymous

---

jφ. Yo, as in the greeting.

dφφd. Dude, used to address a colleague or an unknown person online.

suxφr. Sucks, as in "7h1s suxφr," an example of the φr digram.

l4m3r. Lamer, someone who is lame, an unfair person or someone who isn't fun to be with.

nφφb. Short for noobie, a corruption of newbie. Someone who is new to or is weak at something.

Usage of l33t speak is nonuniform. Some use it exclusively or almost so, while others frown on general use of l33t speak and insist that it should be used only in brief expressions, preferably expression of excitement.

◇ **Exercise A.1:** (No answer provided). Rewrite the following two l33t speak paragraphs in your language.

```
$4n DI3go- feDEr4L @gEN+s $t0rmEd tH3 H0U53$ 0f tW0 $U5p3CTEd TeRr0r15+5 E@RLY
Y35+3rd@Y M0RniNg 4PHTer dEt3rMiNiNg theY WER3 P4Rt opH @ Pl0+ +0 De$TR0y u.5. C1+i3$.

jac0b M4R+Z 4nd cuR+iS hUgH3$, WELL knOWN 1n t3H Pc g4Ming COMMUnI+Y 4$ "W@xX0R"
aND "L00d@|<r1$" resP3C+1vely, 4Re N0w 1N cU5+oDY 4ND @wA1+iN9 4 BA1l HeaRiN9.
```

Among my most prized possessions are words that I have never spoken.

—Orson Rega Card

B
Virus Timeline

This timeline is meant to serve both as a historical survey and as a teaching tool. Most of the viruses described in this appendix have interesting features that make them unique or a first. Those are described here in some detail. Chapter 5 has several detailed descriptions of viruses and worms, including some of the ones mentioned here.

Several timelines of computer viruses can be found on the Internet. One reference is [IbmAntiVirus 05].

1949–50. First attempts to implement self-replicating programs.

1950s. An experimental game in which players use malicious programs to attack each other's computers is developed and used in Bell Labs.

1975. John Brunner publishes *The Shockwave Rider*, a science fiction novel in which computer "worms" spread across networks.

1981. Several of the first viruses seen "in the wild," (i.e., in the public domain) are found on the Apple II operating system, and are designated Apple viruses 1, 2, and 3. These viruses spread through Texas A&M University via pirated computer games.

1982. Another virus found on the Apple II computer and is designated Elk Cloner (the term *virus* was not used).

1983–84. Fred Cohen is the first to consider viruses a serious topic of scientific study and experimentation. He proposes a definition and conducts controlled experiments in virus propagation.

1986. Brain (Section 5.2), perhaps the first widespread virus (a BSI with stealth features), seems to have been written by two brothers in Pakistan who disseminate it on floppy disks with pirated software sold to tourists.

In December, a file infector named Virdem is introduced in Germany as a demonstration. It is quickly followed by the demonstration viruses Burger and Rush Hour.

1987.   This is the first bad year and it signals the shape of things to come. In the fall, the Lehigh virus (Section 5.1), an early file infector, appears at Lehigh university in Bethlehem, Pennsylvania and infects `command.com` files.

The Christmas tree worm paralyses the IBM worldwide network.

In December, the Jerusalem virus appears at the Hebrew University of Israel. It was the first file infector that infected both `.com` and `.exe` executable files and also successfully modified interrupt handling routines so that it could reside in memory and be invoked frequently. A bug in this virus caused it to reinfect programs. The Jerusalem virus was preceded by three variants designated Suriv 1, 2, and 3 (suriv is virus spelled backward) and may have been deployed by the same author.

Two more viruses appear later in the year, the stoned virus (the first master boot record, or MBR infector), apparently written by a student in New Zealand, and the Vienna virus, written by an Austrian high school student. The latter is completely disassembled and analyzed, and its code published.

Last (and perhaps least), a virus appears in South Africa that deletes files on Friday the 13th.

Origins of Friday the 13th

Many stories, anecdotes, and beliefs explain why Friday the 13th is considered by many an unlucky day. Perhaps the most important of those is a historical event. On Friday, October 13, 1307, the Pope of the Roman Catholic church, together with the King of France, sentenced the "Knights Templars" to death and ordered the torture and crucifixion of their leader.

Traditional beliefs have it that Eve tempted Adam with the apple on a Friday, the Biblical Flood, the confusion at the Tower of Babel, and the death of Jesus Christ all took place on a Friday. Also, 13 was the number at the Last Supper following which Judas betrayed Jesus.

The Belgian writer Georges Simenon was born a little after one AM on Friday, 13 February 1903. Being superstitious, his mother Henriette had the birth date officially falsified and recorded as February 12th.

The fear of the number 13 is known scientifically as *tridecaphobia*, and is perhaps the most common of all superstitions.

1988.   The Internet worm (Section 3.4) spreads through the United States DARPA network by exploiting security weaknesses in the `finger` and `sendmail` UNIX utilities. In a rare stroke of luck, its author is promptly identified, tried, and punished.

The first good virus (or anti-virus virus) is released. Its task is to detect and remove the Brain virus. There are two versions of this virus, written by Denny Yanuar Ramdhani in Bandung, Indonesia and named the Den Zuk viruses

This year also sees another innovation, a self-encrypting virus. First found in Germany, the cascade virus is a file infector that encrypts itself with a random key.

The ping-pong virus (also known as "bouncing ball" or "Italian") appears at the university of Turin in Italy in March. It becomes the most common and best known boot sector virus (BSI) and keeps this title for a while. This virus had a small bug that caused it to crash computers based on the Intel 80286 microprocessor and its successors, which made the ping-pong virus easy to detect.

Finally, after several years of attacks, infections, and much damage inflicted by viruses, the topic of malicious software starts attracting the attention of the media. Newspapers and magazines publish articles and news briefs about occurrences of viruses and worms, speculations as to their origins, and descriptions provided by virus detectives.

1989.   The `Dark Avenger.1800` virus is unleashed from Sophia, Bulgaria in January. It is named Dark Avenger after its anonymous creator, and it represents the next step in virus sophistication (some might say, the next generation of viruses). It spreads fast because it infects executable files as they are opened, even if they do not execute. Also, its payload is dangerous. It performs slow data diddling to files on the disk, so that when its damage is finally discovered, even files backed up weeks before are already corrupted.

⬦ **Exercise B.1:** The `Dark Avenger.1800` virus infected executable files as they were opened, even if they did not execute. Why does this make it a fast-spreading virus?

In October, the "Frodo lives" virus emerges from Israel. This is an advanced stealth file infector. It saves the original length of every file infected and displays the lengths when the user asks for a directory listing. It also tries to intercept attempts to read infected files and it sends the original, clean files instead. This virus triggers on September 22 of any year (if it happens to execute on that date), when it displays the message "Frodo lives" and tries (unsuccessfully, because of a bug in its code) to install a Trojan horse. (Frodo Baggins is one of the main characters in the novel *The Lord of the Rings* by J. R. R. Tolkien.)

1990.   The flip virus (a slow file infector also designated flip-2343 because it increases the size of infected files by this number of bytes) escapes from Switzerland and is seen in the wild everywhere. This is perhaps the first successful multipartite virus (both BSI and file infector, Section 2.9) and is also polymorphic (appears as different bit strings, Section 2.21), which delays its identification, isolation, and successful removal. Flip is a slow infector because the only way for it to infect a computer is when a flip-infected file is executed. The file can come from an external disk, can be downloaded from a network, or be an email attachment.

Flip got its name because its payload is to flip horizontally the display on the monitor screen (only EGA or VGA monitors) on the second day of each month, between 16:00 and 16:59. Other flip viruses appear in future years, with other payloads in addition to the relatively harmless flipping.

Symantec Inc., already a recognized company in the field of computer security, launches Norton AntiVirus, one of the oldest anti-virus programs. At the time of this writing, the program still bears the same name and is regularly updated (both the software and the virus definitions).

1991. The tequila virus is a the first widespread polymorph of flip, probably generated by the same person who wrote the original flip virus.

The Bulgarian virus developer Dark Avenger announces in March that he is working on a new, dangerous virus that can mutate in billions of ways. This threat will materialize in 1992 (see MtE).

The first virus kits appear. Version 1 of VCS (virus construction set) appears in March in Hamburg, Germany. It was written by the Verband Deutscher Virenliebhaber (community of German virus lovers). It is followed by VCL (virus construction lab, implemented by Nowhere Man) and in August by PS-MPC.

VCL is an attempt by a virus writer calling himself Nowhere Man to create a user-friendly package that will allow inexperienced programmers to create their own viruses. VCL has menus for the infection type, encryption, and payload, allowing a would-be virus creator to easily generate code in either assembler language or directly as an executable .com file. PS-MPC is a virus code generation file (PS stands for Phalcon/Skism, presumably indicating the anonymous writers) in August.

Virus workers claim that there are upward of 1000 viruses in existence.

1992. Dark Avenger finally releases his long-promised mutation engine (dubbed MtE or DAME). It turns out to be a toolkit that converts ordinary viruses into polymorphic ones.

It takes a while for anti-virus software to get to the point where viruses that employ MtE can be detected. In future years, MtE continues to be a source of inspiration for those planning to implement and unleash polymorphic engines.

> The demo virus which accompanied the [mutation] engine contained the text: "We dedicate this little virus to Sara [sic] Gordon, who wanted to have a virus named after her."
>
> —From [avenger 05].

This year marks the first worldwide panic about a computer virus. The Michelangelo virus (Section 5.3) is touted in the media as a global threat, but turns out to infect very few computers.

Statistics: There are now 1300 viruses in the wild (although many appear to be dead). In response, more and more computer users purchase anti-virus software, encouraging more software makers to jump on this bandwagon (many later alight).

1994. The first major virus hoax, Good Times, appears (hoaxes are discussed in Section 6.5). It warns about a destructive virus that erases an entire disk drive if an email message with the subject "Good Times" is opened. Rumors persist for months, and then resurface in future years.

A destructive, polymorphic virus called Pathogen (or alternatively, SMEG) appears in England. Analysis shows that Pathogen is really two sibling viruses, `SMEG.Pathogen` and `SMEG.Queeg`. The virus author, who calls himself the black baron, claims to have written them in a language he calls the Simulated Metamorphic Encryption Generator (SMEG). The two siblings are highly polymorphic, and mutate to become completely different bit strings in each infection.

In a rare example of successful police work, the author is tracked down by New Scotland Yard's Computer Crime Unit. He is identified as Christopher Pile, is tried in November, and is sentenced to 18 months under the Computer Misuse Act of the United Kingdom.

Ay! Then, Miss Newson, ye had better say nothing about this hoax, and take no heed of it. And if the person should say anything to you, be civil to him or her, as if you did not mind it—so you'll take the clever person's laugh away.

—Thomas Hardy, *The Mayor of Casterbridge*, 1885.

1995.   This is the year of the macro virus (Section 2.10). The first such virus, Concept, is discovered in May. It is written in WordBASIC (an interpreted programming language similar to Visual Basic for Applications and executed by Microsoft Word). Concept infects documents of Word versions 6 and 7 on any computer platforms (Word is supported on Windows and Macintosh). It seems that the only payload of Concept is to display the message "`REM That's enough to prove my point.`" Anti-virus software makers are not prepared for a macro virus. After analyzing Concept they assess it as a weak infector, but in fact it becomes one of the most prevalent viruses in the mid 1990s.

While the good guys try to come to terms with the new macro virus, virus developers decide they like this approach and they write and release a few more macro viruses this year.

1996.   In January, the Boza virus (sometimes misspelled baza) is discovered. Boza is the first virus to spread only under the Microsoft Windows 95 operating system. Even though it has been seen in many geographic locations, it is not considered a serious threat to Windows 95 users. Boza was written by the Australian virus group VLAD and is named after a text string that it contains `Please note: the name of this virus is [Bizatch] written by Quantum/VLAD`.

Two variants, `Boza.B` and `Boza.C` are later released, probably in attempts to correct bugs in the original Boza, but have no noticeable effect.

In July, the anti-virus community learns of a new nondestructive macro virus (promptly named Laroux) that infects Microsoft Excel files (files with an `.xls` extension) for Excel versions 5 and 7 running under Windows 3, Windows 95 and Windows NT, but not on the Macintosh. Once an infected Excel document is opened, the virus will be active every time the Excel program is run, and will infect any workbook that's created or opened. Laroux was written in Visual Basic for Applications (VBA), a macro language based on Visual Basic from Microsoft.

Laroux consists of two macros, `auto_open` and `check_files`. The former is expanded whenever an infected Spreadsheet is opened, followed by the latter macro which determines the startup path of Excel. The virus creates a file titled `personal.xls` with a module called `laroux`, hence its name.

Laroux is one of the most common viruses, but fortunately it has no payload. It just replicates.

Staog is the first Linux virus, discovered in the Fall. It is written in assembler and it infects only Elf-style executable files in the Linux operating system. It copies itself into memory and tries to infect Elf-style executables when they are executed. Staog exploits three known vulnerabilities (mount buffer overflow, tip buffer overflow, and one suidperl bug) in Linux in an attempt to gain superuser status.

Staog is named after the text string "Staog by Quantum/VLAD" that was discovered in it. VLAD is the name of an Australian virus group that also wrote the first Windows 95 virus, Boza

1997.   More hoaxes abound. The following hoax about five viruses is quoted from "Computer Crime: An Emerging Challenge for Law Enforcement," an article by the two PhDs David L. Carter and Andra J. Katz. It was published in the December 1996 edition of the FBI's Law Enforcement Bulletin.

> Virus Introduction
>
> Computer viruses, created for a variety of reasons, can have many different effects, depending on the creator's intent. To illustrate, several new insidious viruses have been found.
>
> "Gingrich" randomly converts word processing files into legalese often found in contracts. Victims can combat this virus by typing their names at the bottom of infected files, thereby signing them, as if signing a contract.
>
> "Clipper" scrambles all the data on a hard drive, rendering it useless.
>
> "Lecture" deliberately formats the hard drive, destroying all data, then scolds the user for not catching it.
>
> "Clinton" is designed to infect programs, but it eradicates itself when it cannot decide which program to infect.
>
> "SPA" examines programs on the hard disk to determine whether they are properly licensed. If the virus detects illegally copied software, it seizes the computer's modem, automatically dials 911, and asks for help.

1998.   In June, the CIH virus, also known as Chernobyl, is discovered in Taiwan. Local authorities point to Chen Ing-hau as the writer of this virus, which derives its name from his initials.

The payload of this virus will first be triggered on April 26, 1999, causing many computer users to lose their data. The total loss is estimated in the hundreds of millions of dollars.

CIH searches for empty, unused spaces in executable files it attempts to infect. On finding such spaces, it breaks itself up into smaller pieces and inserts its code into them. To disinfect a file infected by CIH, anti-virus software looks for these small viral pieces and removes them from the file.

In August, the StrangeBrew virus rears its harmless head. This is the first virus to infect Java files. It can spread from a Java applet or a Java application to another, but only if executed locally, not over the Internet.

The virus searches for existing `.class` files and modifies them to append a copy of itself to the file and include a call to the virus' code in the first instruction. When such a file is later executed, the virus is executed first. The infector routine in StrangeBrew has bugs, as a result of which it rarely infects files in its host correctly. Most of the time it crashes the host when it attempts an infection.

The StrangeBrew virus is based on Java, which makes it capable of executing on virtually any platform that can run Java programs (all Windows and Linux platforms as well as PDA devices that have Java runtime installed).

StrangeBrew does not inflict any damage; it just spreads itself.

1999. March marks the first appearance of the Melissa menace (Section 5.5). The virus (with the official name `W97M_Melissa`) originates in an Internet `alt.sex` newsgroup. This is a macro virus that attacks the Microsoft Word 97 and Word 2000 applications and propagates via email attachments. Melissa executes a macro in a document attached to an email message, and this macro locates the owner's Outlook address book and forwards the document to 50 of the addresses found there. This technique is the reason for its unusually fast spreading. The virus also infects other Word documents and subsequently mails them out as attachments.

At the time of writing, Melissa and variants are still seen in the wild and the very latest about this threat can be found in [melissavirus 05].

An important first this year is the BubbleBoy worm. As soon as email users got used to the idea that email attachments can be dangerous, along comes this worm and teaches them another lesson. Merely *opening* an email message can infect the computer. The worm exploits a security weakness in Internet Explorer 5 (IE, a common Web browser, but the virus affects only IE installations that have Windows Scripting Host) and the fact that Microsoft Outlook, a popular email program, automatically opens email messages in a lower window in the program.

This worm spreads fast because it locates all the Outlook and Outlook Express e-mail address books in the computer and emails itself to every addressee in them. Fortunately, BubbleBoy is relatively harmless. It modifies the owner's email settings by changing the owner's name to BubbleBoy and the organization's name to Vandelay Industries. These are fictitious names taken from a popular television program.

Perhaps the worst feature of this worm is its successful spread, which may tempt other miscreants to come up with similar, but more destructive, worms in the future.

Another first for this year is the tristate macro virus (official name `O97M/Tristate`) and its many variants. This virus is written in Visual Basic for applications (VBA) and its name implies that it infects documents for Microsoft Word, Excel, and PowerPoint, three components of the MS Office 97 suite of applications. An unusual feature of this virus is the large number (at least 11) of its variants.

The virus removes all the macros from the MS Word global template. This, and the fact that it infects the three applications, is its only payload.

2000.   This is the year of Love Bug, also known as the ILOVEYOU virus. First appearing in early May, this virus is the most "successful" email virus to date and is destructive. Within hours of its release it spreads to every continent and infects tens of thousands of computers. The number of machines infected after one day is estimated at 45 million. Its fast spread is attributed to the fact that many users save large numbers of old email messages and also have large address books with many correspondents. The virus can find all these addresses and it automatically generates email messages to all of them (this author has also received one from a student, but was unaffected because he uses a Macintosh and doesn't use Outlook).

This virus arrives as a Visual Basic script attachment in an email message whose subject line claims "I love you." It deletes audio, video, and image files. It also locates usernames and passwords and sends them to its author.

A suspect, 23-year old Reomel Ramones, is located and arrested within a week in Manila, the Philippines. Police charge him with being the originator of this virus, but his relatives blame his girlfriend's sister of creating the virus.

One of the nastiest I've seen.

This worm spreads at an amazing speed.

It began spreading like wildfire, taking out computers left, right and centre.

It's a particularly malicious virus.

It is compromising security and confidentiality.

It can go into private e-mails and forward them to anybody in your contacts book.

I was looking for some deeper meaning in the last two major virus assaults. Each one has seven letters and three vowels, and if you rearrange the letters, MELISSA and LOVE BUG spell: BIG VOLUME SALES.

—Experts' comments on the Love Bug virus.

This year the title "a first" belongs to the Stages worm, the first malware that infects text files. The worm enters a computer as an email attachment named `Life_stages.txt.shs` (`.shs` is the extension of Microsoft Scrap Object files. These files are executable and can contain many different types of objects), but the `.shs` extension is not displayed by the Windows operating system. When the attachment is opened, it is readable (it seems to joke about the male and female stages of life), but a script is simultaneously running in the background, infecting and deleting files. The worm locates addresses in the address books of Outlook, ICQ, mIRC, and PIRCH, and then mails itself as an attachment to all the addressees found. Thus, email users can no longer assume that text attachments to messages are safe.

On Monday, February 7, large, well-aimed and well-planned distributed denial-of-service (DDoS) attacks against Yahoo, eBay, Amazon, and other popular Web sites knock them offline for several hours. What is especially frightening about this attack is that it comes from many servers; it is distributed.

2001. The nimda virus/worm is discovered on September 18. This virus (which affects Windows 95, 98, Me, NT 4, and 2000) has a worm component that spreads by sending email messages with an attachment called `readme.exe`. Nimda (whose name is the reverse of "admin") is a first in two areas (1) it infects files in Web sites and (2) it employs zombies to scan for vulnerable sites. The affected Web sites send the infected files to anyone downloading the files, and the zombies make it possible for nimda to reach Web sites located behind firewalls.

Nimda employs as many as five different methods of replicating and infecting computers, which makes it one of the most sophisticated viruses to date.

Once Nimda infects a computer, it proceeds in four steps as follows:

• Infection. Nimda locates `.exe` files in the computer and infects them. The infected files spread the infection when they are exchanged between computers.

• Mass mailing. Nimda locates email addresses in the address book of the computer's email client. It then searches local HTML files for more addresses. When done, it sends a message with the `readme.exe` attachment to each addressee.

• Web worm. Nimda scans the Internet in an attempt to locate Web servers. Once a server is found, the worm tries to infect it by exploiting several known security holes. If this succeeds, the worm selects Web pages at random on the site and infects them. Visitors downloading these files and executing them will get infected by the virus.

• LAN propagation. The worm component searches for file shares in the local network, either from file servers or from user computers. Once file sharing is found, the worm places an invisible file in any directory that has DOC and EML files. When users later try to open DOC or EML files from these directories, Word, Wordpad, or Outlook will execute the invisible file, thereby infecting the computer.

On February 12, the infamous "Anna Kournikova" worm (formal name `VBS.SST@mm`) starts its rounds. It arrives as an attachment named `AnnaKournikova.jpg.vbs`. When a hapless email reader clicks it, the worm searches the Microsoft Outlook address book and emails itself to every address found in it. On January 26, the worm attempts to direct the computer's Web browser to an Internet address in The Netherlands, which may point detectives looking for its perpetrator in the right direction. An important feature of this worm is that it's written with a virus kit, a tool that makes it easy for beginners to write rogue software. The messages sent by this worm have the subject line "`Here you have, ;o)`" and the message body "`Hi: Check This!`".

In one of those rare success stories that warms everyone's heart, the creator of this virus, 20-year old Jan de Wit of Sneek, The Netherlands, gives himself up, is tried and sentenced, but only to 150 hours community service because he is a first-time offender.

The verdict stated that de Wit "was not a layman in the field of computer viruses. He works in a computer store and collected viruses—about 7,200, according to himself. [The collection was confiscated.] The defendant must have been very aware of the consequences of his acts. The virus he spread was a hindrance, causing worry and annoyance among Internet users worldwide."

Three worms, Sircam, CodeRed, and BadTrans, create headaches for virus workers (and revenues for anti-virus companies).

Sircam spreads as attachments to email messages sent through Windows Network shares. A typical message has one of many sender names and subject lines, but the message body is either `Hi! How are you? I send you this file in order to have your advice`, or something similar. The main innovation of this virus is the way it modifies the default EXE file startup registry key from `HKCR\exefile\shell\open\command` to `""[windows_drive]\recycled\SirC32.exe" "%1" %*"`. This results in an activation of the worm (from its location in folder `recycled`) whenever an `.exe` file is launched; ingenious!

Sircam has two payloads, but because of a bug neither of them works. The first payload is to delete all the files from the startup drive (this occurs on October 16 and in one of 20 cases). The second payload is to create a file and append text to it until it fills up the entire drive. This text contains the string `SirCam`, which is the reason for the particular name of this worm.

In July, CodeRed appears and expands at a terrific rate, much faster than any worm preceding it, infecting approximately 360,000 hosts in its first twelve hours of activity. This worm spreads by exploiting a security hole in the popular Microsoft Internet Information Server (IIS) software. Once it infects a server, it starts scanning the Internet in an attempt to locate other vulnerable servers. Once a month, the worm becomes active. For a few hours it only spreads, then it starts a Denial-of-Service (DoS) attack against `www1.whitehouse.gov` (the White House Web site), and finally it goes back to sleep.

A variant appears in 2002.

In April, the BadTrans worm (formal name `W95/Badtrans.B@mm`) is brought to life. This is a worm that spreads in attachments to email messages sent from computers running any 32-bit version of Windows. Once an email user clicks on the attachment, the worm executes. It places three files in the computer that act as an email worm and a Trojan horse. The worm component spreads itself by automatically sending infected answers to all the unread email messages in the user's inbox. The Trojan horse (file `HKK32.EXE`) is a variant of an older Trojan that steals passwords. It sends all the information it obtains to email address `ld8dl1@mailandnews.com`.

Lots of activity for one year!

2002.   January marks the birth of `SWF/LFM-926`, the first virus to infect Macromedia Flash files (those with extension `.swf`). Flash is a popular program to display animation and special graphics effects. These files can execute scripts, a feature that makes it easy to develop complex animation, but is now found to be a security trap. As it infects `.swf` files, the virus displays the message `Loading.Flash.Movie`, which contributes the `LFM` in its name.

David L Smith, the creator of Melissa (Section 5.5), is sentenced to 20 months in prison.

The success of the Anna Kournikova worm in 2001 has encouraged hackers to continue with worms using celebrity names as a social engineering technique to lure victims, and at least three worms thus named are released in 2002.

• Shakira worm. Released in June, this worm (formal name `VBSWG.AQ`, where `VB` stands for Visual Basic) starts spreading through mIRC chats and email messages sent through Outlook. The subject line is `Shakira's Pictures` and the message body is `Hi: i have sent the photos via attachment, have funn...` The infected attachment is a file titled `ShakiraPics.jpg.vbs`.

This worm is written in Visual Basic Script and was generated with the `VBSWG` virus kit.

• Britney Spears is a very similar worm (appears in March) with the subject line `RE:Britney Pics`, message text `Take a look at these pics...`, and infected attachment `BRITNEY.CHM`.

• Jennifer Lopez worm (named `Loveletter.CN` with `VBS.Lopez.A@mm` as an alias) appears to have been written in Algeria. It arrives in an email with the subject line `Where are you?`, a message body `This is my pic in the beach`, and an infected attached file titled `JENNIFERLOPEZ_NAKED.JPG.VBS`. As part of its payload, this worm places in the Windows registry a key that causes it to execute each time Windows is started.

The Klez worm (actually, a worm/virus combination, dubbed `W95/Klez@mm`) arrives in October, probably from Asia, perhaps from China. Like many other worms, it enters the computer in an email message. It places in the computer a polymorphic `.exe` virus called `ElKern`. The Klez worm employs a variety of subject lines, such as `Hi`, `Hello`, `How are you?`, `Can you help me?`, `We want peace`, `Where will you go?`

As part of its payload, Klez removes autostarting registry keys of security and anti-virus software. As a result, this software or parts of it are disabled next time Windows starts. The virus also stops many processes and corrupts many files, most notably anti-virus checksum files and integrity checker databases. This worm/virus has several variants.

The month of September sees the arrival of the Bugbear worm (`W32.Bugbear@mm`). It attempts to place a keystroke logger and a backdoor in the computer and tries to terminate the processes of various antivirus and firewall programs.

The backdoor installed by Bugbear opens port 36794 and waits for commands from its author. The commands can order the worm to perform several actions as follows:

• Copy files.

• List files and deliver the list to the hacker.

• Delete files.

• Start processes.

• Terminate processes.

• List processes and deliver the list to the author.

• Deliver saved keystrokes to the owner in encrypted form.

- Deliver the following items of information to the owner: (1) Username. (2) Type of processor. (3) Version and build number of Windows. (4) Memory size and availability. (5) Types and physical characteristics of input/output volumes. (6) Network resources and their types.

2003. The slammer worm (`W32.Slammer`, alias Sapphire) appears out of the blue in January. This menace is different from the run-of-the-mill worm because it infects only computers running Microsoft SQL Server 2000 or MSDE 2000, i.e., servers. It uses UDP port 1434 to exploit a buffer overflow weakness in MS SQL servers. End-user machines are not affected. Another uncommon feature is that slammer does not write itself to the disk; it stays in memory until the computer is restarted (but if the computer hasn't been patched against slammer, it is likely to catch the worm again). However, the worm generates a massive amount of data packets, affecting Internet traffic all over the world.

The Blaster worm (`W32.Blaster.C.Worm`) surfaces in August. It exploits a certain vulnerability (with the technical name of DCOM RPC, described in Microsoft Security Bulletin MS03-026) and uses TCP port 135 to target computers running Windows 2000 and XP. In contrast to most other worms, Blaster does not search for email addresses and doesn't mail itself en masse.

Blaster is triggered by the following complex timing condition. From January to July it is triggered every day from the 16th until the end of the month. From 16 August until 31 December, it is triggered every day. The payload is a Denial of Service (DoS) attack on `www.windowsupdate.com`. The obvious aim is to prevent victims from downloading a security patch from Microsoft.

Another fast-spreading worm this year is sobig (`W32.Sobig.F@mm`). This is another mass-mailing worm that looks at many files (more precisely, files with extensions `.dbx`, `.eml`, `.hlp`, `.htm`, `.html`, `.mht`, `.wab`, and `.txt`) for addresses and mails itself to every address. It also spoofs the sender's address in these messages, using addresses found in the victim's computer. Thus, this worm becomes a source of spam. An excellent review of this malware can be found in [Skoudis 05].

Sobig deactivates itself (an unusual feature) on 10 September 2003. However, if the computer clock is out of date, it (the computer) may contribute to the worm's spread past the deactivation date.

Experts estimate that the Blaster and Sobig worms have turned August 2003 into the worst month ever for virus incidents. Obviously, things are getting worse.

2004. January. The MyDoom threat is unleashed. Known as either mydoom or novarg (`W32.Mydoom.A@mm` or `W32.Novarg.A`), this is an email worm that carries an infected attachment with one of the extensions `.bat`, `.cmd`, `.exe`, `.pif`, `.scr`, or `.zip`. Mydoom becomes the most widely-spread worm to date. It is estimated that at its peak, one quarter of all email messages carried this menace.

Mydoom is a sophisticated worm that installs a backdoor by opening TCP ports 3127 through 3198, through which the worm's owner can connect to the computer and to its network resources. The owner can also send any files to the affected computer through these ports. Several pieces of rogue software, among them doomjuice, deadhat, and mitglieder, infect computers through this method.

The worm is triggered on 1 February 2004. There is a 25% chance that the worm will start a DoS attack on that date and continue this until 12 February 2004. If this happens, the worm does not mail itself from the infected computer, but the backdoor stays in the computer indefinitely.

The DoS attack is aimed at the SCO Group, a company that tried to sue several entities for illegally using an open-source version of its UNIX programming language. SCO offers a $250,000 reward to anyone helping in the arrest and conviction of Mydoom's originator(s).

January. The bagle worm (`W32/Bagle-mm`) starts spreading. This is a typical worm that arrives as an email attachment, scans the computer for email addresses and sends itself to all the addresses found. It is sent as a message with a subject line `Hi`, a body that includes the words `Test, yep`, and an attachment with extension `.exe`. Bagle floods computer networks all over the world, but does not have any other destructive payload. Several variants appear in 2005.

March. The Netsky worm (`w32.netsky.d@mm`) pops up. This version and its variant `W32.Netsky.C@mm` are mass-mailing worms. They scan drives `C` through `Z` of a PC for email addresses and email themselves with an infected attachment to all addresses found. The subject, body, and attachment names are selected at random from a set of names, except that the attachment has the extension `.pif`.

In late March, the Witty worm is unleashed to infect Macintosh computers. The worm exploits a vulnerability in BlackICE/RealSecure, firewall software from Internet Security Systems [ISS 05]. The vulnerability is discovered on 8 March with a patch issued by ISS the following day. The details of the vulnerability are published by eEye Digital Security on 18th March, and the worm appears about three days later. It infects every vulnerable Macintosh (about 12,000 computers) within 45 minutes (which translates to about 4.45 computers infected each second).

The witty worm is small, less than 700 bytes, which enables it to send a copy of itself in a single ethernet packet. Once arriving at a computer, it repeats the following two steps: (1) It attempts to replicate itself by generating 20,000 such packets and sending them to random IP addresses with random ports. (2) It locates a point on the hard disk at random and rewrites 65 Kb of data. After several repetitions, the artificial data written by the worm causes a freeze or a crash, and the computer has to be restarted.

Many viruses and worms fail in their destructive mission because of bugs in their code, but the Witty worm is bug free. This implies that it was written by an expert, and from scratch, not from a virus kit. This expert knows how to write Macintosh programs, is willing to wait for the right moment when a vulnerability is discovered, and doesn't mind if his creation infects only a small number of machines. These sad but true conclusions are summarized here.

- Some malware writers are experts, not bored teenagers.

- A worm can be fast propagating and also destructive, not being satisfied with just launching a DoS attack.

- Anti-virus software is useful and important, but it cannot identify new, as-yet-unrecognized malware and therefore does not guarantee a clean computer.

- There will always be users who ignore news and messages about new security patches, or are just too lazy to install them.

- Macintosh computers are relatively, but not absolutely, safe from malware.

May. This is the month of the sasser worm (`W32.Sasser.Worm`). This is a fast-spreading worm that exploits the MS04-011 (LSASS) vulnerability, a security weakness caused by a buffer overrun in the Local Security Authority Subsystem Service (LSASS). This becomes the major security hole of 2004. Because of it, sasser enters a computer through this vulnerability and not as an email attachment. Copy cats hear of the LSASS hole and immediately release a stream of rogue worms with names such as Korgo, Bobax, Cycle, Kibuv, and Plexus.

Upon infecting a computer, sasser starts 128 scanning threads that generate random IP addresses in an attempt to find vulnerable computers. Computers are probed on port 445 which is the default port for Windows SMB communication on NT-based PCs.

Sasser affects computers running Windows XP or Windows 2000 that are connected to the Internet without a firewall. A security patch is quickly issued by Microsoft.

It seems that the only damage this worm inflicts is crashing the computer (probably because of a bug in its code). An 18-year-old German high school student confesses to being the author of the worm. He's suspected of releasing another version of sasser.

A first in 2004 is malicious software that infects cell telephones running the Symbian operating system. Examples of such worms are `Toquimos.A`, `Skulls.A`, and the Cabir family (see year 2005).

Another first in 2004 is vulnerable jpeg images (Section 2.11). Normally, an image file has no executable code, and so cannot be infected. However, Microsoft has a software product that displays such images, and it had a security flaw in the form of buffer overrun. This flaw makes it possible, at least in principle, to construct a jpeg image that when viewed with this software will install a malicious program that can take over the computer and convert it to a zombie. Two malicious programs that take advantage of this flaw appear almost immediately. They are dubbed JPGDownloader and JPGTrojan. Microsoft very quickly issues a security patch to fix this buffer overrun.

2005. A Bagle variant `Bagle.AY` is found in January. Like its older relative `Bagle.AX` the new variant is polymorphic and arrives in email with randomly selected subject and attachment. It also has Peer-to-Peer spreading capabilities and contains a backdoor that waits for commands on TCP port 81. It is programmed to cease its activity on 25 April, 2006.

A new variant of the MyDoom worm, `MyDoom.AI` appears in January and uses social engineering to entice readers to open attachments. It arrives in email messages with infected `exe`, `scr`, `pif`, or `zip` attachments. Some messages contain sexually explicit images and claim that the attachment contains passwords for adult Websites.

A new cell telephone virus, lasco (alias `SymbOS/Lasco.A` and `EPOC/Lasco.A`), also appears in January and infects mobile telephones that run the Symbian operating system, support bluetooth, and are in discoverable mode (see also page 42).

This virus replicates over bluetooth connections and arrives in the message inbox of the telephone hidden inside a file called `velasco.sis`. When the user clicks on this file and agrees to install it, the virus is invoked. It immediately starts looking for new telephones to infect over bluetooth. It also inserts itself into other `sis` files it finds in the telephone. If such infected files are later copied into another telephone, the virus installer will be invoked with the first installation task, and ask the user to accept the installation of Velasco.

Cabir (aliases `SymbOS/Cabir.A`, `EPOC/Cabir.A`, `Worm.Symbian.Cabir.a`, and `Caribe virus`) also infects mobile telephones by exploiting the same vulnerability and is generally very similar to lasco.

A first this year is the `Duts.1520` virus (aliases `WinCE/Duts.1520`, `WinCE.Duts`, and `Dust`) a file infector that attacks the PocketPC platform. Duts affects ARM-based devices only. This is a short program (1520 bytes), apparently written in assembler for the ARM processor and assembled manually. When an infected file is executed, the virus displays a dialog box with the following two-line message asking for permission to infect:

`WinCE4.Dust by Ratter/29A`

`Dear User, am I allowed to spread?`

If granted permission, Duts attempts to infect all `.exe` files in the current directory. It only infects large files (larger than 4096 bytes) that are still uninfected. As an infection marker, the virus writes the string `atar` in the Version field of the `.exe` file header.

The virus infects a file by appending itself to the file and making the last section of the file readable and executable. The entry point of the `.exe` file is set to the beginning of the virus code. Duts contains two messages that are not displayed:

`This is proof of concept code. Also, i wanted to make avers happy.`

`The situation when Pocket PC antiviruses detect only EICAR file had to end ...`

The second message refers to the science-fiction novel *Permutation City* by Greg Egan, where the following sentence appears `This code arose from the dust of Permutation City`.

⋄ **Exercise B.2:** What conclusion can be derived from this timeline?

> On a long enough timeline, the survival
> rate for everything drops to zero.
> —Chuck Palahniuk, *Fight Club* (1996)

Concluding Remarks

This chapter starts with a number of tips for increased security. It continues with a summary of malware and its most important features. The chapter ends with a few final conclusions.

This book has tried to instill in the reader both an awareness of and respect for computer security. Many computer users are aware of security problems simply because of what happened to them, but relatively few have a real respect for security and even fewer give this topic the time and effort it deserves. We therefore start with a short reminder, in the form of a list of security tips. These tips can be found elsewhere in the book but have been collected here as a parting gift from the author to those readers who have got so far in the book.

■ Use strong passwords. Section 8.3 discusses passwords, their applications, and their weaknesses. It describes the features that a strong password should have and it presents examples of weak passwords. Also, passwords should be memorized, not written down, and they should be replaced often.

■ Backup all your data regularly. Backups are discussed on page 143 as well as in other places in the book. This author would like to take this opportunity to stress again the importance of regular and full backups. All files should be backed up, including personal data, application programs, utilities, and operating system files. Those who have sensitive data should keep several generations of backup files, in case corrupted or infected files are discovered in the near future. One last word. If at all possible, check your backups. This is especially true for a large organization (government or commercial) that has sensitive or critical data whose loss may affect many users, customers, or citizens. Checking a backup is time consuming and requires extra equipment. The ideal setup for checking a backup is to have another computer, identical to the one whose files are backed up, and to actually run that computer on the backed-up data, executing programs and looking at data. This does not fully guarantee a clean backup, but will catch most corrupt files and data that had been diddled with.

■ Obtain anti-virus software, update it, and use it regularly. Anti-virus software is mentioned in Section 6.3 and in many other places in the book. While not 100% effective, this software is still the easiest and most cost-effective way to check for, discover, and delete viruses and other types of malware. However, as this book says in several places, it is important to have the latest versions of both the program itself and the virus update, and to run this software regularly (or at least every time a new virus update is released, which is typically 2–3 times a month). If the computer has a removable drive, it is important to set the anti-virus software to automatically check every volume inserted into the drive.

■   Install a firewall and always use it, updating its rules as necessary. Even a simple firewall, just a small piece of software, considerably increases your chances of survival in the Internet jungle. Firewalls are discussed in Section 7.6 and are useful even to those who have a modem and have to dial a number to connect to the Internet.

■   Be suspicious of email attachments. Section 2.4 lists tests that an attachment should pass before a careful user will consider opening it. Email attachments are regularly exploited as carriers of viruses and worms, and no one can count (or even estimate) the number of innocent computer users who became victims of malware by the simple act of clicking on an email attachment (often a love letter purportedly from a known and trusted friend).

(A related principle is to close the preview pane of all email programs. Such a pane permits the user to read a message before it is opened, but can be abused by hackers.)

■   Download all security patches available from software makers. When a security vulnerability is discovered in a widely-used program or operating system routine, its maker often issues a patch to correct the flaw in the software. It is important to use such patches because the existence of a patch doesn't deter hackers from trying to exploit a vulnerability. They know that many users don't install security patches (because of ignorance, laziness, apathy, or sheer plain stupidity) and they exploit this fact to achieve their aims.

■   Finally, try to get in the habit of disconnecting your computer from the Internet as much as possible. Whenever you don't need your computer for communications, physically unplug it from your telephone, your modem, or your router. Many owners of personal computers run their computers continuously, and this may also contribute to security breaches. It is a good idea to either put the computer to sleep (a mode offered by all modern operating systems) or to turn it off completely when not in use (but see Section 4.2 about operating system maintenance done automatically late at night). Many computer users believe that a hard drive lasts longer if allowed to spin continuously, but consider the following: Magnetic disk prices (as well as prices of CD and DVD drives) are coming down all the time, while security risks, attacks, and threats are on the rise. With this in mind, a computer user should answer the following question: Is it better to have a long-lasting disk drive or to have complete backups and turn off the computer as much as reasonably possible?

> User, n. The word computer professionals use when they mean "idiot."
>
> —Dave Barry

Malware: Summary

The discussion of malware in this book can be summarized by looking at the many differences between rogue software and other types of software. There are three main areas where malware exhibits significant differences of behavior.

Generality. An attack (on a computer or a network) that does not involve a virus must be based on a weakness or a flaw in the object attacked. The attacker discovers that a certain security mechanism does not perform the right checks in certain cases, so the attacker creates such a case and thereby gains access to or control of the object. Such an attack generally allows the hacker limited access, so the damage must depend on the amount of access the attacker has.

A virus, however, spreads without exploiting any flaws or bugs in the protection mechanism of the computer, network, or operating system. The virus spreads when users share programs or other resources, and because the virus is a program it can cause any type of damage. We can think of a virus as a team of software installers that distribute a piece of software quickly and automatically. The software being distributed can be benign or malevolent, but the distribution mechanism is the same.

Range. The range of effect of a malicious program is much greater than that of other software. When an attacker breaks into a computer, he can read and delete all the files on that computer. The attacker may steal passwords and use them to break into other computers, but this has to be done manually, computer by computer. When an attacker breaks into a computer and installs a virus, the virus can infect many files on the computer and may propagate itself into other computers either by email, by files sent on the Internet, or by files written on disks and distributed to other computer owners. This feature implies that the range of effect of a virus is far greater than that of other (conventional) software. This feature also applies to benign viruses, which is why such viruses can be very useful.

Persistence. A program is easily deleted, but a virus may be difficult and time consuming to locate, delete, and completely eradicate. When a virus code starts executing, it may check the date, and set itself a target date of, say, three months in the future for releasing its payload. When the time comes to do its damage, the infected program (or programs) may have been backed up, perhaps several times, on several backup devices, for three months. The result is that many copies of the virus may have found their way into all the backups of the computer owner, with the unfortunate consequence that just deleting the virus from the computer is not enough. Keeping up-to-date backups is important, but the backup device itself should be checked for viruses before it is used to restore any infected files.

Perhaps the first thing that comes to mind when an infected program is discovered is to delete it and replace it with a clean copy. Often, this step is performed after the virus has already spread throughout the computer and has infected other programs, with the result that the clean copy is going to be infected soon.

A virus is also persistent because it may find its way to removable storage, such as floppy disks and zip cartridges. In a university environment, it is common to have a computer lab where the computers are connected in a local-area network. It is also common for users to keep files on removable disks and insert the disks into different computers to run programs. Once a virus appears in a file in a computer in such a lab, it will propagate into other files, then into other computers on the network, and then into removable disks. A security person may spend much time cleaning all the computers in the lab, only to have the virus appear again as soon as a user inserts a removable disk into a drive.

A policy that should be adopted in such an environment is to keep the important files (applications, utilities, and operating system) in a locked (read-only) part of the hard drive of each computer, and let the users store their data files temporarily in the unlocked part of the disk. When those files get infected, the unlocked part is simply erased. Another solution is to have computers with no hard drive, and to serve files from a central server that is well-protected by a firewall and by experienced security personnel.

An Internet search unearths real examples of viruses that persisted in an environment for months and kept coming back after each thorough cleaning of the computers involved. An example is the scores virus (Section 5.6).

Over the years, computer users have noticed that viruses written for old versions of an operating systems linger on in the computer even after several newer versions of the operating system have been installed. It is common for computer makers to base a new computer on older models, in order to maintain upward compatibility. This is a useful feature that allows old software, which represents a substantial investment, to run on a new computer, but it also means that viruses written for the old computer may find their way into the new computer and continue their destructive mission for years.

◇ **Exercise Conc.1:** What are well-known examples of computer families with upward compatibility?

Persistence is perhaps the most important feature of benign viruses. Once such a virus enters the environment of a computer or a network, it does its job for years without any supervision or maintenance.

Final Conclusions

Computer security is a vast area that affects the performance of businesses, the quality of services provided by governments, and the daily lives of many on Earth (and perhaps elsewhere in the universe). Security is steadily becoming both more complex and a bigger threat. Security is getting more complex because more security holes are being discovered and because operating systems are becoming more complicated. Security is becoming a bigger headache because of the prevalence of computer networks. The root of all computer security problems is the inability of computers to distinguish good from bad. On a slightly lower level, security threats exist because of the existence of networks and the complexity of modern software. Computer security threats normally arrive at a computer from the outside through a network and they (the problems) thrive on software vulnerabilities.

One natural conclusion from the previous paragraph is that an organization that decides to connect a local-area network of computers to the Internet should stop for a moment and consider the security aspects of this step and how best to handle them.

Similarly, an individual wanting to connect their personal computer to the Internet should first study the security ramifications of this step and be prepared to deal with threats when they arise. Another conclusion is that software users have to balance the advantage offered by new, complex software with the increased security threat that such software poses.

Malware, spam, email dangers, and spyware are bad, but not all bad, as the following quotation shows (by an anonymous writer identified only as `Floydian_99@yahoo.com` and referring to what that writer did while his computer had to be cleaned from viruses or spyware, I forget which).

> Things are not so sad after all, because this break gave me the time to come up with this document. I hope this will stand as a must read for network administrators and security experts out there. As new technologies and new viruses will emerge, some of the information may soon be obsolete, but I think. . .

Another important conclusion from this book is that all security is compromise. It is possible to be very secure, but this can be achieved only at the cost of making the computer less convenient to use. Every security measure, technique, and device results in a slower, less responsive, and clumsier computer. Once this is realized, each computer user has to decide how much security they need. Performing a virus check and file backup every day increases security, but is time consuming. Looking at each email attachment, examining it, thinking about it, and applying tests to it likewise increases security, at the cost of time spent (and higher blood pressure of the user). Installing an activity monitor that detects suspicious or unusual activities also beefs up security, but decreases the user's "quality of life" at the keyboard because of the need to respond to the monitor's discoveries and questions and to constantly make decisions. Even the process of reading this book boosts security by giving the reader confidence, but has the downside of taking time. (Unless you listen to it while you sleep. Ask the publisher to come up with an audio version of the book. Just kidding.)

⋄ **Exercise Conc.2:** The previous paragraph says "all security is compromise," implying that compromise is a general attribute that underlies any type of security. Show an example of this compromise in a non-computer situation.

The goal of this book is to familiarize you, the reader, with the reasons for security threats and with the best security procedures and practices currently available. You should worry about the security of your computer, and this book is trying to teach you to worry correctly. Whether or not this goal is ever reached in your environment is up to the individual reader (but you can still complain to this author when something goes wrong, just to get it off your chest).

Final conclusion: Practice safe computing.

A self test. The following questions will help you decide whether you have read this book carefully.

1. What is the human factor of computer security? (See page xiv.)
2. What does the word "system" mean? (See page xvi.)
3. Why does the problem of computer security exist? (See page 4.)

4. What is the worst thing that can happen to computer security? (See page 8.)

5. How should a computer user/owner start each day? (See page 9.)

6. How should we look at security? (See page 10.)

7. What is the best line of defense against all types of computer security threats? (See page 13.)

8. Does the sentence "people are nosy and machines are noisy" sound familiar? (page 15.)

9. What are the various types of malware?

10. How does a computer virus make sure it gets executed in an infected computer?

11. How can an international organization help in the war against malware? (See Section 3.3.)

12. How safe am I if I have a complete backup of all my files? (See Section 6.4.)

13. Why are virus hoaxes bad? (See Section 6.5.)

14. How do spammers obtain so many valid email addresses? (See Section 7.4.)

15. Can spammers be defeated by legal means? (See case study on page 178.)

16. Does a firewall consist of hardware or software? (See Section 7.6.)

17. What is the most secure biometric authentication technique? (See Section 8.2.)

18. Why is a shredder such a useful tool in the computer security war? (See Section 10.2.)

19. What are the main security concerns of parents? (See Section 11.3.)

20. Why do we trust certain Web sites and mistrust others? (See Section 11.4.)

21. What does the security of an encrypted message depend on? (See Section 12.2.)

It's a rash man who reaches a conclusion before he gets to it.

—Jacob Levin

Answers to Exercises

> A bird does not sing because he has an answer,
> he sings because he has a song.
>
> —Chinese Proverb

Pre.1: Auditing the auditors is fairly easy because the auditors don't write any software and are not supposed to modify existing software. Thus, auditing the auditors is done by making sure they haven't made any changes. This is a straightforward task that can be done by one person who is trusted by the owners/directors of the bank.

Pre.2: One approach to this problem is to sabotage the computer from time to time by creating a short circuit. When the technicians arrive in the computer room, you can cut short your shift and go home. The author isn't recommending such a solution, but similar stories (some perhaps true) have been circulating in the computer security community for many years.

Intro.1: The car industry. A modern car has several computers that control its operations and sense failures. As a result, many millions of small, specialized computers are purchased and installed by car manufacturers every year. Fortunately, there haven't been yet any security problems with those special, embedded computers, but they have become themselves a major source of car trouble.

Intro.2: The question is meaningless. A computer is a machine and as such is neither trustworthy nor untrustworthy. These terms are attributes of humans, which implies that trusting a computer really means trusting those who designed and built it.

> The question of whether computers can think is just like the question
> of whether submarines can swim.
>
> —Edsger W. Dijkstra

Intro.3:   A hacker who has physical access to your computer can replace your keyboard with a rigged one that has a radio transmitter. The hacker would then receive and record all your keystrokes even if you check for spyware and remove all of it.

Intro.4:   Your accent can tell much about your origin, as the following quotation illustrates.

> Simply phonetics. The science of speech. That's my profession; also my hobby. Happy is the man who can make a living by his hobby! You can spot an Irishman or a Yorkshireman by his brogue. I can place any man within six miles. I can place him within two miles in London. Sometimes within two streets.
> —George Bernard Shaw, *Pygmalion* (1916).

Intro.5:   One example is the following: Security holes and weaknesses lurk everywhere and no amount of user testing and expert thinking can find them all. They are discovered slowly, one by one, but every new piece of software written and every new piece of hardware built may contain a new security flaw.

1.1:   Yes, because of two reasons. (1) Most passwords are short enough such that 20% of the password is just one character, which makes it easy to use a brute-force approach to guess the missing character. (2) A computer user may enter the same password several times a day, making it trivial for a spy to complete a missing character.

1.2:   Two things. A hard disk may crash and files may be left open and become inaccessible as a result.

1.3:   Because basements are prone to flooding.

1.4:   The first step is to consult a `whois` data base such as `www.arin.net/whois` to locate the owner of the IP number in question. This is either an ISP or a large organization that has been assigned a block of IP numbers. The second step is to convince the owner to identify the user located at the IP number.

1.5:   Given an unknown data item A, if we repeatedly add to it random numbers that are distributed normally with mean m, we end up with random numbers that are distributed normally with mean $m + A$, thereby allowing an accurate estimation of the unknown data.

2.1:   A personal computer may be used by several users (such as the members of a family). At any given time, only one user can use the keyboard and display, but in principle a user can log in, start a program, and leave, only for another user to log in and start another task. Thus, the operating system of such a computer should allow each user access only to their files and should be able to allocate time slices to several programs. However, an operating system on a personal computer can restrict the use of the computer to one user at a time (a user has to log off before another user can log on) which means that only the programs of one user can reside simultaneously in memory. Even in such a case, the operating system has to protect each program from all the other ones. Thus, the answer is yes, a personal computer can be considered a multiuser computer, with the single exception that only one user sits at the keyboard at any time.

2.2: Here is one in Java (it should be typed on a single line).

```
class s{static public void main(String[]x){String a="class s{static public
void main(String[]x){String a=;System.out.print(a.substring(0,52)+(char)34
+a+(char)34+a.substring(52));}}";System.out.print(a.substring(0,52)+(char)34
+a+(char)34+a.substring(52));}}
```

2.3: Most computer peripherals have moving parts and can be damaged by forcing them to repeat certain operations many times. Here are some examples.

■ A CD (compact disk) is normally read-only, but there are recordable CDs (CD-R) that can be recorded once by the computer, and even recordable rewritable CDs (CD-RW), that can be recorded, erased, and reused by the computer many times. Malicious software can erase such a CD every time it is inserted into the CD drive. Even worse, it can erase the CD many times in a short period of time, thereby shortening its life.

■ The popular flash memories can be damaged in the same way.

■ An uninterruptible power supply (UPS) is the next example. Such a device uses a line-voltage battery to support the computer for a short time in case of a power failure. Recent UPS devices may be connected to the computer with a cable (normally USB) and can launch a utility that closes all the active applications and open files, and turns the computer off when the battery runs low. Malicious software can corrupt this utility such that it opens many files and continually spins the hard drive. When battery power runs out, there is a good chance that the read/write head of the hard drive will crash, thereby physically damaging the drive.

■ Old dot-matrix printers had many small moving parts and it was possible to damage the printing head and the platen in such a printer by printing a dot pattern, backspacing the printing head, and repeating this many times.

■ A CRT has a screen coated with a phosphor compound. When a beam of electrons hits the screen, it is stopped and its kinetic energy is converted to visible light. Screen savers are programs that move the beam continually when the computer is not in use, or simply dim the screen, to make sure that no point on the screen will be exposed to the beam for a long time. Malicious software can corrupt the screen saver so it concentrates the beam at one point on the screen long enough to burn the phosphor coating at the point, and then move the beam to another point, to repeat the damage.

■ Modern personal computers have several cooling fans in them. The fans are turned on and off by the operating system depending on the temperature at various points inside the computer. Rogue software can interfere with this operation in an obvious way and can seriously damage the computer as a result of high temperature.

▪ A computer virus in a laptop can spin the disk continuously and drain the battery very quickly. This does not damage the computer, but is annoying. A similar virus in a cell telephone can achieve the same result even in the absence of a disk.

2.4: When a disk is infected, the virus saves the original boot sector to a different location L on the disk. If an infected disk is reinfected, the virus would save the *modified* boot sector to L. Thus, any virus detective trying to read the boot sector would read the infected version, whether it came from its original position or from L. This would make it easy to identify the virus.

2.5: An extra track may be used for copy protection. Only utilities that know about the track can fully copy the disk.

2.6: The Pareto principle (also known as the 80–20 rule) is named after Vilfredo Pareto, an Italian economist, and was popularized by Joseph M. Juran. It claims that 80% of the results of an operation often stem from 20% of the causes of the operation. This is a useful idea that can be employed as a rule of thumb in many situations, but can also be misused. Examples of this rule are: (1) 80% of the real properties in a certain region may be owned by 20% of the population. (2) 80% of the sales of a company may be due to 20% of its customers. (3) 80% of the execution time of a computer program is caused by 20% of its instructions. However, the claim "80% of the work is done by 20% of the workers" is, in general, wrong.

2.7: The virus selects a few bytes from the middle of the program, and replaces them with a jump instruction to the virus. When execution of the program gets to the jump, it jumps to the virus, which then executes, restores the selected bytes, and resumes the program. This method makes it difficult to detect the virus, but calls for an experienced virus writer, because modern computers have variable-size instructions (an instruction may occupy one byte or several bytes) and the virus has to place the jump between two original instructions, not inside an instruction.

2.8: If the virus came from the boot sector of a removable disk, then the computer has a drive for removable disks and there is a chance that more removable disks will be inserted in the future. If such a virus tries to infect only executable files, it will miss all the future removable disks. On the other hand, if the virus is residing in an executable file (it is a file infector), the computer may not even have a floppy drive or a zip drive, so removable disks will never be inserted and the virus will never propagate.

2.9: The date is different, but the word processor (or other software) has a command, such as "\date," to obtain the date from the operating system, which is why the header is always the same.

2.10: A virus may do nothing because of a bug in its code. Some viruses are written by researchers as a proof of concept, to study a certain aspect of virus propagation or infection, and such a virus may also be benign.

2.11: Changing one bit in a text file modifies one character of text. Often, this may not constitute significant damage, especially since the text in question may have mistypes to begin with. A corrupted character in a poem may never be discovered, even by its author, but legal or medical texts may be sensitive to even small corruptions. Modifying one bit in an image changes the color of one pixel. If the color changes significantly, the modification may be noticeable. In medical (X ray) images and images taken by spy satellites, every pixel may be important, and a corrupt pixel may lead to wrong diagnosis (in the former case) or wrong military decision (in the latter). It's difficult to think of a case where one bad bit in a video file would be noticeable, but a single bad bit in an audio file may be noticed if it changes a short interval of silence to a loud sound. Changing one bit in an executable file corrupts either an instruction or a data item. In either case the program will get corrupted, but may still do its job most of the time. We know that a typical program spends most of its time in small regions (loops) of instructions, while most of its instructions are rarely executed. If one instruction in an error-handling procedure is damaged, the program will still run correctly until the error actually occurs.

2.12: The virus may go into action when the user closes a document in a word processor. Before the virus closes the document, it may make random changes in the text. A sophisticated data diddling virus may simply check every text file found in the computer, scan it for predetermined keywords or phrases, and change each. Thus, each occurrence of "vice president" may be changed to "president" and each "buy" changed to "sell." Another nasty idea is to search for spreadsheet files and change them along the same lines. A file may be changed each time it is saved, or only when the user closes it, or when the virus finds it on the disk. The virus may modify data items or formulas; it may follow guidelines (such as change every "+" to "−" or swap every data item with the one to its left) or may do its damage at random. The point is that it's easy to come up with ideas for inflicting subtle damage, but it is difficult, perhaps even impossible, to correct such damage once it is discovered.

2.13: A vice-president trying to get rid of the president quickly and fill his place. One partner trying to drive the other partner crazy and buy his share of the business awfully cheap. A student trying to have a fellow student fail a class project.

2.14: If a low-clearance user can see the names of high-level files, then S can temporarily modify the name of such a file to signal a 0 or a 1 to R. If S can control the existence of a shared resource, then it can signal a 0 or a 1 by the presence or absence of the resource. Similarly, S can send bits to R by deleting and creating a file each time it receives a synchronization signal from R.

2.15: Because in general it is easier to do evil than to do good, as can be seen by many real-life examples. It takes years to build a large building, but only seconds to bring it down in an earthquake. Similarly, raising a child requires years of effort, but killing someone is much easier and quicker.

2.16: Yes, if the executable file is small to begin with or if it does not compress very well (which happens if it is random or close to random).

2.17: Yes, but I promise to do my best to educate myself and follow the examples, tips, and advice given here and in many other books, articles, and Web sites to try to keep my computer, backups, and network clean.

2.18: (1) Execute a `clear` instruction. Such an instruction clears its operand, which may be a register or a memory location. (2) Subtract register 4 from itself. (3) Prepare the constant zero in location `cons` and execute a `mov` instruction to move that location to register 4. (4) Multiply register 4 by zero. (5) Shift the register n positions to the left or to the right, where n is the register size. (6) Perform an exclusive OR (XOR) of the register with itself.

2.19: On the author's Macintosh, the activity monitor indicates the following: Alias menu (displays a menu of files at the top of the screen, for easy launching), TypeIt4Me (a simple macro processor that types a character string when the user types its name), fax assistant (looking for incoming faxes), Iomega driver (looking for a zip disk inserted into the drive), and Little snitch (a firewall program).

2.20: When a virus senses that new, unfamiliar software has been installed and is scanning disk directories or memory, the virus may react by erasing several important operating system routines from memory (and also deleting them from the disk). This leads to a crash, where the computer behaves erratically or seems frozen. Such a stealth technique is extreme and immediately raises suspicion of a virus, but it may delay the detection and extermination of the virus, or at least may annoy the computer user a while longer.

2.21: Restarting (or rebooting) a computer is done by an interrupt. The user presses a restart button (or a key combination) that generates a special interrupt, and the handling routing for that interrupt closes all the open files and restarts the computer. (On a PC, the key combination CTRL-ALT-DEL is used for this purpose.) This is why a computer can be restarted at any time, even in the middle of a program, and even if the program is stuck in an infinite loop. A virus that infects the reboot interrupt-handling routine can therefore survive a restart. The virus copies itself as a temporary file on the disk, it modifies the operating system routine that boots the computer, and then executes the normal routine for closing down the computer. When the computer restarts, it executes the modified booting routine. The routine boots the computer normally, and then reads the virus from the temporary file, stores it in memory, and deletes the file. As a precaution, the virus may modify the booting routine such that its last step is to remove the modification, leaving nothing suspicious behind.

3.1:   Try to obtain it from the maker of the vulnerable software. A large software maker that sells, for example, a web server (where the hacker has discovered a security hole) will have a list of customers who purchased the software. Such a list will not have the IP numbers, but they can be obtained automatically from the URLs of the customers. The list will not be perfect, but it doesn't have to be.

3.2:   One such example is a dictionary server. The client sends a word, and the server responds by sending back the definition of the word, or its synonyms. Another example is a street-address server, such as [mapquest 04] or [maporama 04]. The client sends the latitude and longitude coordinates of a point on Earth, and the server sends back the street address, if any.

3.3:   It is true that any experiments with rogue software, not just worms, should produce best results if carried out "in the field," rather than in a laboratory. However, the public would have to be notified, and there will be tough resistance to such an experiment, because people are scared of anything they don't understand. Also, the good worm may have a bug in it, that will turn it into a bad worm. Even worse, a hacker may find a way to release a private, bad worm, similar to the good one during the experiment and that worm would spread with the good one, finding no resistance.

3.4:   When a worm generates children and sends them out, each child should get a list of IP addresses as before, but also including the addresses of its older siblings. Thus, if a worm generates children A, B, and C, then B will get a list that has, among other addresses, the address of A, and C will get a list with both A's and B's addresses.

3.5:   We know that it's virtually impossible to completely test and debug a worm (or any other type of rogue software) in the laboratory. Thus, once a worm has been sent into the Internet, its creator may discover a bug in the code. Another reason may be a worm's author who has just finished reading this section and is eager to employ the techniques found here to improve an existing worm.

4.1:   A word processor or an editor runs with a user's own file access privileges, because it must have full access to all the user's files. A Trojan horse in a word processor can therefore read, write, or delete any file opened by the word processor. The horse could, for example, examine the content of the file, and upon finding a keyword (such as `key` or `bomb`), send the entire text to its creator, create a copy that's publicly accessible, or change the access permission of the file to make it generally accessible.

4.2:   Many of the spyware applications discussed in Chapter 9 are Trojans.

4.3:   There aren't many. Perhaps the most important ones are the `mail` routine, the `passwd` routine (to let users change their passwords), the `ps` command (examines the status of all processes in the computer), routine `lquota` (to enforce disk quotas), and the `df` command (which indicates the amount of free disk space).

4.4:   The code of line 3 identifies the fact that the compiler is compiling itself, but this code is weak, because even minimal changes to the source line "`compile(s) {`" will defeat the test of line 3.

4.5:   The original virus can check to see whether a file with a certain name exists. Once the hacker decides that the original virus has done its job, he creates such a file. Whenever any copy of the virus notices the existence of this file, it deletes itself from its host. A variation is to have the original virus itself create this flag file once it has infected the compiler and thus accomplished its mission (see the discussion of antibodies on Page 73).

6.1:   A dentist's office, as discussed on page 144.

6.2:   Yes, to some extent, because many new viruses are created from virus kits and are therefore modified versions of existing viruses, so their codes are similar. Old versions of Norton anti-virus software for the Macintosh, made by Symantec, promised to do just that.

6.3:   An image file tends to be big and is almost always kept in compressed form. Even a small image may consist of a million pixels, each occupying three bytes. Current digital cameras are already in the six megapixel range, and create image files that are at least 18 Mbyte long in uncompressed form. Video files are much bigger. A document with tax information may be needed only once a year. X-ray images in a hospital's archive may remain untouched for years. Pictures taken by astronomical telescopes are stored in archives and may be used years later to compare a newly-discovered astronomical event with the same patch of sky in the past.

6.4:   Because the activity monitor is called by the break routine and this call places another return address at the top of the stack. Thus, when the activity monitor is executing, the address at the top of the stack is the address the activity monitor will use to return to the break routine. The address below it is the address the break routine will use to return to F.

6.5:   Many applications are installed by an installer that decompresses the files needed by the application and writes them in the appropriate places on a disk. When such an installer finds files left from an older version of the application, it may get confused. If the access permission of a folder has changed and the installer can no longer write to it, it may skip part of the installation or terminate abnormally. If power to the computer is cut off during the installation, the installer may not be able to complete its task later.

6.6:   A screen saver. See Section 9.3.

6.7:   When a program terminates normally, it returns control to the operating system by creating an artificial interrupt called a break or a supervisor call. When the hardware senses this interrupt, it invokes an interrupt service routine (part of the operating

system) that either examines user commands that are pending or decides what program
will be next to execute. If the virus writer is familiar with the details of the operating
system, the virus may modify this routine such that it first infects whatever program has
just finished, then executes normally. Notice that in order to infect an operating system
routine, the virus has to obtain high privilege, but such viruses have been detected in
the past.

6.8: The voting circuit cannot decide which result is correct, if any. In such a case,
the circuit can only detect an error and cannot correct it. An improvement is to have
five copies, or even a larger (odd) number of copies.

7.1: Because the association between a URL and its IP may change at any time,
especially if the site in question is hosted by an ISP that provides dynamic IPs.

7.2: Cheap (but possibly bad) prescription drugs, drugs that enlarge or enhance body
parts, herbal remedies, weight loss drugs, get-rich-quick schemes, and financial services
such as mortgage offers or schemes for reducing debts. Qualifications, such as university
degrees or professional titles. On-line gambling. Cut-price or pirated software.

7.3: Just do it.

7.4: At the time of this writing they are `freebieland.net`, `coolfreebielinks.com`,
and `freebielist.com`.

7.5: The term zombie is used in UNIX to indicate a child program that was started
by a parent program but was later abandoned by it. This is not the same as a zombie
computer or a zombie server.

8.1: If you know a person, you can ask him an array of personal questions. If you are
satisfied with the answers, you authenticate the person. If you don't know a person,
you can receive the answers beforehand, and conduct the authentication process by
computer, but this method is still experimental and should not be trusted.

8.2: A natural eye can be distinguished from a glass eye by shining light of varying
intensities on the eye and making sure that its pupil dilates normally.

8.3: Another variation is to prepare a large number of different permutations, then
compute numbers a, b, and so on from the password, and finally perform permutation
a on the password, then apply permutation b on the result, and so on.

8.4: Typical default passwords are the following: help, test, tester, system, system,
manager, sysman, sysop, engineer, ops, operations, central, demo, demonstration, aid,
display, call, terminal, external, remote, check, net, network, phone, and fred.

8.5: Yes, it is secure, because there are so many possible permutations. However, it
may be easier to memorize a random password than to memorize a specific permutation
of 16 characters, again because there are so many permutations.

8.6: It is likely `';lkjh` or `lkjhgf` (look at your qwerty keyboard).

8.7: Products are continually becoming more reliable, easier to use even with a personal computer, and less expensive. Use a search engine and search, for example, under "fingerprint identification."

8.8: Ask a friend to let you use their account. Try to guess a password by using the birthday of its owner, the number of his children, or their birthdays.

8.9: The name of the person, as in Larry's case.

8.10: In the case in question, the hacker identified a computer that ran an early version of `PC AnyWhere`. This software [remotelyanywhere 04] makes it easy to remotely control a PC and the early version had a security flaw that made it possible to login to a remote PC while bypassing the password protection (a classic example of a security compromise). Once gaining control of the computer, the hacker identified its IP address, then used `telnet` software to try nearby IP numbers to break into other computers on campus.

9.1: Are there any complaints on the Internet, especially on popular technical message boards, about the program using deceptive advertising or spam?

9.2: No. If this poor, young, and inexperienced author could come up with such a frightening scenario, imagine what a group of well-determined, well-funded, and well-trained terrorists could come up with when they really put their minds to it. The only remedy to this scenario is for a government agency to check the background of every affiliate network and to scan for a Trojan horse every computer program that seems too good to be true; not very practical.

9.3: A search in early 2005 discloses that James Carter, of Lilburn, Georgia, 30047, an unemployed cardinal health worker, has made two contributions totaling $500 to the campaign of Howard Dean, a 2004 presidential candidate and former governor of the state of Vermont.

9.4: This is easy. A search for "spyware audit" has returned about 260,000 results.

9.5: This is easy. A search for "spyware removal" returns several million results, among them [Spybot 04], makers of *SpySweeper*; [snapfiles 04], that advertises *Spyware Doctor*; [lavasoft 04] with its *Ad-Aware*; and [SearchAndDestroy 04] that offers free spyware removal.

10.1: This author cannot think of any.

10.2: (1) Open a text file, copy the individual characters of the password one by one, and paste each character where you need to type the password. (2) Start by typing a string of `as`, then type the characters of the password in random order in between the `as`, and finally delete the `as` with the delete key. As an example, consider password `ChHaakon`. It can be typed surreptitiously in the following steps

aaaaaaaa → aaaaakaaa → aaaHaakaaa → aaaHaakaoaa →

aCaaHaakaoaa → aCaaHaakaoana → aCahaHaakaoana → ChHaakon.

(3) Use a virtual keyboard. This is a program that displays a keyboard on the screen. The user clicks on keys, and the corresponding characters are displayed at the cursor's location. An example of a virtual keyboard is [corallosoftware 05]. These methods are safe but tedious, which illustrates the tradeoff between security and ease of use.

10.3: Here are some examples: (1) A bank statement with cancelled checks. A sophisticated thief can wash off any traces of ink from a check, then use it in an obvious way. (2) A box full of newly-printed checks. (3) A preapproved credit card offer. It is always a good idea to opt out of such offers and in the United States this is possible by calling 888-5-OPT-OUT. (4) New credit cards issued for old, expired ones. (5) Letters (with checks, official forms, or money orders) you leave in your mailbox for the mailman to pick up.

10.4: Marketers and spammers send unwanted advertisements and spam targeted by IP numbers. Hackers and snoops track a victim's Internet surfing habits by his IP address, which increases one's chances of becoming a victim of identity theft.

10.5: Profiling and targeted advertising are popular applications of cookies. You surf to a magazine's site and decide to read an article on weight loss. The site sends your computer a cookie that identifies you as one who is interested in weight loss. On every subsequent visit to the magazine's site, the cookie is read by the site, which then displays ads for weight loss.

The biggest online advertising company is DoubleClick. Relatively few have heard of this company and even fewer have visited their Web site. However, chances are that you have a cookie in your browser from DoubleClick even if you have never visited that site [cookiecentral 04]. This is a third-party cookie, sent by a site that you have visited. When you visit a commercial Web site X that employs DoubleClick as its online advertising company, X retrieves any DoubleClick cookies that you may have and sends them to DoubleClick, which then sends X ads based on those cookies for you to watch. Site X then sends you another DoubleClick cookie identifying you as a visitor of X.

10.6: By spreading false rumors about a new, revolutionary product about to be released by Microsoft and including a link to his site for anyone to click on instead of typing.

10.7: You cannot. A search at [Network solutions 04] indicates that this domain has already been registered (by Alon Swartz) and so have virtually all the domain names that are typographically similar to `microsoft.com`.

11.1: A news agency may want to customize news it carries in its Web site by time zones.

11.2: A redundancy. Similar to phrases such as absolutely necessary, advance warning, boiling hot, hot water heater, my personal opinion, and newborn baby.

11.3: Yes, because a child, especially a pre-teen, may not fully grasp the risk of opening an email attachment or may easily forget any warnings they received about this danger.

11.4: Here is an example of such a set.

■   Search the Internet for Web sites that carry news about new malware. Browse 2–3 such sites every morning. The few minutes that this takes are time well spent. Search the Internet for security news and white papers on security.

■   Obtain a firewall, use it, and update its rules as needed.

■   Obtain anti-virus software, update it and run it regularly.

■   Shut down your computer when you are not using it.

■   Enable other operating system services only when necessary and only on a temporary basis.

■   Use robust passwords that include letters, digits, and other characters in a hard-to-guess string. Remember! Sophisticated dictionary attacks are being carried out all the time.

■   Keep up to date with security patches for (1) your operating system, (2) your Web browser, and (3) other software, especially any servers or communications software.

■   Keep a sharp eye out for domain name trickery.

■   Never download anything from any source you don't know and trust, and be sure it really is the source you think it is. As this book explains elsewhere, it's easy to create a convincing fake version of any Web site.

■   Delete, without reading or opening, email attachments from anyone you don't know and trust. Be wary of attachments even from known, trusted persons, whose computers may have been compromised.

12.1: The number of 64-bit keys is $2^{64} = 18{,}446{,}744{,}073{,}709{,}551{,}620$ or approximately 1.8×10^{19}. The following examples illustrate the magnitude of this key space.

1. 2^{64} seconds equal $584{,}942{,}417{,}355$ years.

2. The unit of electrical current is the Ampere. One Ampere is defined as 6.24×10^{18} electrons per second. Even this huge number is smaller than 2^{64}.

3. Even light, traveling (in vacuum) at 299,792,458 m/s, takes 61,531,714,963 seconds (about 1,951 years) to cover 2^{64} meters. This distance is therefore about 1951 light years.

4. In a fast, 5 GHz computer, the clock ticks five billion times per second. In one year, the clock ticks $5 \cdot 10^9 \cdot (3 \cdot 10^7) = 1.5 \cdot 10^{17}$ times.

5. The mass of the sun is roughly $2 \cdot 10^{31}$ kg and the mass of a single proton is approximately $1.67 \cdot 10^{-27}$ kg. There are therefore approximately 10^{58} protons in the sun. This number is about 2^{193}, so searching a keyspace of 193 bits is equivalent to trying to find a single proton in the sun (ignoring the fact that all protons are identical and that the sun is hot). The proverbial "needle in a haystack" problem pales in comparison.

6. The term *femto*, derived from the Danish *femten*, meaning *fifteen*, stands for 10^{-15}. Thus, a femtometer is 10^{-15} m, and a cubic femtometer is 10^{-45} cubic meters, an incredibly small unit of volume. A light year is 10^{16} meters, so assuming that the universe is a sphere of radius 15 billion light years, its volume is $(4/3)\pi(15{\times}10^9{\times}10^{16})^3 = 1.41372 \times 10^{79}$ cubic meters or about 10^{124} cubic femtometers. This is roughly 2^{411}, so searching a keyspace of 411 bits is like trying to locate a particular cubic femtometer in the entire universe.

These examples illustrate the power of large numbers and should convince any rational person that breaking a code by searching the entire keyspace is an illusion. As for the claim that "there is a chance that the first key tried will be the right one," for a 64-bit keyspace this chance is 2^{-64}. To get a feeling for how small this number is, consider that light travels 1.6×10^{-11} meters (about the size of 10 atoms laid side by side) in 2^{-64} seconds.

12.2: Follow each letter in the key `polybiuscher` with its first successor that is still not included in the key. Thus, `p` should be followed by `q` and `o` should be followed by `p`, but because `p` is already included in the key (as are `q`, `r`, and `s`), the `o` is followed by `t`. This process produces first the 22-letter string `pqotlmyzbcikuvswhnefrx` which is then extended in the same way to become the 25-letter string `paqdogtlmyzbcikuvswhnefrx`.

12.3: Yes, as is easy to see by examining the following examples (notice the two occurrences of 22 in the ciphertext and how they produce different plaintexts):

Plaintext	+	66	05	66	11	61		Ciphertext	−	**22**	**61**	**88**	**22**	**27**
Key		66	66	22	11	66		Key		66	66	22	11	66
Ciphertext		**22**	**61**	**88**	**22**	**27**		Plaintext		66	05	66	11	61

12.4: The average word size in English is 4–5 letters. We therefore start by examining 4-letter words. There are 26 letters, so the number of combinations of four letters is $26^4 = 456,976$. A good English-language dictionary contains about 100,000 words. Assuming that half these words have 4 letters, the percentage of valid 4-letter words is $50000/26^4 \approx 0.11$. The percentage of 5-letter words is obtained similarly as $50000/26^5 \approx 0.004$. Random text may therefore have some short (2–4 letters) words, and very few 5–6 letter words, but longer words would be very rare.

12.5:   When an encrypted message is sent by Alice to Bob, it can be intercepted by Eve and copied. When the key is later sent, Eve may intercept it and use it to decrypt the message.

12.6:   Mixing salt and pepper is a one-way operation in practice (in principle, they can be separated). Heat flow from high to low temperature in a closed system is a one-way process in principle. Giving birth is one-way in principle, while squeezing glue out of a tube is one-way in practice.

12.7:   This is a direct result of the properties of the modulo function. In step 3, Alice computes

$$\beta^a \bmod 13 = (5^b \bmod 13)^a \bmod 13 = 5^{b \cdot a} \bmod 13,$$

and Bob computes the identical expression

$$\alpha^b \bmod 13 = (5^a \bmod 13)^b \bmod 13 = 5^{a \cdot b} \bmod 13.$$

12.8:   The final key is computed, in step 3, as $L^{a \cdot b} \bmod P$ (or, identically, as $L^{b \cdot a} \bmod P$), so it is an integer in the range $[0, P-1]$. Thus, there are only P possible values for the key, which is why P should be large. If we allow values L greater than P, then a user may accidentally select an L that is a multiple of P, which results in a key of 0, thereby providing an eavesdropper with useful information. If P is a prime and if $L < P$, then P is not a prime factor of L^x, so $L^x \bmod P$ cannot be zero.

A.1:   No answer provided, but if you cannot easily read that (and I hope that you cannot), then you are not a good hacker.

B.1:   Imagine an anti-virus program that does not yet recognize `Dark Avenger.1800`. The program works by opening executable files and checking them, with the result that they all become infected even though they are not executed.

B.2:   Grim.

Conc.1:   The IBM S/360 family was succeeded by the S/370, and 3080, 3090, and 43xx families, all upward compatible. The DEC PDP-11/20 was the first model (made in 1970) of the famous PDP-11 family of upward compatible mini and microcomputers, whose last descendant was the Micro PDP-11/94 (made in 1990).

Conc.2:   Banks have to transfer large amounts of cash and they spend much effort and money on securing these transfers. They employ specially-designed armored trucks, trained security personnel, and special cameras and other security equipment. It would be easier and cheaper (and not much slower) to simply use a delivery service such as Federal Express to perform this task, but it would also be extremely nonsecure. The compromise in this case is extreme.

Compromise

Noun:

1. A middle way between two extremes.
2. Accommodation in which both sides make concessions.

Verb:

1. Make a compromise; arrive at a compromise.
2. Settle by concession.
3. Expose or make liable to danger, suspicion, or disrepute.

The only exercise some people get is jumping to conclusions, running down their friends, side-stepping responsibility, and pushing their luck!

—Anonymous

Glossary

Access control. Safeguards that prevent unauthorized access to a computer or a computing facility. An access control can be physical, such as lock or guard, or software-based, such as a password or a firewall.

Account harvesting. The process of collecting account names and passwords on a computer or a database.

Active content. Executable code (often in Java) embedded in a Web page. When the page is read, downloaded, and displayed by a Web browser, the embedded code is executed and may release a harmful payload.

ActiveX. A technology that extends the capabilities of a web browser (from Microsoft).

Activity monitor. Techniques that attempt to prevent malware infection by looking for suspicious or unusual activity in the computer.

AES. Advanced Encryption Standard, adopted by NIST as a replacement for the DES.

Anti-virus software. Software that searches for viruses and other malware. (See also Heuristic scanner.)

Applet. A small application. This term normally refers to Java applets.

ASCII code. (although Unicode is becoming a competitor). ASCII stands for American Standard Code for Information Interchange. It is a $(1+7)$-bit code, meaning 1 parity bit and 7 data bits per symbol. As a result, 128 symbols can be coded. They include the upper- and lowercase letters, the ten digits, some punctuation marks, and control characters. (See also Byte, Unicode.)

Asymmetric algorithm. A cryptographic algorithm where different keys are used for encryption and decryption. Most often a public-key algorithm. (See also Public-key algorithm.)

Attachment. Any file, data or executable, attached to an email message.

Attack. (1) An approach used by a codebreaker to decrypt encrypted data or to reveal hidden data. An attack may use brute force, where every key is tried, or a sophisticated approach such as differential cryptanalysis. An attacker may use only known ciphertext or known ciphertext and plaintext. (2) An attempt to break into a computer or a network or to hamper their operations.

Audit Trail.   A record of all of a computer's activities during a certain time period. A trail is produced automatically by an operating system routine or a special utility and is saved as a log file. It can later be used by administrators or security experts to identify improper or unauthorized use of the computer.

Auditing.   The process of collecting and analyzing information in order to ensure a proper level of security, as well as compliance with the policies of an organization.

Authentication. The process of verifying a user's identity or authority. Alternatively, the process of establishing the validity of a message. (See also Biometrics.)

Authorization.   The process of empowering someone to perform an operation or to have access to restricted resources.

Availability.   A computing resource (such as a file server of an organization) should be available to legitimate users. It often happens that malicious persons attack the availability of a resource thereby making it unusable without damaging the resource itself. (See also DoS, DDoS.)

Backdoor. A hidden feature in a piece of software that gives certain people special privileges denied to others. A typical example is a backdoor placed in an encryption algorithm by its author. The author can use the backdoor to decrypt messages without knowing the encryption key. In 1997 the American Senate approved a bill that would have banned the manufacture, distribution, or import of any encryption product that did not include a backdoor for the federal government, but that bill never became a law.

Backdoor Trojan.   A Trojan horse that enables a remote user to access and control a computer. This constitutes unauthorized access.

Bacterium. Another name for a computer virus that's not a rabbit. (See also Virus, Rabbit.)

Backup.   The process of creating a true copy of a set of data files.

Bandwidth.   The capacity of a communications channel. Measured in amount of data per unit time, such as bits per second (baud).

Bayesian filtering.   A statistical method that determines whether email is spam. It is based on Bayesian probability theory that computes the probability of an event A given that another event B has occurred.

Biometrics. Identifying or authenticating a person by checking certain physical characteristics such as fingerprints or eye and facial features. (See also Authentication.)

BIOS. An acronym that stands for Basic Input/Output System. BIOS is the lowest level of the operating system routines that control input/output operations. It interfaces directly with hardware.

Bitrate. Bits per second. A measure of the speed of a process such as encrypting or decrypting a file.

Blackhole list. A published list, usually commercial, of addresses known to be sources of spam. (See also Real-time blackhole list.)

Blacklist. A list of email addresses and domains from which no email will be accepted. Used by firewalls and email filters.

Block cipher. A symmetric cipher that encrypts a message by breaking it down into blocks and encrypting each block separately. DES, IDEA, and AES are block ciphers.

Boot sector. The part of the operating system that is first read into memory from disk when a computer is turned on or restarted. The program in the boot sector is then executed, which in turn loads the rest of the operating system. (See also Booting.)

Boot sector virus. A virus that resides in the boot sector of a disk.

Booting. The process of turning a computer on. The main task of booting is to load the operating system from disk. (See also Boot sector.)

Browser. A computer program that locates a Web site (a server), downloads data from it in html format, and displays it as text and graphics. (See also Web browser.)

Brute-force attack. An attempt to break an encrypted message by trying every possible key.

Buffer overflow. An unusual situation that occurs when a program tries to store data past the end of a buffer (an array). Such data overwrites the instructions or data located past the array, and so may cause unexpected results. This is a common technique exploited by hackers to corrupt or infect executable code. To solve such a problem, the program has to check every index used to store data in the array and make sure indexes never point outside the array.

Bug. An error in the design or implementation of a computer program.

Byte. A set of eight bits. This is often the smallest addressable unit in a computer's memory. The number 8 was chosen because one character (ASCII) code or two decimal digits can be stored in 8 bits. (See also ASCII.)

Caesar cipher. A cipher where each letter is replaced by the letter located cyclically n positions in front of it in the alphabet. (See also Affine cipher.)

CGI. An acronym for Common Gateway Interface. A standard employed by a Web server to run programs or scripts and send the output to a user's Web browser.

Checksum. The result of a computation that involves all the bits of a piece of data (a file or a message). The checksum is later used to verify the validity of the data, because virtually any modification of the data will change its checksum.

Cipher.   An encryption algorithm that depends on a key.

Ciphertext.   The encrypted result produced by a cipher. (See also Plaintext.)

Client.   Software that requests and uses a service provided by another program (a server). Often, the server may itself be a client of some other server. (See also Server.)

Code.   A symbol that represents another symbol (also a set of symbols that represent other symbols). The ASCII code, for example, represents a set of 128 characters by a set of 128 8-bit codes.

Code (in cryptography).   A cryptographic technique that uses a codebook to replace words and letters in the plaintext with symbols from the codebook.

Companion virus. A virus that exploits a feature in certain operating systems that allows for two programs with the same name but different extensions. The operating system uses the file extension to decide which program to execute.

Complex dictionary checking.   A feature of anti-spam software that locates (in a dictionary) words often used in spam, even if letters are replaced with lookalike numerals or characters (such as "1nterest r@te").

Computer Emergency Response Team (CERT).   An organization that responds to attacks on computers and networks. CERT publishes alerts concerning vulnerabilities and threats, and offers other information to help improve computer and network security.

Computer Network.   See Network.

Cookie.   A small amount of data that stores information in a computer with the user's permission. Cookies are normally used to enable a Web site to track visits and remember visitors' information.

Corruption.   An accidental or intentional modification of computer programs or data.

Covert channels.   Physical means by which information is sent between two parties secretly using normal network and computing procedures.

Cryptanalysis. The science and art of breaking encryption (recovering plaintext from ciphertext when the key is unknown). (See also Attack.)

Cryptanalyst. One who tries to break encrypted codes.

Cryptographer. One who develops encryption methods.

Cryptography. The art and science of using mathematics to obscure the meaning of data by applying transformations to the data that are impractical or impossible to reverse without the knowledge of some key. The term comes from the Greek for "hidden writing."

Cryptology. The branch of mathematics concerned with secret writing in all its forms. It includes cryptography, cryptanalysis, and steganography.

CSV. An acronym for Comma Separated Values. CSV is a file format where values (for example, the values from an Excel spreadsheet) are displayed separated by commas. The format does not support macros, so that it cannot spread macro viruses.

Daemon. An operating system routine that runs continuously and forwards input/output requests to other programs or processes as appropriate. The term daemon originated in Unix. The Windows operating system refers to daemons as system agents and services.

Data diddling. Alteration of data. This term refers to what a malicious virus may do to data files it locates in an infected computer.

Data encryption standard (DES). A block cipher based on the work of Horst Feistel in the 1970s that is widely used in commercial systems. DES is a 64-bit block cipher with a 56-bit key organized in 16 rounds of operations.

Data leakage. The theft of data (including software).

DDoS. See Distributed denial of service.

Decryption. The process of converting ciphertext back to plaintext by means of a key. The inverse of encryption. (See also Ciphertext, Encryption, Plaintext.)

Denial of service attack. An attempt to prevent the use of a Web server by sending a vast number of simultaneous messages or requests.

Dictionary attack. Brute-force software that bombards a mail server with email addresses that are generated alphabetically, looking for valid addresses. The same method can be used to guess passwords.

Diffie–Hellman (DH). A public-key cryptography algorithm that generates a shared secret key between two entities after they publicly share some randomly-generated data.

Digital. An approach where all types of data—text, images, audio, and video—are represented in terms of digits (normally bits).

Digital signature. Data value generated by a public-key algorithm based on the content of a block of data and on a private key. It generates an individualized checksum.

Digram. A pair of consecutive symbols.

Disassembly. The process of translating a program in machine language to assembler language.

Disaster-recovery plan (DRP). A procedure developed and periodically rehearsed and revised to ensure quick and complete recovery of an organization from various disasters.

Distributed denial of service. A denial of service attack coming from many computers. (See also Denial of service.)

Domain hijacking. An attack where a hacker takes over a domain by first blocking access to the domain's name server and then replacing it with his own name server.

DoS. See Denial of service.

Downloading. The transfer of data into one's computer. The opposite of uploading. (See also Uploading.)

Dumpster diving. Obtaining private and personal data by searching through discarded documents, disks, and other media. (See also Scavenging.)

DVD. An optical disc, similar to a CD but with seven times the data capacity. A DVD can have 1, 2, or 4 tracks (or layers), with capacities of up to 17.08 Gb. The acronym may either refer to "digital video disc" or "digital versatile disc," or may stand for nothing.

Eavesdropping. Unauthorized interception of data being transmitted.

Electronic fund transfer (EFT). A computerized transaction that can quickly and securely transfer funds electronically between organizations without the need to fill out paper documents.

Emanations analysis. Spying on computer operations by collecting and analyzing signals that are emitted by hardware components.

Encryption. The process of converting plaintext back to ciphertext by means of a key. The inverse of decryption. (See also Ciphertext, Decryption, Plaintext.)

Ethernet. A technology for avoiding message collisions in a local area network (LAN). The ethernet standard is IEEE 802.3.

Eve. A term used in cryptography discussions and examples for the ubiquitous eavesdropper.

Exclusive-OR (XOR). A logical (Boolean) operation that is also its own inverse, which makes it useful in cryptography. It is identical to adding two bits modulo 2. (See also XOR.)

Exploit. A ready-to-run program that takes advantage of a known weakness. These can often be found in hackers' newsgroups. (See also Hoax.)

Factor. Given an integer N, a factor is any integer that divides it without a remainder.

Factoring. The process of finding the prime factors of an integer.

False positive. A report about a virus or a source of spam that turns out to be wrong.

File infector. A virus that infects executable files and runs each time an infected file is executed. (See also Parasitic virus.)

File server. A computer where data is stored that can be downloaded by authorized computers. (See also Client, Server.)

Firewall. Security software that is placed between the Internet and an organization's local network, or between a network and a computer. The firewall software is governed by rules and passes only network traffic authorized by the rules.

Gateway. A computer that either serves for the transfer of data (for example, a mail gateway that handles all the mail coming into an organization), or a computer that converts data from one protocol to another.

Giga. The quantity giga is defined as $2^{30} = 1,073,741,824$. In contrast, a billion is defined (in the United States) as 10^9. (See Mega.)

Greylist. Email senders who are not blacklisted (excluded) or whitelisted (accepted) can be placed on a greylist and requested to prove that they are sending legitimate mail.

Hacker. Someone who tries to break into computers. A more lenient term is "a computer enthusiast."

Ham. Email that a recipient believes isn't spam.

Harvesting. Scanning the internet for email addresses that can be added to spammers' mailing lists.

Heuristic scanner. A program that detects viruses by using general rules about what viruses are like or how they behave. Conventional anti-virus software looks for known signatures of viruses and is therefore much slower a heuristic scanner. (See also Anti-virus software.)

Hoax. A report about viruses or other security threats, often spread by email, that is intended to deceive. (See also False positive.)

Honeypot. A computer on the internet that used specifically to attract and trap spammers and hackers.

HTML. An acronym for Hypertext Markup Language. The standard for text and images on a Web site.

HTTP. An acronym for Hypertext Transport Protocol. A protocol used by Web servers and clients (browsers) to transfer data to Web browsers.

HTTP scanning. Real-time scanning of HTTP traffic for viruses.

Hypertext. Text that has links to other texts and images.

Integrity. The correctness of a piece of data. An attack on integrity tries to damage data by changing bits. This is why a checksum, normally in the form of CRC, is important.

Internet. THE network that connects many networks and computers all over the world.

Internet protocol (IP). A set of rules governing how data is sent from one computer to another on the Internet.

Interrupt. The way the computer responds to urgent or unusual events. Interrupts involve both hardware and software.

IP Address. A unique 32-bit number assigned to each computer on the Internet. It is used as the unique address of the computer by Internet protocols. There can be 2^{32} IP addresses (about four billion).

ISO. The International Standards Organization. This is one of the organizations responsible for developing standards. Among other things, it is responsible (together with the ITU) for the JPEG and MPEG compression standards. (See also ITU.)

ITU. The International Telecommunications Union, the new name of the CCITT, is a United Nations organization responsible for developing and recommending standards for data communications.

Java. A platform-independent higher-level programming language designed specifically for the Web. Programs written in Java are either applications or applets. (See also Java applet, Sandbox.)

Java applet. A small application normally used to display text and graphics on Web pages. Applets are run by the browser in a safe environment and cannot make changes to the client's computer. (See also Java, Sandbox.)

JFIF. An acronym for JPEG File Interchange Format. JFIF is a graphics file format that makes it possible to exchange JPEG-compressed images between different computers. The main features of JFIF are the use of the YCbCr triple-component color space for color images (only one component for grayscale images) and the use of markers to specify features missing from JPEG, such as image resolution, aspect ratio, and features that are application specific.

JPEG. A sophisticated lossy compression method [Salomon 04] for color or grayscale still images (not movies). It also works best on continuous-tone images, where adjacent pixels have similar colors.

The main idea behind JPEG is that an image exists for people to look at, so when the image is compressed, it is acceptable to lose image features to which the human eye is not sensitive.

The term JPEG is an acronym that stands for Joint Photographic Experts Group. This was a joint effort by the CCITT and the ISO that started in June 1987. The JPEG standard has proved successful and has become widely used for image presentation, especially in Web pages.

Kerckhoffs's principle. An important principle in cryptography (Section 12.2). It states that the security of an encrypted message must depend on keeping the key secret and should not depend on keeping the encryption algorithm secret.

Key (cryptographic). A string of bits used to encrypt and decrypt messages. In non-computer cryptography the key is a string of any symbols. (See also Key distribution.)

Key distribution. The process of distributing a secret cryptographic key to all the locations of an organization. [See also Key (cryptographic).]

Key space. The number of possible key values. For example, there are 2^{64} key values for a 64-bit key. (See Exercise 12.1.)

Leet. Slang used by hackers to obfuscate discussions in newsgroups and other "gathering places" on the Internet. Examples of leet are "warez" (for pirated software), "pr0n" for pornography, and "sploitz" (for exploits).

Link virus. A virus that corrupts directory entries so that they point to the virus file, allowing it to execute when the user types the name of a legitimate application.

Logic bomb. Malicious software, normally a Trojan horse, left in a disk or inside another file to be triggered by a certain event. A disgruntled employee about to be sacked can plant such a bomb in a central file server, waiting to damage files when the employee's id number is deleted from the list of employees. (See also Rogue Software, Time Bomb.)

Macro. A set of instructions and/or data that's assigned a name. When the user types the name, the macro is expanded. Certain applications, such as Microsoft Word and Excel, support a macro facility.

Macro virus. A virus disguised as a macro and infecting data files.

Mail drop. An email address set up by a spammer specifically to receive responses to spam. The spammer opens and closes such accounts frequently.

Malicious software. See Rogue Software.

Malware. See Rogue Software.

Mantrap. A device to prevent unauthorized access to a room without employing a guard. A small booth between two doors where a door can open only when the other door is closed.

Master boot record. The boot sector on a bootable disk. Also known as the partition sector. The first sector that's read and executed when a computer is booted or is restarted.

Mega. Mega is defined as $2^{20} = 1{,}048{,}576$. In contrast, a million is defined as 10^6. (See Giga.)

Memory-resident virus. A virus that copies itself in memory when it is first executed. It modifies certain interrupt handling routines, so it is executed each time any of the routines is invoked.

Modem. An acronym that stands for MOdulator/DEModulator. Modem is hardware that converts data (bits) between computer form and a form that can propagate through telephone lines, radio or satellite link.

Monoalphabetic substitution cipher. A cryptographic algorithm with a fixed substitution rule.

Multipartite virus. A virus that infects both boot sectors and executable files.

Munging.   Disguising email addresses so that they cannot be harvested. Recipients are told how (or use their intelligence) to decode the address.

National Computer Security Center (NCSC).   A United States government organization that evaluates computing equipment for high-security applications.

National Institute of Standards and Technology (NIST).   An agency of the United States government that establishes national standards.

National Security Agency (NSA). A branch of the United States Department of Defense responsible for intercepting foreign communications and for ensuring the security of United States government communications.

Network.   A set of computers or computer installations connected by communication channels.

Newsgroup.   An electronic forum where users post articles, questions, and followup messages on specific topics.

Obfuscation. A term that refers to (1) disguising email addresses so that spammers cannot harvest them and (2) spammers' attempts to hide messages so that they will not be detected.

One-time pad. An encryption method that employs a large key (as long as the message) to securely encrypt and decrypt a single message. Each encrypted message has to use a fresh key.

Open relay.   An SMTP email server that allows the third-party relay of email messages. Spammers and other hackers can hijack such servers and use them to send spam and malicious software.

Operating system. A set of programs that provide important services to the user. In a multiuser computer, the operating system also supervises users. The most common services an operating system provides are file handling (display, save, rename, move, and delete), data handling (editing text and compiling programs), and input/output (high-level routines that handle interrupts and simplify the transfer of data).

Packet.   Long messages transmitted over a network are broken up into small chunks called packets (or data packets). This is why a computer network is often referred to as a packet-switching network. The advantage of packets is reliability. If one packet is lost on its way or arrives garbled, only that packet has to be resent. All the packets of a long message contain the same destination address, same identification number, and individual serial numbers. The serial number are used to combine the packets into one message at the destination.

Parasitic virus. See File infector.

Password.   A string of symbols (normally letters, digits, and certain punctuation marks) used to identify an authorized computer user. It is important to select strong passwords, keep them secret, and change them periodically.

Password sniffing. Wiretapping a network in order to harvest passwords.

Patch. An update released by a software maker to eliminate bugs and security holes in existing programs.

Phishing. Tricking users into submitting confidential information or passwords by creating a replica of a legitimate Web site or by social engineering methods.

Phreaking. Hacking telephones. Manipulating the way telephones work to void paying for telephone use.

Piggybacking. Sneaking into a restricted facility by following someone while a door is open. Same as Tailgating.

Plaintext. An as-yet unencrypted message. (See also Ciphertext.)

Polyalphabetic substitution. A cryptographic technique where the rule of substitution changes all the time.

Polymorphic virus. Self-modifying virus that changes its code in an attempt to make itself harder to detect. (See also Virus.)

Port. A port is similar to a door in that accessing a network opens up a port in the computer. Each packet of data that arrives at the computer has a port number and certain ports are dedicated to certain network protocols. A port can be thought of as an integer that identifies the endpoint of a communications channel. Once a port is opened on a computer, only one process can listen on it for input.

Port scan. Each port is associated with a process (a program) that listens for input arriving to the port from the outside. Imagine a hacker who discovers a weakness in a certain program that's used to listen to port P. The hacker may decide to send probing messages to port P in all the computers whose IP numbers are in a certain interval. When a computer responds, the hacker adds its IP to the list of potential victims that can later be attacked.

Program. A set of instructions that specifies actions a computer should perform. A program is normally written in a higher-level language and is translated by a compiler into a set of machine instructions. (See also Software.)

Program virus. See File infector.

Protocol. A set of rules, often to standardize procedures for computer communications.

Proxy serve. A server that makes requests to the Internet on behalf of another computer. It sits between a local network and the internet and can be used for security purposes.

Public-key algorithm. A cipher that uses a pair of keys, a public key and a private key, for encryption and decryption. Also called an asymmetric algorithm. (See also Asymmetric algorithm.)

Public-key cryptography. Cryptography based on methods involving a public key and a private key.

Public-key cryptography standards (PKCS). Standards published by RSA Data Security that describe how to use public-key cryptography in a reliable, secure, and interoperable fashion.

Rabbit. A computer virus that does not attach itself to another piece of software and does its damage by monopolizing some computing resource, such as CPU time, memory, or disk space. (See also Bacterium, Virus.)

RAM. Acronym for Random Access Memory, but a misnomer. RAM is really read/write memory. Currently, most computer memories are of this type, which is volatile. It loses its content when power is turned off. (See also ROM.)

Real-time blackhole list (RBL). A list that rejects all email, valid or not, from addresses that are blacklisted because they are known to send spam or to host spammers. Such a list can be employed by ISPs to take anti-spam measures and thereby greatly help their users. (See also Blackhole list.)

Reverse DNS check. Checking an email's sender address against the database of a domain name server to ensure that it originated from a valid domain name or Web address.

Rogue software. A computer program specifically written to damage computing resources. (See also Malicious software, Malware, Virus, Worm, Trojan Horse, Logic Bomb.)

ROM. Acronym for Read Only Memory. ROM is nonvolatile and is therefore used to store permanent data such as the bootstrap loader, Section 2.6. (See also RAM.)

Root kit. A program that's specially designed to hide the fact that a computer's security has been compromised. A root kit may replace an operating system program, thereby making it impossible for the user/owner to detect the presence of the intruder by looking at activity inside the computer.

Router. A hardware device that receives messages for computers in a network and forwards them to the individual computers in the network based upon IP addresses.

RSA Data Security, Inc. (RSADSI). A company [RSA 04] primarily engaged in selling and licensing public-key cryptography for commercial purposes.

Sandbox. A mechanism for executing programs in a controlled environment, often used with Java applets. (See also Java.)

Scavenging. Probing a computer (or even discarded old disks) at random for data useful to a hacker. (See also Dumpster diving.)

Secure socket layer (SSL). A protocol enabling the secure transfer of sensitive information on the Internet. The sensitive data is encrypted by a block cipher, and the SSL protocol is used to select a random key for each transfer and communicate it securely through unsecured channels.

Security (computer). The field that has to do with guaranteeing the availability, confidentiality, and integrity of computing systems.

Server.   A program that provides data in response to requests from other programs called clients. If a computer is dedicated to running servers, it is also called a server. (See also Client, File server.)

Session.   A process where an entire network protocol is executed between two computers (hosts).

Session hijacking.   The process of taking over a session that someone else has started.

SHS.   A 3-letter file extension for Windows "scrap object" files. These files can include virtually any code and execute when clicked on. The extension itself may be hidden.

Smart card.   A plastic card that includes a chip. The chip is either a microprocessor or memory. The smart card authenticates its owner and permits certain transactions such as using a pay telephone or public transportation, or withdrawing money from an ATM.

SMTP.   An acronym for Simple Mail Transport Protocol. The protocol for delivering Internet email.

Sniffer. A program that captures passwords and other data while it (the data) is in transit either within the computer or between computers or routers on a network

Social engineering. A general term for methods that exploit human weaknesses. A hacker may discover someone's password by calling and pretending to be an official, by looking over someone's shoulder while they type their password, or by sending email that poses as an official notice asking for sensitive information. Even though no special software may be needed and no software weakness is exploited, this is still a tool used by many.

Software.   A set of instructions (in assembler) or statements (in a higher-level language) that carry out a task on the computer. Computers are useful because the same computer can execute many programs and thus perform many different tasks. However, without a program, a computer can do nothing. (See also Program.)

Spam.   Commercial and bulk email sent unsolicited and in large quantities in an attempt to trap a small percentage of the receivers into buying useless products and services.

Spambot.   Software used by spammers to find and harvest email addresses from the Internet.

Spoofing. The term spoof means to pretend to be someone else. Spoofing is forging the sender's address in email. It is used mostly to hide the origin of spam, or to convince recipients that the email came from a familiar or reliable source.

Spyware. Software that tracks user activity without the user's knowledge and reports this information to its "owner."

Surge suppressor. See UPS.

Tarpitting. Any technique to monitor email in order to discover sources of large quantities of email that may be spam.

Tarpit. An email server that's kept intentionally slow in order to trap spammers that use harvesting robots.

TCP/IP. Acronyms for Transmission Control Protocol/Internet Protocol. The collective name for the two chief Internet protocols.

Threat. A potential for a security violation. A threat exists when someone discovers a security weakness and attempts to exploit it for harmful purposes.

Time Bomb. A logic bomb triggered at a certain point in time. (See also Logic Bomb, Rogue Software.)

Trapdoor. See Back door.

Trojan horse. Malicious (rogue) software that hides itself in the computer in an attempt to harm. A typical Trojan horse may collect keystrokes and transmit them to its owner who may be looking for passwords and other personal information typed by the user. (See also Rogue Software.)

Trust. The process of determining who gets what permissions and who can perform certain actions on a computer.

Unicode. A new international standard code, the Unicode, has been proposed, and is being developed by the international Unicode organization (`www.unicode.org`). Unicode uses 16-bit codes for its characters, so it provides for $2^{16} = 64K = 65,536$ codes. (Notice that doubling the size of a code much more than doubles the number of possible codes. In fact, it *squares* the number of codes.) Unicode includes all the ASCII codes in addition to codes for characters in foreign languages (including complete sets of Korean, Japanese, and Chinese characters) and many mathematical and other symbols. Currently, about 39,000 out of the 65,536 possible codes have been assigned, so there is room for adding more symbols in the future. (See also ASCII.)

Uninterrupted Power Supply (UPS). A device that "cleans" the power supplied by the power grid. A UPS employs special circuits to suppress power surges and uses a battery to temporarily supply electrical power when the voltage drops.

Unix. A popular multiuser, multitasking operating system that originated at Bell Labs in the late 1960s by a handful of programmers. Unix was originally envisioned as a small, flexible operating system used exclusively by programmers, but has developed over the years in response to changing demands and technological innovations. Today, Unix is the operating system of choice of many unsophisticated computer users.

Uploading. The transfer of data from one's computer. The opposite of downloading. (See also Downloading.)

URL. An acronym for Uniform Resource Locator. A Web address.

User. A person, an organization, or a process that accesses a computer. A user can be authorized or not.

VBS. Acronym for Visual Basic Script. VBS is executable code embedded in an application, document, or a Web page that can run as soon as the page is viewed.

Vernam cipher. Cipher developed for encrypting teletype traffic by computing the exclusive OR of the data bits and the key bits. This is a common approach to constructing stream ciphers. (See One-time pad.)

Virus. Malicious (rogue) software that infects other programs. In practice, viruses tend to harm the computer they are in, and also replicate themselves and send copies outside. (See also Rogue Software.)

Virus identity. A detailed description of virus features used by anti-virus software for virus recognition.

Virus scanner. Anti-virus software. Most scanners are virus-specific, they identify and delete only viruses that are already known. (See also Anti-virus software, Heuristic scanner.)

Vulnerability. A flaw or weakness in the design, implementation, or operation of a piece of hardware or software that could be exploited to violate security.

Vulnerability scanner. A program especially designed to quickly check computers on a network for known weaknesses. A port scanner is a special case. It's a program that attempts to find open ports on a target computer or ports that are available to access the computer. A firewall is a piece of hardware or software that defends computers from intruders by closing off all unused ports.

WAP: Wireless Application Protocol. Internet-type protocol that provides information to mobile telephones.

Web. See World wide web.

Web browser. Client software to access and display the html content of Web sites. The HTTP protocol is used to transfer html documents. (See also Browser.)

Web bug. A small image inserted in an email or Web page that alerts a spammer when a message is read or previewed.

Web server. A computer connected to the Internet that stores a Web site in html format and can make it accessible with the HTTP protocol.

Whitelist. A list of trusted email addresses from which email is accepted without checking it for spam and/or viruses.

Wiretapping. Intercepting data as it moves along a communications channel.

Workstation. A single-user computer, often connected to a network. Nowadays, there is no difference between a workstation and a personal computer, but in the past workstations were more powerful.

World Wide Web. The collection of Web servers all over the world.

Worm. Rogue software that replicates and transmits copies of itself through a network. A worm may damage its host, or is designed to use the host's computing resources for the benefit of its owner. (See also Rogue Software.)

WWW. See World Wide Web.

XOR. See Exclusive OR.

Zombie. A computer that has been hijacked and is under the remote control of a hacker. Zombies are used to send spam or launch a denial of service attack.

Bibliography

3M (2004) is `http://cms.3m.com/cms/US/en/2-68/iclcrFR/view.jhtml`.

absolute (2005) is URL `http://www.absolute.com/public/main/`.

ACA (2005) is URL `http://www.und.nodak.edu/org/crypto/crypto/`.

Aegean Park Press (2001) is URL `http://www.aegeanparkpress.com/`.

AFAC (2005) is URL `http://www-vips.icn.gov.ru/`.

Agrawal, Rakesh, and Ramakrishnan Sirkant (2004) "Privacy-Preserving Data Mining," available from
http://www.almaden.ibm.com/software/quest/Publications/papers/sigmod00˙privacy.pdf.

Akamai (2004) is `www.akamai.com`.

Amiga (2004) is URL `http://www.amiga.org/`.

Anderson, Ross, Roger Needham, and Adi Shamir (1998) "The Steganographic File System," in David Aucsmith (ed.) *Proceedings of the Second Information Hiding Workshop, IWIH*, pp. 73–82, April. Also available from URL
`http://citeseer.nj.nec.com/anderson98steganographic.html`.

anonymizer (2005) is URL `www.anonymizer.com`.

APWG (2004) is `http://www.antiphishing.org/`.

arin (2004) is `http://www.arin.net/whois/`.

Arnold, Michael, Martin Schmucker, and Stephen D. Wolthusen (2003) *Techniques and Applications of Digital Watermarking and Content Protection*, Boston, Artech House.

Asonov, Dmitri and Rakesh Agrawal (2004) "Keyboard Acoustic Emanations," *IEEE Symposium on Security and Privacy*, Oakland, California, pp. 3–11, May. Available at
`http://www.almaden.ibm.com/software/quest/Publications/papers/ssp04.pdf`.

attrition (2004) is URL `http://www.attrition.org/`.

attrition-mirror (2005) is URL `http://www.attrition.org/mirror/attrition/`.

Aura, Tuomas (1996) "Practical Invisibility in Digital Communication," in *Proceedings of the Workshop on Information Hiding*, Cambridge, England, May 1996, pp. 265–278, *Lecture Notes in Computer Science* **1174**, New York, Springer Verlag. Also available from URL `http://www.tcs.hut.fi/Personnel/tuomas.html`.

avenger (2005) is `http://www.research.ibm.com/antivirus/SciPapers/Gordon/Avenger.html`.

badguys (2005) is URL `http://www.badguys.org/`.

Bamford, James (2002) *Body of Secrets: Anatomy of the Ultra-Secret National Security Agency*, New York, Anchor books (Random House).

Barker, Wayne G. (1984) *Cryptanalysis of Shift-Register Generated Stream Cipher Systems*, Laguna Hills, Calif., Aegean Park Press, vol. **C-39**.

Barker, Wayne G. (1989) *Introduction to the Analysis of the Data Encryption Standard (DES)*, Laguna Hills, Calif., Aegean Park Press, vol. **C-55**.

Barker, Wayne G. (1992) *Cryptanalysis of the Single Columnar Transposition Cipher*, Laguna Hills, Calif., Aegean Park Press, vol. **C-59**.

Bauer, Friedrich Ludwig (2002) *Decrypted Secrets: Methods and Maxims of Cryptology* 3rd edition, Berlin, Springer Verlag.

bbbseal (2005) is URL `www.bbbonline.org`.

bbc (2004) is `http://www.bbc.co.uk/dna/h2g2/A787917`.

Bell, D. E., and L. J. LaPadula (1974) "Secure Computer Systems: Mathematical Foundations and Model," Technical report, MITRE.

Blakley, G. R. (1979) "Safeguarding Cryptographic Keys," in *AFIPS Conference Proceedings*, **48**:313–317.

Blowfish (2005) is URL `http://www.schneier.com/blowfish.html`.

Boneh D., and D. Brumley (2004) "Remote Timing Attacks Are Practical," available from `http://crypto.stanford.edu/%7Edabo/abstracts/ssl-timing.html`.

BPCS (2003) is URL `http://www.know.comp.kyutech.ac.jp/BPCSe/` file `BPCSe-principle.html`.

Brenner, Susan W. (2002) "Organized Cybercrime? How Cyberspace May Affect the Structure of Criminal Relationships," *North Carolina Journal of Law and Technology*, **4**(1).

business.com (2004) is `http://www.business.com/directory/computers_and_software/security/hardware/tracking_and_theft_prevention/`.

CA (2004) is `http://www3.ca.com/securityadvisor/virusinfo/default.aspx`.

Calif-gov (2005) "Your Social Security Number: Controlling the Key to Identity Theft," available online at URL `http://www.privacy.ca.gov/sheets/cis4english.htm`.

Campbell, K. W., and M. J. Wiener (1993) "DES Is Not a Group," *Advances in Cryptology, CRYPTO '92*, New York, Springer Verlag, pp. 512–520.

Casanova, Giacomo (1757) *Histoire de Ma Vie*, in 12 volumes. Translated by Willard R. Trask as *The History of My Life*, Baltimore, Johns Hopkins University Press, 1967, reissued 1997.

CDC (2004) is `http://www.cdc.gov/`.

CERT (2004) is URL `http://www.cert.org/other_sources/viruses.html`.

chatdanger (2005) is URL `http://www.safekids.com/chatdanger.htm`.

Chomsky, Noam, and George A. Miller (1958) "Finite State Languages," *Information and Control*, **1**(2)91–112, May.

Code Red II (2001) "Code Red II: Another Worm Exploiting Buffer Overflow In IIS Indexing Service DLL," CERT Incident Note IN-2001-09, Aug. 6. Available online at `http://www.cert.org/incident_notes/IN-2001-09.html`.

Cohen, Fred (1987) "A cryptographic checksum for integrity protection,' *Computers and Security*, **6**(6)505–510, December 1.

Cohen, Frederick B. (1994a) *A Short Course on Computer Viruses*, 2nd edition, New York, NY, John Wiley.

Cohen, Frederick B. (1994b) *It's Alive! The New Breed of Living Computer Programs*, New York, NY, John Wiley.

comscore (2004) is URL `http://www.comscore.com/`.

Conceptlabs (2004) is URL `http://www.conceptlabs.co.uk/alicebob.html`.

cookiecentral (2004) is `http://www.cookiecentral.com/faq/#2.9`.

Coppersmith, Donald, and Philip Rogaway (1994) "A Software-Optimized Encryption Algorithm," *Fast Software Encryption, Cambridge Security Workshop Proceedings*, New York, Springer-Verlag, pp. 56–63.

Coppersmith, Donald, and Philip Rogaway (1995) "Software-Efficient Pseudorandom Function and the Use Thereof for Encryption," United States Patent 5,454,039, 26 September.

corallosoftware (2005) is `http://www.corallosoftware.com/index.html`.

Cox, Ingemar J. (2002) *Digital Watermarking*, San Francisco, Morgan Kaufmann.

Crap (2005) is URL `http://www.mat.dtu.dk/people/Lars.R.Knudsen/crap.html`.

creditexpert (2005) is URL `https://www.creditexpert.com/`.

creditreporting (2005) is URL `http://affiliates.creditreporting.com/`.

Cryptologia (2005) is URL `http://www.dean.usma.edu/math/pubs/cryptologia/`.

Cryptology (2005) is URL `http://link.springer.de/link/service/journals/00145/`.

CSE (2005) is URL `http://www.cse.dnd.ca/`.

csrc (2004) is `http://csrc.nist.gov/CryptoToolkit/tkhash.html`.

CVE (2001) is CVE-2001-0500, *Buffer overflow in ISAPI extension*, available online at `http://cve.mitre.org/cgi-bin/cvename.cgi?name=CVE-2001-0500`.

cyberpatrol (2005) is URL `http://www.cyberpatrol.com/`.

CyberSitter (2005) is URL `http://www.cybersitter.com/`.

cypherpunks (2004) is `ftp://ftp.csua.berkeley.edu/pub/cypherpunks/steganography/`.

Dawkins, Richard (1990) *The Selfish Gene*, 2nd Edition, New York, Oxford University Press.

Day (2004a) is `http://www.csse.uwa.edu.au/~pd/securing_mac_os_x.pdf`.

Day (2004b) is `http://www.csse.uwa.edu.au/~pd/securing_mac_os_x_present.pdf`.

Denning, Peter J. (1990) *Computers Under Attack: Intruders, Worms, and Viruses*, New York, ACM Press and Addison Wesley.

DES2 (1993) is `http://www.itl.nist.gov/fipspubs/fip46-2.htm`.

DES3 (1999) is `csrc.nist.gov/publications/fips/fips46-3/fips46-3.pdf`.

digitalenvoy (2004) is `www.digitalenvoy.net/`.

dodgeit (2004) is `http://www.dodgeit.com/`.

DSD (2005) is URL `http://www.dsd.gov.au/`.

dslreports (2004) is URL `http://www.dslreports.com/scan`.

Duke (2005) is URL `http://www.oit.duke.edu/helpdesk/filesharing/`.

Dunham W. (1990) *Journey Through Genius: The Great Theorems of Mathematics*, New York, John Wiley.

dvdbook (2005) is URL `http://www.dvdforum.org/tech-dvdbook.htm`.

eBates (2005) is URL `https://www.ebates.com/`.

eeggs (2005) is URL `http://www.eeggs.com/`.

EICAR (2004) is URL `http://www.eicar.org/`.

Encyc1 (2004) is `http://www3.ca.com/securityadvisor/virusinfo/browse.aspx`.

Encyc2 (2004) is `http://securityresponse.symantec.com/avcenter/vinfodb.html`.

ensuretech (2004) is URL `http://www.ensuretech.com/`.

equifax (2005) is URL `http://www.equifax.com/`.

Feige, Uriel, Amos Fiat, and Adi Shamir (1988) "Zero Knowledge Proofs of Identity," *Journal of Cryptology*, **1**(2)77–94.

Feistel, Horst (1973) "Cryptography and Computer Privacy," *Scientific American*, **228**(5) 15–23, May.

FIPS-180 (2005) is `http://www.itl.nist.gov/fipspubs/fip180-1.htm`.

FIPS-185 (2005) is `http://www.itl.nist.gov/fipspubs/fip185.htm`.

FIPS-186 (2005) is `http://www.itl.nist.gov/fipspubs/fip186.htm`.

Flannery, Sarah, and David Flannery (2001) *In Code: A Mathematical Journey*, Workman Publishing Company.

FreeBSD Words (2005) is URL `ftp://www.freebsd.org/usr/share/dict/words`.

freedom (2005) is URL `www.freedom.net`.

Friedman, William F. (1996) *The Index of Coincidence and Its Applications in Cryptanalysis*, Laguna Hills, Calif., Aegean Park Press, vol. **C-49**.

f-secure (2005) is URL `http://www.f-secure.com/`.

ftc (2004) is URL `http://www.ftc.gov/opa/2003/09/idtheft.htm`.

FTC-CONT (2005) is URL `www.ftc.gov/bcp/conline/pubs/online/sitesee.html`.

FTC-infosecurity (2005) is URL
`http://www.ftc.gov/bcp/conline/edcams/infosecurity/index.html`.

FTC-privacy (2005) is `http://www.ftc.gov/privacy/index.html`.

FTC-work (2005) is `http://www.ftc.gov/bcp/workshops/spyware/index.htm`.

fundrace (2005) is URL `http://fundrace.org/citymap.php`.

Gaines, Helen Fouché (1956) *Cryptanalysis: A Study of Ciphers and Their Solutions*, New York, Dover.

Garfinkel, Simson (1995) *PGP: Pretty Good Privacy*, Sebastopol, Calif., O'Reilly.

GCHQ (2003) is URL `http://www.gchq.gov.uk/`.

gemplus (2005) is URL `http://www.gemplus.com/`.

Gerrold, David (1988) *When HARLIE Was One*, Bantam Spectra (Random House), Updated edition.

getnetwise (2005) is URL `www.getnetwise.org/`.

getnetwise-ctrct (2005) is URL `www.getnetwise.org/tools/toolscontracts.php`.

GnuPG (2004) is `http://www.gnupg.org/`.

Golomb, Solomon W. (1982) *Shift Register Sequences*, 2nd edition, Laguna Hills, Calif., Aegean Park Press.

Google (2005) is URL `desktop.google.com`.

Gordon, Sarah (2005) "Virus Writers: The End of The Innocence?" available at URL `http://www.research.ibm.com/antivirus/SciPapers/VB2000SG.htm`.

Grampp, F. T., and R. H. Morris (1984) "UNIX Operating System Security," *Bell Laboratories Technical Journal*, **63**(8)1649–1672, October.

gregorybraun (2005) is URL `http://www.gregorybraun.com/PassKeep.html`.

Guillou, Louis, and Jean-Jacques Quisquater (1988) "A Practical Zero-Knowledge Protocol Fitted to Security Microprocessors Minimizing Both Transmission and Memory," in *Advances in Cryptology, Eurocrypt '88 Proceedings*, pp. 123–128, Berlin, Springer-Verlag.

Guinness (2004) is `www.guinnessworldrecords.com/`.

Gutenberg (2005) is URL `http://www.gutenberg.net/`.

Guthke, Karl S. and Robert C. Sprung (1991) *Traven: The Life Behind the Legends*, Chicago, IL, Lawrence Hill Books.

Harley, David, Robert Slade, and Urs Gattiker (2001) *Viruses Revealed*, Berkeley, CA, Osborne/McGraw-Hill.

HastaLaVista (2004) is `http://www.hastalavista.com` (but don't use it, even at your own risk).

Hinsley, F. H., and Alan Stripp (eds.) (1992) *The Codebreakers: The Inside Story of Bletchley Park*, Oxford, Oxford University Press.

homograph (2005) is the PDF document at `http://www.cs.technion.ac.il/~gabr/papers/homograph_full.pdf`.

honker (2004) is URL `http://www.cnhonker.com/`.

House (2004) "Spyware: what you don't know can hurt you." Hearing before the subcommittee on commerce, trade, and consumer protection, April 29, 2004, serial no. 108-89. Available at `http://www.access.gpo.gov/congress/house/house05ch108.html`.

Hydan (2005) is URL `http://www.crazyboy.com/hydan/`.

IANA port (2004) is URL `http://www.iana.org/assignments/port-numbers`.

IbmAntiVirus (2005) `http://www.research.ibm.com/antivirus/`.

idtheftcenter (2004) is `http://www.idtheftcenter.org/index.shtml`.

IIS (2004) is `www.microsoft.com/iis`.

Information Week (2004) is URL `http://www.informationweek.com/story/showArticle.jhtml?articleID=52601698`.

insecure (2004) is URL `http://www.insecure.org/nmap/`.

intelius (2005) is URL `http://find.intelius.com/`.

IOCCC (2004) is `http://www.ioccc.org/`.

iridiantech (2005) is URL `http://www.iridiantech.com/`.

ISIS (2005) `http://www.imrg.org/8025696F004581B3/pages/imrg+Resources`.

ISS (2005) is URL `www.iss.net`.

ITU (2005) is URL `http://www.itu.int/home/index.html`.

Jack Moratis (2004) is `http://home.comcast.net/~educbc5454/software.html`.

Jargon (2004) is URL `http://www.catb.org/~esr/jargon/`.

Johnson, Neil F., et al. (2001) *Information Hiding: Steganography and Watermarking—Attacks and Countermeasures, Advances in Information Security*, volume 1, Boston, Kluwer Academic.

junkbusters declare (2005) is URL `http://www.junkbusters.com/declare.html`.

Kahn, David (1996) *The Codebreakers: The Comprehensive History of Secret Communications from Ancient Times to the Internet*, revised edition, New York, Scribner.

Katzenbeisser, Stefan, and Fabien A. P. Petitcolas (eds.) (2000) *Information Hiding Techniques for Steganography and Digital Watermarking*, Norwood, Mass., Artech House.

Kerckhoffs, Auguste (1883) "La Cryptographie Militaire," *Journal des Sciences Militaires*, **9**:5–38, 161–191, January–February. Also available in html format from URL `http://www.petitcolas.net/fabien/kerckhoffs/la_cryptographie_militaire_i.htm`.

Knowspam (2004) is URL `http://www.Knowspam.net/`.

knowyourloanrate (2005) is URL `https://www.knowyourloanrate.com/`.

Knuth, Donald E. (1984) *The TEXBook*, Reading, Mass., Addison-Wesley.

Konheim, Alan G. (1981) *Cryptography: A Primer*, New York, John Wiley and Sons.

Kuhn (2004) is URL `http://www.cl.cam.ac.uk/TechReports/UCAM-CL-TR-577.pdf`.

Larson, P. Å., and A. Kajla (1984) "Implementation of a Method Guaranteeing Retrieval in One Access," *Communications of the ACM*, **27**(7)670–677, July.

Lavasoft (2004) is `http://www.lavasoftusa.com/` or `http://www.lavasoft.de/`.

Levy, Steven (2002) *Crypto: How the Code Rebels Beat the Government Saving Privacy in the Digital Age*, Penguin Putnam.

Mailblocks (2004) is URL `http://www.Mailblocks.com`.

MailFrontier (2004) is URL `http://www.MailFrontier.com/`.

mailinator (2004) is URL `http://www.mailinator.net/mailinator/Welcome.do`.

Maiwald, Eric and William Sieglein (2002) *Security Planning and Disaster Recovery*, Berkeley, CA, Osborne/McGraw-Hill.

maporama (2004) is `http://www.maporama.com/share/`.

mapquest (2004) is `http://www.mapquest.com/maps/latlong.adp`.

MathWorld (2005) is html file `Gram-SchmidtOrthonormalization.html` in URL `http://mathworld.wolfram.com/`.

McAfee (2004) is URL `http://www.mcafee.com/us/`.

McDonald, Andrew D., and Markus G. Kuhn (1999) "StegFS: A Steganographic File System for Linux," in *Proceedings of Information Hiding*, New York, Springer-Verlag, LNCS **1768**, pp. 463–477. Also available from `http://www.mcdonald.org.uk/StegFS/`.

MD5 (2004) is `ftp://ftp.umbc.edu/pub/unix/rfc/rfc1321.txt.gz`.

melissavirus (2005) is URL `www.melissavirus.com/`.

Merkle, R. C., and M. Hellman (1981) "On the Security of Multiple Encryption," *Communications of the ACM*, **24**(7)465–467.

missingkids (2005) is URL `http://www.missingkids.com/`.

Mitnick, Kevin D. and William Simon (2002) *The Art of Deception: Controlling the Human Element of Security*, New York, John Wiley.

Moore, Dan Tyler and Martha Waller (1965) *Cloak and Cipher*, Indianapolis, IN, Bobbs-Merrill, 1962; London, Harrap.

MS04-028 (2004) is `http://www.microsoft.com/technet/security/bulletin/MS04-028.mspx`.

MSoffice (2005) is URL `http://office.microsoft.com/en-us/officeupdate/`.

MSsecurity (2005) is URL `http://www.microsoft.com/security/`.

MStechnet (2005) is URL `http://www.microsoft.com/technet/security/`.

MTX (2005) is URL `http://www.f-secure.com/v-descs/mtx.shtml`.

NCM (2005) is URL `http://www.nsa.gov/museum/`.

netnanny (2005) is URL `http://www.netnanny.com/`.

Network solutions (2004) is URL `http://www.networksolutions.com/en_US/whois/index.jhtml`.

networkusa (2005) is URL `http://www.networkusa.org/fingerprint.shtml`.

Newton, David E. (1997) *Encyclopedia of Cryptology*, Santa Barbara, Calif., ABC-Clio.

Nicetext (2005) is URL `http://www.nicetext.com/`.

NIST (1992) "The Digital Signature Standard, proposal and discussion," *Communications of the ACM*, **35**(7):36–54.

NIST (2004) is URL `http://csrc.nist.gov/virus/`.

NIST Handbook (2004) is available at `csrc.nist.gov/publications/nistpubs/800-12/handbook.pdf`.

NISTunits (2004) is `http://physics.nist.gov/cuu/Units/binary.html`.

NSA (2004) is `http://www.nsa.gov/`.

NSA-SEC (2005) is URL `http://www.nsa.gov/snac/`.

NSA-venona (2004) is `http://www.nsa.gov/venona/`.

onion-router (2005) is URL `http://www.onion-router.net/`.

OpenPGP (2005) is `http://www.openpgp.org/`.

opensecrets (2005) is URL `http://www.opensecrets.org/indivs/`.

OpenSSL (2004) is the OpenSSL project, located at `http://www.openssl.org`.

Orebaugh, Angela D. and Gilbert Ramirez (2004) *Ethereal Packet Sniffing*, Rockland, Mass., Syngress.

packet-sniffing (2004) is URL `http://www.packet-sniffing.com/`.

pchell (2005) is URL `http://www.pchell.com/virus/mtx.shtml`.

PCPhoneHome (2004) is `http://www.pcphonehome.com/`.

performics (2005) is `http://www.performics.com/about/press/code_of_conduct.pdf`.

Petitcolas (2003) is URL `http://www.petitcolas.net/fabien/steganography/bibliography/`.

Pfitzmann, B. (1996) "Information Hiding Terminology," in *Information Hiding*, New York, Springer *Lecture Notes in Computer Science*, **1174**:347–350.

ping (2004) is URL `http://ftp.arl.mil/~mike/ping.html`.

PKCS (2004) is `http://www.rsasecurity.com/rsalabs/node.asp?id=2124`.

Pohlmann, Ken (1992) *The Compact Disc Handbook*, 2nd edition, Middleton, Wisconsin, A-R Editions.

privacyalliance (2005) is URL `http://www.privacyalliance.org/`.

privacyrights (2005) is URL `http://www.privacyrights.org/fs/fs21-children.htm`.

protectkids (2005) is URL `http://www.protectkids.com/`.

purityscan (2005) is URL `http://www.purityscan.com/`.

qspace (2005) is URL `http://qspace.iplace.com/`.

Quova (2004) is `www.quova.com/`.

Raymond (2004) is URL `http://www.catb.org/~esr/faqs/`.

Reiter, Michael K. and Aviel D. Rubin (1998) "Crowds: Anonymity for Web Transactions," *ACM Transactions on Information and System Security*, **1**(1)66–92 remotelyanywhere (2004) is URL `http://www.remotelyanywhere.com/`.

Rescorla, Eric (2000) *SSL and TLS: Designing and Building Secure Systems*, Reading, Mass., Addison Wesley.

RFC-862 (2004) is at URL `www.faqs.org/rfcs/rfc862.html`.

RFC-864 (2004) is at URL `www.faqs.org/rfcs/rfc864.html`.

rfc1321 (2005) is URL `http://www.ietf.org/rfc/rfc1321.txt`.

RFC-1738 (2004) is at URL `www.faqs.org/rfcs/rfc1738.html`.

RIAA (2005) is URL `http://www.riaa.com/about/members/`.

Ritter (2005) is URL `http://www.ciphersbyritter.com/ARTS/PRACTLAT.HTM`.

Ritter, Terry (1990) "Substitution Cipher with Pseudo-Random Shuffling: The Dynamic Substitution Combiner," *Cryptologia* **14**(4)289–303. An updated version is available at `http://www.ciphersbyritter.com/DYNSUB.HTM`.

Rivest, R. (1991) "The MD4 Message Digest Algorithm," in Menezes, A. J., and S. A. Vanstone, (eds.), *Advances in Cryptology: CRYPTO '90 Proceedings*, pp. 303–311, New York, Springer-Verlag.

Rivest, R. (1992) "The MD4 Message Digest Algorithm," RFC 1320, MIT and RSA Data Security, Inc., April.

Rochlis, J., and M. Eichin (1989) "With Microscope and Tweezers: The Worm from MIT's Perspective," *Communications of the ACM*, **32**(6):689–698, June.

Roman, Steven (1999) *Writing Word Macros*, Sebastopol, CA, O'Reilly Assoc.

Rosenberger (2005) is URL `http://www.vmyths.com/fas/fas1.cfm`.

RSA (2001) is URL `http://www.rsasecurity.com/rsalabs/challenges/factoring/` file `faq.html`.

RSA-MD4 (2005) is `http://www.rsasecurity.com/rsalabs/node.asp?id=2253`.

RSASecurID (2004) is `http://www.rsasecurity.com/node.asp?id=1157`.

RSAsecurity (2004) is URL `http://www.rsasecurity.com/`.

safekids (2005) is URL `http://www.safekids.com/`.

SaftLite (2005) is available at `http://haoli.dnsalias.com/shared/saft_lite.hqx`.

Salomon, David (2003) *Data Privacy and Security*, New York, Springer Verlag.

Salomon, David (2004) *Data Compression: The Complete Reference*, 3rd edition, New York, Springer Verlag.

Salomon, David (2005) *Coding for Data and Computer Communications*, New York, Springer Verlag.

Savard (2005) is URL `http://home.ecn.ab.ca/~jsavard/crypto/jscrypt.htm`.

scc-inc (2004) is `http://www.scc-inc.com/SccVsLexmark/`.

Schneier, Bruce (1993) "Fast Software Encryption," in *Cambridge Security Workshop Proceedings*, pp. 191–204. New York, Springer-Verlag. Also available from `http://www.counterpane.com/bfsverlag.html`.

Schneier, Bruce (1995) *Applied Cryptography: Protocols, Algorithms, and Source Code in C*, 2nd edition, New York, John Wiley.

Schneier, Bruce (2003) is URL `http://www.counterpane.com/crypto-gram.html`.

Schneier, Bruce (2004) *Secrets and Lies: Digital Security in a Networked World*, Hoboken, NJ, John Wiley & Sons.

Schnorr, Claus Peter (1991) "Efficient Signature Generation for Smart Cards," *Journal of Cryptology*, **4**(3)161–174.

Schotti, Gaspari (1665) *Schola Steganographica*, Jobus Hertz, printer. Some page photos from this old book are available at URL
`http://www.cl.cam.ac.uk/~fapp2/steganography/steganographica/index.html`.

SearchAndDestroy (2004) is URL `http://www.SearchAndDestroy.com/`.

secunia (2004) is `http://secunia.com/`.

send-safe (2005) is URL `http://www.send-safe.com`.

Shamir, Adi (1979) "How to Share a Secret," *Communications of the ACM*, **22**(11)612–613, November.

Shamir, Adi and Eran Tromer (2004) "Acoustic cryptanalysis," available online in html format at URL `http://www.wisdom.weizmann.ac.il/~tromer/acoustic/`.

Shannon, Claude E. (1949) "Communication Theory of Secrecy Systems," *Bell System Technical Journal*, **28**:656–715, October.

Shannon, Claude E. (1951) "Prediction and Entropy of Printed English," *Bell System Technical Journal*, **30**:50–64, January.

Shoch, John and Jon Hupp (1982) "The Worm Programs—Early Experience With a Distributed Computation," *Communications of the ACM*, **25**(3)172–180. Reprinted in [Denning 90].

Simovits, Mikael J. (1996) *The DES, an Extensive Documentation and Evaluation*, Laguna Hills, Calif., Aegean Park Press, vol. **C-68**.

Singh, Simon (1999) *The Code Book*, New York, Doubleday.

Sinkov, A. (1980) *Elementary Cryptanalysis: A Mathematical Approach* (New Mathematical Library, No. 22), Washington, D.C., Mathematical Assn. of America.

smartcardalliance (2005) is
`http://www.smartcardalliance.org/industry_info/index.cfm`.

Skoudis (2005) is `http://infosecuritymag.com/skoudis`

snapfiles (2004) is URL `http://www.snapfiles.com/`.

sophos (2005) is URL `www.sophos.com/virusinfo/hoaxes`.

Sorkin, Arthur (1984) "Lucifer, A Cryptographic Algorithm," *Cryptologia*, **8**(1):22–41, January. An addendum is in **8**(3)260–261.

spam (2004) is URL `http://media.hormel.com/templates/knowledge/knowledge.asp?catitemid=14&id=94`.

spam abuse (2004) is URL `http://spam.abuse.net/others/sites.shtml`.

SpamArrest (2004) is URL `http://www.SpamArrest.com`.

spambob (2004) is `http://spambob.com/`.

spamcop (2005) is URL `http://www.spamcop.com/`.

spamgourmet (2004) is `http://www.spamgourmet.com/`.

Spamhaus (2005) is URL `http://www.spamhaus.org/`.

spamhauslasso (2005) is `http://www.spamhaus.org/statistics.lasso`.

SpectorSoft (2004) is `http://www.SpectorSoft.com/`.

Spybot (2004) is `http://www.spybot.info/en/index.html`.

Spy Sweeper (2005) is URL `http://www.webroot.com/`.

spywareguide (2004) is URL `http://www.spywareguide.com/`.

spywareguide-country (2004) is URL `http://www.spywareguide.com/articles/country_code_extensions_look_u_45.html`.

spywareinfo (2004) is URL `http://www.spywareinfo.com/`.

ssa-gov (2004) is URL `https://s044a90.ssa.gov/apps6/isss/bp-7004home.jsp`.

ssa-form (2004) is `http://www.ssa.gov/online/ssa-7004.pdf`.

ssa-stat (2005) is URL `https://s044a90.ssa.gov/apps6a/isss/main.html`.

Stallings, William (1998) *Cryptography and Network Security: Principles and Practice*, Englewood Cliffs, N.J., Prentice-Hall.

Staniford, Stuart, Vern Paxson, and Nicholas Weaver (2002) "How to 0wn the Internet in Your Spare Time," *Proceedings of the 11th USENIX Security Symposium (Security '02)*. Available online at `http://www.icir.org/vern/papers/cdc-usenix-sec02/index.html`.

Steganosaurus (2004) is URL `http://www.fourmilab.to/stego/`.

Stego (2005) is URL `http://www.stego.com/`.

Stoll, Clifford (1988) "Stalking the Wily Hacker," *Communications of the ACM*, **31**(5) 484–497, May.

Stoll, Clifford (1990) *The Cuckoo's Egg*, Bodley Head.

Stoll, Clifford (2004) `http://www.ocf.berkeley.edu/~stoll/`.

storagereview (2000) is URL
`http://www.storagereview.com/guide2000/ref/hdd/index.html`.

Strunk, William Jr. (1918) *The Elements of Style*, Ithaca, NY, W. P. Humphrey, (also NY, Bartleby.com 1999).

sweetcocoa (2005) is URL `http://homepage.mac.com/sweetcocoa/lapcop/`.

Symantec (2004) is URL `http://www.symantec.com/index.htm`.

takedown (2004) is URL `http://www.takedown.com/`.

technet (2004) is `http://www.microsoft.com/technet/archive/community/columns/security/essays/10imlaws.mspx`.

theinquirer (2004) is UTL `http://www.theinquirer.net/?article=19159`.

Thomas, Steven A. (2000) *SSL and TLS Essentials: Securing the Web*, New York, John Wiley.

Thompson, Ken (1984) "Reflections on Trusting Trust," *Communications Of The ACM*, **27**(8)172–180.

TransUnion (2005) is URL `https://www.freecreditprofile.com/`.

Trithemius, Johannes (1606) *Steganographia*. Available (for private use only) from URL `http://www.esotericarchives.com/tritheim/stegano.htm`.

truste (2005) is URL `http://www.truste.org/`.

Unicode (2005) is URL `http://www.unicode.org`.

Unicode Standard (1996) *The Unicode Standard*, Version 2.0, Reading, Mass., Addison-Wesley.

van Eck, Wim (1985) "Electromagnetic Radiation from Video Display Units: An Eavesdropping Risk," *Computers and Security*, 4:269–286.

Verisign (2004) is `http://www.verisign.com/products-services/security-services/pki/unified-authentication/`.

versiontracker (2005) is URL `http://www.versiontracker.org/`.

Virus bulletin (2005) *Virus Bulletin: The International Publication on Computer Virus Prevention, Recognition, and Removal*. Available online at `http://www.virusbtn.com/magazine/`.

vmyths (2005) is URL `http://www.vmyths.com/`.

vote-smart (2005) is `http://www.vote-smart.org/pdf/vsdm2004/vsdm-2004.pdf`.

WatermarkingWorld (2005) is located at URL `http://www.watermarkingworld.org/`.

Wayner, Peter (1992) "Mimic Functions," *Cryptologia*, **XVI**(3)193–214, July.

Wayner, Peter (2002) *Disappearing Cryptography*, 2nd edition, London, Academic Press.

Webopedia (2004) is URL `http://www.webopedia.com/`.

webroot (2004) is URL `http://www.webroot.com/`.

Western digital (2004) is URL
`http://www.wdc.com/en/products/Products.asp?DriveID=35`.

Wild List (2004) is URL `http://www.wildlist.org/`.

Witten, Ian H. (1987) "Computer (In)security: Infiltrating Open Systems," *ABACUS*, **4**(4)7–25. Also available from `http://cryptome.org/compinsec.htm` and in [Denning 90].

Wright, Peter (1989) *Spycatcher: The Candid Autobiography of a Senior Intelligence Officer*, New York, Random House.

Wyatt, Allen (2004) *Cleaning Windows XP for Dummies*, New York, John Wiley.

Zalewski, Michal (2005) *Silence on the Wire: A Field Guide to Passive Reconnaissance and Indirect Attacks*, San Francisco, CA, No Starch Press.

Zimmermann, Philip (1995) *PGP Source Code and Internals*, Cambridge, Mass., MIT Press.

Zimmermann, Philip (2001) is `http://www.philzimmermann.com/`.

> When you re-read a classic you do not see in the book more than
> you did before. You see more in you than there was before.
> —Clifton Fadiman

Index

This long index reflects this author's belief that a detailed index is invaluable in a scientific/technical book. A special effort was made to include full names (first and middle names instead of initials) and dates of persons mentioned in the book. Any mistakes, inaccuracies, and omissions found in the index and reported to the author will be included in the errata list and corrected in any future editions of the book.

$\mathcal{Z}_N$, 277

A Clockwork Orange (novel), 285
absolutely secure ciphers, 269–270
acoustic keyboard eavesdropping, xii, 18–19
activity monitor (and viruses), 82, 316
activity monitor (anti-virus software), xvii, 150–152, 318
Ad-Aware (anti-spyware software), 221
Adams, Douglas (1952–2001), xxi
add-on virus, 54
Adleman, Leonard M. (1945–), 274
Advanced Encryption Standard (AES), 327, 329
adware, xviii, 211, 215, 225
 and children, 256
 definition of, 225
 spyware, xviii, 227–228
AES, *see* advanced encryption standard
affiliate network, 217, 218
Agrawal, Rakesh, 30
Amiga (vulnerability to viruses), 66
Ampere (electrical current), 322
Anna Kournikova worm, 297, 299
anonymizer.com (useful internet service), 235, 252

anonymizers, 252–253
anonymous proxy server, 216, 236
anti-phishing working group, *see* APWG
anti-spyware software, 220
anti-virus software, xvii, 145–155, 302, 305
 activity monitor, 150–152
 and polymorphic engines, 40
 as preventive measure, 154
 behavior blocker, 146
 behavior checkers, 150–152
 BSI, 50
 checks CRC, 79
 compressed files, 145, 150
 decompress .com files, 133
 defeated by stealth, 84
 disassembled, 79
 disinfecting, 150
 file size modified, 79
 firewall, 154
 fooled, 77
 generic, 150–152
 integrity checker, 146
 modified file size, 77
 MTX malware, 135
 mutating viruses, 80
 not transparent, 147

preventive techniques, 152–155

scanner, 341

specific, 73

tail chasing, 82

updates, 9, 140

virus signatures, 333

virus specific, 148–150

antibody, 73–74, 318

antiphishing toolbars, 242

Apple virus, 289

APWG (anti-phishing working group), 242

Aristotle (384–322 B.C., no hacker), ix

arithmetic and logic unit (ALU), 85

ASCII (character code), 327, 340

Asonov, Dmitri, 19, 284

attachments to email, 44, 45, 66, 82, 144, 153, 204, 306

identity theft, 206

keystroke loggers, 221

macro, 129, 295

MTX, 135

SirCAM, 128

spyware, 233

attack (on encrypted or hidden data), 328

audit

anti-virus tool, 132, 142

network traffic control, 110, 187

authentication, xviii, 189–209, 319, 328

biometrics, xviii, 189–196, 310

consumer, 189, 243

passwords, 196–206

author's email address, xviii

Back, Adam, 276

backdoor, xi

code red II, 94

definition of, 34, 328

in a campus, 208

in literature, 220

in MTX, 135

in spyware, 220

into an organization, 208

opener virus, 134

backup (files), xvii, 67, 68, 82, 116, 143, 154, 155, 305, 307

bacterium (computer virus), 328

Baez, Joan Chandos (1941–), 80

Baggins, Frodo, 291

bagle worm, 301, 302

Banks, Iain Menzies (1954–), 285

Barry, Dave, 306

basic input/output system, see BIOS

Bates, Jim, 107

baza virus, see boza virus

bcc field in email, 180

behavior blocker (anti-virus software), 146

behavior checker (anti-virus software), 150–152

Bell-LaPadula model, 70–72

Berger, John, 24

Bertillon, Alphonse (1853–1914), 190

biometric authentication, xviii, 189–196, 310, 328

BIOS (basic input/output system), 47, 76

bitrate (definition of), 329

Blair, Eric Arthur (George Orwell, 1903–1950), 285

Blaster worm, 300

boot sector infector, see BSI

boot sector viruses, 46–51, 76–77

booting a computer, 34, 49, 57, 86, 88, 127, 154, 316, 329

bootstrap loader, 49–50, 64, 338

bouncing ball virus, see ping-pong virus

boza virus, 293

brain virus, 36, 51, 126–127, 289

detection of, 290

break interrupt, 86, 151, 318

Britney Spears worm, 299

Brunner, John, 91, 289

BSI (boot sector infector), 46–51, 76–77

buffer overflow, see buffer overrun (security weakness)

buffer overflow vulnerability, 61, 302, 329

buffer overrun (security weakness), 60–62, 93, 108, 329

Bugbear worm, 220, 299

bugging a compiler, xvii, 117–124

BugMeNot.com (useful internet service), 235

Buonarroti, Miguel Angel (Michelangelo 1475–1564), 127

Burch, Frank (and iris scan), 193

Burger virus, 290

Burgess, Anthony (John Anthony Burgess Wilson, 1917–1993), 285

cabir worm, 303

Caesar cipher, 329

Campbell, Robert, 143

Carter, David L., 294

Carter, James, 320

Carvalho, David Nunes (1848–1925), 209

Casanova, Giacomo Girolamo (1725–1798), 48

cascade virus, 291

Catlett, Jason, 249

CCS (cryptographic checksum), 159

cell telephone security threats, 302–303, 314

chain letters, 161–162

Chargen (and DoS), 182

Chernobyl virus, *see* CIH virus

children's online privacy, 253–258, 310

Chinese remainder theorem, 277

Christmas card virus, 131–132, 142

CIH virus, 53, 294

ciphers
  absolutely secure, 269–270
  knock, 267
  monoalphabetic substitution, 265–267, 335
  nihilistic, 267
  one-time pad, 269–270, 336
  polyalphabetic substitution, 268, 275, 337
  Polybius monoalphabetic, 265–267
  Polybius polyalphabetic, 268
  public-key, 273–274, 338
  RSA, 274–278
  Vernam, 269, 341

Clancy, Thomas Leo Jr. (1947–), 229

classification of viruses, 46–48

click of allegiance, 217, 223, 229

code red I worm, 93–94, 298

code red II worm, 94

Cohen, Fred (origins of virus), 37, 289

Commanger, Henry Steele (1902–1998), 2

companion virus, 38, 46, 55–56, 330

compiler (rigging or bugging), xvii, 117–124

computer crime, vii

computer emergency response team (CERT), 11

computer incident advisory capability (CIAC), 11

computer operations, audit, and security technology (COAST), 11

computer security, 339

computer security (laws of), 5–10, 262, 305–306, 322

Concept virus, 293

concluding remarks, 305–310

continuous-tone image, 334

cookies (Internet), 238–239
  anonymizing, 253

coregistration (email addresses), 173–174

Cornwall, Hugo, 238

Counterpane Internet Security, 11

covert channels, 70, 72–73

CRC (cyclic redundancy code), 79, 159, 333

credit and bank monitoring services, 241–242

Crichton, Michael (1942–), 220

cruncher virus, 79, 133, 146

cryptanalysis (definition of), 330

cryptanalyst (definition of), 330

cryptographer (definition of), 330

cryptographic checksum, *see* CCS

cryptography, 263–284
  definition of, 330
  Diffie–Hellman–Merkle key exchange, 272–273
  public-key, 273–274, 338
  rules of, 8, 265, 267, 270, 271, 334

cryptology (definition of), 330

cyclic redundancy code, *see* CRC

daemon (a background process), 108, 331

DAME, *see* polymorphic engine

Dark Avenger.1800 virus, 291, 324

data diddling, 67, 68, 72, 291, 315, 331

data encryption standard (DES), 329, 331

data wiping, 237

Daugman, John, 193

Day, Paul, 28

DDoS (distributed denial of service), 177, 217, 218

de Hoffman, Frederick, 202

Dean, Howard, 320

defacing web sites, 168, 206–208

degaussing, 237

denial of service, *see* DoS

dictionary attack (password cracking), 199–201

Diffie, Bailey Whitfield (1944–), 272–274

Diffie–Hellman–Merkle key exchange, 272–273, 331

digest (of a message), 280

digital signature, 80, 280, 281

digrams, 286, 287, 331

Dijkstra, Edsger Wybe (1930–2002), 311

direct mail sender (spamware), 170

direct memory access (DMA), 87

disassembler, 106

   definition of, 148

disassembling

   a program, 106, 117

   a virus, 47, 148–149

   a worm, 103, 106

   anti-virus software, 79

   rogue software, 105

disaster recovery planning, 23, 28–29

disinfecting files, 150

disk directory, 35

   and boot sector, 48

   and brain virus, 126

   damaged, 116

   modified by viruses, 50, 53, 78

   search rules, 55

disposable email address (DEA), 29

DNS

   attacked, 177–178

   poisoning, 167–168, 206

domain name server, see DNS

DoS (denial of service), viii, xviii, 2, 67, 68, 177, 181–184, 186, 296, 298

   blaster, 300

   MIM attack, 167

   mydoom, 301

   stone age, 7

drive-by download, 219, 221, 233

dual-infection virus, see multipartite virus

dumpster diving, xii, 24, 205, 332

Dunaway, Sean, 179

duts virus, 303

DVD (digital versatile disc), 332

easter eggs (surprise software), 74

eavesdropping spying, xii

Echo (and DoS), 182

Egan, Greg, 303

Elk Cloner virus, 289

Ellis, James H., British cryptographer (1924–1997), 275

email address of author, xviii

email attachments (and malware), 44, 45, 66, 82, 144, 153, 204, 306

   identity theft, 206

keystroke loggers, 221

   macro, 129, 295

   MTX, 135

   SirCAM, 128

   spyware, 233

email obfuscation, 174

embedded computers (no security problems), 311

encryption

   one-way, 197–198

   reasons for, 10

entry point obscuring, see EPO

Enzer, Matisse J., 342

EPO (entry point obscuring), 53

   in MTX, 135

error-control codes, 25, 157–158

ethernet, 332

ethical issues, 172, 194, 249

EULA (end user license agreement), see software license

examples of malware, xvii, 125–137

exclusive OR (XOR), 316, 332, 342

exploit, xii, 332

extension of a file name (as a security measure), 154

face recognition (biometric authentication), 194

Fadiman, Clifton, 356

femto (definition of), 323

Feynman, Richard Phillips (1918–1988), 202

file infector viruses, 51–55, 77–83, 332, 336, 337

file permission in Unix, 69

finger (UNIX utility), 91, 108, 290

fingerprints (biometric authentication), 191–192

firewalls, 164, 184–187, 220, 223, 235, 306

   as preventive measure, 154

flip virus, 291, 292

flip-2343 virus, 291

Franklin, Benjamin (1706–1790), 8, 111

free gifts, 174, 250

Friday the 13th (origins of), 290

Frodo lives virus, 291

Gabrilovich, Evgeniy, 245

Galilei, Galileo (1564–1642, a hacker?), ix

Garbo, Greta (Greta Lovisa Gustafsson 1905–1990), 248
Gauss's theorem, 277
Gauss, Karl Friedrich (1777–1855), 237
general application virus, 47
geolocation, 248–249
Gerrold, David, 37
giga (definition of), 266, 333
glass eye, 193, 319
Gontmakherm, Alex, 245
good time virus, 161
google desktop search, 226
Gordon, Sarah (virus researcher), 40, 292
Grampp, F. T., 200
Grant, David, 30
grayscale image, 334
GT-Spoof virus, 161
Guzman, Onel de (LoveLetter writer?), 41

hacker, ix–xiv
hackers tools
    dumpster diving, xii
    eavesdropping spying, xii
    exploit, xii, 332
    optical spying, xii
    root kit, xiii, 338
    scavenging, xii
    shoulder spying, xii
    side-channel attacks, xii
    sniffer, xii, 339
    social engineering, xii, 339
    Trojan horse, xi, 340
    virus, xi, 341
    vulnerability scanner, xii, 341
    worm, xi, 342
hacktivist, xi
halon (fire extinguisher gas), 20
Hardy, Thomas (1840–1928), 293
Harley, David, 3
harvesting email addresses, 174
hashing (MD5), 280
Havel, Václav (1936–), 285
Heinlein, Robert Anson (1907–1988), 23
Hellman, Martin E. (1945–), 272
hiding methods for viruses, 76–80
hoaxes, xvii, 160–162, 294
    Clinton, 294
    Clipper, 294
    Gingrich, 294

good times, 292
    Lecture, 294
    SPA, 294
Homer (Ομηρος, Greek poet), 113
homograph threat, 245–246
honeypot, xiii
hooks, see interrupts (and viruses)
Howard, Jane, 187
Hughes, Howard Robard (1905–1976), 9

I/O interrupt, 86
Ibragimov, Ruslan, 170
ICMP (Internet control message protocol), 183
IDEA (block cipher), 329
identity theft, xviii, 3, 9, 214, 231–246
iframe security flaw, ix, 61–62
ILOVEYOU virus, see love bug virus
image
    continuous-tone, 334
    grayscale, 334
infomediaries, 252–253
Ing-hau Chen (CIH virus creator), 294
integrity checker (anti-virus software), 146
intelligence
    artificial, 4, 61, 194, 257, 260
    artificial (lack of), 5
    human, 153
    military, 15
    natural, 19, 203, 336
international standards organization, see ISO
Internet control message protocol, see ICMP
Internet research provider (IRP), 227
Internet worm, xvii, 36, 69, 73, 91, 108–111, 142, 200, 290
interrupts, 35
    activity monitor, 151, 318
    and viruses, 44, 46–48, 54, 64, 83–88
    break, 86, 151, 318
    I/O, 86
    invalid instruction, 52, 86
    memory protection violation, 85
    timer, 35, 86
interstitials (ads), 225
intrusive virus, 46, 54
invalid instruction interrupt, 86
iris scan (biometric authentication), 192–193
ISO, 334

ISO 7816 smart card standard, 195
Italian virus, *see* ping-pong virus
ITU, 334

Java applets (and Trojans), 118
Jaynes, Jeremy, 178
Jennifer Lopez worm, 299
Jerusalem virus, 290
JFIF, 334
Jiang, Juju, 233
Johnson, Lyndon Baines (1908–1973), 262
jokes, xiv, xvi, 13, 35, 42, 114, 127, 241, 246, 260, 309
JPEG, 334
    vulnerability to viruses, 59–61, 153, 302
JPGDownloader virus, 59, 302
JPGTrojan virus, 59, 302
Juran, Joseph M. (1904–), 314
Jurassic Park (novel), 220

Kahn, David A. (1930–), 19
Kaiser, Henry John (1882–1967), 87
Kaspersky, Eugene, 116, 179, 219
Katz, Andra J., 294
Kerckhoffs' principle, 8, 265, 267, 271, 334
Kerckhoffs, Auguste, *see* Nieuwenhoff
Kerst, Donald William (1911–1993), 202
key (in cryptography)
    asymmetric, 273, 327, 337
    distribution problem, 271, 273, 275
    public, 273–274
    symmetric, 273
key space, 265, 335
    exhaustive search of, 265, 266, 323
Keychain (Macintosh utility), 199
keystroke loggers, xi, 18, 19, 88, 115, 211, 213–215, 220, 221, 239
    by radio, 312
Klez worm, 299
knock cipher, 267
Krause, Doug, 127

laptop security, 7, 26–27
laroux virus, 293
lasco worm, 42, 303
laws of computer security, 5–10, 262, 305–306, 322
l33t Speak, xiii, xviii, 285–287, 335
LeGuin, Ursula Kroeber (1929–), 285

Lehigh virus, 125–126, 290
Levin, Jacob, 310
Li, Hao (author of Saft Lite), 246
license (software), 223, 225
link virus, 335
logic bomb, 335
    definition of, 34, 37
love bug virus, 296
LoveLetter virus, 41
Luján, Rosa Elena, 9

Macintosh
    file forks, 76
    file permissions, 69
    FireWire target disk mode, 69
    opener virus, 134–135
    viruses, 130, 308
    vulnerability to viruses, 27–28, 56, 65, 293, 302
    Witty worm, 301
macro
    definition of, 47, 57
    security weakness, 58
macro virus, 39, 45, 47, 57–59, 70, 75, 76, 129, 154, 293, 295, 335
malware
    definition of, xi, 33
    examples, xvii, 125–137
man in the middle, *see* MIM
mantrap (secure access), 21
marketscore (researchware), 227–228
McLuhan, Marshall (1911–1980), 207
McMahon, Ed (6 March 1923–), 127
MD5 hashing, 280
mega (definition of), 266, 335
Melissa virus, 43, 58, 129–130, 295, 298
memory protection interrupt, 85
memory resident virus, 47, 64, 87, 335
Merkle, Ralph C., 272
Michaelangelo virus, 67, 127, 292
Michelangelo (Michaelangelo), *see* Buonarroti
Microsoft Word (and macro viruses), 57–59
Miller, Henry (1891–1980), 31
MIM (man in the middle), 167
misdirection virus, 53, 78
Mitnick, Kevin, 166
modulus (as a one-way function), 272, 275

monoalphabetic substitution ciphers, 265–267, 335
Morris R. H., 200
Morris, Robert Tappan, 110, 111
MPEG, 334
MSBlast worm, ix
MtE (polymorphic engine), 292
MTX virus/worm, 82, 135–137
multipartite virus, 47, 56–57, 335
mutating viruses, 80–82, 145, 149
Muuss, Mike (ping author), 184
MyDoom worm, 300, 302
Müller-Uri, Ludwig, 193

National Infrastructure Protection Center, 11
National Institute of Standards and Technology (NIST), 327, 336
National Rifle Association (NRA), 41, 261
national security agency, *see* NSA
Netscape Communications, Inc. (SSL developers), 278, 283
netsky worm, 301
network security, xviii, 163–246
Nieuwenhoff, Jean Guillaume Hubert Victor François Alexandre Auguste Kerckhoffs von (1835–1903), 265
nihilistic cipher, 267
nimda virus/worm, 94–95, 297
Nineteen Eighty-Four (novel), 285
NIST, *see* national institute of standards and technology
nonoverwriting virus, 46, 54, 77
North, Oliver (1943–), 237
Norton AntiVirus, 291
novarg worm, 300
NOVEC 1230 (fire extinguisher fluid), 20
NSA (national security agency), 336

obfuscation, 336
  of email, 174
Odysseus (son of Laertes), 113
one-time pad cipher, 269–270, 336
one-time password, 244
one-way encryption, 197–198
one-way function, 272–274
online
  privacy, xviii, 247–258
  trust, xviii, 258–261, 310

opener virus, 134–135
operating system, 34–35
  definition of, 6, 34, 83, 336
  its maintenance, 117, 306
  open source, 152
  protection provided by, 7, 69
operating system virus, 47
optical spying, xii
overwriting virus, 46, 52–54, 77, 83

Palahniuk, Charles Michael (Chuck, 1961–), 303
Panov, Alexey, 170
parasiteware (definition of), 218
parasitic virus, 332, 336
Pareto principle, 53, 314
Pareto, Vilfredo (1848–1923), 314
password cracking, xviii, 3, 7, 196–206
  dictionary attack, 199–201
password encryption, 196–199
password keeper (Windows utility), 199
passwords, 196–206, 305
  bad, 200
  default, 200, 319
  secure, 201–204
Paxson, Vern, 92
payload (of rogue software), 37, 66–75, 99, 100, 102, 106, 132, 158
perturbed data (and privacy), 30, 215
pest control (and security), 10
pestware, 215
phishing, xviii, 239–246, 337
  of passwords, 109
phreaker, 208
physical threats, 20–25
  data integrity, 24
  data protection, 23
  disaster-recovery plan, 23
  electrical power, 20
  fire, 20
  hard copy, 24
  magnetic fields, 22
  mantrap, 21
  principles of security management, 25
  spies, 24
  static electricity, 22
  theft, 21
  user tracking, 22

pif (program information file), 135
Pile, Christopher (virus author), 293
ping of death, 183–184
ping-pong virus, 291
placebo (in cryptography), 267
PocketPC security threats, 303
political contributions (and privacy), 218–219, 320
polyalphabetic substitution ciphers, 268, 337
  compared to RSA, 275
Polybius cipher
  monoalphabetic, 265–267
  polyalphabetic, 268
polymorphic engine, 39, 40, 292
  MtE, 292
polymorphic virus, 337
polymorphism in viruses, 40, 80–82, 291, 292
pop-ups (ads), 225
port scanner, xviii, 3, 164–165
Powell, Anthony Dymoke (1905–2000), 369
privacy (children), 253–258, 310
privacy (online), xviii, 247–258
privacy protection, 29–31
processor status flag (and activity monitor), 151
program counter (PC), 85
program information file, *see* pif
program virus, 337
programs (self printing), 36, 118–119, 313
proxy server, 236
PS-MPC, *see* virus code generation
public-key cryptography, 273–274

rabbit (computer virus), 34, 67, 338
Ralsky, Alan, 171, 173
Ramdhani, Denny Yanuar (good-virus writer), 290
Raymond, Eric Steven (1957–), x, xiv
Recording Industry Association of America, *see* RIAA
redundancy and error-control codes, 158
remote reporting, xviii, 222–224
remote-access Trojan (RAT), 178
renepo, *see* opener virus
Reno, Janet (1938–), x
replay (network attack), 168
researchware (spyware), xviii, 211, 215, 227–228
resident virus, 88

retina scan (biometric authentication), 193–194
retrovirus, 148
RIAA (and spyware), 215–217
Rifkin, Stanley Mark, xv
rigging a compiler, xvii, 117–124
Ritchie, Dennis MacAlistair (1941–), 117
Rivest, Ronald L., 274
Rochefoucauld, François de La (1613–1680), 137
Rogers, William Penn Adair (1879–1935), 124
rogue software, 33–162, 338
  cell telephones, 302–303, 314
  defenses against, xvii, 139–162
  definition of, xi
  easter eggs, 74
  payload, 37, 66–75, 99, 100, 102, 106, 132, 158
  PocketPC, 303
  prevention of, xvii, 139–162
root kit, xiii, 338
RSA cryptography, 274–278
  cycling attack, 277
  encryption (and timing attacks), 17
  multiplicative property of, 277
RSA SecurID, 243–244
RSA Security, 12, 278, 338
Rush Hour virus, 290
Rush-Killer virus alert, 161

salt (in a password), 197, 198
Sandmaier, Marian, 246
sasser worm, ix, 302
Scarfo, Nicodemo, 215
scavenging, xii
Schneier, Bruce (1963–), 12
scores virus, 130, 308
screen capture, xii, 18, 116
script virus, 57–59
secure hash algorithm (SHA-1), 280
secure passwords (guidelines for), 201–204
secure socket layer, *see* SSL
security (definition of), 1
security weakness
  and CCDC, 107
  Bell-LaPadula model, 72
  buffer overrun, 60–62, 93, 108, 329

finger, 91
iframe, ix, 61–62
in BIND, 167
in TCP, 165
in UNIX, 108
JPEG, 59
list of, 139
macros, 58
network vulnerability, 163
open source software, 152
social engineering, 204
spyware, 228
war dialing, 208
worms looking for, 95
self-printing programs, 36, 118–119, 313
self-referencing software, 122
sendmail (UNIX utility), 91, 109, 290
Shakira worm, 299
Shamir, Adi, 274
shareware viruses, 142
Shaw, George Bernard (1856–1950), 312
shell virus, 46, 52
Shimomura, Tsutomu, 166
shoulder spying, xii
shredding, 21, 24, 205, 234, 236–238, 310
side-channel attacks, xii, 15–19
    timing attacks, 17
simple virus, 46, 55
Sircam worm, 128–129, 298
Sirkant, Ramakrishnan, 30
Sklodowska-Curie, Maria (1867–1934), ix
Skulls.A worm, 302
slammer worm, ix, 300
smart card (biometric authentication), 194–
    196, 243
Smathers, Jason, 178
Smith, David L. (Melissa writer), 43, 130,
    298
smurf attack, 184
Snepscheut, Jan L. A. van de, 146
sniffer, 339
sniffing, xii, 163, 205
snoopware, 231
sobig worm, 170, 300
social engineering, xii, 204–205, 251, 339
    definitions, 205
    in worms, 299
    mydoom, 302
social security number, 200, 234, 238

and identity theft, 232
and passwords, 201
on checks, 234
software capable of damaging hardware, 39,
    313–314
software license, 223, 225
spam, 68, 169–181
spam proxie (hijacked computer), 170
spamware (malware), 170
Spark, Muriel (1918–), v, xviii
spawning virus, see companion virus
spider, see Web crawling
spoofs, xviii, 3, 165–167, 339
    sobig, 300
SPYBLOCK (spyware legislation), 211–212
Spybot (anti-spyware software), 220
spyware, xviii, 3, 18, 24, 67, 115, 211–229,
    339
    adware, xviii, 211, 225
    and terrorism, 217–218, 320
    definition of, xi, 212–213
    google desktop search, 226
    legislation, 211–212
    political contributions, 218–219, 320
    remote reporting, xviii, 222–224
    removal, 320
    researchware, xviii, 211, 215, 227–228
    ten basic facts, 228–229
    users of, 213–215
SQL database vulnerability, ix
SSL (secure socket layer), 168, 278–284, 338
SSL certificates, 280–284
stages worm, 296
Staniford, Stuart, 92
staog virus, 294
statistical distribution (and privacy), 30
stealth technique of viruses, 77, 83–84
Stoll, Clifford, xvii, 200, 204
stoned virus, 290
StrangeBrew virus, 295
Strunk, William Jr. (1869–1946), xvii
Sutton, Willie (bank robber 1901–1980), xv
Swiss Amiga virus, 131
system (a vague term), xvi, 108
system administration, networking, and se-
    curity (SANS), 11

tail-chasing effect, 82

Tempest (NSA keyboard eavesdropping), 19
tequila virus, 292
ternary digit, *see* trit
terrorism (and spyware), 217–218, 320
The Dispossessed (novel), 285
The Lord of the Rings (novel), 285, 291
The Memorandum (novel), 285
The Player of Games (novel), 285
Thompson, Kenneth (1943–), 117
time bomb, 340
  definition of, 34, 37
time slices, 86
timeline of viruses, xvi, xviii, 289–303
timer interrupt, 35, 86
timing attacks, 17
Tippett, Peter, viii
Tolkien, John Ronald Reuel (1892–1973),
    285, 291
Toquimos.A worm, 302
Torvalds, Linus Benedict (1969–), x
trapdoor, 88–89, 340, *see also* backdoor
  definition of, 89
traps, *see* interrupts (and viruses)
Traven, B. (1890?–1969), 9
tridecaphobia (fear of 13), 290
tristate virus (macro), 295
trit (ternary digit), 267
Trojan horse, xi, xvii, 39, 113–124, 246, 340
  definition of, 34, 36
  living, xv
  ultimate parasite, 122
trust (online), xviii, 258–261, 310

Unicode (character code), 327, 340
Unix, 340
  permissions, 69
  vulnerability to viruses, 65
unsolicited commercial email (UCE), 169
unsolicited email, 162, 169, 179, 180
user (meaning of the term), xvii, 306
users of spyware, 213–215

vaccine for viruses, 157
VBS.KAK worm, 45, 132–133
VBSWG virus kit, 299
Velasco, Marcus (virus writer), 42
VeriSign unified authentication scheme, 244
Vernam cipher (one-time pad), 269, 341
Vernam, Gilbert S. (1890–1960), 269

Vienna virus, 290
Virdem virus, 290
virus, xi, xvii, 33–88, 341
  add-on, 54
  and interrupts, 44, 46–48, 54, 64, 83–88
  antibody, 73–74, 318
  Apple, 289
  bacterium, 328
  boot sector infector, 46–51, 76–77
  boza, 293
  brain, 36, 51, 126–127, 289, 290
  Burger, 290
  cascade, 291
  Christmas card, 131–132, 142
  CIH, 53, 294
  classification, 46–48
  companion, 38, 46, 55–56, 330
  cruncher, 79, 133, 146
  Dark Avenger.1800, 291, 324
  definition of, 34, 38, 56
  disassembling of, 148–149
  dual-infection, 56
  duts, 303
  Elk Cloner, 289
  file infector, 51–55, 77–83
  flip, 291, 292
  flip-2343, 291
  Frodo lives, 291
  general application, 47
  good time, 161
  GT-Spoof, 161
  hidden in an extra track, 50, 76
  hiding, 76–80
  hoaxes, xvii, 160–162, 292, 294
  in shareware, 142
  infect only large files, 77
  intrusive, 46, 54
  Jerusalem, 290
  jpeg vulnerability, 59–61, 153, 302
  JPGDownloader, 59, 302
  JPGTrojan, 59, 302
  laroux, 293
  Lehigh, 125–126, 290
  link, 335
  love bug, 296
  LoveLetter, 41
  Macintosh, 130, 308

macro, 39, 45, 47, 57–59, 70, 75, 76, 129, 154, 295, 335
  Concept, 293
Melissa, 43, 58, 129–130, 295, 298
memory resident, 47, 64, 87, 335
Michaelangelo, 67, 127, 292
misdirection, 53, 78
MTX, 82, 135–137
multipartite, 47, 56–57, 335
mutating, 80–82, 145, 149
nimda, 297
nonoverwriting, 46, 54, 77
opener, 134–135
operating system, 47
overwriting, 46, 52–54, 77, 83
parasitic, 332, 336
ping-pong, 291
plural of, 36
polymorphic, 337
polymorphism, 40, 80–82, 291, 292
program, 337
psychological factor, 77
rabbit, 34, 67, 338
resident, 88
retrovirus, 148
Rush Hour, 290
Rush-Killer alert, 161
scores, 130, 308
script, 57–59
shell, 46, 52
simple, 46, 55
SirCAM, 128–129
spawning, 55
special case of a Trojan horse, 39
staog, 294
stealth technique, 77, 83–84
stoned, 290
StrangeBrew, 295
survives rebooting, 88, 316
Swiss Amiga, 131
tequila, 292
timeline, xvi, xviii, 289–303
tristate, 295
vaccine, 157
Vienna, 290
Virdem, 290
writers, 40–43
virus code generation (PS-MPC), 292
virus construction lab (VCL), 292

virus construction set (VCS), 292
virus kit, 39, 40, 147, 292, 297, 301, 318
  PS-MPC, 292
  VBSWG, 299
  VCL, 292
  VCS, 292
virus writers, 40–43
voting principle (in hardware), 159, 319
vulnerability scanner, xii, 341

Walton, Gertrude, 217
war dialers, 208–209
  origin of name, 208
War Games (movie), 208
warhead, *see* payload (of rogue software)
warm colors
  harder to read, 258
  preferred by readers, 258
Weaver, Nicholas C., 92
Web crawling, 249–250
Web site of this book, xviii, 28
Wheeler, Wayne, 369
Wilde, Oscar (1854–1900), 25
Wit, Jan de (author of Anna Kournikova virus), 297
Witten, Ian, 13
Witty worm, 301
worms, 91–111, 342
  Anna Kournikova, 297, 299
  bagle, 301
  Bagle.AY, 302
  Blaster, 300
  Britney Spears, 299
  Bugbear, 220, 299
  cabir, 303
  code red I, 93–94, 298
  code red II, 94
  definition of, xi, 34, 36–37, 91
  Internet, xvii, 36, 69, 73, 91, 108–111, 142, 200, 290
  Jennifer Lopez, 299
  Klez, 299
  lasco, 303
  Lasco.A, 42
  MSBlast, ix
  MyDoom, 300
  MyDoom.AI, 302
  netsky, 301

nimda, 94–95
novarg, 300
sasser, ix, 302
Shakira, 299
Sircam, 298
Skulls.A, 302
slammer, ix, 300
sobig, 170, 300

stages, 296
Toquimos.A, 302
VBS.KAK, 45, 132–133
Witty, 301
www (Web), 334

zombie computer, 68, 96, 175–179, 218, 319
spam proxie, 170

If you don't find it in the index, look very
carefully through the entire catalogue.

—*Sears, Roebuck, and Co. Consumer's Guide*, 1897

Colophon

The idea for this book was proposed to this author in mid 2004 by Wayne Wheeler, the computer science editor of Springer Verlag. Most of the material was written in late 2004 and early 2005. It is based on the author's own experience with computer security issues, on topics discussed in many books on computer security, and on material found on the Internet about recent problems and attacks and how to fight them. The chapter on cryptography has improved and extended material from [Salomon 03]. The many inserts with quotations have been included to liven up the book and also to push the text up or down in order to improve the page breaks.

The book was designed by the author and was typeset by him in plain TeX (plus about 150 macros). The figures and diagrams were drawn in Adobe Illustrator. The following numbers convey an idea of the amount of work that went into the book:

- The book contains about 180,000 words, consisting of about 1,100,000 characters.

- The text is typeset mainly in font cmr10, but about 30 other fonts were used.

- The raw index file has about 1850 items.

- There are about 190 cross references in the book.

  As the Preface promises, this is not a fact-free book.

"I'm afraid I haven't read any of your books. I believe you write books, don't you? I hope you won't mind that." I was in process of picking out one of the several routine replies designed to bridge this not at all uncommon conversational opening—a phrase that at once generously accepts the speaker's candour in confessing the omission, while emphasizing the infinite unimportance of any such solicitude on that particular point—when need to make any reply at all was averted by a matter of much greater interest to both of us. This was entry into the room of Widmerpool and the Quiggin twins.

—Anthony Powell, *Hearing Secret Harmonies* (1975)